Spirits of the Air

Smilax lævis Lauri folio non Serrato, baccis nigris.

Spirits *of the* Air

BIRDS & AMERICAN INDIANS IN THE SOUTH

SHEPARD KRECH III

The University of Georgia Press ATHENS AND LONDON

Pica cristata cærulea.
The crested Jay.

A WORMSLOE
FOUNDATION
PUBLICATION

Designed by Richard Hendel

Set in Arno and The Sans types by Copperline Book Services

Printed and bound by Kings Time Printing

The paper in this book meets the guidelines for permanence
and durability of the Committee on Production Guidelines
for Book Longevity of the Council on Library Resources.

Printed in China

13 12 11 10 09 C 5 4 3 2 1

Library of Congress Cataloging-in-Publication Data

Krech, Shepard, 1944–

Spirits of the air : birds and American Indians in the South /
Shepard Krech III.

    p. cm. — (Environmental history and the American South)

Includes bibliographical references and index.

ISBN-13: 978-0-8203-2815-7 (hardcover : alk. paper)

ISBN-10: 0-8203-2815-4 (hardcover : alk. paper)

    1. Indians of North America — Southern States — Antiquities.
2. Indians of North America — Southern States — Social life and
customs.   3. Indians of North America — Southern States — Rites
and ceremonies.   4. Birds — Southern States.   5. Birds — Religious
aspects.   6. Bird remains (Archaeology) — Southern States.
7. Human-animal relationships — Southern States.
8. Southern States — Antiquities.   I. Title.

E78.S65K74   2009

975'.01 — dc22   2008016949

British Library Cataloging-in-Publication Data available

In memory of
my grandfather,
Shepard Krech,
and my father,
Shepard Krech Jr.,
and for my daughter,
Teal

Contents

Foreword

In the fall of 2003, the University of Mississippi's Department of History hosted a symposium on "The Environment and Southern History." The meeting brought together most of the usual suspects — scholars such as Mart Stewart, Tim Silver, Jack Temple Kirby, and Don Davis, all of whom had been working diligently to persuade southern historians to take the environment seriously and environmental historians to pay some attention to the South. The symposium program also included a few interlopers, relative strangers to the southern terrain that was its focus. At the time, I fell into that latter category, as did Shepard Krech III — although he was a decidedly more distinguished interloper than was I. We had not met, but I knew Shep Krech's scholarship well — particularly his influential study of American Indian environmental history and myth, *The Ecological Indian* (1999). His personal acquaintance and a growing interest in the possibilities of southern environmental history were two of the most valuable things I carried away from that weekend in Oxford, Mississippi.

The title of Krech's symposium talk was "American Indians and Birds in the South: An Environmental History." I remember it as an endlessly stimulating and lavishly illustrated talk, but also as hurried and overstuffed. It was clear to many of us in the audience that the full contours of this fascinating topic spilled well beyond the confines of a short essay; I imagine that Krech had come to the same conclusion well before we did. It remained for the keen-eyed Christa Frangiamore, who was there that day representing the University of Georgia Press, to convince Krech that his exploratory "ethno-ornithology" was a book-in-the-making. *Spirits of the Air* is the happy result, and I am thrilled to have it appear as a volume in our Environmental History and the American South book series.

Shepard Krech's hook is a deceptively simple one: why is it, he asks, that our "most persistent visual image of the indigenous people of the New World is that they were feathered?" That is such an obvious question, once one hears it asked. And yet no one has explored in a comprehensive way this or the many other facets of the relationship between American Indians and birds — until now. Indeed, as one of the scholars who reviewed *Spirits of the Air* for the press aptly put it, "Krech's manuscript is one of those rare instances in reading where I hit my head and wondered aloud why this had not been done before. That is the beauty of it — Krech shows the subject to be so obvious and pertinent that one wonders how it could ever have been overlooked."

Spirits of the Air assesses the place of birds in the lives and cultures of the indigenous peoples of just one region of North America, what we now know as the U.S. South. On one level, this was a practical choice, for to chart this relationship over an entire continent would have been daunting, if not impossible. But there are also good reasons, beyond pragmatic narrowing, to home in on the South. As Krech points out, the region was and remains the host to tremendous avian abundance and diversity, and bird life has in turn helped to define the region. The recent furor over the apparent rediscovery of the ivory-billed woodpecker, which long haunted the region's mature bottomland hardwood forests before they were decimated, is but one example. Moreover, and perhaps more importantly, the region has been the home to distinctive indigenous cultures and societies that, despite tremendous diversity among them, provide a coherent basis for broad generalizations as well as intraregional comparisons. Finally, the region boasts a tremendously rich set of sources on Indian-avian relations and interconnections, sources that have been crying out for the sort of synthesis that Krech has provided here.

Spirits of the Air is several books in one. At its most basic, it is an old-fashioned ethnography, encyclopedic in its approach to the relationship between southern Indians and the birds that enriched their lives, materially as well as spiritually. Krech has systematically sifted through the historical literature, oral traditions, archaeological artifacts, and numerous other sources, and his fine mesh has captured even the smallest of insights on how southern Indians perceived, utilized, and gave meaning to birds. One cannot but be impressed by the detective work. On another level, *Spirits of the Air* is a stunning visual tour through the art and material culture that have constituted, reproduced, and illuminated this relationship. Thumb through the scores of beautiful illustrations contained herein, and it will not take you long to realize that birds were everywhere in this corner of native North America, hiding in plain sight. On yet another level, this is a passionate book about the birds of the South, past and present. Here, too, Krech is a brilliant guide, for he is an avid and accomplished birder who knows the region's avian fauna and their habitats well enough to make remarkable sense of often fragmentary evidence. Indeed, Krech's ornithological expertise gives this study a critical animus. Finally, *Spirits of the Air* is a revealing transect through the region's larger environmental history. As Krech himself points out, "birds represent an important slice of nature, in terms of numbers, biomass, diversity, and so on, and to fathom the relationship between them and humans is to comprehend our relationship with an important part of the natural world."

Spirits of the Air is more than just a tour-de-force explication of a bygone set of human-avian interactions. Lurking quietly at the very core of this book is a reminder of the cultural depth and specificity of our own interconnections with the avian world. Shepard Krech has written one of those rare books that, by asking a simple question, opens up a whole new field of vision.

PAUL S. SUTTER
Athens, Georgia

Preface

In 2003, Charles Reagan Wilson and Robbie Ethridge, professors in the departments of history and anthropology, respectively, at the University of Mississippi, invited me to join a symposium on southern environmental history at the Center for the Study of Southern Culture. Hoping for something related to an earlier work on Indians, ecology, and conservation (*The Ecological Indian: Myth and History*), they gracefully accepted my proposal to talk about native people and birds. Christa Frangiamore, at the time acquisitions editor for the University of Georgia Press, was in the audience and urged me to work up a longer version of the presentation for the Press. Thus began this book, and I thank all three for their support and persistence.

In important ways, however, this project's roots are far deeper. When I was a boy, my family moved from New York to Maryland's Eastern Shore, and in the years before I was sent away to school, like my father and grandfather in earlier times, my parents took my sister and me out of the local school and headed for Thomasville, Georgia, to spend the month of February with my paternal grandparents, who wintered there.

This was in the 1950s. As isolated — and southern — as the Eastern Shore was in those days, it did not compare to the deep South. I remember trips by car and by train. By car, the two-day journey took us on U.S. 301 south through Virginia and the Carolinas, past, on the border between North and South Carolina, the emporium South of the Border, with cotton fields for cotton-pickin' Yankees — and thence into what seemed to me to be an alien world.

The landscape became increasingly rural, a succession of fields and forest broken by barns and sharecroppers' houses. Briars crawled over field edges, and vines choked gullies. No doubt some of the green was the invasive species kudzu, which had been rooting in southern soil for twenty years and more and, as the "plant that ate the South," strangles pretty much everything within reach. Southern pines dominated roadside forests and Spanish moss draped trees the further south we drove. Water overflowed ditches and flooded the ground beneath trees. In my young imagination, alligators lurked in every ditch and inundated forest.

In Thomasville I played hooky for a month — albeit with daily lessons prepared by my school so I would stay up to speed — and to judge from memory and family lore and photographs, spent as much time as I could with my grandfather. My grandparents and their kin managed the land for quail, which for me meant tagging along on the mule-drawn wagons that took hunters in their white coats, and pointers with names like Preacher, Poacher, and Pluto, about the plantation in pursuit of quail. I also shot — rabbits at first, flushed ahead of deliberate periodic burnings of the pine grasslands to maintain optimal habitat for game birds, then graduating to ducks, doves, and finally, when older and safe in the field, to quail.

Birds were everywhere in Georgia: the game birds, of course, but also hawks, owls, woodpeckers, nuthatches, chickadees, thrashers, mockingbirds, towhees, sparrows, warblers, wrens, and others. Even though I knew about both, try as I might I could not conjure an ivory-billed woodpecker or a Bachman's warbler. Hunters, for whom quail were real birds, were not terribly interested in the little ones that they lumped together as "dicky birds." Somehow I ultimately became interested in them individually, even the little sparrows. Once I told my father, for whom life was competition, that I had seen a fox sparrow at the feeder. He refused to believe it, and sensing opportunity, I promptly bet him five dollars, an exorbitant sum in those days, and won!

As a boy, I was definitely into birds. I grew up in settings in which paintings or lithographs of birds hung on the walls, miniature carvings of birds rested on shelves, decoys nested in bushel baskets in the basement during the off-season, and, of course, real birds could be found outside or cooking in the oven. It was normal to line up game birds such as ducks, geese, doves, quail, and turkeys in the sights of a gun and then put them in the pot; and to feed all kinds of inedible ones outside winter windows with suet and seed or, as my grandfather Krech did with catbirds (and chipmunks and squirrels), canned cherries. My grandfather fed my interest with gifts of a watercolor of black-capped chickadees by a friend of his working on a book of the birds of Long Island; his copy of Ernest Thompson Seton's *Wild Animals I Have Known*, which he had received as a gift in 1899 at age eight; and, shortly after it was published, Thomas Burleigh's massive tome, *Georgia Birds*. I hung the watercolor on the wall and devoured the books, and they fueled a lasting interest in birds.

Much later came an undergraduate major in anthropology at Yale (and Harold Conklin's seminar on ethnoscience), graduate studies at Oxford and Harvard, and ethnography on the changing trapping patterns of the Gwich'in of northwestern Canada. From the field I sent occasional notes on birds to Gardner Stout, a keen birder and conservationist (and editor of the acclaimed *Shorebirds of North America*), friend, and president of the American Museum of Natural History. From all this evolved an abiding interest in human-environment relationships in native North America — and a suspicion that one day I just might combine my interests in birds and indigenous people.

Many people helped as my research took shape, and I wish here especially to thank them:

Tim Silver, for sharing his vast knowledge of the environmental history of the South, and Carolyn Merchant, for fundamental insights on nature; in the 1990s, we three led "Nature Transformed," a National Endowment for the Humanities institute at the National Humanities Center that brought to the seminar table dedicated high school instructors who taught us as much as we tried to teach them.

Ian Brown, Robbie Ethridge, Raymond D. Fogelson, Christa Frangiamore, Charles

Hudson, Jerald Milanich, and Vincas Steponaitis, who read earlier drafts of the manuscript.

Steve N. G. Howell, who over the years has shared his deep knowledge of avian ecology and behavior (and chocolate), changing forever how I thought about birds.

Teal Chapin Krech Paynter, a writer and journalist and my daughter, who read the entire manuscript and sent (from Tanzania) numerous suggestions for improvements, a real labor of love.

Celeste Sullivan, my indispensable research assistant, who located, ordered, and secured permissions for illustrations, brought accuracy and consistency of style to the bibliography, and saw to the completion of other tasks too numerous to detail.

Paul Sutter, for his trenchant critique and insistence that this work be published in his series, Environmental History and the American South; the anonymous readers for the University of Georgia Press, who offered many valuable suggestions; and Nicole Mitchell, Andrew Berzanskis, Jon Davies, and Barb Wojhoski for seeing the manuscript through the Press.

Colleagues, friends, and kin who generously helped me think through my argument, identified objects and sources, responded to various requests, contributed information, opinions, or advice, or patiently listened to me go on about this project — David Aftandilian, Rumee Ahmed, John Bourgoin, Sabine Eiche, J. Frederick Fausz, Christian Feest, Sheila ffolliott, William Fowler, Arlene Fradkin, Pat Galloway, T. Grand, Gary Graves, Davis Hammond, Warren Hofstra, Donald Holly, H. Edwin Jackson, Karl Jacoby, J. C. H. King, the late Shepard Krech Jr., Susie Low, John F. Reiger, Patricia Rubertone, David Harris Sacks, Claudio Saunt, Joanna Scherer, Michael D. Scholl, Elaine Shirley, Kevin P. Smith, Michele Hayeur Smith, John Strong, the late William C. Sturtevant, Sarah Thimmesch, Greg Waselkov, Marianne Wason, and Diana Wells.

The archivists, curators, photographers, and others in libraries, museums, and other repositories who helped secure images and permissions (with apologies to any inadvertently omitted): Jackie Donovan, American Antiquarian Society; Robert James, American Gourd Society; Anibal Rodriguez, Lindsay Calkins, and David Thomas, American Museum of Natural History; Isabel Simó Rodríguez and Antonio Sánchez de Mora, Ministerio de Cultura, Archivo General de Indias (Seville); Laura Miani and Rita de Tata, Biblioteca Universitaria di Bologna; Ann Dodge, Pat Sirois, Andrew Moul, and Alison Bundy, John Hay Library, Brown University; Patrick Yott, Robin Rao, Ben Tyler, Ann Caldwell, Elizabeth Coogan, Jill Wood, and Hans-Dieter Gomes, Rockefeller Library, Brown University; Richard Ring, Heather Jesperson, Norman Fiering, Lynne Harrell, Susan Danforth, John Minichiello, Leslie Tobias-Olsen, Richard Hurley, and Dennis Landis, John Carter Brown Library, Brown University; Michael S. Harris, Florida Atlantic University; Elise LeCompte and Jeff Gage, Florida Museum of Natural History; Anne Lewellen, Fort Caroline National Memorial; Dana Yarbrough, Gilcrease Museum; Charles E. Hilburn, Gulf States Paper Company; Julie

Brown, Peabody Museum of Archaeology and Ethnology, Harvard University; Helen Najarian, Peabody Museum Press, Harvard University; Linda Sanns, Huntington Museum of Art; Anna Peele, Indian Temple Mound Museum, Fort Walton Beach, Florida; Glenn Anderson, Museum of Science and History, Jacksonville, Florida; Katie Anderson and Judith Magee, Natural History Museum, London; Fred G. Meijer, Netherlands Institute for Art History; John Powell, Newberry Library; Julie Droke, Sam Noble Museum, University of Oklahoma; Paul Tarver, New Orleans Museum of Art; Duryea Kemp and Martha Otto, Ohio Historical Society; Joyce Harwell, Pennsylvania State University Libraries; Victoria M. Cranner, Robert S. Peabody Museum of Archaeology, Phillips Academy, Andover; Cécile van der Harten and Els Vorhaak, Rijksmuseum, Amsterdam; Alicia Sell, the Virginia Room at the Roanoke Public Libraries; Bruno Svindborg, Royal Library, Copenhagen; Lou Stancari, National Museum of the American Indian, Smithsonian Institution; Becky Malinsky, Daisy Njoku, Felicia Pickering, National Museum of Natural History, Smithsonian Institution; Richard Sorenson and Lizanne Garrett, National Portrait Gallery, Smithsonian Institution; Leslie Green, Smithsonian American Art Museum; Suzanne White, South Florida Museum; Steve Cox, Tennessee State Museum; Mary Suter, University of Arkansas Museum; Alison Miner, University of Pennsylvania Museum; Jeffrey Makala, Thomas Cooper Library Rare Books and Special Collections, University of South Carolina; Jefferson Chapman and Lynne P. Sullivan, Frank H. McClung Museum, University of Tennessee; William Fowler and Hunter Darrouzet, Vanderbilt University; David Grabarek and William C. Luebke, the Library of Virginia; Cassandra Parsons, the Wallace Collection; Donna Anstey, Yale University Press; and Virginia Anderson, Deanna Brandon, James A. Brown, Don Contreras, James Dorian, Raquel Espejo, Justin Gillespie, Brian Gohacki, Anne Goodyear, Frank Goodyear, Katherine Grimaldi, Kyle Matthews, Jerald Milanich, Tiziana Milano, Simone Poliandre, Susan Power, Barbara Purdy, David Ray, Mark Slankard, Keats Sparrow, Vincas Steponaitis, John Strong, Norman Trahan, Choua Vang, Ryan J. Wheeler, and John Whitehurst.

Last but certainly not least, the National Humanities Center, for a John D. and Catherine T. MacArthur Foundation Fellowship in the Ecological Humanities, and the Haffenreffer Museum of Anthropology, Brown University, for research and publication support.

Needless to say, I alone am responsible for omissions and shortcomings.

Spirits of the Air

FIGURE 1.
Largest White Bill'd
Woodpecker (ivory-
billed woodpecker).
*Hand-colored etching
by Mark Catesby,*
Natural History
*(1771), plate 16. The
iconic bird in the
American South.
(Catesby's titles differ
slightly in his text and
inscription; unlike this
one, most come from
his text.) John Carter
Brown Library at
Brown University.*

Birds & American Indians

The announcement, in a press conference in Washington, D.C., on April 28, 2005, was electrifying: an ivory-billed woodpecker had been spotted in Arkansas. The Lord God Bird still lived! The news, which included a short video clip as evidence, made international waves: front-page coverage in papers, segments on radio and television, and endless chatter on Web sites and blogs. The spectacular-looking bird, long believed extinct, was suddenly in the forefront of people's minds, nonbirders and birders alike. Many who had never before given the bird — or any bird — a thought found themselves riveted.

As the bird shook off the certainty of extinction after almost sixty years, reporters and others picked up on its nickname from years past, the Lord God Bird. Its fans had never given up on the name, even if they had largely lost hope that the bird was still alive. And now! Well, it is enough to say that more than a few ordinarily unflappable people got goose bumps. Some cried. If, like me, you had ever looked at what flew through southern landscapes, especially woodpeckers with crests, in unfulfilled hope for the ivory-billed, you were sure to be in here somewhere.

Known primarily to dedicated birders, ornithologists, and conservationists, this magnificent bird now enthralled the wider public. To most who were aware of it, the ivory-billed had long since been one of the most important symbols of extinction alongside the dodo and dinosaurs.[1] But to the few who searched for it high and low, the ivory-billed was the Grail Bird. New reports of sightings in Florida's panhandle made public eighteen months after that press conference gave additional reason to hope that the story of the Arkansas bird would not become the tragedy of the last remaining ivory-billed. Whatever the outcome — and there is vigorous debate — this bird's iconic status is forever secure.[2]

The Lord God Bird is the largest and showiest woodpecker and is on everybody's short list of avian stars in North America. Its rediscovery cries out for reconsideration of the reasons for its demise. In fact, these are well known. Always going against it was its need for a large territory, its dependence on large cerambycid beetle larvae, its shyness, and its shaky breeding and fledgling success.

Compounding these ecological demands and biological challenges was humankind: specifically, commodification of the bird or its habitat by people ranging from American Indians to newcomers of European descent. Most destructive was the insatiable desire of mercantilists and industrialists for mature bottomland forests, the ivory-billed's haunts — a sad story of decline that coincided, ironically, with the efforts of the very people who cared most about the birds and who documented them at their nests, as lumber companies destroyed their habitat. Indeed, habitat preservation is the key to the ivory-billed woodpecker's future, if there is one. Even with the latest reported sightings, the deck is stacked against the survival of the species, but stranger things have happened in stories of near-death and extinction.[3]

INTERSECTIONS OF INDIANS AND BIRDS

That Americans of European descent commodified ivory-billed woodpecker habitats should come as no surprise. But why might American Indians have made a commodity of the bird? What were the reasons — cultural, ecological, gustatory, or other — for their interest in this woodpecker? For that matter, did their interest translate into an impact on the ivory-billed's population? These questions come easily. This book addresses them — even if they are far simpler to pose than to answer — not just for the ivory-billed but for birds in general in one particular region of North America: the South.

As yet no sustained analysis exists of the relationship between native people and birds in the South or any other region of North America. This is most likely because for many people birds simply don't come up on the radar. For example, birds are largely absent compared to other living things in the basic anthropological literature on North American Indians. For over a century, anthropologists interested in the relationship between indigenous people and the natural world in North America have tended to focus on the intersection of people's lives with large animals such as buffalo, deer, caribou, and sea mammals; with salmon and other major salt- and freshwater species of fish; and with maize and other plants domesticated or gathered.

This research has often unfolded in the context of what are known as culture areas; based on biomes, or natural areas, these are major regions, like the Arctic, the Northwest Coast, the Plains, or the South (Southeast), within which people shared certain traits (like hunting sea mammals or buffaloes or domesticating maize) to a far greater degree than with people in other areas. This is often the first thing learned about North American Indians. But one problem is that although culture areas facilitate comparative insights on native people, they run the risk of eliding what the anthropologist Alfred Kroeber called "finesses." One such finesse comprises birds, which remain largely invisible on a continental scale.[4]

Yet birds represent an important slice of nature, in terms of numbers, biomass, diversity, and so on, and to fathom the relationship between them and humans is to comprehend our relationship with an important part of the natural world. In plumbing that relationship, it seems important first to establish if and where intersections between humans and birds existed, then to determine their nature, and finally to interpret and, if possible, explain them.

As it happens, there is much to explain about humans and birds: why, for example, native people consumed certain birds but tabooed others; why birds figure in contexts of kinship, descent, power, religion, sickness, well-being, performance, and narrative;

and why some birds were visible and named while others seem not to have been. The evidence for the intersection of humans and birds is extensive and rich. In the pages that follow, I make sense of it by framing it anthropologically — privileging ecological, cultural, and temporal contexts; sharpening observations on the South with comparisons elsewhere; and emphasizing, through incident and anecdote, individual agency that both reveals and creates relationships with birds.

THE SOUTH

As in other parts of North America, the bird-human relationship is largely invisible in the South. Competing in this region for the attention of scholars, and winning, are weighty matters such as the timing and extent of the domestication of plants; the reconstruction of traditional pre-European-arrival social and political organization; the impact of newcomers from Europe (and Africa), including the exchange of cloth and other goods for white-tailed deer hides; and the disastrous removal of native people in the nineteenth century. That these topics should command attention is due to their cultural and historical importance. But this still leaves a substantial gap in our knowledge of the intersections of humans and a big slice of the natural world, a lack of awareness addressed throughout this work.

As for why the South, first, avian life was (and to a degree still is) incredibly rich in this region; in the past it included healthy populations of birds that today are extinct or nearly so. Second, there is broad consensus that this region is distinctive with respect to indigenous people, who shared important aspects of society, culture, and history, yet still differed substantially in language and other ways — opening up the possibility of general statements about and comparison within the region. Third, despite the general lack of attention to the human-bird relationship in North America, archaeolo-

FIGURE 2.
(Left) Ceramic wood stork or pelican. *Choctawhatchee Beach Cemetery Site, Walton County, Fla., ca. AD 1350–1500, 4.25 in. high. This elegant effigy possesses features — curved mandible, pigmentation (dark head and neck versus pale body) — that suggest a wood stork; a pelican is also possible. Courtesy of the Indian Temple Mound Museum Collection, City of Fort Walton Beach Heritage Park and Cultural Center, Fla., 1089.*

FIGURE 3.
(Right) Ceramic bird jar. *Franklin County, Fla., ca. AD 900, 8 in. high. A stylized bird difficult to identify — if indeed based on a specific bird. National Museum of the American Indian, Smithsonian Institution, 17-4088. Photo by NMAI Photo Services Staff.*

gists, ethnologists, and others have long made clear that the representation of birds is prominent in the material record of the South; what is still lacking, however, is synthesis.

One final reason for focusing on the South is that it is perhaps today the most self-consciously distinct region in America. Defined variously in geographical, ecological, historical, and cultural terms, most consider the heart as equivalent to the Confederate core — Alabama, Arkansas, Florida, Georgia, Louisiana, Mississippi, North Carolina, South Carolina, Tennessee, eastern Texas, and Virginia. Many add Kentucky and the southern and eastern parts of Maryland to these states. The details might be debated but not the area in general represented by these states and portions of states, which are taken as the South in this book. There is no great difference between this South and the anthropological South or Southeast culture area.

Asked what epitomizes the South, people most often list distinctive accent and food, Dixie, plantations, slavery, gospel music and the blues, King Cotton, the Confederacy, Jim Crow, lynching, kudzu, Baptists, guns, stills, textiles, rural poverty, country music, rural blacks, illiteracy, writers, racism, and NASCAR. Birds and Indians never appear. It goes without saying that before 2005, it would not have crossed anyone's mind to include the ivory-billed woodpecker. But now there cannot be any question that it belongs, even if the case must still be made that birds in general — or Indian people, or the two as they intersect with each other — deserve mention.[5]

A NOTE ON TIME, SOURCES, AND METHODS

Did birds hold the attention, then, of indigenous people in the South? Were they consumed? Were they socially or materially useful or culturally meaningful? Were they visible?

The use of the past tense indicates an interest here mainly in former, not current, intersections of birds and native people. This should not be taken to mean that the intersections of today's native people with birds are unworthy of note. Rather, it reflects the primary focus on the long period of native residence in the South, from the earliest traces in the archaeological record through several centuries marking the arrival and settlement of newcomers from Europe, even including the cataclysmic nineteenth-century removals that divorced most native people from their southern homelands.

There is ample evidence bearing on how the lives of native people and birds intertwined in the South during these millennia. Following removal west, change was practically inevitable given the death of older people and their knowledge — a loss native people bemoan — and novel circumstances. In the West, southern Indians who survived came in far greater contact with one another than previously, encountered new

FIGURE 4. Wooden bird head. *Key Marco, Collier County, Fla., AD 1450–1550, 4.2 in. high. Despite a short and curved bill, the bulging lower mandible of this graceful sculpture suggests a pelican's pouch. University of Pennsylvania Museum, 40708.*

Indians who lived there, and adapted to new environments presenting a fresh selection of living things, including birds. This affected much, including thoughts about and relationships with birds.

Given these fundamental changes, it is not surprising that the ways in which people had used, conceptualized, and categorized and named birds prior to the forced march west altered or disappeared. Yet counterbalancing these changes was persistence — in language, in involvement in recognizably southern institutions with recognizably southern cultural meanings, and in selected aspects of culture. Moreover, some southern Indians remained in the South, where they evolved along their own trajectories, retaining, in the most isolated cases, remnants of former ways of constituting culture. For these reasons, we draw cautiously and selectively here on native testimony from Oklahoma as well as the postremoval East, elicited as recently as the mid- and late-twentieth century by anthropologists, historians, folklorists, and others — native and nonnative people — because it enriches substantially the story of the relationship between people and birds in the South.

The evidence for a relationship with birds comes principally from an extensive record in archaeology, history (oral and written), visual materials, material culture, ethnography, native studies, and folklore. This documentation holds the key to questions concerning the knowledge of birds that indigenous people possessed; how people used birds in subsistence and material culture; the ways that birds figured in ideology, religion, narrative, and social and political relations; and the impact of native people on bird populations — all of which are taken up in this book. Like all evidence, it must be approached skeptically and weighed carefully for assumptions and biases; not surprisingly, it presents a range of methodological challenges that are addressed in their turn in the text and notes.[6]

FIGURE 5. Ceramic bowl with bird head and tail on the rim. *Walton County, Fla., ca. AD 1350–1500, 8 in. diameter. Even though abstract, the upright head with a notched crest evokes a gallinaceous bird. Courtesy of the Indian Temple Mound Museum Collection, City of Fort Walton Beach Heritage Park and Cultural Center, Fla., 1264.*

THE PEOPLE

The South is vast, encompassing some five hundred thousand square miles, and has been home to indigenous people for roughly 11,500 years. For the first 6,000 years, they hunted, gathered, and fished; generalized foragers, they also domesticated the dog. They drew on a broad range of resources; plant foods alone at first consisted of nuts, acorns, berries, seeds, and more. During the next several thousand years, native people settled near estuaries and other promising sites on the coast as well as along rivers in the interior. As early as 4,500 years ago, people began to alter gourds, squashes, sunflowers, maygrass, goosefoot, knotweed, and other plants, nudging them toward domestication and codependence; as they did so, they moved about less except to per-

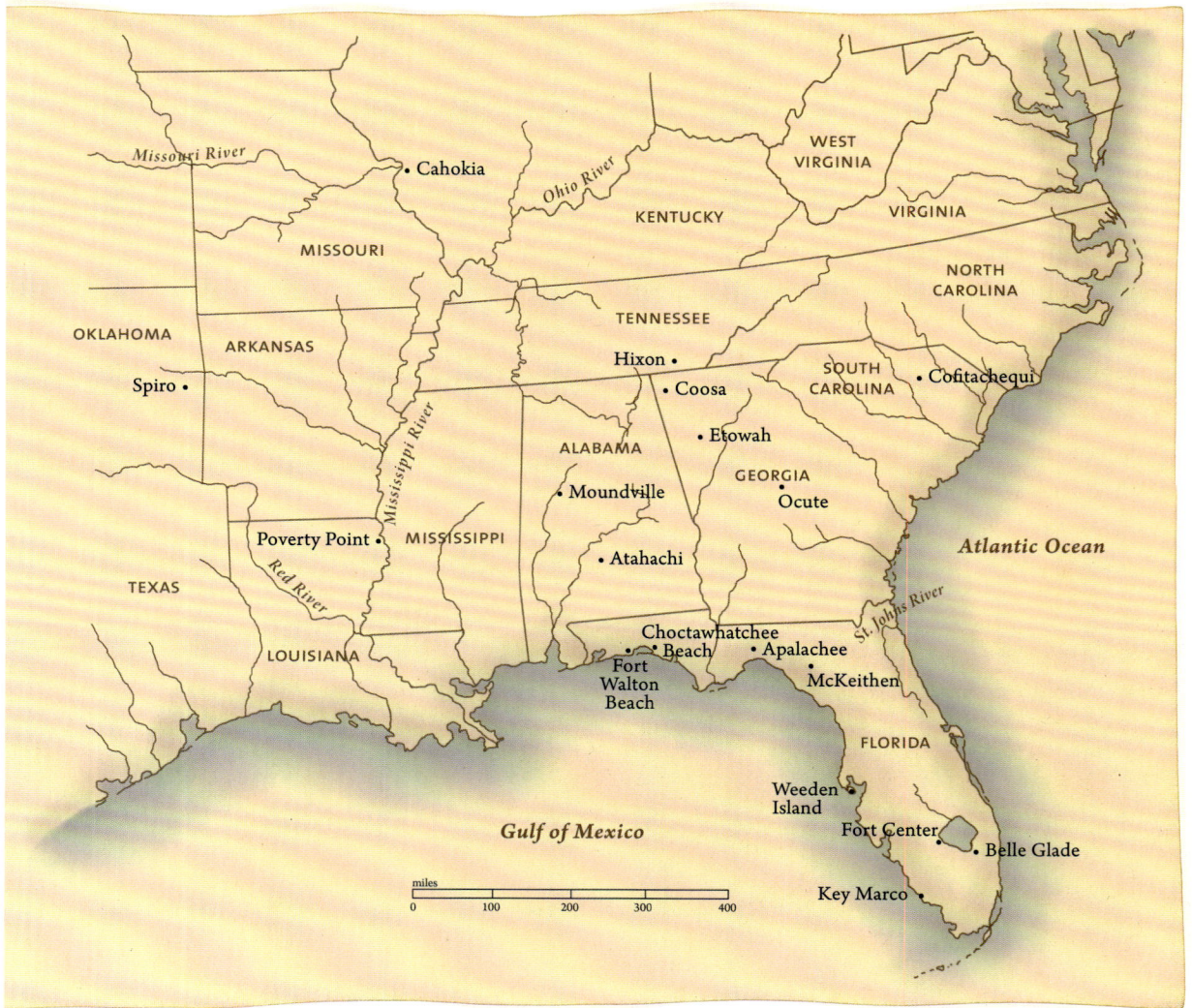

Map showing the southeastern United States with labeled states, rivers, bodies of water, and archaeological sites including: Missouri River, Cahokia, Ohio River, WEST VIRGINIA, KENTUCKY, VIRGINIA, MISSOURI, NORTH CAROLINA, OKLAHOMA, ARKANSAS, TENNESSEE, Hixon, SOUTH CAROLINA, Cofitachequi, Spiro, Coosa, Etowah, ALABAMA, GEORGIA, Ocute, Mississippi River, Moundville, Poverty Point, MISSISSIPPI, Atlantic Ocean, Red River, Atahachi, TEXAS, St. Johns River, LOUISIANA, Choctawhatchee Beach, Apalachee, Fort Walton Beach, McKeithen, FLORIDA, Gulf of Mexico, Weeden Island, Fort Center, Belle Glade, Key Marco.

miles
0   100   200   300   400

MAP 1. *Some mounds, towns, and other sites, 2000 BC– AD 1600.*

form seasonal tasks, built houses and storage facilities, developed distinctive styles in ceramics and other artifacts, and participated in extensive trade networks.[7]

As their populations grew larger and increasingly sedentary, societies went through periods during which they shared regionwide cultural patterns, even as each society gave its own slant to the pattern. The most important of these periods were known as Woodland and Mississippian, which together lasted some 2,200 years, from 700 BC to AD 1500, overlapping at the close with the arrival of newcomers from Europe. These two millennia saw a continuation of hunting and collecting alongside the steady increase in the production of domesticated plants, eventually focusing on maize, squash, and beans; the development of specialized production of a variety of artifacts; the elaboration of tribute and long-distance exchange; an increase in social hierarchy, rank, and stratification; and widespread platform-mound construction and the related development of a divine hereditary elite who received, at death, special mortuary treatment including burial with exotic funerary objects.[8]

In many parts of the South, fortified power centers — chiefdoms — evolved with different histories and trajectories. In a climate of endemic warfare and constant jockeying for stressed resources, some of these polities were flashes in the pan, but others lasted generations. Platform mounds appeared all over the region, but three Mississippian-era power centers (two of them outside the boundaries of the South set here) had vast influence over the region: Cahokia in present-day Illinois, the earliest and largest and the first of the three to dissolve, between the twelfth and fourteenth centuries; Spiro in eastern Oklahoma (AD 850–1450); and Moundville in Alabama (AD 1050–1500), which was the last to emerge and still in existence when Europeans arrived in the mid-sixteenth century, although by then it had declined to insignificance.

When they came to the South, Europeans encountered native people almost everywhere. Many lived in mutually antagonistic chiefdoms. Several societies were notable for the extent of stratification as well as the reach of tribute, authority, and power: Apalachee in north-central Florida, Cofitachequi in north-central South Carolina, Coosa in northwestern Georgia, and Ocute in central Georgia. A bewildering profusion of ethnonyms testifies to numerous ethnic identities and to local social and cultural variation. No fewer than six major indigenous language families — Muskogean, Iroquoian, Siouan-Catawba, Algonquian, Caddoan, and Timucuan — were spoken in the region. Yet many native people shared certain cultural and adaptive features. All foraged for and hunted deer, small mammals, shellfish, fish, turkeys, passenger pigeons, migratory waterfowl, and so on, where they were available. All gathered wild plants, and most farmed maize, squash, and other cultivated domesticated plants. Away from the coast and north of southern Florida, deer and corn were of great importance. Many southern Indians lived in populous societies whose leaders were capable of organizing labor for monumental building projects, limiting access to basic resources, controlling trade and tributary villages, and coordinating ritual expressions. Trade linked communities and sent both exotic and ordinary objects over networks of long-established trails.

Because Europeans introduced epidemic disease, their arrival in the sixteenth century proved to be a watershed event. Many native people died in the wake of the mid-century expeditions of Hernando de Soto and Juan Pardo into the heart of the South and following various English, French, and Spanish forays along the Atlantic coast. The survivors either moved about or stayed put, and reorganized themselves socially and politically. In some cases the erosion of a society's power and influence was rapid. Many formerly sovereign societies disappeared, along with their ethnonyms, replaced by newly coalescent societies whose names remain familiar today: the Catawba, the Creek, the Alabama, the Yuchi, the Chickasaw, the Choctaw, the Cherokee, the Seminole, the Natchez, the Caddo, and others (see map 2). All native people were caught up

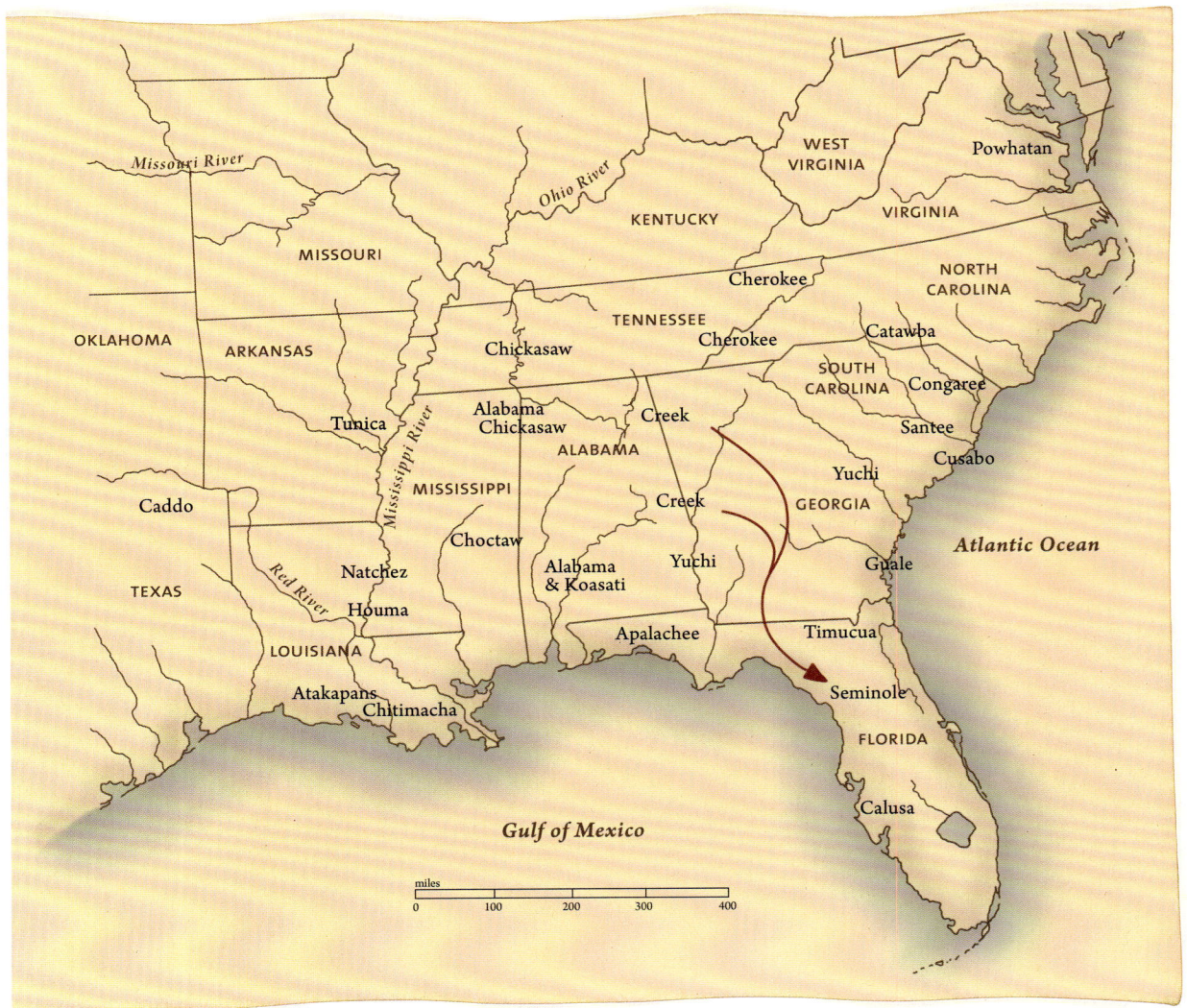

MAP 2.
Native people in the South. Locations are approximate and changing, sixteenth–nineteenth centuries.

in the European play for commodities, power, and empire as it unfolded in the South, and in conflicts ranging from internecine to international in scope that involved a fluid selection of allies and opponents and often resulted in slavery and death.

In the nineteenth century, the United States forcibly removed most native people from the South, marching them to Indian Territory in today's Oklahoma. Catering to the demands of land-hungry immigrants and states' rights advocates over the objections of the Supreme Court, the nation's executive and legislative branches sanctioned this deeply troubling event. Profoundly traumatic, removal was an immediate tragedy for Indian people. The forced dislocation destroyed lives, fractured families, and shattered communities. For the Cherokee, the trek was their Trail of Tears. Ironically, those most affected were the Five Civilized Tribes (the Cherokee, the Chickasaw, the Choctaw, the Creek, and the Seminole), so-called because of political, economic, and social institutions that included literacy for the Cherokee, and farming and slavery for all.

Quite a few native people managed to avoid removal and continued to live in the South in scattered communities and homesteads, including over one thousand Choctaws, several hundred Cherokees, Creeks in Alabama, Seminoles in Florida, and other Indians in Virginia, North and South Carolina, Louisiana, Texas, and elsewhere. Many had families with people of African and European descent. Many were landless and destitute and deliberately kept a low profile. Yet they formed the core of no less than thirty-eight separate southern Indian tribes and groups that have federal or state recognition today, the base for a twentieth-century demographic resurgence and remarkable recent cultural and ethnic rebirth powered by casinos and other economic development projects, and celebrated in powwows (in which birds and their feathers figure in old and new ways) — but this is getting ahead of a story that must first set the stage by taking up the diversity and numbers of birds in the South.[9]

PLATE 76.

FIGURE 6. Virginian Partridge (northern bobwhite). *Hand-colored engraving by Robert Havell from a painting by John James Audubon,* Birds of America, *vol. 1 (1827–30), plate 76. A dramatic narrative: a red-shouldered hawk attacks a covey of northern bobwhites that explodes in all directions. The bobwhite, or quail, was an important food bird that also figured in native story and myth; in contrast, the red-shouldered hawk, a common bird in the South, was little remarked on. Rare Books and Special Collections, Thomas Cooper Library, University of South Carolina.*

The Birds

Fray Sebastián de Cañete, a cleric who accompanied the Spanish explorer Hernando de Soto on his earth-shaking expedition through the heart of the South in 1539–43, recalled eye-catching numbers of birds in "all parts" of the region, including "an infinite number" of "partridges" (northern bobwhites) and "turtledoves" (mourning doves), "many turkeys," and "many other kinds of very good birds."[1]

Was Cañete on the mark? The short answer is yes. Birds were everywhere. They still are today, albeit in greatly diminished numbers. Over three hundred species of birds occur regularly in the region. Some are resident year-round. Others arrive from the North and spend the winter. Still others migrate through the South in fall or spring, or both. Most North American bird families can be found somewhere in the region: loons, grebes, ducks, geese, swans, gulls, terns, herons, storks, ibises, rails, sandpipers and other shorebirds, turkeys and grouse, vultures, hawks, falcons, owls, pigeons, doves, goatsuckers (nighthawks and nightjars), hummingbirds, flycatchers, swallows, crows, jays, titmice, nuthatches, wrens, northern mockingbirds, thrushes, vireos, warblers, blackbirds, orioles, tanagers, finches, sparrows, and others.[2]

Such great diversity is not surprising. After all, the South is vast. Today, it is thought of as hot and humid, plagued by hurricanes, and overrun by kudzu. Like most stereotypes, however, this distorts and oversimplifies; it also fails to distinguish the exotic or invasive — kudzu — from the endemic. Far better to start with the region's "environmental images" invoked by Timothy Silver, an environmental historian: palmetto-covered coastal plains, southern pine forests, moss-heavy live oaks, blood red soil, smoky mountains, canebrakes, and cypress swamps. In short, the region presents a complex environment with distinctive zones ranging from the coastal plain and the alluvial Mississippi Valley to the Piedmont and the heights of the Appalachian Mountains.[3]

Birds could be found in all zones and habitats. Individual Europeans missed many species because the birds were unevenly distributed, evident briefly during migration, or gone for seasons at a time; even so they collectively made note of much of the diversity over the course of several centuries. One must read their avian lists and descriptions with the skepticism of the historian firmly in place and vet their language for exaggeration and propaganda, yet this contemporary (or nearly so) record, with which we begin, provides if nothing else an introduction to avian resources considered worthy of note over hundreds of years.

There is no better place to start than with Cañete and other members of the mid-sixteenth-century de Soto expedition, who found "many wild fowl … as large as peafowls,

FIGURE 7.
Sharp-shinn'd
Hawk. Redstart.
Yellow-rump
(yellow-rumped
Warbler). *Hand-
colored engraving by
Alexander Lawson
based on drawing
by Alexander
Wilson*, American
Ornithology, *vol. 5,
1808–14, plate 45.
All three were
common birds in
the South. John Hay
Library at Brown
University.*

small partridges like those of Africa, cranes, ducks, turtledoves, thrushes, and sparrows" as well as "certain black birds which [were] larger than sparrows and smaller than starlings" and "goshawks, falcons, sparrowhawks, and all the birds of prey found in Spain."[4]

In the same century, Jean Ribault, a French Huguenot on the Florida and Georgia Atlantic coasts, remarked, "[T]he sight of the fair medowes is a pleasure not able to be expressed with tonge, full of herons, corleux, bitters, mallards, edertes, woodkockes, and of all other kinde of smale birdes."[5] He noted, "[There are] guinea foule and innumerable wildfoule of all sortes, and in a lyttell ilande at the entrye of this haven . . . there is so great numbre of egretes that the bushes be all white and covered with them, so that one may take of the yong ones with his hande as many as he will carry awaye. There be also a nombre of other foule, as herons, bytters, curleux, and to be shorte, so many smale birdes that yt is a straung thing to be sene."[6] A few years later, René Laudonnière, another Huguenot with interests in colonization on the northern Florida Atlantic coast, listed "Indian chickens, partridges, parrots, pigeons, doves, turtledoves, blackbirds, crows, hawks, falcons, shrikes, herons, cranes, storks, wild geese, ducks, cormorants, white, red, black, and grey herns."[7]

Farther up the coast, in seventeenth-century Virginia, the English explorer and settler John Smith found in winter "great abundance" of swans, sandhill and whooping cranes, herons, geese, brant, wigeon and other ducks, dotterel, oxeyes, and parrots and pigeons, but in summer, "not any, or a very few to be seene." He remarked that "more plentie of swannes, cranes, geese, duckes, and mallards, & divers sorts of fowles none would desire." His birds included eagle, sparrow hawk, lanaret, goshawk, falcons, osprey, northern bobwhite, wild turkey, woosels or red-winged blackbirds, thrushes, and "diverse sorts of small birds, some red, some blew, scarce so bigge as a wrenne, but few in Sommer."[8]

Thomas Harriot, a colonist trained in geography at Oxford, listed "fowl" that included "Turkie cockes and Turkie hennes: Stockdoves: Partridges: Cranes: Hernes: & in Winter great store of Swannes & Geese." He also mentioned "Parats, Faulcons, & Marlin haukes," remarking, "[A]lthough with us they bee not used for meate, yet for other causes I thought it good to mention."[9]

FIGURE 8.
The Small Bittern
(green-backed
heron). *Hand-colored
etching by Mark
Catesby*, Natural
History *(1731–43),
plate 80. A common
wading bird in the
South. John Carter
Brown Library at
Brown University.*

Others involved in the late sixteenth- and early seventeenth-century effort to colonize Virginia (today's North Carolina and Virginia) agreed with this vision of useful abundance, describing a land "full of Deere, Conies, Hares, and Fowle, even in the middest of Summer, in incredible aboundance," and an "infinite number" not just of deer but of "turkeys, swans, and all kinds of fowl." In winter, rivers and creeks were "covered with swans, Geese, Ducks, & several other kinds of waterfowle." At that season there was "such a Multitude of Swans, Geese, Brants, Sheldrakes, Ducks of several Sorts, Teal, Blewings, and many other Kinds of Water-Fowl, that the Plenty of them [was] incredible." William Strachey, a Londoner with an interest in natural history, described larger winter populations of waterfowl, venturing, "[They are of such] aboundaunce as I dare avowe yt, no Country in the world may have more." On shore and in marshes and grasslands could be found "Plenty of other Game, of all Sorts, as Cranes, Curlews, Herons, Snipes, Woodcocks, Saurers, Ox-eyes, Plover, Larks, and many other good Birds for the Table that they ha[d] not yet found a name for," and lands inland had "the Advantage of Wild Turkeys, of an incridible Bigness, Pheasants, Partridges, Pigeons, and an Infinity of small Birds."[10]

These adventurers and explorers based many of their bird names on species known at home in Europe or from travels abroad. Some birds remain obscure, but most can be narrowed to several or two species, or can even be identified. For example, Harriot's "Stockdoves" were probably passenger pigeons, "Hernes" were great blue herons, "Parats" were Carolina parakeets, "Faulcons" were peregrine falcons, and "Marlin haukes"

FIGURE 9.
Indians Fishing.
Watercolor over black lead by John White, ca. 1585. Almost incidental to this scene of Indian fishing methods are birds in flight: at top left is possibly a pelican; below and to the right in flight are long-tailed waterfowl—perhaps swans (left) or terns, gannets, or other birds. © The Trustees of the British Museum, 1906,0509.1.6.

were merlins.[11] Among the less obvious birds in the lists mentioned so far, "swans" were probably tundra or trumpeter swans (or both), "teal" were green-winged teal, "blewings" were blue-winged teal, "sheldrakes" were northern shovelers, "bitters" were bitterns, "cranes" were sandhill or whooping cranes (or both), "white herns" and "red herns" were various egrets, "grey herns" were great blue herons, "curlews" and "corleux" were whimbrels and/or long-billed and Eskimo curlews, "saurers" were soras, "ox-eyes" were dunlin, "plover" were black-bellied plovers, "lanaret" was the peregrine falcon, "pheasants" were ruffed grouse and greater prairie-chickens, "partridges" were northern bobwhites, "pigeons" were passenger pigeons, "turtledoves" were mourning doves, "parrots" were Carolina parakeets, and "larks" were eastern meadowlarks.[12]

The depictions of Virginia and North Carolina birds not only distinguish waterfowl populations by season — plentiful in winter, scarcer in summer — but show a continuing emphasis on birds useful for consumption as well as grudging admission that other birds, such as various hawks and falcons or the Carolina parakeet, were worthy of note. The acknowledgment of the raptors betrays, no doubt, the great interest in falconry in Europe, and the Carolina parakeet was a gaudy, raucous bird hard to overlook.

In this light, the description of George Percy, a colonist of aristocratic upbringing, is of interest not only because he mentions "a store of Turkie nests and many Egges" but because of the broad range of birds he observes: "Black Birds with crimson wings, and divers other Fowles and Birds of divers and sundrie collours of crimson, Watchet [light blue], Yellow, Greene, Murry [reddish purple or blood red], and of divers other hewes naturally without any art using." Although colorful, these descriptions are unfortunately too general to identify specific birds other than the red-winged blackbird; "Watchet," for example, could refer to the eastern bluebird, indigo bunting, or blue grosbeak.[13]

Bird life in the mid-seventeenth- and early eighteenth-century Carolinas and Georgia evidently did not differ appreciably from what has just been described, except for apparently even more robust coastal populations of shorebirds, gulls, and other species. Regarding the Georgia and southern South Carolina coast, William Hilton and other explorers noted, "[They abound] with . . . Turkeys, Quails, Curlues, Plovers, Teile, Herons; and as the Indians say, in Winter with Swans, Geese, Cranes, Duck, and Mallard, and innumerable other water-Fowls, whose names we know not, which lie in the Rivers, Marshes and on the Sands."[14]

On the Carolina coast in winter in the early eighteenth century, the English naturalist-explorer John Lawson, whose powers of observation were unusual and notes on birds invaluable, spoke of killing "good Plenty of Fowl, as Curleus, Gulls, Gannets, and Pellicans, besides Duck and Mallard, Geese, Swans, Teal, Widgeon, &c." Near the mouth of one river were "great Numbers of Deer and Turkies . . . as also great Store of Partridges, Cranes, and Conies, in several Places." On one river Lawson found "great Store of Ducks, Teal, Widgeon," on another, "numerous Train of Swans, and other sorts of Water-Fowl, not common, though extraordinarily pleasing to the Eye."[15]

FIGURE 10.
Long-tailed Duck.
Summer D. (wood
duck). Green-winged
Teal. Canvas-back
Duck (canvasback).
Red-headed D.
(redhead). Mallard.
*Hand-colored
engraving by
Alexander Lawson
based on drawing
by Alexander
Wilson,* American
Ornithology, *vol.
8, 1808–14, plate
70. These were all
common food birds
consumed by natives
and newcomers. John
Hay Library at Brown
University.*

Lawson's remarks on swans are of great interest. He distinguished "two sorts": "[T]he one we call Trompeters" from their noise, which are "the largest" and "come in great flocks in the Winter," where they remain in fresh water in the rivers until spring when they go away somewhere to lakes to breed. The other were "call'd Hoopers," and were smaller in size, stayed more in salt water, and were "equally valuable, for Food."[16]

Today we call these the trumpeter swan and the tundra swan. The trumpeter, which is the largest North American waterfowl, is now rare in the South, but formerly both species were evidently common in parts of the region and in some seasons. In winter, the trumpeter was abundant on the coasts of North Carolina, Texas, Louisiana, Mississippi, and western Alabama. Whether it bred in the South is uncertain; unfortunately most historical references are to "swans" generically. Everywhere trumpeter swan numbers were greatly reduced from the seventeenth through the beginning of the twentieth centuries because Europeans and people of European descent commodified their skins for quills and feather products and disturbed and eventually destroyed many of their preferred habitats.[17]

In fall and winter, Lawson's party killed swans, geese, cranes, turkeys, ducks, mallards, parakeets, and "other small Fowls, as Curlues and Plover, &c." In the forests he described "great Flocks of Parrakeeto's." Inland, some Indians had "abundance of

Woanagusso. The Swann.

Storks and Cranes in their Savanna," and others lived near prairies "plentifully stor'd with Cranes, Geese, &c and the adjacent Woods with great Flocks of Turkies." Lawson was struck by the great number of turkeys; in one spot, "Flocks of these Fowl" came out of a swamp at sunrise, "containing several hundreds in a Gang, who fe[d] upon the Acorns, it being most Oak that gr[ew] in these Woods." In some places "great Flocks" contained up to five hundred birds. On many occasions Lawson's men ate turkeys that they killed or that were given to them by Indians; "barbacu'd Turkeys," some weighing dozens of pounds, were a favorite.[18]

Inland in the mid-eighteenth century, the Scots-Irish trader James Adair found turkeys relatively tame and easy to run down on horseback in the season when they were fat with acorns; he also described waterfowl and passenger pigeons in plentiful numbers.[19] Lt. Henry Timberlake, whose mission was to bring several Cherokee leaders from their nation to London, found time to remark on the "turkey, geese, ducks of several kinds, partridges, pheasants, and an infinity of other birds" in Cherokee country.[20] And on several occasions, the Philadelphia Quaker and naturalist William Bartram wrote of being awed by the lushness, beauty, and sheer abundance of birds and other wildlife. On one "bird isle," a small hammock of several acres "almost every tree of which was loaded with nests of various tribes of water fowl," he remarked, "It is incredible what prodigious numbers there were, old and young, on this little islet, and the confused noise which they kept up continually."[21]

The picture is much the same in eighteenth-century French Louisiana, where "prodigious quantities" of ducks, geese, bustards, and other waterfowl were attracted to Lake Pontchartrain in winter and killed.[22] Antoine-Simon Le Page du Pratz, a Dutch-born planter with a concession in Louisiana from 1718 to 1734, was struck by the "hideous noise of the numberless water-fowls that [were] to be seen on the Missisippi, and every river or lake near it, such as cranes, flamingo's, wild geese, herons, saw-bills, ducks, &c." At various times and places, away from the settlements, he reported "flocks of swans," country "stored with game of every kind, including partridges, ducks, and ring-doves"; forests "abound[ing] with" turkeys and partridges; and other lands as a retreat for "flocks of turkeys." He remarked that for every wild duck seen in France, "you may count here a thousand."[23] Like others, Le Page places the emphasis on "game" — on birds for sport and consumption — and he is more forthright than many about comparing the bounty of the New World with depletions in the Old.

Just to the north in the territory of the Quapaw along the Arkansas River in the mid-eighteenth century, the French naval officer Jean-Bernard Bossu depicted "all

FIGURE 11.
Trumpeter Swan. *Pen and ink with watercolor, associated with John White, ca. 1585–1600. Inscribed: "Woanagusso. The Swann." Both trumpeter and tundra swans wintered in the Carolinas; with its large black bill lacking yellow on the lores (forward of the eyes), this one is probably based on the trumpeter. Sloane volume. © The Trustees of the British Museum, SL,5270.82.*

kinds of game" including "turkeys, hazel grouse, pheasants, partridges, quails, doves, wood pigeons, swans, bustards, ducks of all kinds, teals, loons, marsh hens, golden plovers, woodcocks, snipes, thrushes, starlings, and other birds that [were] not seen in Europe." On one particular lake could be found "[t]oward the end of autumn a multitude of geese, bustards, teals, water hens, and ducks of all kinds." In a generalized account of natural history, Bossu mentioned many more birds, including the "carrion crow," or black vulture; the flamingo; red-winged blackbirds "so numerous" that "one hundred of these edible birds [could] be killed with a single shot"; parakeets and jays; egrets "whose extremely white feathers [were] used to make aigrettes for the ladies"; and the mockingbird, painted bunting, cardinal, blue grosbeak, goldfinch, hummingbird, wood duck, pelican, and roseate spoonbill.[24] Farther west in Caddo territory, a seventeenth-century Spanish Franciscan missionary reported numerous wild ducks of several kinds, prairie-chickens, "many kinds" of birds like herons, quail, partridges, and "endless number of birds that [sang] very melodiously in the spring."[25]

In sum, the numbers and — to the more discriminating naturalists — different kinds of birds seemed phenomenal, sometimes to the point of defying belief. The sources, as cautioned, must be read carefully in light of the well-known tendency for some to write

FIGURE 13.
Common Coot
(American coot).
Purple Gallinule.
Gray Phalarope
(Wilson's phalarope).
Red Phalarope.
Wilsons Plover.
*Hand-colored
engraving by J.
Warnicke based on
drawing by Alexander
Wilson,* American
Ornithology, *vol. 9,
1808–14, plate 73. In
the South, the coot
was common and
the phalaropes rare;
both the coot and
purple gallinule were
consumed. John Hay
Library at Brown
University.*

FIGURE 14.
Urogallus minor
(greater prairie-
chicken). *Hand-
colored etching by
Mark Catesby,* Natu-
ral History *(1731–43),
plate appendix 1.
The greater prairie-
chicken, or "heath
hen," which ultimate-
ly was extirpated
from the South, was
commonly consumed.
John Hay Library at
Brown University.*

propaganda or depict the flush of "strawberry time" rather than the season of want, to appeal to would-be emigrants and colonists from the Old World. As will be seen, however, in many cases cautious methodological skepticism gives way to sheer wonder at the apparent reality of the natural bounty.

PASSENGER PIGEONS

One bird that almost everyone seemed to mention was the passenger pigeon. Nearly always, remarks focused on their vast numbers. In the winter of 1564–65, for example, René Laudonnière, the Huguenot sent by France to establish a post on the St. Johns River in northern Florida, reported, "[A] great flock of doves came to us, unexpectedly and for a period of about seven weeks, so that every day we shot more then two hundred of them in the woods around our fort." These were surely passenger pigeons, not mourning doves or some other kind of dove. Laudonnière was not alone in calling a bird that resembled a European dove in appearance yet was the same length as the European wood pigeon a "dove"; in the Old World, birds that are today called doves were formerly called pigeons, and vice-versa. This is less important, however, than the numbers. Did Laudonnière exaggerate? Two hundred pigeons per day over seven weeks amounted to a total of ten thousand birds killed out of the "great flock."[26]

Actually, Laudonnière was probably circumspect. Reports of passenger pigeons came from across the region through time, with estimates in the millions and even billions. Pigeons wintered in the South and nested in Kentucky, Mississippi, and perhaps elsewhere in the region.[27] They awed those who observed them. In seventeenth-century Virginia, William Strachey remarked,

> [There is a] kynd of wood-pidgion we see in the wintertyme, and of them such numbers, as I should drawe (from our Homelings here such who have seene peradventure scarse one more then in the markett) the Credit of my Relation concerning all the other in question, if I should expresse what extended flockes and how many Thowsandes in one Flock I have seene in one day wondring (I must confesse) at their flight, when like so many thickned Clowdes, they (having fed to the Nor-ward in the daye tyme) returne againe more Southwardly towardes night to their Rowst, but there be many hundred witnesses who may Convince this Report, if herein testefieth an untruith.[28]

Later in the century the Oxford-trained rector and naturalist John Banister wrote, "I cannot omit (though it be allmost incredible) to relate, that here are some years such clouds of pidgeons, they darken the air, the wind of their wings is like the noise of great waters, & they sit so thick, where they roost that their weight break down great limbs of trees."[29]

At the beginning of the eighteenth century, Lawson remarked that passenger pigeons wintered (but did not spend the summer) in the Carolinas. One winter, he recounted,

[I] saw such prodigious Flocks of these Pigeons . . . that they had broke down all the Limbs of a great many large Trees all over those Woods, whereon they chanced to sit and roost; especially the great Pines, which are a more brittle Wood, than our sorts of Oak are. These Pigeons, about Sun-Rise, when we were preparing to march on our Journey, would fly by us in such vast Flocks, that they would be near a Quarter of an Hour, before they were all pass'd by; and as soon as that Flock was gone, another would come; and so successively one after another, for great part of the Morning.[30]

And the naturalist and artist Mark Catesby remarked that "incredible numbers" of pigeons wintered in Virginia and the Carolinas (especially when there was little food for them northward). He noted, "[In Virginia] I have seen them fly in such continued trains three days successively, that there was not the least interval in losing sight of them, but that somewhere or other in the air they were seen to be continuing their flight south."[31] William De Brahm, a cartographer and surveyor, reported in the 1760s that all passenger pigeons in North America "seem[ed] to make Georgia and East Florida their Home during the Winter Season, when their Game afford[ed] Diversion, and supplie[d] the Table in lieu of Poultry."[32]

The story was much the same farther west. In Louisiana, Le Page offered a similar account of wintering passenger pigeons: "[They are present] in such prodigious numbers, that I do not fear to exaggerate, when I affirm that they sometimes cloud the sun." Once he heard a "confused noise" from "a legion of wood-pigeons, who kept continually flying up and down successively among the branches of an ever-green oak, in order to beat down the acorns with their wings."[33]

In the early nineteenth century, the ornithologist Alexander Wilson reported in much the same vein that when beech nuts were abundant, so were pigeons in "corresponding multitudes," commuting back and forth at distances of up to eighty miles between a food source and a roosting site. The latter are "always in the woods, and sometimes occupy a large extent of forest," and, as Wilson continued, when the birds use a roost "for some time the appearance it exhibits is surprising. The ground is covered to a depth of several inches with their dung; all the tender grass and underwood destroyed; the surface strewed with large limbs of trees, broken down by the weight of the birds clustering above one another; and the trees themselves, for thousands of acres, killed as completely, as if girdled with an axe. The marks of this desolation remain for many years on the spot; and numerous places could be pointed out where for several years after scarce a single vegetable made its appearance."[34]

"VERY GOOD BIRDS"

Not only were passenger pigeons frequently mentioned and the subject of anecdotes, they were one of the "very good birds," by which Europeans meant useful for subsistence. That phrase, "very good birds," quickly became a refrain. Most observers of European extraction who remarked on birds led their lists with those that possessed food

FIGURE 17.
Black or Surf Duck
(surf scoter).
Buffel-headed D.
(bufflehead). Canada
Goose. Tufted duck
(ring-necked duck).
Golden eye (common
goldeneye).
Shoveller (northern
shoveler). *Hand-
colored engraving by
Alexander Lawson
based on drawing
by Alexander
Wilson*, American
Ornithology, *vol. 8,
1808–14, plate 67.
Where they occurred,
most, if not all, of
these ducks were
commonly pursued
and consumed. John
Hay Library at Brown
University.*

value, were large or showy with plumes, were predators, had brightly colored feathers, or reminded them of species they knew in the Old World, perhaps because they used birds like them in falconry or accessorized fashionably with their plumes. The exceptions were natural historians like John Lawson and ornithologists like Mark Catesby, Alexander Wilson, and John James Audubon, who noticed a far greater range of birds and wrote about them not just in light of what they managed to glean from the writings of others but from personal experience.

On most observers' lists were waterfowl, egrets, cranes, herons, raptors, turkeys, and passenger pigeons — but few were held in common beyond these. Sometimes a list was even more tightly focused on what the surveyor William De Brahm thought of as important "natural Products": turkeys "in great Abundance," ducks "in incredible Quantity," uncountable passenger pigeons, quail that became accustomed to human settlement and fed alongside domesticated poultry, and woodcocks and snipe. Many observers noted birds that were useful for the pot and tasty, and some compared them to home; Jean-Bernard Bossu reported being treated to wild ducks that smelled marshy and fishy but "taste[d] as good as the ducklings that I ate in Rouen on my way to le Havre," which he attributed to a diet of wild grains.[35]

KNOWING BIRDS

The newcomers who came to America focused on "very good birds" useful for food and other purposes, yet their knowledge about birds did not stop there. The question of what they did know is not idle, for knowledge constrained what they wrote. As the historian Keith Thomas and others have shown, Europeans and European Americans who wrote about things like birds during the early-modern era (ca. AD 1500–1800) held notions about the natural world that were quite different from today's ideas based in science. It is surely not surprising that knowledge about nature could change over a period lasting several hundred years. In this instance, the shift was from a foundation in folk systems to one in natural history, and it was reflected throughout conceptions of the natural world, including names for birds and ideas about birds.[36]

For example, prior to the eighteenth and nineteenth centuries, the English, whose observations appear repeatedly here, widely anthropomorphized birds, assigned them moral characteristics, and considered some auspicious and others unlucky. As in Exodus and Deuteronomy, where it was linked with God, or in a twelfth-century Latin bestiary, in which it led the list of birds and was believed to present its offspring to the rays of the sun or to come down from on high like a thunderbolt, the eagle signified courage and strength and was a highly privileged bird. Some thought that the bittern made its booming call by inserting its bill into a reed or the mud; that the jack snipe and snipe were male and female of the same species rather than two separate species; that swans lived three hundred years; and that swallow ashes were a remedy for failing sight.

Many also believed in metamorphosis: barnacle geese grew from and dropped off barnacles and metamorphosed into feathered birds, robins morphed into redstarts, garden warblers changed into blackcaps, and in winter corncrakes became water rails until spring, when they changed back again into corncrakes (the Scots, in their fashion, thought that the corncrake, a lucky bird, semihibernated in a torpid state in winter).

Some birds were augural: a green woodpecker calling or a grey heron flying low foretold rain; a pied wagtail that wagged its tail more or less than nine times after it landed was unlucky to the person keeping track; a killed robin (an ill omen for many) or swallow would bring bad luck. Some considered the carrion crow, the rook, and the raven ominous, but others thought the raven a powerful bird useful in divining. When calling, the bittern, which some branded the night raven, was greatly feared as an omen of death; owls were ill omens, and the Welsh named both the tawny and the barn owl "corpse bird"; the magpie was not simply an ill omen but could morph into human form; and some, calling it "corpse-hound," believed that the nightjar (the only European member of the goatsucker family) caused distemper in calves, sucked goats dry of their milk at night, or housed the wandering souls of unbaptized infants.[37]

Until the nineteenth century, people of European descent had uneven success identifying birds in the South, especially ones that lacked any kind of familiarity. Most hardly noticed birds, but a few stood out in their knowledge of natural history. One was the naturalist John Lawson, who listed in his "Natural History of Carolina" 120 different kinds of birds, ranging from waterfowl, shorebirds, pigeons, and raptors to thrushes, woodpeckers, swallows, and the martin, the catbird, the mockingbird, and the oriole.[38]

Lawson even listed "Hedge-Sparrows" — New World sparrows resembling the European dunnock (a small, widespread bird streaked brown and gray commonly known as the hedge sparrow) — but it is striking in retrospect how few observers noticed flycatchers, warblers, sparrows, wrens, vireos, and other families, which are conspicuous in their absence from lists. Other than Lawson, the exceptions were the artist-naturalists and ornithologists Mark Catesby, Alexander Wilson, John James Audubon, and a few others. On the whole, small birds went underreported, unreported, or overgeneralized. Among them were sparrows and other birds known for being skulkers or unremarkable in plumage or behavior, the classic "dicky birds" or "little brown jobs."[39]

The nineteenth-century ornithologist and painter Alexander Wilson spoke about the persistence of popular European beliefs about birds, as well as about convergences in Indian and European beliefs. For example, he commented that Indians regarded the whip-poor-will "like the Owl and other nocturnal birds," with "suspicious awe, as a bird with which they wish[ed] to have as little to do as possible." Night plagues the superstitious, Wilson thought, with "kindred horrors . . . apparitions, strange sounds and awful sights," and the "solitary inoffensive" whip-poor-will "being a frequent wanderer in these hours of ghosts and hobgoblins, [was] considered by the Indian as being by habit and repute little better than one of them." Some Indians, Wilson said, "treated these silly notions with contempt," but of greater importance is that the "superstition of the Indian differs very little from that of an illiterate German, a Scots Highlander, or the less informed of any other nation. It suggests ten thousand fantastic notions to each, and these, instead of being recorded with all the punctilio of the most important truths, seem only fit to be forgotten. Whatever, among either of these people, is strange and not comprehended, is usually attributed to supernatural agency; and an unexpected sight, or uncommon incident, is often ominous of good, but more generally of bad fortune, to the parties."[40]

Wilson was on the right track in suggesting a parallel sensibility about birds in Indian and European folk belief, even while his language reflects the growing tension between folk-biological and natural-historical — in time, scientific — explanation. Naturalists of European descent eventually considered early-modern beliefs at first quaint and then bizarre, but for centuries this avian folklore led observers to fear certain birds, admire and privilege others, and deem many barely worthy of notice. And certain beliefs proved remarkably difficult to dislodge, like the one about swallows entering torpor and submersing in water or muck during winter rather than migrating to some warmer, insect-filled clime — an explanation encouraged in America, as the historian Andrew

FIGURE 18. Red Owl (eastern screech-owl). Warbling Flycatcher (warbling vireo?). Purple Finch. Brown Lark (American pipit). *Hand-colored engraving by Alexander Lawson based on drawing by Alexander Wilson,* American Ornithology, *vol. 5, 1808–14, plate 42. Other than the screech-owl, these birds did not appear to figure significantly in the lives of native people. John Hay Library at Brown University.*

FIGURE 19.
Carolina Parrot
(Carolina parakeet).
Canada Flycatcher
(Canada warbler).
Hooded F. (hooded
warbler). Green,
black-capt F. (Wil-
son's warbler). Hand-
colored engraving by
G. Murray based on
drawing by Alexander
Wilson, American
Ornithology, vol.
3, 1808–14, plate
26. The Carolina
parakeet was con-
sumed and used,
but warblers, even
brilliant migrants or
ones that remained
to breed, largely
escaped notice. John
Hay Library at Brown
University.

Lewis suggests, by a climate of intellectual permissiveness in natural history.[41]

INDIGENOUS KNOWLEDGE OF BIRDS

To name something is to know it. Apparently, few people of European descent bothered to name the little birds that the English called collectively "dicky birds." Today we might say that these "little brown jobs" simply didn't come up on their screens. But what about native people? What did *they* do? Did they name the same birds as Europeans or different ones? Did their names reflect similar knowledge or partitioning of the natural world? Did birds named or unnamed provide insight into indigenous environmental and cultural knowledge?

Forty years ago, the anthropologist Claude Lévi-Strauss declared, against any who assumed that indigenous people such as American Indians lived in "intellectual poverty," that for all human beings, "the universe is an object of thought at least as much as it is a means of satisfying needs." Therefore, things such as birds "are not known as a result of their usefulness; they are deemed to be useful or interesting because they are first of all known." In other words, as Lévi-Strauss had developed in an earlier work, birds are not just useful in a narrow utilitarian sense or, as he put it, "good to eat"; they are also good for thinking, that is, good to think about or reflect upon.[42]

Lévi-Strauss's proposition, and the questions raised earlier, are serious given certain assumptions about knowledge of the natural world, like the greater the number of names, the greater the knowledge of the intimate details that distinguish one living thing from the next and establish difference in the natural world. But these questions are not the easiest to settle for the period immediately following the arrival of Europeans in the New World, at least not for an ethno-ornithology of the South. Unfortunately, knowledge of native naming (and classification) will always be incomplete prior to the eighteenth century. John White, the remarkable London artist (and governor of the Roanoke colony in 1587), did manage to record sixteenth-century Algonquian names for birds in North Carolina, but only for roughly twenty different kinds. They include the common loon, red-breasted or common merganser, surf scoter, osprey, sandhill crane, pileated woodpecker, towhee, red-wing blackbird, Baltimore oriole, northern cardinal, blue jay, and barn swallow. Others are not so easily identified — yet White's range from water to land, large to small, raptor to passerine, is striking.[43]

Thomas Harriot, the geographer, and William Strachey, the Englishman curious about nature, also recorded names of birds in the Algonquian languages spoken in sixteenth- and seventeenth-century North Carolina and Virginia. Harriot elicited terms for eighty-six different kinds of birds: "Of al sorts of fowle I have the names in the countrie language of fourescore and six of which number besides those that be named, we have taken, eaten, & have the pictures as they were there drawne with the names of the inhabitaunts of severall strange sorts of water foule eight, and seventeene kinds more of land foul, although wee have seene and eaten of many more, which for want of leasure there for the purpose coulde not bee pictured." Unfortunately, this list has disappeared.[44]

William Strachey's inventory included over one dozen water birds such as "duck" (mallard?), "another duck," "sheldrake," "wigeon," "a bird called divedapper" (a small diving bird), "fowl like a teal with a sharp bill like the blackbird," "waterfowl in bigness of a duck finely colored with a copit crown" (probably copple, referring to a "tuft of feathers on a fowl's head" or "a crest" and perhaps the multihued crested wood duck), "brant," "goose," "another goose," "goosling," "swan," and "gull." Strachey also lists raptors like "eagle," "sparrow hawk," and "owl" and game birds like "turkey" (two separate labels) and "turkey cock." Two wading birds are mentioned: a "bird like a lapwing" and a "crane." Land birds include "pigeon" (mourning dove?), "wood pigeon" (passenger pigeon?), "parrot" (Carolina parakeet), "robin red breast" (American robin), "bird with carnation-colored wings," "watchet-colored bird," and "small bird of diverse colors." There are also words for "chicken," "small bird or chicken," and "bird," which might be another specific bird or the general category. Often obscure, the names on this list nevertheless privilege, like their European counterparts and perhaps because of Strachey's biases, waterfowl, raptors, and other useful or noticeable birds.[45]

As we come closer in time to the present, the data remain frustratingly uneven. Nineteenth- and twentieth-century dictionaries reveal little about birds — a reflection of the erosion of native knowledge, the limited interest or scant ornithological knowledge of the linguists and others who compiled the dictionaries, and the impact of novel categories or names in English or other European tongues or in the languages of other native people with whom southern Indians came into contact following removal to Indian Territory in Oklahoma.

FIGURE 20. Barn Swallow. White-bellied S. (tree swallow). Bank S[wallow]. *Hand-colored engraving by J. Warnicke based on drawing by Alexander Wilson,* American Ornithology, *vol. 5, 1808–14, plate 38. Swallows were present in vast numbers in some seasons but were seemingly unnoticed. John Hay Library at Brown University.*

Chúwquaréo. The blackbyrd.

Weeheépens. The Swallowe.

Kaiauk. A gull as bigg as a Duck.

Qvúnziuck. Of the bignes of a Duck.

FIGURE 21. *(Above, left)* Red-winged Blackbird and Barn Swallow. *Pen and ink with watercolor, associated with John White, ca. 1585–1600.* Inscribed: "Chúwquaréo. The blackbird." "Weeheépens. The Swallowe." *Like many bird names in the South, the Algonquian name for the red-winged blackbird is onomatopoeic. Sloane volume. © The Trustees of the British Museum, SL,5270.90.*

FIGURE 22. *(Above, right)* Herring Gull. *Pen and ink with watercolor, associated with John White, ca. 1585–1600.* Inscribed: "Kaiauk—A Gull as bigg as a Duck." *This heavy-billed gull with dark tail and primaries (and curious dark wing coverts) was probably an immature (second-winter) herring gull. Gulls are largely invisible in the ethno-ornithology of the South. Sloane volume. © The Trustees of the British Museum, SL,5270.83.*

FIGURE 23. *(Right)* Red-breasted or Common Merganser. *Pen and ink with watercolor, associated with John White, ca. 1585–1600.* Inscribed: "Ovúnziuck. Of the bignes of a Duck." *This bird combines features of the red-breasted and the common merganser: it has the former's distinctive crest and flanks, and head, throat, and eye colors; and the latter's contrast of a whitish breast and green throat and head. In the South, native people sculpted and consumed mergansers. Sloane volume. © The Trustees of the British Museum, SL,5270.79.*

For example, two late twentieth-century Chickasaw dictionaries list only some fifty to sixty different kinds of birds. In the first, finch, nuthatch, sparrow, thrasher, and thrush are *foshi*, "bird"; blackbird, grackle, and brown-headed cowbird are lumped into the category *chulha losa* (*losa* is "black"); other names translate directly from a bird's habitat (for example, gull is *oka foshi*, "water bird") or from appearance (for instance, *foshi lakna*, "bird yellow," is some yellow bird other than "warbler" — perhaps the yellow warbler — or the exotic canary, which are lumped into their own named category).[46] In the second and more recently published dictionary, many familiar birds are named, such as the eastern bluebird, cardinal, chickadee, crow, raven, scissortailed flycatcher (*hilowifoshi'*, "thunder bird"), great horned owl, (ruby-throated) hummingbird, mockingbird (one name is *foshi' taloowa'*, "bird-singer"), and whip-poor-will. At least four different kinds of owls are distinguished: great horned, screech-, short-eared, and a fourth. There are five kinds of eagles (*osi'*) — bald (literally, white-headed), golden, red-headed, striped with one stripe around the body, and big. And three hawks (*akankabi'*): chicken (literally, "kill-chicken"), red-tailed ("kill-chicken tail red"), and "smaller kill-chicken." Several woodpeckers (*bakbak* or *aboowa bo'li'*, "house pound") are named: *bakbak ishkobo'homma*, "woodpecker head red"; *bakbak ishto'*, "woodpecker big"; *chapchap* (a small woodpecker); *itti' cha'li'*, "tree pound." And the flicker receives two names. There is even a "little brown job" or "dicky bird" on the list: *aachompa' foshi'*, "town/store/trading post bird," presumably the invasive European house sparrow. The greatest lexical elaboration is reserved for a different kind of exotic bird, the chicken (*akanka'*), which we return to later.[47]

In a compilation that is far more satisfactory because the interviewer himself was knowledgeable about birds, Chief Sam Blue, a twentieth-century Catawba, provided names for over sixty kinds of birds ranging from ducks, grebes, herons, and raptors to shorebirds and a variety of small birds. Some names, like those for killdeer and screech-owl, are onomatopoeic; others, like "big chicken" for turkey, "very small bird" for a wren, and "bird black with red wings" for red-winged blackbird, describe appearance (although "big chicken" is odd given that the turkey was endemic and the chicken introduced, unless a domesticated turkey is the reference). Yet others signal some characteristic, such as "tree bird" for wood duck, "fish catching bird" for kingfisher, "bird hollering at night" for common nighthawk, "sucking bird" for ruby-throated hummingbird, "shypoke" for green heron, and "wild ancient sure enough eats all carrion" for turkey vulture (the last being descriptive both of a mythological role and foraging behavior). Chief Blue did not always depict a one-to-one correspondence between a Catawba name and a scientific species. He often generalized a name from one specific bird to others perceived as related. At times he gave only one name for two species (e.g.,

FIGURE 24.
The Baltimore-Bird (Baltimore oriole). *Hand-colored etching by Mark Catesby,* Natural History *(1771), plate 48. A common spring and summer resident and a striking bird with a musical song, this oriole nevertheless does not seem to figure importantly in the ornithology of native people in the South. John Carter Brown Library at Brown University.*

FIGURE 25. *(Left)* Magnolia Warbler. *Drawing by William Bartram. A beautiful, small (and largely invisible) migrant in the South. Botanical and zoological drawings, 1756–1788, the Botany Library, no. 64 (Ewan 2), © Natural History Museum, London.*

FIGURE 26. *(Right)* The Nuthatch. The small Nuthatch (white-breasted nuthatch [L]; brown-headed nuthatch [R]). *Hand-colored etching by Mark Catesby,* Natural History *(1731–43), plate 22. Both nuthatches are resident in much of the South, but neither is especially visible in the region's ethno-ornithology. John Carter Brown Library at Brown University.*

great horned owl and barred owl; whip-poor-will and chuck-will's-widow) or more than two, apparently because he regarded them as different sexes of the same species. Interestingly, the turkey vulture and black vulture received one label in Catawba but two in English. Many birds remained unnamed.[48]

The data are even richer for the Cherokee, who collectively distinguished 110 kinds of birds in the category *jisgwa* (bird), one of five major kinds of animals. They named both highly visible species like various hawks (sharp-shinned, Cooper's, red-tailed, red-shouldered, broad-winged, and marsh hawks are all distinguished), falcons, eagles, and the osprey, as well as less flashy or conspicuous birds like winter wren, golden-crowned kinglet, least flycatcher, bank swallow, and pine siskin. Their names are largely either onomatopoeic or descriptive of appearance or perceived behavior: "Climbing up and down on a round thing" (white-breasted nuthatch), "imitator" (brown thrasher), "white dirt" (northern flicker, from the conspicuous white rump of this ground feeder), "love sick" or "hawk big" (red-tailed hawk; the first name is from its whistle, perceived as a sign of loneliness), "fire on head" (golden-crowned kinglet), "head eating" (northern mockingbird; to eat the head of this bird is to make one intelligent).

Most birds named by the Cherokee correspond to species in Western science (or to genera represented by single species), such as the wild turkey, the American goldfinch, and the pileated woodpecker. Yet sometimes the Cherokee lumped two or more species into a single category: for example, there is one name (tanager) for the scarlet and the summer tanager; one for the downy and the hairy woodpecker; one (blackbird) for the red-winged blackbird, rusty blackbird, brown-headed cowbird, and common grackle; one, apparently generalized from the moorhen, for it, the coot, and several species of rails; one label (sandpiper, "they put their legs in water") for nine species of shorebirds except for the snipe and the woodcock (which are lumped together as one category) and the killdeer, which is distinct in name; one label (sparrow) for seventeen species of sparrows and allies; one (duck) for over twenty species of waterfowl (relatively uncommon in Cherokee country); one (gull, "turnip" for some reason) for gulls; one (water thrush) for the very similar northern and Louisiana water thrush; and one ("stripe on eyes") for the red-eyed vireo and the white-eyed vireo (which are very different in appearance, behavior, habitat, and voice) and for several warblers.

Despite lumping together the two water thrushes, and several warblers with two vireos, the Cherokee did distinguish many conspicuous breeding and migrant warblers: black-and-white warbler, ovenbird, worm-eating warbler, Blackburnian warbler, chestnut-sided warbler, hooded warbler, redstart, and yellow-breasted chat all received individual names. Sparrows, however, present a puzzle: collectively they are "the real or principal bird" or "really the bird," and the Cherokee separated by name the song sparrow, the fox sparrow, and the white-throated sparrow but apparently not others in this numerous but inconspicuous category of small brown birds similar in appearance.

Individual Cherokees varied in their ability to identify birds and did not always agree on naming. For example, some considered the red-winged blackbird and the common grackle as the same kind of bird, others gave the same name to the red-winged blackbird and the brown-headed cowbird, and at least one person distinguished these birds according to where they lived (e.g., in the swamp) or by tint (e.g., bluish). Some called the red-headed woodpecker, yellow-bellied sapsucker, and red-breasted nuthatch by the same name, "deaf" (because they seemed fearless in the presence of humans), but others did not. Some considered the red-headed woodpecker to have been a witch who turned herself into a bird to escape people coming to execute her; but others thought that the yellow-bellied sapsucker was the former witch. As we shall see, this is the tip of the iceberg in the intersection of the world of birds and other-than-human or other-than-avian beings: the Cherokee category "bird" embraced spirit birds and beings with birdlike attributes — that is, they have feathers or fly — prominent among which was a mythical raptor, as it excluded, at least at first, chickens and other exotic domesticated fowl.[49]

Even though this information on the Cherokee is comparatively robust, all the bird lists are based on the limited knowledge of a few people and represent the collective knowledge of those few; and as others have remarked with regard to the distribution of knowledge and the naming of things like birds in any society, no single person is omniscient. For these reasons, as well as the loss through time of much former cultural information and the success with which European American naming and systematics

FIGURE 27. Green-backed Heron. *Drawing by William Bartram. A common and active small heron, whose shy or retiring nature is reflected in the Catawba word for it. Botanical and zoological drawings, 1756–1788, the Botany Library, no. 17 (Ewan 44), © Natural History Museum, London.*

FIGURE 28.
Spotted Sandpiper.
Bartram's S. (upland
sandpiper). Ring
Plover (semi-
palmated plover).
Sanderling P.
(sanderling). Golden
P. (American golden
plover). Killdeer P.
(killdeer). *Hand-
colored engraving by
J. Warnicke based on
drawing by Alexander
Wilson,* American
Ornithology, *vol.
7, 1808–14, plate
59. Most of these
shorebirds are
common migrants in
the South or, in the
case of the killdeer,
a breeder, but none
appears to register
significantly in native
thought. John Hay
Library at Brown
University.*

supplanted the indigenous system, firm conclusions on nomenclature remain difficult. At this late date the more subtle distinctions formerly made among birds might be very hard to ascertain. The Cherokee data show that despite in-depth collaboration between knowledgeable native people and anthropologists, no Cherokee names have been recorded for approximately one-half of the species that lived in or passed through their territory. Yet the data also suggest that even though many species apparently remained invisible, these people distinguished by name not merely birds that were important in subsistence, the economy, and material culture, or that were visible in size, coloration, or behavior, but also those that on the surface seem not to have been especially important in these contexts; but this needs further investigation.[50]

It does, however, seem safe to assume that prior to the period when they were forcibly removed from the South, the Cherokee and other southern Indians possessed profound knowledge of the region where, for generations, they had made a living, a knowledge equal to that of indigenous people elsewhere; and that among the living things recognized and named were many kinds of birds corresponding to the species and genera of Western science.

Yet to underscore a point made earlier, this means not that indigenous knowledge was the equivalent, or shared the rationality, of today's Western ethology, ornithology, or science, but only that it existed with its own logic. Examples must be legion of indigenous people who, despite encyclopedic knowledge of the environment, assert as fact (as some do in eastern Indonesia and Papua New Guinea) that certain birds are celibate or switch sexes, that males in nature are really females and vice versa, that a falcon decapitates its prey with its wing, or that a bird produces low-pitched vocalizations with its anus. Thus it cannot be surprising that in the American South, a twentieth-

FIGURE 29. *(Left)* Brown Thrush (brown thrasher). Golden-crowned Th. (ovenbird). Cat Bird. Bay-breasted Warbler. Chestnut-sided W[arbler]. Mourning W[arbler]. *Hand-colored engraving by Alexander Lawson based on drawing by Alexander Wilson,* American Ornithology, *vol. 2, 1808–14, plate 14. The thrasher is a resident throughout the South, the catbird less so, and the warblers are migrants; none is especially significant despite showy plumage (the migrants) or strong vocal abilities (the catbird and the thrasher). John Hay Library at Brown University.*

FIGURE 30. *(Right)* American Siskin (pine siskin). Rose-breasted Grosbeak. Green black-throated Warbler (black-throated green warbler). Yellow rump[ed] W[arbler]. Coerulean W[arbler]. Solitary Flycatcher (blue-headed vireo). *Hand-colored engraving by Alexander Lawson based on drawing by Alexander Wilson,* American Ornithology, *vol. 2, 1808–14, plate 17. Mainly migrants in the South, these birds include some that also winter there. John Hay Library at Brown University.*

century Pamunkey Indian thought that soras turned into frogs, and frogs into soras, when each appeared or disappeared. Of course, given what has been said about early-modern European folk beliefs about metamorphosis, it is an open question whether this belief was ancient or influenced by people of European descent.[51]

Nor does vast environmental knowledge mean that all species were visible in no-menclature. Indeed, the great global range in indigenous naming of birds — from people who label every bird that flies (or walks) to others who lump into a residual category many birds that fail, for various and often unpredictable reasons, to cross the threshold of salience — gives pause to drawing blanket conclusions about southern In-dians, for whom much former cultural knowledge is a distant and fragmented memory or entirely lost.[52]

FIGURE 31. Wild Turkey. *Hand-colored engraving by William Lizars from a painting by John James Audubon,* Birds of America, *vol. 1 (1827–30), plate 6. The most important bird in the South for its flesh and material products. Rare Books and Special Collections, Thomas Cooper Library, University of South Carolina.*

Subsistence

Gabriel Archer, a gentleman and leader of the Jamestown colony in 1607–10, remarked that the Powhatan "kill[ed] fowle [in] aboundance." One century later, the Virginia-born Robert Beverley, drawing here, perhaps, as he did elsewhere on the natural historian John Banister, noted that these Indians "solemnize[d] a day for the plentiful coming of their Wild Fowl, such as Geese, Ducks, Teal, etc. for the returns of their Hunting Season."[1]

On the surface, the Powhatan seemed far from alone in the South in their interest in hunting birds for subsistence or their success in doing so. But were they in fact typical? What birds did southern Indians consume? Which were most important, and which were less so? Did native people prohibit the consumption of any birds? Did they domesticate and raise birds before or after Europeans arrived? How did they hunt birds, and did they find it essential to protect domesticated crops against marauding bird pests? We explore these and other questions related to native subsistence in the South in the pages that follow.

What is clear at the outset is that Indians throughout the region based subsistence on nut- and seed-bearing plant foods, shellfish, fish, small mammals, white-tailed deer, and domesticated plants. But everywhere, birds were an important supplement, especially turkeys, passenger pigeons, northern bobwhites, ducks, and geese; the eighteenth-century Caddo were typical in their interest in turkeys, geese, ducks, "partridges," cranes, northern bobwhites, "and other birds that are on the beach or on the banks and margins of the rivers."[2]

Nowhere were birds of greater importance than white-tailed deer or, when they became available, domesticated crops. Yet faunal analysis at archaeological sites (and other evidence) leads to three broad conclusions about birds in the diet. First, away from the coast, turkeys and (where they occurred) migratory and wintering ducks loomed large. Second, on the coast, where fish and mollusks were especially favored, birds rose in importance through time. And third, birds became more critical for subsistence when white-tailed deer were scarce.

TURKEYS

Turkeys, as indicated, were especially important; an estimated five million lived in the fifteenth-century South, especially in oak and chestnut habitats. Accounts of flocks of birds numbering in the hundreds were common; there were even reports of concentrations of over a thousand birds. Southern Indians hunted turkeys all year long but favored winter and early spring, when men were likely to be hunting deer and also finding many edible birds. The Timucua, for example, hunted "turkey cocks" in winter, and Virginia Algonquians and Carolina Indians hunted waterfowl in winter and turkeys in March and April. In early spring, gobblers competed for hens on strutting grounds, hens were eager to copulate, and hunters easily called them both into range of their traps and weapons. Lawson remarked that in "Hunting-Quarters" inland, turkeys were abundant and "a roasted or barbakued Turkey, eaten with Bears fat, [was] held a good Dish." Here as elsewhere, turkeys were prepared by roasting or boiling and sometimes left undressed. Indians also consumed turkey eggs.[3]

PASSENGER PIGEONS

Given what has been said about the multitude of passenger pigeons, it is not surprising that many Indians hunted them at roosts or when they passed through their territory. Indians sought especially fat, oily young squabs, eating them on the spot or, like Indians in the Carolinas, rendering them for oil that they preserved and carried on winter hunts.[4]

Lawson's description of the vast numbers killed at a wintertime roost near the Yadkin River in North Carolina is famous:

> [W]e went to shoot Pigeons, which were so numerous in these Parts, that you might see many Millions in a Flock; they sometimes split off the Limbs of stout Oaks, and other Trees, upon which they roost o' Nights. You may find several *Indian* Towns, of not above 17 Houses, that have more than 100 Gallons of Pigeons Oil, or Fat; they using it with Pulse, or Bread, as we do Butter, and making the Ground as white as a Sheet with their Dung. The *Indians* take a Light, and go among them in the Night, and bring away some thousands, killing them with long Poles, as they roost in the Trees. At this time of the Year, the Flocks, as they pass by, in great measure, obstruct the Light of the day.[5]

Lawson concluded, "[W]here Pigeons are plentiful, [Indians] get their Fat enough to supply their Winter Stores."[6]

The ornithologist Alexander Wilson also commented on the use of pigeons by native people: "By the Indians, a Pigeon roost, or breeding place, is considered an important source of national profit and dependence for that season; and all their active ingenuity is exercised on the occasion. The *breeding place* differs from the former in its greater extent." Wilson mentioned one Kentucky rookery that "stretched through the woods in nearly a north and south direction; was several miles in breadth, and was said to be upwards of forty miles in extent! In this tract almost every tree was furnished with nests, wherever the branches could accommodate them." Passenger pigeons arrived in mid-April and left with their young before the end of May.[7]

Given the descriptions of millions of passenger pigeons and evidence that native people had a gustatory interest in them, it seems curious, the archaeologist Thomas Neumann has suggested, that pigeon remains are not more abundant in archaeological sites. Perhaps, he proposes, pigeon numbers first spiked prior to the well-documented free fall to extinction, as a result of people of European descent who killed off the competition (turkeys, deer, squirrels) for what botanists call mast (beechnuts, acorns, and other forest nuts and fruit), whose diseases eliminated yet more competition (native people), and who created ecological niches in the woodlands where these birds flourished.

As clever as this sounds — and even if he is ultimately right about an increase in numbers — Neumann unfortunately slights or misses several key early sources indicating great abundance of these birds in the South. In other words, that there were vast numbers of passenger pigeons on the cusp of, or shortly after, the arrival of Europeans cannot be in question. Furthermore, H. Edwin Jackson demonstrates in a recent synthesis of zooarchaeological research in the Southeast that pigeons were both widely distributed in the South and widely represented in the Mississippian archaeological faunal record. Perhaps, he suggests, in an ecological argument parallel to Neumann's, pigeon numbers increased because a new domesticated food source, maize, became widely available to them at the same time that human pressure on traditional mast lessened — both happening centuries before the arrival of European newcomers.[8]

OVER SEVENTY-FIVE SPECIES

As important as they were, turkeys and passenger pigeons do not begin to represent the whole story of native consumption of birds. Much that we know today comes from the analysis of faunal remains in archaeological sites. Despite their friability, especially in acidic or poorly drained soils, bird bones and feathers do not decay immediately, and many bones no longer fall through sifting-screen mesh as they did when archaeologists had only larger prey in mind.[9]

Today we know that the record of bird consumption in the South is impressive. Middens on the coastal plain have yielded over fifty species of birds, and sites inland from thirty to eighty species. The coastal list regularly includes remains of mallard, lesser scaup, hooded and red-breasted merganser, common loon, double-crested cormorant, great blue heron, great egret, and turkey vulture; also found are those of American coot, pied-billed grebe, common murre, razorbill, gannet, black vulture, caracara, sharp-shinned hawk, anhinga, white ibis, limpkin, king rail, sandhill crane, various gulls and geese, wood duck and other ducks, and even great auk. Overall, one can find in refuse heaps in the South ducks, geese, swans, cranes, herons, rails, gulls, eagles, crows, and various small songbirds, and American bittern, American coot, raven, red-tailed hawk, barred owl, barn owl, screech-owl, long-eared owl, turkey vulture, passenger pigeon, greater prairie-chicken, northern bobwhite, wild turkey, and ivory-billed woodpecker.[10]

FIGURE 32. Eine wilde amerikanische Taube (A wild American pigeon). *Colored drawing by Philip George Friedrich von Reck, Georgia, 1736. Von Reck provides names in Creek (Pat-schi) and Yuchi (Zuntschipá) for the passenger pigeon. Courtesy of Det Kongelige Bibliotek, Copenhagen, NKS 565 4to 06r.*

FIGURE 33.
The round-crested
Duck (hooded
merganser). *Hand-
colored etching
by Mark Catesby*,
Natural History *(1771),
plate 94. A common
food bird. John Carter
Brown Library at
Brown University.*

FIGURE 34.
The Pied-Bill
Dopchick (pied-billed
grebe). *Hand-colored
etching by Mark
Catesby*, Natural
History *(1771), plate
91. Some southern
Indians consumed
this small diving bird.
John Carter Brown
Library at Brown
University.*

The record probably embraced even more species whose remains were not recovered due to their size and to decay. The early twentieth-century Catawba reported to the anthropologist Frank Speck that they hunted various birds asleep at night during the winter, blinding them with lit splinters of "fat-wood" (lightwood) and killing such birds as "a red bird or black bird or snow bird or blue jay or the small bird [song sparrow] and also the dove." They told Speck, "There are birds of all kinds. Do go bird brushing."[11]

PROHIBITIONS ON EATING BIRDS

The "bird brushing" Catawba also remarked, "[If we] find an old buzzard . . . we will let him go. He stinks so much we cannot eat him." Like all people, the Catawba preferred certain foods to others — including birds. But did they and other southern Indians prohibit or taboo certain birds and define them as inedible? There should be little doubt that they consumed most of the birds that turn up in archaeological middens — for example, ducks, geese, turkeys, sandhill cranes, herons and gulls, eagles, crows, red-tailed hawks, various small song birds, and even the great auk and ivory-billed woodpeckers. Moreover, ethnographic and historical data make clear that indigenous people not only consumed many different kinds of birds but relished turkeys, and some apparently preferred blue-wing teal "to all other water fowl." But it is not always possible to conclude that birds were fair game and eaten, and questions might be raised about midden evidence of birds such as turkey and black vultures as well as barred and long-eared owls.[12]

According to James Adair, the Scots-Irish trader who spent decades in the mid-eighteenth century among the Chickasaw, the Cherokee, and other southern Indians, the Catawba considered the turkey vulture as "a most impure fowl, as it lives on putrid carcasses," and southern Indians thought "all birds of prey, and birds of night, to be unclean, and unlawful to be eaten." Eagles, ravens, crows, vultures, swallows, and "every species of" owl (as well as bats and insects, among things that fly) appear on his list of tabooed foods.[13]

Adair had an uncommon interest in food prohibitions because of his theory (shared with others both before and after his day) that American Indians were the descendants of the lost tribes of Israel. In fact, his list of tabooed birds recalls such "abominations" in Deuteronomy and Leviticus as vultures, eagles, kestrels, other raptors, ravens and the other corvids, the ostrich, the eagle owl and other owls, the white stork and other storks, the hoopoe, and bats.[14]

It is unfortunate that so little evidence exists either to corroborate or to refute Adair, yet hints of what might once have existed are contained in scattered sources. For example, Indians apparently shunned raw eggs in favor of ones thoroughly cooked — "boiled so much," Adair remarked, "as to be blue." Some Indians showed an aversion to cooking flesh from birds and other animals together: an eighteenth-century Saponi Indian expressed concern when deer and turkeys were boiled together, saying, "[W]e Shou'd for the future kill nothing, because the Spirit that presided over the Woods would drive all the Game out of our sight."[15] Some prohibited the consumption of birds in the belief that they affected a person adversely during his or her life cycle: a pregnant Cherokee woman, for example, was supposed to avoid eating ruffed grouse, else her child would

FIGURE 35.
Ein Seiden Schwäntz-gen, Buttervogel (A silk tail, butterfly). *Colored drawing by Philip George Friedrich von Reck, Georgia, 1736. Von Reck gives Yuchi and Creek names for the "Silk Tail" (Blue Jay) — Tsee and Ta-si, respectively — as well as for the tiger swallowtail. The manner of hanging the blue jay — by a thread from decorative feathers — is curious and perhaps indigenous. Courtesy of Det Kongelige Bibliotek, Copenhagen, NKS 565 4to 07r.*

FIGURE 36.
The White-Face Teal
(blue-winged teal).
*Hand-colored etching
by Mark Catesby,
Natural History
(1731–43), plate 100.
A highly esteemed
food bird. John Carter
Brown Library at
Brown University.*

FIGURE 37.
The Turkey Buzzard
(turkey vulture).
*Hand-colored etching
by Mark Catesby,
Natural History (1771),
plate 6. An important
bird in the ethno-
ornithology of the
South. John Carter
Brown Library at
Brown University.*

not live; a Creek lad was to refrain from eating "turkey cocks" and "fowls," among other things, on the threshold to manhood.[16] Some Indians refused, apparently, even to touch certain birds. For example, one Chickasaw woman would not butcher a hawk "for fear of contracting pollution, which she called the 'accursed sickness,' supposing disease would be the necessary effect of such an impurity." Yet this personal taboo could not have been universally observed, for on another occasion Choctaw hunters touched, cooked, and, presumably, ate a hawk.[17] In later times, the Chero-kee prohibited the consumption of vultures, eagles, hawks, owls, wrens, swallows, ospreys, American crows, common ravens, whip-poor-wills, woodcocks, belted kingfishers, and northern cardinals — a long list indeed.[18]

The anthropologist Charles Hudson suggests that southern Indians might not ordinarily have consumed flesh-eating birds, which also happens to be one explanation for the Old Testament's forbidden birds. Carnivorous, they were seen as different, even anomalous, and judged as defiling and unclean — even if other meat or fish eaters were not. Of perhaps greater importance than a diet based in flesh was one perceived as unclean because of a connection to human excreta and flesh. But the problem with applying this formula to the indigenous American South is not just that information on dietary taboos is woefully incomplete but that concepts of cleanliness or anomaly are derived from culture, not nature. That said, however, it would not be surprising if numerous and variously meaningful prohibitions, now long since lost to memory, formerly affected consumption habits across the region, for the simple reason that such taboos, endlessly variable, are universal.[19]

DOMESTICATION

William Strachey, the natural historian and Jamestown resident in 1610–11, remarked that Virginia Indians did not "bring up tame poultry . . . nor keepe byrds, squirrells, nor tame Partridges, Swan, duck, nor Geese."[20] Following Strachey and others, most scholars conclude that southern Indians did not domesticate birds — despite the odd reference to birds kept, like an eagle raised in captivity and then presented to a visiting dignitary. Peter Martyr commented that Indians on the coast kept "a great variety of chickens, ducks, geese, and other similar fowl," but little credence is given to this except, at most, as an idiosyncratic observation or isolated occurrence.[21]

John Lawson's intriguing reference to domesticated wading birds — storks and cranes — is more difficult to dismiss. The Congaree, he said, "have abundance of Storks and Cranes in their Savannas" and "take them before they can fly, and breed 'em as

tame and familiar as a Dung-hill Fowl [chicken]." "Cream-colored" cranes are "easily bred up tame, and are excellent in a Garden to destroy Frogs, Worms, and other Vermine." Both sandhill and whooping cranes were seasonal residents of the Carolinas. Which one was "easily bred" depends on which one's colors are closest to yellowish white cream. Adult whooping cranes are white and adult sandhills gray in winter and rust in summer; juveniles intersperse brown with the adult colors. Unless Lawson had brown, rust, and gray in mind as the colors of cream, his cranes were probably whooping cranes. In his watercolor of Indians who visited New Orleans in 1735, Alexandre de Batz pictured an Illinois Indian grasping an ambiguous pale crane around the top of its neck; the pale color is that of a whooping crane, but the absence of a red malar stripe below the eye resembles the sandhill crane.[22]

TURKEYS

Some like Lawson also remarked occasionally on Indian people raising young turkeys or using them as decoys. Indeed, turkey bones and eggshells are common in inland archaeological sites, which, together with the well documented taste of the Choctaw, Chickasaw, Powhatan, and others for birds' eggs, suggests to some that Indians domesticated turkeys for eggs, meat, and, presumably, feathers. Yet the evidence is thin.

FIGURE 38. Ruffed Grous or Pheasant (ruffed grouse). *Hand-colored engraving by J. Warnicke based on drawing by Alexander Wilson,* American Ornithology, *vol. 6, 1808–14, plate 49. According to the Cherokee, a pregnant woman must not consume this bird because grouse chicks suffer high mortality (and so might a woman's children). John Hay Library at Brown University.*

FIGURE 39.
Sandhill Crane.
*Pen and ink
with watercolor,
associated with John
White, ca. 1585–1600.
Inscribed: "Taráwkow.
The Crane." An
important food
bird and perhaps
tamed by some in
the Carolinas. Sloane
volume. © The
Trustees of the British
Museum, SL,5270.76.*

Strachey spoke about the "great store of Turkeys" in Virginia, but he evidently meant wild, not tame, birds.[23] Lawson commented more fully but, again, ambiguously. Sometimes, he remarked, Indians took wild turkeys hatched at home (by European colonists, he implied) to serve as decoys to attract others to roost (and be shot) near their cabins. Even though the adult birds might feed alongside domesticated turkeys, they "yet retain[ed] a wild Nature," overcome, Lawson hazarded — presumably assuming that warm milk would induce tractability — by dipping the eggs in "a Bowl of Milk-warm Water."[24] Farther west in French Louisiana lived people reputed to raise turkeys "without any other care than that which they [took] for young chickens," but firmer evidence for the domestication of turkeys is sketchy.[25]

Complicating a definitive answer to the question of domesticated eastern wild turkeys prior to the arrival of Europeans were, as Lawson implied, domesticated turkeys possessed by the settlers. A century before Lawson's remarks that eggs taken from wild turkeys could be hatched under tame birds (and that the wild and the tame interbred), John Smith commented on "wilde Turkies . . . as bigge as our tame" in Virginia.[26]

Lawson's and Smith's tame birds were the descendants of domesticated forms of the Mexican wild turkey (*Meleagris gallopavo gallopavo*) that had been transported from Mexico to Italy and Spain in the early sixteenth century. The Spaniards were no fools when it came to the domesticated turkey, which, according to Bernardino de Sahagún, a Franciscan priest in sixteenth-century Mexico, "leads the meats; it is the master," the hen especially being "tasty, healthful, fat, full of fat, fleshy, fleshy-breasted, heavy-fleshed." In a matter of decades, these turkeys became barnyard fixtures throughout Europe, including England. Their descendants were then brought to America, including Jamestown, South Carolina, and Biloxi in the seventeenth century. Common in Jamestown by the 1630s, turkeys spread throughout the South in immigrant and, eventually, Indian hands, mingling and mixing with the larger eastern (*M. g. silvestris*) and Florida (*M. g. osceola*) subspecies of the wild turkey — there being no impediment to mating — and producing, over time, offspring that were more tractable, at least when young, than the notoriously wild feral birds. They shaped both domesticated stock and wild populations — and even allowed for a small export market.[27]

It was probably one of these domesticated forms, with at least partial origin in European stock, that de Batz painted in his 1735 watercolor of native people and commodities in New Orleans. This bird is odd. Its head resembles somewhat a turkey's on a mid-sixteenth-century map of Port Royal, South Carolina, by the Huguenot Jacques Le Moyne de Morgues, but its serpentine, egret- or swanlike neck is peculiar, and the tail recalls ostrichlike or gallinaceous birds pictured on Old and New World maps. Admittedly peculiar, this bird is undoubtedly a turkey. But is it an eastern wild turkey tamed by native people or a domesticated turkey descended from birds whose origin was Mexico via the Old World? The pale color and fleshy growth on the head suggest the latter. Eastern wild turkey hues are ordinarily darkly metallic and only rarely light. In contrast, domesticated turkeys acquired many hues, including gray and white, which were noted in print and drawn or painted in Mexico and Europe as early as the sixteenth century. Moreover, compared to the eastern wild turkey, the domesticated turkey has heavier, more prominent wattles and caruncles (the fleshy head, throat, and neck appendages that turn red or blue and become large or small with changing hor-

FIGURE 40. Louisiana Heron (tricolored heron). Pied Oyster-catcher (American oyster-catcher). Hooping Crane (whooping crane). Long billed Curlew. *Hand-colored engraving by Alexander Lawson based on drawing by Alexander Wilson,* American Ornithology, *vol. 8, 1808–14, plate 64. Of these the whooping crane was important, and the tricolored heron figured during the late nineteenth-century plume trade, but the others are rarely mentioned. John Hay Library at Brown University.*

FIGURE 41.
Domestic Fowl.
Oil on oak panel by Albert Cuyp (1620–91). Chickens domesticated in Southeast Asia and turkeys tamed in Mexico soon became stalwarts in European barnyards, from which they were taken to the North American South. One turkey's pale plumage shows the effects of domestication and is not uncommon in seventeenth- and eighteenth-century representations. Groeningemuseum Bruges, 0.585.I. Image courtesy of Reproductiefonds.

monal states), especially the conelike one (the snood) on the forehead of the male that swells, elongates, and hangs over and below the bill at breeding time.[28]

CHICKENS

In addition to turkeys, Europeans also transported chickens (*Gallus gallus domesticus*) to the American South; they were the ordinary yard fowl first domesticated in Southeast Asia and then soon common throughout the Old World. The English often called them dunghill fowl, and they and other Europeans brought these birds to the American South in the sixteenth century, where immigrants and indigenous people alike incorporated them into the economy through breeding, consumption, and exchange.[29]

The history of the chicken in the South reduces to one eventual outcome — the fowl eventually took hold everywhere — but otherwise resists generalization. In early seventeenth-century Virginia, animal and human predation, hard winters, and consumption demand led to such attrition among domesticated animals that it became a capital crime for a European colonist to kill any. That included chickens, yet by midcentury poultry were said to be "without number." As for Indian demand, it is of interest that among Powhatan's requests from John Smith were swords, a grindstone, and "a cock and a hen." Perhaps more to the point, far to the south in Florida, 50 percent of the remains of domesticated species in two sixteenth-century native sites were chicken bones; there is no question that Indians here welcomed them.[30]

Yet what is to be made of Lawson's statement that early eighteenth-century Siouans kept "many Cocks, but seldom above one Hen"? Or the Jesuit priest Jacques Gravier's curious report from French Louisiana in 1700 about "few Villages in france where there are more hens and Cocks than in that of the houmas," because native people "never kill any, and will not even eat any of those that their Dogs quite often kill." Gravier continued, "When one wishes to obtain chickens from them, He must not say that he intends to kill or eat them. They would give them with reluctance; but they willingly sell these fowls when they are not killed in their presence, or when they are told that they will be taken away to be reared as with them. The hens have little chickens at all times, And in the month of december there were some in all the Cabins, since they keep Warm in the Cabins, — which the people are Careful to keep clean, and which they sweep out 2 or 3 times a day."[31]

Why would Carolina Siouans keep roosters but not hens, if not for some utilitarian, ornamental, or spiritual advantage obscure today? Far to the west, the Caddo desired rooster feathers for decorative purposes. We do not know whether Carolina Siouans had identical needs, but their reasons were surely among those given elsewhere for keeping roosters, but not more hens than necessary: because, as Frederick Simoons states, people consider cocks to be sacred or auspicious, connect them to gods or myth, use them in divination, desire them for tail feathers, or are awakened by their crowing at first light.[32]

The second question, why might the Houma have prohibited the consumption of chickens? returns us to food taboos. The Houma seem not to have minded commodifying and profiting from these fowl or doing what was necessary to protect their investment. They were not alone; like the Houma, the nearby Choctaw raised "dunghill fowls and a very few ducks," yet rather than consume them took them instead "for profit" to the market in Mobile some 120 miles away. There they were exposed to what the historian Daniel Usner has called "cross-cultural food marketing," which in theory included firsthand encounters with consumers who regarded chickens as edible.[33]

One possible reason for a prohibition on consumption might be that these birds were novel at a time when there was no need to use them as food, because the supply of endemic fowl and animals was up to the subsistence demand. To follow this line of argument, as traditional sources of meat became scarce through time, and native people traveled less from one season to the next, they became more sedentary, more able to accommodate keeping chickens, and finally more willing to drop the taboo and consume chickens.

However, even though the supply of wild animals did decrease and Indians did curtail seasonal movements, the correlation with an increased acceptance of chickens as food is far from clear. In fact, when the Choctaw and the Houma marketed chickens instead of eating them in the eighteenth century, a swelling number of immigrants from Europe pressured turkeys and other animals, making game, in the words of the surveyor Bernard Romans, "so scarce" among the Choctaw in the 1760s – 1770s that one-half of the men had never killed a deer or a turkey.[34]

The Creek and the Cherokee, in contrast, drew on oft-plentiful game as well as domesticated fowl: the Creek on a "very abundant" supply of deer, bear, and turkeys as well as an "abundance of small cattle, hogs, turkeys, ducks and dunghill fowls (all of which [were] very good in their kind)" that they raised, ate, and traded where there was a market; the Cherokee on deer, bear, rabbits and "turkeys, . . . wild fowl, and domestic poultry," all of which they consumed.[35] The late eighteenth-century Creek kept "a great many poultry" or "great number of fowls," selling or bartering them for the equivalent of one cent each or, to traders, for six cents (and twice that for capons). And the nineteenth-century Seminole possessed "chickens, more than they [were] willing to use," perhaps because northern bobwhites, turkeys, and ducks, which they hunted, remained abundant.[36]

Given this contradictory picture, we turn instead to possible cultural explanations for the prohibition on the consumption of chickens. It is useful to keep in mind that indigenous people worldwide have tabooed chickens as food as often as they have eaten them and that they have not automatically considered chickens, exotic or familiar, to be the same order of "persons" as endemic birds, or even as "birds." In many African societies, where chickens are common, women are not supposed to eat them lest their fertility or ability to conceive healthy children be adversely affected; men, on the other hand, both sacrifice and use chickens for various ends — and consume this privileged food. In other parts of the world, women are not permitted to eat chickens and eggs because of similar beliefs about the adverse impact on sex and fertility; or both men and women avoid them because they perceive the scavenging, even predatory, diet of chickens as filthy, and instead raise them for sale to those without such prejudices.[37]

To return to the American South, Adair's assertion that Indians perceived a connection between diet and abilities or character is highly suggestive — if it is not fatally colored by his fixation on the Indian-Israelite connection. According to Adair, southern Indians thought that people who consumed domesticated animals, especially the chicken, or the lethargic bear, instead of deer, risked severe consequences: "[H]e who feeds on venison, is according to their physical system, swifter and more sagacious than the person who lives on the flesh of the clumsy bear, or helpless dunghill fowls, the slow-footed tame cattle, or the heavy wallowing swine."[38]

It is, of course, the dunghill fowl that is of interest in this list. And some southern Indians, at least, considered them problematic not simply because they were "helpless" but because of what they ate. Given the diet and habits of chickens — the dunghill could contain human excreta as well as other waste — it is not odd that some might have regarded them as impure. Adair related how an ill Chickasaw woman, who worked for traders, ascribed her sickness to having "eaten a great many fowls after the manner of the white people," fowl that contained "accursed blood." She recovered but then "strictly abstain[ed] from tame fowls, unless they [were] bled to death, for fear of incurring future evil, by the like pollution." When the Choctaw, who linked diet and disease, wished to eat a chicken, they first shut it up and fed it by hand "until what it had foraged for itself was out of it." At first, the Choctaw were among those who refused to eat chickens (and pigs) "because, they sa[id], 'these animals eat filth'"; for these and other people, consuming something that visibly eats carrion, vermin, or human excrement and flesh was taboo. But in time they grew accustomed to these fowl through contact and intermarriage with people of European descent; in Adair's time, Indians commonly possessed "fowl-houses" or chicken coops separate from but near their own houses. As for consuming what they raised, it is entirely conceivable that many Indians emulated the traders and others of European extraction who lived in their midst, married native women, and formed families; that is, ultimately they grew accustomed to eating, not just raising and selling, chickens.[39]

Adding another layer to how southern Indians perceived chickens (and people of European descent) was their tendency to call white people, "despitefully," according to Adair, "helpless timorous dunghill fowls." All Indians, remarked Adair, "formerly despised the English, as a swarm of tame fowls, and termed them so, in their set speeches." Cherokees who killed whites in North Carolina were said to become great warriors "'by killing swarms of white dung-hill fowls, in the corn-fields, and asleep' according to their war-phrase." Some Indians took umbrage at the disparaging epithet "eater of dunghill fowls," if directed at them.[40]

This might help us understand why, in 1814, the great Choctaw orator and statesman Pushmataha, weary of factionalism, war, land cessions, and the opportunistic intervention of non-Indian land speculators and militia, as well as the contradictions involved in resisting the machinations of Tecumseh and being allied with the United States during the War of 1812, attached a suit of military clothing given to him by Andrew Jackson to a cord, dragged it behind him through the town where he lived, and at each house stopped and shot a chicken with his bow and arrow. Then, after "unceremonious" preparation, he held a feast.

The Choctaw villagers all laughed. Pushmataha clearly amused them, but why? Above all, why did he shoot chickens? The key might well be in the link made by native people between white people and dunghill fowl. Pushmataha's fellow villagers had a ready explanation relating birds and human behavior, which Pushmataha evoked each time he shot a chicken — a tame, pale-fleshed, excrement-consuming dunghill fowl. Not only can Pushmataha's behavior be seen as thinly veiled commentary on white men (domesticated fowl) against Indians (wild birds), and on the chicken as ironic symbol of misgiving, spite, conflict, and an uncertain future; his action was perhaps the only one possible against an ally that had proven to be as much an enemy as a friend to Choctaw interests. In another context altogether, the anthropologist Stanley Brandes argues that animal metaphors emerge or find expression especially when there is disturbance or conflict; such seems also to be the case with Pushmataha and his chickens.[41]

In the beginning, some native southerners might have considered chickens not only exotic but abhorrent, but in time all native people indigenized them, making them their own. Over time, the changing population and status of chickens were reflected in lan-

FIGURE 42. Pushmataha, Choctaw. *Oil on wood by Charles Bird King, 1824. Painted in the year of his death, Pushmataha, the great Choctaw war leader and chief, a poor but generous and respected man, and the subject of many humorous and ironic anecdotes, wears plumes in his hat—a virtual signature of office in the South. The Warner Collection of Gulf States Paper Corporation and on view in the Westervelt-Warner Museum of Art, Tuscaloosa, Ala.*

guage. The Chickasaw, for instance, came to distinguish different kinds of chickens (*akanka'*), including striped, bearded, spotted, yellow, red, black, white, tailless, curly-headed, and others. In compound words, they linked *akanka'* to chickens of different ages and sexes as well as to guinea fowl, gamecocks, chicken pox, chicken hawks, chicken coops, chicken dumplings, chicken eggs, castor beans, tomatoes, and ketchup.[42]

THE MUSCOVY DUCK

According to Bernard Romans and others, the Choctaw, Houma, and Creek domesticated ducks and sold them in the market. These surely were the same Muscovy ducks (*Cairina moschata*) noted by Le Page du Pratz, who branded them "ducks of India" because "they [were] native to the country." Le Page depicted these ducks in detail: "They are almost completely white and have only a few gray feathers. They have on both sides of the head flesh of a brighter red than that of the turkey and are larger than our dabs. The flesh of the young ones is delicate and of a very good flavor, but that of the old and above all of the males smells of musk. They are as timid as those of Europe." Le Page's description of this duck was accurate, but he was mistaken about the Muscovy duck's origin in South Asia. These ducks both flew wild and were domesticated by local

FIGURE 43. Peacocks and Ducks. *Oil on canvas by Melchior de Hondecoeter, ca. 1680. A family of Muscovy ducks appears in the left foreground, below the peacock, of this European scene. Introduced to the Old World from the New, they soon became familiar (and hybridized) in European barnyards. European settlers brought them to the American South with domesticated chickens and turkeys. Southern Indians highly esteemed peacock feathers and ostrich plumes; rare and costly, they appeared on heads and in turbans of leading men. The Wallace Collection, London, P64.*

indigenous people from central Mexico and the Greater Antilles south. As with turkeys, Europeans carried them home across the Atlantic and brought their descendants back to the New World. Unlike turkeys, in France, Muscovy ducks were crossed with domesticated ducks, the descendants of mallards, to produce sterile hybrids (*mulards*), whose flesh and livers were esteemed, and were returned to a part of the New World where they had never been established. The Creek called this hissing, distinctive-looking bird, with bare skin from its bill to its eyes, *fuco sule*, "buzzard-duck."[43]

PROTECTING FIELDS AND GARDENS

Long before they kept chickens and ducks, southern Indians cultivated and harvested domesticated plants, such as maize, that were susceptible to birds, and the question of the impact of those birds on crops and daily life comes naturally. There can be no doubt

FIGURE 44.
The Purple Jack Daw (common grackle). *Hand-colored etching by Mark Catesby,* Natural History *(1731–43), plate 12. A common agricultural pest to natives and nonnatives alike, and present in massive numbers in the South.* John Carter Brown Library at Brown University.

of the potential damage of birds where their numbers were great. In the early nineteenth century, John James Audubon remarked that farmers killed "immense numbers" of common grackles in Louisiana, unfairly vilifying them, he thought, because they ate not just grain but worms and other pests. Red-winged blackbirds were construed similarly, as possessing "the most nefarious propensities" because they destroyed rice, corn, and all grain, but they also, Audubon remarked, ate millions of grain-consuming insects.[44]

Alexander Wilson also remarked on the damage to grain that birds like blackbirds and grackles could effect. He focused in particular on the devastation brought by a large migratory or wintering flock of red-winged blackbirds. Because this must have been a common problem for Indian as well as immigrant farmers, it is worth quoting him at length:

Before the beginning of September these flocks have become numerous and formidable, and the young ears of maize, or Indian corn, being then in their soft, succulent, milky state, present a temptation that cannot be resisted. Reinforced by numerous and daily flocks from all parts of the interior, they pour down on the low countries in prodigious multitudes. Here they are seen, like vast clouds, wheeling and diving over the meadows and devoted corn fields, darkening the air with their numbers. Then commences the work of destruction on the corn, the husks of which, tho composed of numerous envelopements of closely wrapt leaves, are soon completely or partially torn off; while from all quarters myriads continue to pour down like a tempest, blackening half an acre at a time; and, if not disturbed, repeat their depredations till little remains but the cob and the shriveled skins of the grain; what little is left of the tender ear being exposed to the rains and weather is generally much injured. All these attacks and havoc made at this time among them with the gun, and by the Hawks, several species of which are their constant attendants, has little effect on the remainder.[45]

At the time, Wilson continued, Indians, "who usually plant their corn in one general field, keep the whole young boys of the village, all day patrolling round and among it; and each being furnished with bow and arrows, with which they are very expert, they generally contrive to destroy great numbers of them."[46]

Wilson and Audubon were mainly concerned with the relationship between birds and farmers of European descent at the outset of the nineteenth century. But together they help to frame inferences about the relationship between native people and the birds that ate their crops, both in their day and in earlier times. Unsurprisingly, it turns out that Indians with economies based on the domestication of plants faced many of the same problems, and developed similar responses, as the nonnative farmer. René Laudonnière, for instance, on the north Florida Atlantic coast in the mid-sixteenth century, said, "So many birds . . . continually attack the corn that the Indians have to guard it, for otherwise they would lose their entire harvest." Native people, he reported, erected "houses" in some fields "for the persons who guarded the corn."[47]

This was a common strategy. In sixteenth-century North Carolina cornfields, Indians built observation platforms, as John White reported (and imaged): "[A]s yt weare a scaffolde wher on they sett a cottage like to a rownde chaire . . . wherin they place one to watche. for there are suche number of fowles, and beasts, that unless they keepe the better watche, they would soon devoure all ther corne. For which cause the watchman maketh continual cryes and noyse."[48] Little changed as the years progressed. In the mid-eighteenth century, Adair noted a novel way of controlling avian pests: the Chickasaw planted corn in fields ripe with fruit, in the hope that birds would ignore kernels. As insurance, older women, "who fret[ted] at the very shadow of a crow," mounted scaffolds in melon fields from which they frightened birds away.[49] Later in the same century, Bartram reported: "The youth, under the supervisal of some of their ancient people, are daily stationed in their fields, who are continually whooping and hallooing, to chase away crows, jackdaws, black-birds and such predatory animals, and the lads are armed with bows and arrows, who, being trained up to it from their early youth, are sure at a mark, and in the course of a day load themselves with squirrels, birds, &c."[50]

Both Indians and European and American settlers also protected their gardens against destructive bird and insect pests by enticing birds like purple martins to nest there and drive the unwanted ones away. In the eighteenth century, Lawson remarked that settlers from Europe "put Gourds on standing Poles, on purpose for these Fowl to build in, because they [were] a very Warlike bird, and best the Crows from the Plantations." Catesby also commented that colonists encouraged purple martins to breed in gourds because they were "of great use about houses and yards, for pursuing and chasing away crows, hawks, and other vermin, from the poultry."[51]

Prior to Lawson's and Catesby's times, native people in seventeenth-century Virginia attracted, according to the naturalist John Banister, "the swallow or Martin kind," by which he meant barn swallows and either tree swallows (the nearest equivalent to the Old World house martin) or purple martins. Providing gourds for houses attracted martins, which were useful not just to protect crops but, as Catesby suggested, to warn chickens, after Indians had adopted them, about predators like crows and hawks. In

FIGURE 45. The red wing'd Starling (red-winged blackbird). *Hand-colored etching by Mark Catesby,* Natural History *(1731–43), plate 13. Another common agricultural pest—but one whose red shoulders are explained in myth.* John Carter Brown Library at Brown University.

FIGURE 46.
The Village of
Secoton. *Watercolor
over black lead by
John White, ca. 1585.
Three fields of corn,
or maize, appear at
different stages of
growth—"newly
sprong," green, and
ripe—and in the last
is a small elevated
hide in which to sit
and scare birds away.
Nearly all the men
who dance or sit in
the foreground wear
feathers in their hair
or on their heads.*
© The Trustees of
the British Museum,
1906,0509.1.7.

the early nineteenth century, Alexander Wilson remarked, "Even the solitary Indian seems to have a particular respect for this bird [the purple martin]. The Chactaws and Chickasaws cut off all the top branches from a sapling near their cabins, leaving the prongs a foot or two in length, on each of which they hang a gourd, or calabash, properly hollowed out for their convenience." And Audubon reported a different purpose for the martin: Indians put up a calabash near their camp, and a purple martin took up residence, was vigilant, and drove off any vulture interested in the skin or meat of white-tailed deer.[52]

In the late nineteenth century, the anthropologist James Mooney remarked that

FIGURE 48.
Gourds above a
Cherokee house and
garden in Atoah
Creek, North Carolina,
1890. *The Cherokee
and other southern
Indians hollowed
gourds and mounted
them on poles to
provide nesting sites
for purple martins
and other birds, which
nested and defended
territories against
birds interested in
kitchen-garden crops
or domestic fowl.
Speck,* Gourds of the
Southeastern Indians,
*fig. 80. Courtesy of
the American Gourd
Society (http://www
.americangourdsociety
.org/).*

for the Cherokee, the "black house-martin [purple martin] is a favorite . . . attract[ed] by fastening hollow gourds to the tops of long poles set up near their houses so that the birds may build their nests in them." The anthropologist Frank Speck concluded from his own research, including ethnography in the early twentieth century, that the Cherokee, the Creek, and various other Indians in Virginia and the Carolinas used gourds for over two dozen specific ends, including housing martins near domestic and agricultural spaces. Gourds that were hollowed, holed in the side for an entrance, punctured in the bottom for drainage, and hung from high poles planted in gardens attracted purple martins, swallows, and wrens, which nested, protected their territories, issued alarm calls, consumed insects, and drove away grain-eating avian pests.[53]

These were not the only birds found in or near domesticated spaces in the South. Lawson, Catesby, Wilson, and Audubon all remarked that southerners of European origin kept different kinds of birds for their amusement (the smaller ones in cages), ranging from water species such as Canada geese to parakeets, cardinals, brown thrashers, Baltimore orioles, mockingbirds, and painted buntings, all seemingly adapted to captivity. Indigenous people apparently did not keep pet birds themselves (or not many), although they might have participated in meeting the European and American demand by capturing birds for an exchange that stretched as far as to Europe. Audubon said that in Louisiana from April through October thousands of painted buntings were caught for the cage trade, bought by middlemen for six pence each in New Orleans, and sold for three guineas each in London.[54]

HUNTING AND KILLING BIRDS

To hunt and kill birds, southern Indians used equipment ranging from snares and traps to bows and arrows, decoys and calls, and fire and dogs. The most famous weapon prior to the close of the nineteenth century, by which time it was obsolete, was the blowgun. Bernard Romans, the Dutch surveyor in Florida and Georgia in the 1760s–1770s, was struck by the use and accuracy of the blowgun. Native hunters, he remarked, blew it "so expertly as seldom to miss a mark fifteen or twenty yards off"; their marks were first of all birds and small animals like squirrels and rabbits.[55]

The Catawba, Choctaw, Cherokee, Yuchi, Creek, Chitimacha, and other native people used blowguns to hunt birds. These weapons ranged in length from five to ten feet; the Creek blowgun was "about as long as a man is tall." The Choctaw made blowguns of cane after clearing out the joints and shot from them darts made of pine or cane fifteen to eighteen inches in length, wrapped in the lower portion — nearest the mouth of the user — with thistle down, cotton, or soft, tanned skin. Birds were a frequent target, but if larger game were the quarry, hunters aimed at the eye because of the weapon's inherent weakness.[56]

In 1930, the anthropologist Frank Speck accompanied Joe Saunders, a Catawba Indian, hunting birds with a cane blowgun made for the occasion, and reported that the Catawba cut canes from three-quarters to one and one-half inches in diameter from tall cane brakes, kept them straight with weights while they were seasoned, and bored them with a heated iron rod (that they were bored in earlier times is clear, but how is not). Catawba darts were similar to Choctaw darts: eight- to ten-inch-long sharpened slivers of pine, oak, or cedar with a plunger of downy chicken or goose feathers, or rabbit tail tufts; how appropriate, Speck mused, to blow a feathered or furred dart at feathered or furred quarry. The Catawba shot robins, thrushes, doves, and other birds that flooded into their territory in winter and roosted in evergreen trees at night; "in early evening," Speck said, "the roosting birds could be picked off without noise to alarm them." The Catawba blew their darts some one hundred feet but penetrated skin at only twenty-five to thirty feet; a dart that struck the eye of a target such as a grouse or a quail was fatal.[57]

FIGURE 49.
The Painted Finch (painted bunting). *Hand-colored etching by Mark Catesby,* Natural History *(1731–43), plate 44. A common summer coastal resident in the South, this bunting—one vernacular name was nonpareil—quickly became an international commodity as a cage bird. John Carter Brown Library at Brown University.*

Southern Indians also hunted birds with bows and blunt or sharpened cane arrows, nets, baited traps, snares, decoys, calls, bolas, fire, and dogs. The Rappahannock, for example, spread corn or grain to attract turkeys, quail, and small birds to log traps called "scratch traps" or "log houses"; set a special perforated, boxlike "quail trap" for these birds; trapped juncos in a "snatch trap" consisting of a board held aloft by a stick released by pulling on a long string; captured sparrows, juncos, and other small birds with a pyramidal-shaped splint "bird trap" that fell over them; and caught juncos and robins on bent pins placed inside worms, which were swallowed by the birds. In the 1940s, some Rappahannocks recalled killing birds that visited during the winter, but not those resident all year round, and others remembered killing and eating, in addition to the robins, thrushes, mourning doves, and other birds already mentioned, cedar waxwings, common grackles, eastern meadowlarks, rusty blackbirds, brown-headed cowbirds, passenger pigeons, "marsh" birds, and others.

To hunt turkeys, many southern Indians used a decoy like the head of a turkey and imitated a turkey's calls with their voices or with the aid of tube-shaped instruments crafted from turkey wing and other bones, with which they made sucking and grating noises. Indians regularly drove turkeys into trees, where they made easy targets. The Creek drove turkeys from one grove of trees to the next, killing a few at every stop; the Natchez and the Powhatan employed dogs to chase turkeys into trees, where they were shot; the Powhatan hunted other land birds with dogs. The Alabama evidently were able to kill many turkeys, especially if they remained perched in trees, with de-

FIGURE 52.
(Left) The Fieldfare of Carolina (American robin). *Hand-colored etching by Mark Catesby*, Natural History *(1731–43), plate 29. The robin was commonly hunted and consumed. John Carter Brown Library at Brown University.*

FIGURE 53.
(Right) The Yellow-rump (yellow-rumped warbler). *Hand-colored etching by Mark Catesby*, Natural History *(1771), plate 58. Southern Indians used both traps and snares to hunt birds large and small, including migrating and wintering warblers. John Carter Brown Library at Brown University.*

coys: several Indians would place turkey skins on their shoulders and scarlet cloth on their heads that fluttered and attracted birds, which were then shot quietly by others with bows and arrows.[58]

Indians also used fire to hunt birds: Sewee Indians hunted by "firing the Canes Swamps, which [drove] out the Game, then taking their particular Stands, kill[ed] great Quantities of both Bear, Deer, Turkies, and what wild Creatures the Parts afford[ed]." Both the Cherokee and the Catawba used firebrands to locate, confuse, and surround roosting birds at night.[59]

One possibly unique hunting method in the South was that of the Quapaw, who were reported to obtain "geese, bustards, teals, water hens, and ducks of all kinds" by "placing tame waterfowl or stuffed birds on the water," then diving beneath the surface as wild birds trolled in, grabbing the feet of the birds and hooking them to belts, and bringing them back alive to clip their feathers, place them in pens, and save them for the time when food was short. As apocryphal as this account may sound, the technique of capture is similar to that in other parts of North America, even if the end result is different. Far to the west, for example, the Paiute were said to camouflage their heads with moss, wade out among canvasbacks and others ducks, and then pull birds under, crush their heads and break their legs, and secure them beneath the water to a loop around their waists.[60]

FIGURE 54. The Large Lark (eastern meadowlark). *Hand-colored etching by Mark Catesby,* Natural History *(1731–43), plate 33. Hunted and eaten by the Catawba and others, the meadowlark was also invoked by Cherokee men in spells intended to win over women. John Carter Brown Library at Brown University.*

TIME AND PLACE NAMES

Time and place names often reflect the location, or the coming and going, of animals and plants important in a people's subsistence. In the South, birds work their way into the names of both places and months, not overwhelmingly but appropriately given their role in subsistence. Thus the Creek named Wattooluhhaugau hatche (Crane Creek) after *wvtolv*, "sandhill crane," and Ochoccola (Peckerwood Creek) from *cvkvlv*, "red-headed woodpecker." The Creek's Whooping Creek of myth was named for those large cranes that assembled and filled the air with their calls. Towns also received the names of birds: Choctaw towns included "Whooping Crane" and "Wild Goose Crying"; and Creek towns Woc-co-coie from nests of the "blow-Horn" (herons like the *wvko-racco*, "great blue heron"), Pin-e-hoo-te (Turkey House) from *penwv*, "wild turkey," and Pad-gee-li-gau (Passenger Pigeon Roost) from *pvce*, "passenger pigeon."[61] The last is one of many pigeon names on the landscape in Muskogean (Parchelagee Creek in Georgia and Patsaliga in Alabama) and English (Pigeon Creeks in Alabama and Florida, Little Pigeon Creek in Tennessee, Pigeon Roost in Kentucky, and Pigeon Roost Creek in Mississippi), a reflection of the great importance of this bird relative to others.[62]

As with the landscape and human settlement, so with the seasons and months, in

FIGURE 55.
Ben Percy Harris
(Catawba), with
sandhill crane. *Black-
and-white gelatin-
glass negative,
photograph by
De Lancey W. Gill,
1899. Harris wears a
headdress of turkey
feathers and holds
a sandhill crane
pierced by an arrow
fletched with what
seems to be a turkey
feather. National
Anthropological
Archives, Smithsonian
Institution, glass
negatives of Indians
BAE GN 03814B/
broken negative file
06679700.*

FIGURE 56. Wilson
Cypress (Seminole)
skinning a wild
turkey. *Black-
and-white copy
negative, unknown
photographer, 1910.
Skinning and plucking
were alternative
ways to begin to
prepare the most
often consumed bird
in the South. National
Anthropological
Archives, Smithsonian
Institution, glass
negatives of Indians
55323.*

FIGURE 57. Passenger Pigeon. Blue-mountain Warbler. Hemlock W[arbler]. *Hand-colored engraving by J. Warnicke based on drawing by Alexander Wilson,* American Ornithology, *vol. 5, 1808–14, plate 44. The two warblers might be blackpoll and pine warblers, respectively, in various plumages. John Hay Library at Brown University.*

which birds figure again in proportion to their role in subsistence, that is, not large. Nevertheless, the Powhatan called winter *cohonks,* an onomatopoeic name from the calls of geese (and others called this month the time of the eagle); North Carolina Siouans and the Tuscarora called March – April the time "when Turkey-Cocks gobble"; and the Choctaw called the month straddling July – August "crane month."[63] Furthermore, birds figured (with much else) in Natchez celebrations of each "new moon." The Natchez made presentations to their leader the Great Sun during these lunar feasts, consuming what they had hunted or gathered in the preceding month. They wore distinctive colored feathers in March, white for the Great Sun and red for his brother, the

Great War Chief, and, symbolically, the enemy; presented "skewered ducks" in April and birds in August; feathered themselves (white or red, as in March) in September for a ball game between sides led by the Great Sun and the war chief; celebrated October as the time that turkeys sought out nettles to eat; and feted January as the month when "many bustards, geese, ducks, and other similar kinds of game [were] to be had." Despite their secondary status in subsistence, birds were rarely far from mind.[64]

FIGURE 58.
An Indian painted
for the hunt
or ceremony.
*Watercolor over black
lead by John White,
ca. 1585. Accessorizing
with feathers was
common not just for
decorative purposes
but because feathers
signaled status and
leadership in politics,
war, and ritual. The
quiver holds arrows
fletched presumably
with wild turkey or
raptor feathers.
© The Trustees of
the British Museum,
1906,0509.1.12.*

*The manner of their attire and
painting them selues when
they goe to their generall
huntings, or at theire
Solemne feasts.*

Material Culture

That southern Indians ate many different kinds of birds is without doubt, but did they use them in other ways? Were birds — their feathers, bones, and skins — important in material culture, that is, the objects or artifacts that people made and used? To answer this question we examine a range of evidence from written accounts to the archaeological record and museum collections. Unfortunately, because bird feathers are relatively friable and ephemeral, and because formerly the recovery of faunal remains targeted much larger prey, the remains of objects made of feathers are rare in southern Indian archaeological and museum collections.[1]

In fact, archaeological evidence might lead us to conclude that birds were fairly unimportant in the material world. Yet there is evidence from Spiro, Oklahoma — just beyond the western fringe of the South, albeit among an important people whose influence was felt well inside the South — of textiles dated AD 1100–1400 made of the downy feathers of swans, Canada geese, and turkeys, the feathers often dyed black (geese), red (swans), or both (turkeys), the garments perhaps of the elite at an important ceremonial center.[2]

Despite the paucity of archaeological evidence, the visual and documentary record suggests pervasive use of bird feathers and other parts. In fact, the most persistent visual image of the indigenous people of the New World is that they were feathered. From the sixteenth through the twentieth century, a succession of woodcuts, engravings, lithographs, watercolors, drawings, oil paintings, photographs, and other images of American Indians from the South and elsewhere show them in feather capes, crowns, sashes, and headdresses. The anthropologist William C. Sturtevant argued that the representations at first were based on the South American Tupinamba (they were "tupinambized," as he said) and that they evolved through a succession of images, including a series of allegorical Americas, of Indians wearing feathered headdresses.[3]

Many southern Indians were represented visually wearing feathers, bird parts, and even entire birds. On the surface these representations support the general conclusion that indigenous people were feathered. But were they faithful to real Indians?[4] As always, we must make note of the lens through which they were produced, and the most important consideration is that Europeans who visualized, or remarked on, feather use in the South held assumptions about clothing and accessories formed in the Old World, where feathers were associated with the upper class, the court, fashion, processions, pageantry, balls, armor, and portraiture. People of European descent almost certainly were predisposed to certain conclusions that made sense in their cultural framework but didn't necessarily apply to the indigenous people they were documenting. Thus, the probability that the evidence is not straightforward or watertight dictates a cautious approach.[5]

ORNAMENTATION

We begin in 1524–25 with the maritime explorer Giovanni da Verrazzano, who was on a fast track north along the Atlantic coast for the glory of France yet had time to remark that Indians in the Carolinas wore "garlandes of byrdes feathers." This might be the earliest documentary evidence that Indians in the South were plumed and indeed seems borne out by later data that make clear that Indians throughout the region inserted feathers or plumes into their hair — described by some as "crowns" — and decorated themselves with feathers, bird parts, or entire bird skins. Some had elaborate hairstyles, shaving one side of the head and ornamenting the other, or inserting feathers into a topknot. Despite great regional variation in feather use, one common thread was that men tended to accessorize with feathers more than women. This is not because they were merely being fashionable "dandies," for while feathers were ornamental and possessed clearly visible aesthetic qualities, they also, as will become apparent, resonated symbolically in important contexts.[6]

Fifteen years after Verrazzano, the chroniclers of Hernando de Soto's expedition, especially Garcilaso de la Vega, also remarked on feather use from the instant the expedition encountered twenty Indians "painted red and adorned with feathers" ashore on Florida's Gulf Coast. Not far inland appeared "four young Indian nobles with a great many plumes on their heads, which [were] the principal adornment they [wore]." Further north at Cofaqui, in today's central Georgia, "many nobles handsomely equipped with bows and arrows and great plumes" came out to greet the strangers.[7]

The pattern continued. At Cofitachequi in South Carolina, a young man sent as an emissary by others said to be chiefs or nobles appeared "very elegantly attired, as befitted an ambassador on such a mission, and wore on his head a large plume made of a pleasing combination of vari-colored feathers that added to his gracefulness." Farther along, an estimated one thousand "nobles" appeared at Coosa in northwestern Georgia wearing mantles of pelts and "long plumes on their heads, which [were] the decoration and adornment that the Indians of this great kingdom must [have] value[d]." The chronicler notes, "These men were well disposed, as those of that country generally are; their plumes stood up half a fathom high and were of many and varied colors." In central Alabama, Tascaluza, the chief of Atahachi, appeared seated in a litter surrounded by one hundred nobles "richly dressed in fine mantles of various kinds of furs with long plumes on their heads." The connection between feathers, on the one hand, and social position and political events, on the other, seems apparent in these accounts and is explored in greater detail below.[8]

Farther north and later in the same century, John White, the artist, surveyor, and governor of Roanoke colony, painted North Carolina Algonquians ornamented with single and sometimes large feathers in their hair, behind their ears, or on their fore-

heads, and one man with a dark bird on the right side of his head.[9] Southward, the Cusabo on the South Carolina coast wore feathers in their hair for "Ornament or Gallantry" and "hung" a chief's house "with feathers of different colors, to the height of a pike."[10] In Florida, the Timucua, according to Jacques Le Moyne de Morgues, the artist who accompanied René Laudonnière and Jean Ribault, wore "many pieces of a stuff made of feathers," ornamented with reeds of different colors. The French sailor Le Challeux added, "[They] esteem nothing richer or more beautiful than bird feathers of different colors."[11]

In the seventeenth century, the evidence for feather use accumulated. In Virginia, the Powhatan often stuck long feathers in the knots of their hair. The "Common People" were said to go about "bare-headed, only large shining feathers about their Heads, as their fancies [led] them," the feathers being those of turkeys, hawks, and ruffed grouse (or greater prairie-chickens). Feathers were used both by "common people," who, as Gabriel Archer reported of Indians in the vicinity of Jamestown in 1607–10, stuck "long fethers" in a knot in their hair, and by chiefs, who sometimes wore long feathers in their headgear.[12] John Smith reported, "Some on their heads weare the wing of a bird or some large feather with a Rattell. Those Rattels are somewhat like the chape of a Rapier but lesse, which they take from the taile of a snake. Many have the whole skinne of a hawke or some strange fowle, stuffed with the wings abroad."[13]

The evidence was similarly rich farther west in the region. Chitimacha women, for example, apparently decorated their hair with feathers from about age eight until they

lost their virginity or married. Lower Mississippi River girls wore a type of skirt consisting of a net from which depended "claws of birds of prey like eagles, tiercelets, buzzards, etc." that "made a kind of clicking which please[d] them" when the girls walked about.[14] West of the Mississippi, the seventeenth-century Caddo put red-tinted swan and duck down in their hair, and in the early eighteenth century, they tied feathers to the back of long hair "in a very curious manner," remarked a Franciscan friar, each looking "like a sprout." Indians collected feathers from the chickens that the Spaniards brought with them, keeping them in chests to wear "at their brightest." The Spaniards' accounts give the impression of Indians who "like[d] fine feathers," stored ornamental feathers carefully away in "hollow clean reeds" and other containers, and used turkey-tail fans in dances.[15]

Many Indians perforated their ears, hanging from them or their hair a variety of objects, including feathers and bird parts. From their ears, the Powhatan suspended pearls, bones, copper, animal claws, and "with a great pride certayne Fowles leggs, Eagles, Hawkes, Turkeys, etc." One pair of ear ornaments worn by a chief consisted of "a Birds Claw through it beset with fine Copper or Gold."[16] Regarding Indians in North Carolina, John Lawson remarked, "[They wear] great Bobs in their Ears, and sometimes in the Holes thereof they put Eagles and other Birds, Feathers, for a trophy. When they kill any Fowl, they commonly pluck off the downy Feathers, and stick them all over their Heads." The Timucua also inserted bird claws in holes in their ears, and on the late seventeenth-century Gulf Coast along Florida's panhandle, Spanish explorers discovered, in a village from which Indians had fled, bird claws, downy white feathers, and the feathers of turkeys, cardinals, and other birds.[17]

The use of feathers and bird parts in the ears and elsewhere continued unabated in the eighteenth century, when turkey spurs ornamented thigh-length deerskin boots, and Chickasaw men tucked a feather into a beaded headdress or more elaborately "fasten[ed]," as James Adair reported, "several different sorts of beautiful feathers, frequently in tufts; or the wing of a red bird, or the skin of a small hawk, to a lock of hair on the crown of their heads." Swan feathers were said to be "great ornamants" among the Chickasaw, who killed swans in ponds at night with the aid of torches. The Cherokee decorated their hair with feathers, the skin of a small hawk, a northern cardinal's wing, or goose's down, and placed heron and egret feathers in their hair or ears; the Creek hung "soft white plumes of heron feathers" from perforated ears.[18]

Finally, decorative feathers and plumes, at times held in place by metal headbands, also appeared in the turbans worn by Creek, Seminole, and Yuchi men in the eighteenth and nineteenth centuries. The turban had been in vogue as early as the sixteenth century (when the de Soto chroniclers likened one chief to a Moor because of his headgear), and if a myth about the regional trickster Rabbit hiding an object in the folds of his turban is ancient, then the turban might be even older than the sixteenth century and in some way connected to earlier headdresses.[19] The more immediate predecessor might have been a crown of feathers or a plain headband. In the eighteenth century some men wore simply a headband, which did not mean an undiminished role for feathers. In Bartram's description, "A very curious diadem or band, about four inches broad, and ingeniously wrought or woven, and curiously decorated with stones, beads, wampum, porcupine quills, &c. encircles their temples, the front peak of which is embellished with a high waving plume, of heron or crane feathers."[20]

In short, evidence was abundant through time and across the region that Indians ornamented themselves with feathers and bird parts. For those so inclined, fashion, or "finery," for whatever ends, could take time. Late eighteenth-century Creeks, who were said to be "very fond of dress," dedicated part of the day to fashion; one Creek Indian guide regularly "employed about two hours at his toilet."[21] According to Le Page du Pratz, young Indian men in French Louisiana were also "as much taken up by dress, and as fond of vying with each other in finery as in other countries." He noted, "[T]hey paint themselves with vermilion . . . ; they deck themselves with bracelets . . . ; they wear necklaces like the women, and sometimes have a fan in their hand; they clip off the hair from the crown of the head, and there place a piece of swan's skin with the down on; to a few hairs that they leave on that part they fasten the finest white feathers that they can meet with."[22]

Not surprisingly, not everyone dressed so elaborately. Some men reportedly "usually" went about "almost naked." But the young were said to "indulge" themselves with

FIGURE 61.
(Left) Hysac, or the Woman's Man. Engraving, after a pencil drawing of 1790. This Creek Indian man's turban is adorned with a thin feather tucked into its folds. Trumbull, Autobiography, plate 19. National Anthropological Archives, Smithsonian Institution, negative 1169-L-2.

FIGURE 62.
(Right) Stimafutchki, or Good Humour— of the Coosades, Creeks. Engraving, after a pencil drawing of 1790. Wispy plumes from a peacock or another exotic bird adorn this man's head and ears. Trumbull, Autobiography, plate 20. National Anthropological Archives, Smithsonian Institution, negative 1169-L-3.

Hysac, or the Woman's Man
N. York July 1790 J.T

Stimafutchki, or Good—Humour—
of the Coosades, Creeks.
New York July 1790 J.T

FIGURE 63.
Seminolee. *Pencil drawing by George Catlin, 1838. All but one of the men in this drawing are plumed (and armed), the boy is modestly feathered, and the woman wears no feathers — a typical pattern. Collection of the New-York Historical Society, plate 68, neg. 33068.*

FIGURE 64.
Mico Chlucco the Long Warior or King of the Siminoles. *Engraving by James Trenchard from a drawing by William Bartram,* Travels, *frontispiece. This Seminole warrior is decorated with feathers tucked into a headband (perhaps a sign of his status) and on ear ornaments, and wears a feather mantle covering his shoulders, upper arms, and, presumably, upper back. John Carter Brown Library at Brown University.*

"decorations" especially for festivals or weddings, or at dances performed as a prelude to war.[23]

Yet as these remarks suggest and the ethnologist John Swanton reminds us, it would be a mistake to conclude that feathers worn ostensibly for decorative or ornamental purposes were somehow devoid of meaning. For the Choctaw, for example, feathers traditionally signified quite specific skills or association with birds: "a doctor who could cure rheumatism would put a buzzard feather in his hair"; men who "claimed that they could stop the hooting of a common owl (ōpa), considered a sign of bad luck, . . . wore the feather of this same owl"; most men wore the feather of a "peafowl," which "calls out before daybreak" and "stands for prosperity and happy anticipations"; an "active, intelligent man" wore the feather of a hawk; chiefs (and some others) wore crow feathers when mourning death in the family; turkey feathers "distinguished a good turkey hunter and also a good hunter of birds in general"; a weather prophet wore the feather of the "tall crane" when rain was on the way; and "a tall, stout man, or one mentally strong or conspicuously honest," donned eagle feathers.[24]

A change from endemic to exotic feathers — some chiefs later inserted six ostrich feathers in place of six crane feathers in their silver headbands or headdresses — signified that newly available exotic plumes of high value had become the insignia of office. Just as decorative plumes carried meaning, so did their absence: according to the dependable "enthusiast" Henry Halbert (as Swanton termed him), when in mourning, the Choctaw eschewed plumes and other ornamentation.[25]

CLOTHING, BLANKETS, AND MATS

In late April 1540, Hernando de Soto arrived at Cofitachequi, a chiefdom in present-day South Carolina ruled by the Lady of Cofitachequi, whose superior status was signaled by her being carried about on a litter or reclining on cushions shaded by an awning in a large dugout canoe. She presented the Spaniards with freshwater pearls and told them that there were more where these pearls came from. The Spaniards were quite clearly taken by this powerful woman and by the many things they noted about Cofitachequi, including feather headdresses and garments. Indians here wore white, green, red, and yellow "feather mantles" deemed "elegant and suitable for winter" and gave the Spaniards "feather blankets" for their horses.[26]

This account was the first significant mention of large feather garments or coverings seen by Europeans in the South. Until the nineteenth century, Indians across the region transformed the skins of birds, as well as deerskins, bison hair, moss, palmetto, and other plant and animal materials, into mantles, robes, blankets, coats, skirts, and mats for summer and winter use.[27] Feathers were used nearly everywhere. In seventeenth-century Virginia they made "mantels . . . of Turky feathers, so prettily wrought and woven with threeds that nothing could bee discerned but the feathers." John Smith thought them "exceeding warme and very handsome."[28] In the eighteenth-century Carolinas, according to John Lawson, Siouans made "Match-Coat[s] of Hair, Furs,

Feathers, or Cloth" for both men and women. The feather coats were "very pretty, especially some of them, which [were] made extraordinary charming, containing several pretty Figures wrought in Feathers, making them seem like a fine Flower Silk-Shag; and when new and fresh, they [became] a Bed very well, instead of a Quilt." Others, Lawson remarked, "are made of the green Part of the Skin of a Mallard's Head, which they sew perfectly well together, their Thread being either the Sinews of a Deer divided very small, or Silk-Grass. When these are finish'd they look very finely, though they must needs be very troublesome to make."[29]

Farther west, a Franciscan mentioned that the seventeenth-century Caddo were "neatly attired in dressed skins adorned with feathers" and some specifically wore clothing "made . . . very skillfully of turkey feathers fastened by means of small strings."[30] In the next century, Houma and Tunica men and women wore turkey-feather mantles and robes, and Le Page, the planter with a concession at Natchez in the 1720s, reported that native women in general wore cloaks "of the feathers of swans, turkies, or India [Muscovy] ducks," and men and women used feather blankets in winter. He suggested that swans were of "great value," both for "large" feathers, presumably primaries, for "the diadems of their sovereigns, hats, and other ornaments," and for "small" feathers woven "as the peruke-makers [wove] hair" for "coverings . . . for their noble women." Swan skins, with the down intact, became tippets or neck coverings for young people.[31]

To make these garments, Indians everywhere apparently worked feathers into a fiber netting formed of beaten and spun strands of inner bark from mulberry trees or other plants.[32] In French Louisiana, according to Jean François Benjamin Dumont de Montigny, a French soldier who lived there in the 1720s – 1730s, native people made "a kind of mantle" from thread from the basswood tree and then covered the mantle "with the finest swan feathers fastened on this cloth one by one." And Le Page observed, "[F]eather mantles are worked on a frame similar to that on which wig makers work hair. They lay out the feathers in the same manner and fasten them to old fish nets or old mulberry-bark mantles. They place them in the manner already outlined one over another and on both sides. For this purpose they make use of little turkey feathers. The women who can obtain feathers of the swan or Indian duck make mantles of them for the women of the Honored class."[33]

Feather garments remained fashionable throughout the eighteenth century, when the Choctaw, according to Bernard Romans, made "blankets and other coverings out of the feathers of the breasts of wild turkies by a process similar to that of [European] wig makers, when they knit hair together for the purpose of making wigs."[34] James Adair added, "[Indians make] turkey feather blankets with the long feathers of the neck and breast of that large fowl — they twist the inner end of the feathers very fast into a strong double thread of hemp, or the inner bark of the mulberry tree, of the size

FIGURE 66.
Mrs. Dabney Burkett
with turkey-feather
mantle. *Mrs. Burkett,
of Montgomery
County, Va., is
holding a mantle
she apparently
made prior to 1910;
a rare photograph
of a turkey-feather
mantle, albeit in the
hands of a woman
whose ethnicity is
currently unknown.
Mosby and Handley,
Wild Turkey in
Virginia, fig. 2.*

and strength of coarse twine, as the fibres are sufficiently fine, and they work it in the manner of fine netting. As the feathers are long and glittering, this sort of blankets is not only very warm, but pleasing to the eye."[35] Even in the nineteenth century, the Creek apparently wore textiles of slippery-elm bark ornamented with iridescent turkey feathers.[36]

William Bartram, the great naturalist and romantic, remarked that some men wore "a short cloak, just large enough to cover the shoulders and breast . . . most ingeniously constructed, of feathers woven or placed in a natural imbricated manner." He said that the feathers were "of the gayest color" and that they included "usually . . . the scarlet feathers of the flaningo."[37]

There is little doubt about Bartram's short cloak, but what about "flaningo" feathers? Today, except for escapes, the greater flamingo is not found north of the Yucatan. Yet this bird, which can be found both in shallow saline waters, its preferred habitat, as well as where fresh and salty waters converge, was identified as one of the two "chiefe" birds in sixteenth-century Florida "fresh rivers." Furthermore, both Bossu and Le Page mentioned the flamingo in the early to mid-eighteenth century, and in 1832, Audubon saw flamingos in Florida, remarked that many were killed in the Keys and along the west coast of Florida, and reported that others had been seen on the Texas coast. For-

A Flamineo.

merly, this bird bred or wintered, or both, in both the Caribbean and along the Gulf Coast.[38]

But there are two other possibilities for flamingo-colored feathers: the scarlet ibis and the roseate spoonbill. In recent times, the scarlet ibis, a resident of South America and the southern Caribbean, has been vagrant in the United States, but formerly, according to Mark Catesby, it "frequent[ed]" the Bahamas, and after Bartram's time, Alexander Wilson stated that it could be found along the Atlantic coast from the southern Carolinas south in the early nineteenth century. Although it is uncertain whether Catesby or Wilson wrote from firsthand knowledge of this exotic and commonly traded ibis, Audubon, a better source, wrote that he saw several in Louisiana in the early 1820s.

The roseate spoonbill raises fewer questions. It seems always to have been common in the South, and abundant in coastal habitats, except when plume hunters hounded it and other wading birds in the late nineteenth and early twentieth centuries. Even though it is barely scarlet, the roseate spoonbill possesses impressive bright pink wings, flaming red shoulders, and an orange tail. Its plumage is altogether striking and eminently suited for feather garments covering the shoulders, and it is of more than passing interest that a common vernacular name for this bird is "flamingo."[39] Thus it is entirely possible that Bartram was correct, but it would be no surprise to find the feathers of these other two species also in the material culture of southern Indians.

ARROWS, AWLS, FANS, AND POUCHES

Before they were overwhelmed by the disease and social upheaval that followed the initial arrival of the Spanish in their lands, the Apalachee, who lived in the eastern panhandle of present-day Florida, stunned de Soto with the power of their long bows. Renowned archers, they shot cane arrows with enough force to pin a rider's armored leg to his horse, pierce trees, and penetrate mail. The Apalachee were especially skilled and feared, but all Indians in the South developed a strong and effective bow-and-arrow technology. Archers shot quickly and far. Accurate, they were able to "hit a flying bird" at a distance with arrows stabilized, for the most part, with three or four fletched feathers.[40]

In addition to consuming birds and ornamenting and covering themselves with the feathers of birds, southern Indians also converted feathers and bird parts into a range of products like fletching for arrows, arrow points, and wrist guards, at least until firearms made bow-and-arrow technology obsolete. Many, like the Powhatan, favored turkey

FIGURE 69.
Roseate Spoonbill.
*Hand-colored
engraving by
Robert Havell from
a painting by John
James Audubon,* Birds
of America, *vol. 4
(1835–38), plate 321.
Although it is quite
invisible in what is
known about the
ethno-ornithology
of the South, this
striking bird, whose
vernacular name was
"flamingo," might
well have been used
for decorative and
other purposes. Rare
Books and Special
Collections, Thomas
Cooper Library,
University of South
Carolina.*

feathers for fletching. Others preferred hawk feathers, which the Yuchi, linking performance in bird and weapon, said came from a bird "swift and sure in its flight." Archers made points of various raw materials, from the Apalachee's fire-hardened cane to the turkey spurs and bird bills used by the Powhatan, the Cherokee, and others. To protect their arms when shooting arrows, Indians used a variety of materials, including wrist guards "made of thick feathers," which ran the entire length of the inner lower arm. And to hunt turkeys, some Indians enticed them into range with turkey wing-bone callers.[41]

Native people also turned bird bones into tubes, awls, tubular beads, pins, and fish-hooks. Many preferred turkey bones for these purposes; for example, they often fashioned the tarsometatarsus — the fused lower bones of the foot — into an awl.[42] They also used feathers for various other purposes, including wiping after meals, as among the Powhatan and other Indians in Virginia and the Carolinas. According to John Smith, one woman tended the chief Powhatan when he ate meat, brought him water before and after; another "waiteth with a bunch of feathers to wipe them instead of a Towell, and the feathers when he hath wiped are dryed againe."[43]

Another product was the wing or tail-feather fan, which was widespread. Older Yuchi men used turkey tail feathers strung together by the quills as fans to flick away insects, as an accompaniment to gestures, and as a sign of leadership in dances.[44] In

FIGURE 70.
Louisiana Indians.
Drawings in black india ink and watercolor by Jean Benjamin François Dumont, dit Montigny, in Louisiana, 1719 – 37. Five of six Indians imaged hold or wear something related to birds: a fletched arrow (top left), a feathered calumet (top center), a bird shot with "modern" weaponry (top right), a turkey-tail fan (bottom left), and a turkey- or goose-feather mantle (bottom center). Courtesy Edward E. Ayer Collection, the Newberry Library, Chicago, Ayer MS 257 no. 17 (top) and no. 15 (bottom).

eastern Texas, the Caddo held turkey-feather fans in dances, and in Louisiana, young men sometimes carried turkey-feather fans — and in a novel adaptation, the French were said to make an "umbrella" from the tail feathers of four turkeys (whether domesticated or wild was not specified).[45] Feathers were also used to tickle the throat to induce vomiting (the Choctaw) and to skim oil off the top of a container of acorn meal and water (the Creek).[46]

Even the quill and splintered bones were put to use: the Catawba used a sharpened eagle quill to penetrate the skin and allow medicine to flow into the cut, and Creek women might have marked designs in clay pots with a turkey-feather quill.[47] Both the Cherokee and the Creek scratched people with bird bones: the Cherokee with a comb-like "scratcher" of sharpened splinters of a turkey leg or wing bone lashed into a small wooden frame used to bleed ballplayers, preparing them ritually before engaging in the

FIGURE 71.
Belted Kingfisher.
Black and yellow
Warbler (magnolia
warbler). Black-
burnian W[arbler].
Autumnal W. Water
Thrush (northern
waterthrush). *Hand-
colored engraving by
Alexander Lawson
based on drawing by
Alexander Wilson,
American Ornithol-
ogy, vol. 3, 1808–14,
plate 23. The migrant
warblers, which all
breed in the North, do
not seem to appear
in lore, artifact, or
subsistence, but the
belted kingfisher is
a figure in myth and
perhaps medicine.
John Hay Library at
Brown University.*

ball game; the Creek with "Splinters of Turkey bones" used to scratch women who had committed incest.[48]

Southern Indians also fashioned bird skins into tobacco pouches: one Indian brought Mark Catesby, the English naturalist and artist, "the entire skin" of a whooping crane being used to hold tobacco; a second tobacco pouch was made of a swan skin.[49] Among the miscellaneous uses of bird bones and skins, perhaps the most esoteric was reported by Dumont de Montigny, who said,

> [Indians in French Louisiana] make use of the body of a certain bird which in many places is called a "fisher." After having dried it, some of them cut it into many small pieces which they put here and there on their skins. Others reduce it to a fine pow-der, which they scatter over the skins side of the hair. In whatever way one makes use of it, it is certain that the odor of this bird drives away moths and all other de-structive creatures which might be able to injure the peltries. It is asserted that the martin (martinet), a kind of bird which resembles the swallow, has the same virtue and the same properties.[50]

The first bird ("the fisher") that prevented moths from consuming the pelts of animals was probably the belted kingfisher (*martin-pecheur*). Candidates for "the martin" are the tree swallow — which resembles the European martin — or another swallow, the purple martin, or perhaps the chimney swift.

EUROPEAN TRADE AND FASHION: CLOTHING AND PLUMES

In seventeenth-century Virginia, John Banister, the naturalist (and rector), noticed that some Indians took up woolen trade cloth to "cover their naked-ness." They were not the first, and would not be the last, southern Indians to adopt the clothing of the newcomers from Europe. Across the region, im-ported European duffel, stroud, and other trade cloth steadily replaced native materials and dress. The pat-tern differed from one part of the region to the next. In Florida, Indians stripped Europeans they intended to kill of their clothing. They did not merely replace their own clothing but instead probably added the new to their old, or wore the new on special occa-sions. Here, the demand for European cloth and clothing was too great for Franciscans to satisfy.[51]

In similar fashion, after their attack on the French in Louisiana in 1729, the Natchez spared the lives of two men "kept," according to Le Page, "for their talents." One was a carter who made what was required to haul away the furnishings and arms of the French. The other was a tailor whose job it was to modify and fit, for native wear, the uniforms and other dress taken from the French, dead or alive. If the clothes "were too narrow, as they often were, he enlarged them with other pieces of fabric in a different color, which pleased them more than if it had been the same color." Such was the demand for European cloth and clothing.[52]

By the beginning of the nineteenth century, Creek Indians had taken on what the historian Kathryn Holland Braund calls "a decidedly Scottish look" in their dress. British traders, including some of Scottish extraction, had long been resident among the Creek and had native wives and families; thus this novel appearance was not perhaps so surprising. Even though changes like these did not happen overnight, traditional wear had fallen away by the mid-nineteenth century, especially feather mantles, blankets, and accessories. Once the process started, there was no stopping it. The major impetus behind this transformation was the exchange by native people of deerskins and other products for European cloth (and other trade items), as well as the influence of European ideas about clothing and fashion. When southern Indians possessed the means, position, or inclination, or when circumstances were appropriate, they added to, or replaced, their own clothing and accessories with the offerings of European and American traders in their midst. The Creek, as Braund has written, were consumers interested in cloth second only to guns — but such was the demand in the region that the southern exchange, usually known as the deerskin trade, might as well have been named the "cloth trade."[53]

FIGURE 72.
The American Swallow (chimney swift). *Hand-colored etching by Mark Catesby,* Natural History *(1731–43), plate appendix 8. A fast flyer that once nested in large numbers in hollow trees, the chimney swift was invoked by Cherokees for success in the ball game. John Hay Library at Brown University.*

Southern Indians abandoned feather clothing and blankets but did not, as indicated earlier, entirely give up wearing feathers. In fact, feathers occasionally figured in the exchange — as in the mid-eighteenth century, when Jean-Bernard Bossu, a French naval officer who traveled widely in Alabama, Georgia, and Florida, wrote that one Alabama leader arrived with "feathers on his head" wearing "a scarlet coat with gold braid and English cuffs," beneath which were a white shirt, a loin cloth, and moccasins; Bossu promptly gave him "a blue coat, a waistcoat with gold braid, a plumed hat, and a white shirt with embroidered cuffs."[54]

Feathers and plumed hats turn up in southern trade inventories in small numbers, primarily, it seems, as gifts or special considerations for leaders and others deemed important. In 1797, for example, one Creek Indian requested "1 hat, a good one, black

feather," and French traders exchanged plumes for deerskins or gave them as presents on four occasions in Louisiana in the period 1701–63.[55]

As European and American explorers and colonists quickly became aware of the various uses to which southern Indians put feathers, so must Indians have been cognizant of the desire on the part of men and women of European descent for feathers. Alexander Wilson remarked that "long plumes" of great egrets had "at various periods been in great request" in Europe, especially in France and Italy, for ornamenting women's hats, and that Indians who "prize[d] them for ornamenting their hair, or top-knot" could also occasionally be seen "wandering through the market-place of New Orleans with bunches of those feathers for sale."[56]

Indeed, Wilson's comment prompts the question, what might Indians have seen through time in the dress of Europeans or European Americans encountered either in their own Indian lands or in colonial settlements, American towns, or Europe? Aside from people of Puritan or Quaker leaning, who were sober in dress, the newcomers — such as upper-class Virginians, who thought of themselves as "stylish" compared to Puritans — indulged what at times was an extravagant taste for feathers. In America from the mid-eighteenth through the first half of the nineteenth century, women of fashion liked to dress their hair and hats with plumes or feathers from ostriches, birds of paradise, roosters, and other birds, colored black, blue, yellow, green, brown, white, and so on. They displayed these in casual settings and on formal occasions, from riding to promenades and balls. Near the end of this period, bonnets were so heavily plumed that one woman resembled (in the words of "a wit") "a shuttlecock, for she was all cork and feathers."

In seventeenth- through nineteenth-century America, feathers were associated in particular with military uniforms and formal wear. In early seventeenth-century Virginia, men's hats and helmets were plumed, and women at times carried feather fans or wore feathers in their hair or hats. Later in the same century, men decorated their hats with ostrich feathers, and women accessorized with feather fans and feathers at their waists. In the eighteenth century, men fancied hats plumed around the crown, and women wore feathers in the hats of their riding habits. In the late eighteenth century, women, influenced by the court in France and elsewhere in Europe, decorated high coiffures and hats with plumes and feathers; military men wore red plumes and cockades in their hats, with feathers and colors coded by rank — in 1780, majors wore black-and-white feathers in their hats, brigadier generals wore white feathers, and the aides

FIGURE 74. *(Left)* Há-tchoo-túc-knee, Snapping Turtle, a Half-Breed. *Oil on canvas by George Catlin, near Fort Gibson, Indian Territory, 1834. Catlin feathered this Choctaw historian—also known as Peter Pitchlynn, educated at the University of Nashville, and a frequent and wide traveler—in a style affected by Plains Indians in Indian Territory. Yet Charles Dickens, who met him, remarked that Pitchlynn dressed as he, Dickens, and others did every day. Smithsonian American Art Museum, gift of Mrs. Joseph Harrison Jr., 1985.66.296.*

FIGURE 75. *(Right)* Matoaka als Rebecca filia potentiss: Princ: Powhatani Imp: Virginiae. *Copperplate engraving by Simon van de Passe, 1616. In this important engraving, Pocahontas (Matoaka was her secret name and Rebecca her baptismal name), the daughter of the chief Powhatan, is feathered in a fashion similar to English women of her time and station. Her adornment—a plume accessorizing her hat and a dainty plumed fan in her hand—signals that she is an aristocrat in her own land as well as, perhaps inadvertently, an American Indian.* Baziioologia: A Booke of Kings, *London, 1618. National Portrait Gallery, Smithsonian Institution, NPG.77.43.*

de camp of the major generals sported a green feather and those of the commander in chief a white and green feather. In the early 1780s, the infantry wore black plumes, and in the following decade, different legions of infantry and artillery were distinguished by different colored plumes in hats or helmets: white, red, yellow, and green.[57]

Indians exposed to these fashions in America surely made note of them, as did those who traveled to Europe — unwillingly, as captives, or voluntarily, as members of delegations or in other capacities. They could not have avoided European fashion, including accessorizing with plumes, which was far more elaborate in England and on the Continent than in America. Trimming and accessorizing with feathers was more widespread and elaborate in some periods and settings than in others. For example, in sixteenth- and especially seventeenth-century England, men commonly trimmed their hats with feathers of ostriches, herons, or other birds. On the Continent, feathered

The Three Cherokees, came over from the head of the River Savanna to London 1762

1 Their Interpreter that was Poisoned.

hats reached the height of fashion for men and women in the eighteenth century, especially the 1770s–1780s. Somewhere in Europe from the fifteenth through nineteenth centuries, men or women trimmed their hats with plumes and used feathers in fans and other accessories — fashion statements that Indians who traveled there must have noticed.[58]

For their part, Indians found themselves subject to intense scrutiny in Europe. In 1762 in London, Englishmen remarked on Ostenaco and two other Cherokees, who adorned their heads "with Shells, Feathers, Earrings, and other trifling Ornaments." Three decades before, in 1730, Alexander Cuming brought seven Cherokees to London, where the feathers in their hair evoked comment about a "natural" accessory. Indians who survived these voyages returned home with knowledge of European fashion at court, in social gatherings, and among the various classes. Perhaps, like some who went to New Spain and admitted to "imitating [the] dress" of people there, or others who found themselves in the company of new Americans in their settlements and towns, Indians also picked up ideas for potential new fashions, including feather use that while different in certain respects (especially gender) was similar in others. Whatever ensued, there is little doubt that both Indians and Europeans left impressions on each other.[59]

FIGURE 78.
Crested woodpecker
plaque. *Key Marco,
Collier County, Fla.,
AD 1450–1550, 16.5 in.
long. As explored in
the text, the design
evokes the ivory-
billed woodpecker.
The original cypress
plaque on which the
drawing is based was
found during the
1896–97 expedition
led by Frank
Hamilton Cushing
and has decayed.
Drawing by Wells
Sawyer. National
Anthropological
Archives, Smithsonian
Institution, MS 241259.*

Imagery

We've established that southern Indians ate a wide variety of birds, accessorized with their feathers, and used their skins and other body parts in everyday life. Now we take up the role of birds in other contexts and the challenge, discussed earlier, introduced by the anthropologist Claude Lévi-Strauss: Were things like birds good for thinking (and not just good to eat or to make certain products)? Did they figure, for example, in social and political understandings, worldview and ideology, religion, myth, art, ritual, tales, or theories of sickness and well-being?[1]

A CRESTED WOODPECKER

These questions will preoccupy us for the next six chapters of this book. For initial insight we begin with the ethnologist and archaeologist Frank Cushing, who, deep in a watery, mosquito-ridden late fifteenth- or early sixteenth-century Calusa site at Key Marco on Florida's Gulf Coast in 1897, made the startling discovery of a wooden board on which was painted the striking image of a woodpecker with a crest. Rare for reasons concerning preservation, few wooden objects survive the ages; fewer still represent or image birds. They include, as we shall see, sculpted duck heads (one resembling a dabbling duck, the other a merganser), a pelican, a great horned owl over six feet in length, and raptors, waterfowl, and other birds in a mortuary context.[2]

Cushing knew that he was onto something unusual and exciting. He had been pulling from the muck painted wooden masks holed in the top for attachments such as feathers, with detachable and movable wings, and sculpted wooden animals. Then he found "a thin board of yellowish wood" some sixteen inches long on which was painted "an elaborate figure of a crested bird . . . in black, white, and blue pigments." He was ecstatic. It was his "crowning find," an "altar tablet of cypress wood" on which could be seen a "distinct though faded painting of the King-Fisher-God bearing his double paddle as insignia, with word signs issuing from his mouth — precisely as in paintings of the Central American and higher Mexican codices."[3]

Misled perhaps by the extensive light blue pigmentation, Cushing was quite wrong that this was a painting of a kingfisher, a blue jay, or some mythological bird with elements of both.[4] The wooden board started to decay the instant it was exposed to air, but fortunately the image on it was copied faithfully, and what it shows is clearly a crested woodpecker based on either the ivory-billed or the pileated. Both woodpeckers are large and crested. But they differ so much in size, behavior, voice, and other characteristics that biologists assign them not just to different species but to separate genera. Like

FIGURE 79.
Ivory billed Wood-
pecker. Pileated
W[oodpecker].
Red headed
W[oodpecker]. *Hand-
colored engraving by
Alexander Lawson
based on drawing by
Alexander Wilson,
American Ornithol-
ogy, vol. 4, 1808–14,
plate 29. In the
ethno-ornithology
of the South, ivory-
billed and red-headed
woodpeckers loom
larger than all others.
John Hay Library at
Brown University.*

the ivory-billed in nature, the painted woodpecker has a white bill and a line of white feathers from its auricular area down the neck. Somewhat like the ivory-billed, white swirls appear on the back above the scapulars of the wing. These artistic details seem based more on the ivory-billed than on the pileated. The ivory-billed in nature also has a prominent patch of all-white secondaries (and inner primaries) at rest, but other than being set off from the painted bird's mantle (like the ivory-billed), the abstract geometry of the secondary patch bears no resemblance to either woodpecker in life. When it came to the secondaries and the belly and vent (painted with chevron bands or teardrop-shaped sections of color), the artist had other-than-avian considerations in mind.

Moreover, this painted woodpecker has feet with two toes forward and one back, and on each foot and leg the nails (which merge with the digits) and tarsus are strong in appearance. They are curious. Most birds have three toes forward and one back, and no bird has only three toes. Woodpeckers (and the osprey and cuckoos) have a zygo-dactylic toe pattern, in which two toes are forward and two back. Few birds have as long digits or as strong claws as those represented on the board. One category that does

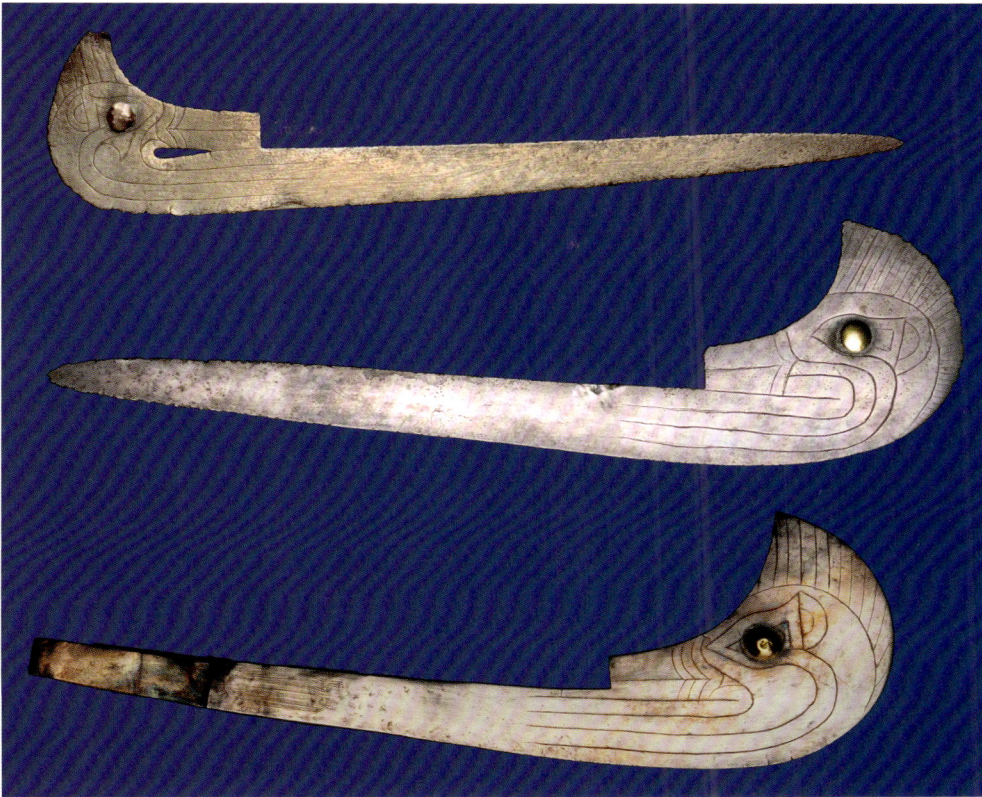

FIGURE 80.
Silver crested-woodpecker hairpins. *Glades County, Fla., ca. AD 1500–1600; silver, with gold or copper inset eyes, 9.6 in. long. Men likely placed these pins in their turbans or headbands. South Florida Museum, Bradenton, Fla.*, top to bottom: *4512, 6184, 8552.*

consists of raptors, whose predatory characteristics the arrangement on the painted bird might well reference. The small animal outlined in white just beneath the talons, if prey and part of the composition, is consistent with this interpretation.[5]

Odder still are four circular objects pigmented white, blue, and red that depend in a line from the bird's bill. Enigmatic, they might be related to the origin or capacity for speech — although this is highly speculative. The globular objects were connected by a thin tongue line disappearing into the bill and throat, which recalls the beaded segments of tongues represented in woodpecker bills etched onto artifacts from Moundville, the prominent Mississippian site in Alabama. Here and elsewhere woodpecker (and raptor) tongues are represented prominently, with curious angular terminal parts. This may be no accident. Woodpecker tongues, especially those of the ivory-billed and the pileated, are extremely long — when withdrawn they curve inside what are known as hyoids in the skull — and have prominent backward-oriented barbs at pointed tips. No wonder they are a focus of artistic representation.[6]

In addition to Cushing's discovery, crested woodpeckers show up repeatedly on artifacts before and after Europeans arrived in the South, from gorgets and a tortoise-shell hair ornament from the Mississippian site of Etowah in Georgia to sixteenth-century silver, gold, and copper ornaments from central Florida that the elite probably inserted into headbands or turbans (one, in fact, was discovered in association with a human skull and metal headband).[7]

FIGURE 81.
(Left) Raptor
sculpted in wood.
*Fort Center, Glades
County, Fla., ca. AD
200–800, 7.25 in.
long. A small elegant
sculpture evoking
a raptorial bird in
repose. Collections of
the Florida Museum
of Natural History,
62355.*

FIGURE 82.
(Right) Duck head
sculpted in wood.
*Belle Glade Site, Palm
Beach, Fla., ca. AD
200–1500, 7.3 in.
high. Naturalistic,
the head of this bird
evokes the fulvous
whistling duck or
a related water
fowl. Department
of Anthropology,
Smithsonian
Institution, 383868.*

These crested woodpecker representations were most likely based on the ivory-billed. Just as it has recently captured the imagination of people worldwide, the ivory-billed has always been a bird to be reckoned with. Before and after Mississippian times, this big, spectacular black-and-white bird flew directly through and over mature bottomland and upland forests, emitted loud and distinctive nasal calls, drummed with a resonant double-rap cadence, and used its strong chisel-like bill to carve off huge slabs of bark and get at larvae beneath. It was as hard to ignore in the past as today. Culturally important, the ivory-billed was an object of exchange, curiosity, and spiritual interest, and (as discussed later) its skins and bills have been found far from its presumed range. Compared to the ivory-billed, the pileated was slightly smaller in size, more common, required one-thirtieth the territory, and simply might not have measured up; the Cherokee, for one, considered it "lazy and stupid" and thoroughly minor as a bird.[8]

CARVED, WOVEN, TATTOOED, AND SCULPTED BIRDS

Across the region, Indians represented birds not just in wooden sculpture or in pigments on wood, but in various other media. Eighteenth-century Carolina Indians, for example, in John Lawson's words, "[make baskets] of a very fine sort of Bulrushes, and sometimes of Silk-grass, which they work with Figures of Beasts, Birds, Fishes, &c." Other native people wove representations of birds into baskets, tattooed them onto their bodies, etched them into shells, and sculpted them in stone and other materials. The people of Cofitachequi in South Carolina made figures representing birds from pearls. Siouans and the Chickasaw worked "figures of animals" into mulberry cloth and

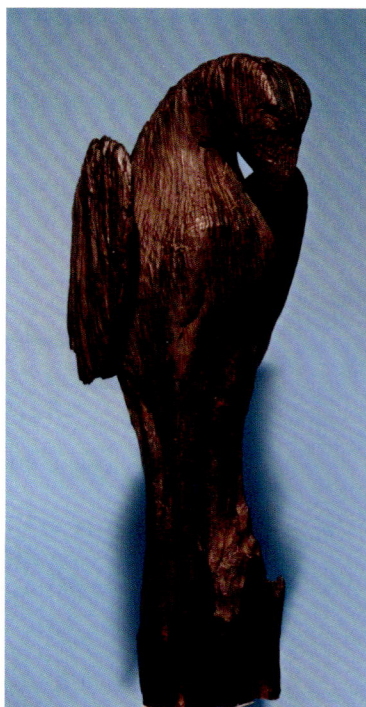

baskets. "The better sort" of Powhatan women wore skin mantels decorated with the figures of birds and other animals. Algonquian women tattooed on their bodies figures of birds and other animals — "fowles, fishes, beasts," George Percy called them — as did Caddoan men and others. And the Caddo kept in cane baskets or wooden chests objects such as "little platters or vessels of black wood like circular shields, all curiously worked and having four feet," some of which "represented little ducks." The exact reasons for these representations are not known but were conceivably related to kinship and descent or to a spiritual alliance with an other-than-human being rather than merely to aesthetics.[9]

Much of the material worked with avian themes and known from documentary records was friable — the skins, cloth, and baskets especially. But from an early period in Florida come stone plummets resembling the heads of shovelers and other ducks, which were sometimes interred with the bodies of women and might have weighted the bottoms of fishing nets or, less likely, been suspended from people's belts.[10] Also sculpted from stone and widespread in the eastern woodlands are enigmatic artifacts shaped like abstract or pop-eyed birds. Known as birdstones, their function is unknown, which has not halted speculation that it was utilitarian, decorative, ceremonial, amuletic, or totemic. Probably it was basely practical, birdstones serving as weights bringing greater stability and accuracy to weapons like darts thrown with the aid of atlatls, or spear-throwers. Yet the care taken with aesthetics speaks to the evocation of aerial beings in the flight of a dart, to a magical sympathy, that is, with the targets of darts.[11]

THE SOUTHEASTERN CEREMONIAL COMPLEX

Dating birdstones is an uncertain business, but some are ancient and betray a long-standing avian interest in the region. In fact, the evidence for fascination with birds is abundant in works of clay, shell, and stone over thousands of years, beginning, notably, with Poverty Point, an Archaic period site in northeastern Louisiana, where among massive earthworks erected between 1730 and 1350 BC can be found two bird-shaped mounds some forty-five to sixty feet high as well as numerous small owl-shaped artifacts. An avian fixation developed and intensified during the succeeding eras known as Woodland (700 BC – AD 1000) and Mississippian (AD 1000 – 1500), which together lasted over two thousand years. Woodland people shaped clay into vessels in the form of owls, ducks, and other birds and decorated ceramic rims with the heads and tails of ducks, vultures, and other raptors. They also incised stone tablets with designs ranging from abstract to natural, some representing vultures and other birds.

The precise function of these objects is obscure. At least some of the vessels might have held the infusion known as black drink, a bitter purgative decoction of leaves and twigs of the yaupon (*Ilex vomitoria*), a southern holly, brewed until black in color. Conceived as an esoteric "white" drink from a beloved tree, black drink was ingested by southern Indian men in prescribed ways to purify themselves on ritual occasions,

FIGURE 83. *(Left)* Stone plummets representing birds. *Left to right, top to bottom: the head of a wild turkey; cormorant, red-breasted merganser, or similar water bird; northern shoveler; and cormorant, red-breasted merganser, or similar water bird. Southern Indians sometimes suspended objects from belts around their waists, but these are probably plummets used to weight fishing nets. Most represent expert fishers and other water birds or powerful land birds such as the turkey. Top, left to right: Turkey Creek Mound, Brevard County, Fla., AD 200–500, 3.38 in. long, 3.75 in. long. National Museum of the American Indian, Smithsonian Institution, 047338, 047339. Photos by NMAI Photo Services Staff. Bottom left: Cedar Keys, Levy County, Fla., 3.5 in. long. National Museum of the American Indian, Smithsonian Institution, 104273. Photo by NMAI Photo Services Staff. Bottom right: Turkey Creek Mound, Brevard County, Fla., ca. AD 200–500, 5.38 in. long. Division of Anthropology, American Museum of Natural History, DN/749.*

FIGURE 84. *(Right)* Birdstones. *Widespread in the northeastern woodlands (but relatively rare in the South), often poorly dated, birdstones were sculpted in different styles; many had cylindrical popeyes or fan tails. Why they were made is unknown, but they probably functioned as counterweights for spear-throwers, which, if aimed at birds, achieved sympathy with the prey. Top to bottom: Greenstone birdstone, Floyd County, Ga., ca. 1500–1000 BC, courtesy of the Division of Anthropology, American Museum of Natural History 1869-90-81; Granite birdstone, Big Sandy River, W.Va., ca. 500 BC, Huntington Museum of Art, Huntington, W. Va., 1977.65; Steatite birdstone, Mingo, W.Va. or Ohio, 5.18 in. long, Huntington Museum of Art, Huntington, W. Va., 1980.206.187.*

including the ceremony that marked the ripening of green corn. Men of high rank or special status passed around shell cups and other vessels incised with bird-human imagery, each taking a drink of the purifying beverage, some vomiting, purging themselves of pollution, and readying themselves for purity and peace.[12]

Avian imagery was especially abundant during the half-millennium represented by the Mississippian era. The most famous objects are gorgets, whelks, circular disks, celt handles, and copper plates associated with what is commonly known as the Southeastern Ceremonial Complex (SECC). Essentially homegrown and built on a Woodland base, this ritual complex was widespread in the South and is best known from three mortuary sites where artifacts concentrated remarkably through time: Spiro in eastern

FIGURE 85. *(Left)* Stone owlets. *Northeastern Louisiana, 2000–1000 BC, 0.6–1.4 in. high. These miniature abstract sculptures of rotund, earless owls, based perhaps on the barred owl, as well as the large, possibly bird-shaped mounds associated with the Archaic site of Poverty Point, betray an early and intense interest in birds in the South—even if questions about what they meant remain unanswered. Given the widespread association of owls with present and future malevolent events, these small figures might have been made and presented, carried, or worn for purposes of protection or fortune. Poverty Point State Historic Site, Pioneer, La., Louisiana Department of Culture, Recreation, and Tourism. Photo by Robert Rickett.*

FIGURE 86. *(Right)* Ceramic bowls with the head and tail of a duck on the rim. *Near Nashville Tenn., Mississippian. The blunt foreheads, hint of crests on the heads, and small bills recall wood ducks, common residents (and tree-cavity nesters) in the South. Thruston Collection, Department of Anthropology, Vanderbilt University, courtesy of William R. Fowler. Photo by Hunter Darrouzet.*

Oklahoma, Moundville in Alabama, and Etowah in Georgia. By the time of its height in the thirteenth and fourteenth centuries, the SECC either reflected a set of region-wide understandings about authority and religion indigenized by each southern Indian group in its own culturally specific way or consisted of closely related but separate complexes.[13] Today there is vigorous debate over whether the SECC represents anything regionwide or whether the concept occludes more than it reveals: such is the emphasis on the local, not regional, distribution of ideas; the importance of sites outside the South, like Cahokia; and a healthy skepticism over what, precisely, the material record means.[14]

However this issue is ultimately resolved, it is agreed that Mississippian artifacts represent a robust range of birds and avian beings. Like their predecessors, they vary in style from naturalistic to abstract. Some seemingly represent birds in nature, and others apparently serve as models for other-than-human beings with combined human and avian elements.

Despite the wide variety, most birds fall into several categories: woodpeckers with

Anas cristatus elegans.
The Summer Duck.

T 97

FIGURE 87.
The Summer Duck
(wood duck). *Hand-
colored etching
by Mark Catesby*,
Natural History
*(1771), plate 97.
This common and
spectacularly hued
tree-nesting duck was
often represented in
the material culture
of the South. John
Carter Brown Library
at Brown University.*

crests; raptors like vultures, owls, falcons, and eagles; ducks; and the wild turkey. All lent their forms to ceramic or stone artifacts or appeared engraved on shells. Some objects are quite remarkable: stone tobacco pipes in the form of ducks and owls and other raptors, which continued the Woodland interest in naturalistic representation; a stone bowl representing what surely is, given its remarkable verisimilitude, a vulture with its head on the outside of the bowl; wooden celt handles in the form of crested-woodpecker heads and necks, each with a copper celt hafted in an open bill; jars in the form of owls and other birds; bowls with rims featuring the heads of ducks, owls and other raptors, and other birds; and vessels incised with representations of turkeys, among others.[15]

Many birds represented are powerful, even aggressive, species or families, making for muscular symbols. This is especially true of woodpeckers with crests, if they are the ivory-billed, and turkeys. Like the ivory-billed woodpecker, turkeys are strong birds in nature. Gobblers in particular have a reputation for pugnacity during the breeding season, when they strut, display, and readily engage in daylong combat against other males, resulting in debilitating wounds and even death. And while somewhat awk-ward in the air, turkeys are powerful runners, trotting ten miles per hour and going full bore at twenty-five. In the Mississippian world, which was marked by ranked societies run by powerful elites, differential access to basic resources, contests of authority and

FIGURE 88. *(Left)* Copper celts with crested-woodpecker handles. *Wood, copper, and shell, Spiro Temple Mound, LeFlore County, Okla., AD 1200–1350, longest blade 8.625 in. long, longest handle 17 in. long. The wooden-handled crested woodpeckers have open bills with protruding tongues, as if they were dead. Even if these objects were used for ceremonial purposes, the putative link between large woodpeckers and a complex defined by power, aggression, and war is apparent. National Museum of the American Indian, Smithsonian Institution, 18-9077. Photo by Carmelo Guadagno.*

FIGURE 89. *(Right)* Diorite crested-bird bowl. *Moundville, Tuscaloosa County, Ala. AD 1250–1500, 15 in. high. An elegant long-necked waterbird bowl, carved of hard stone; when the pattern is flattened, the cross-hatched design on the neck, head, and bill appears serpentine; some bill marks might indicate that the mandibles are sewn together. The length of the neck and the prominent crest—the most notable morphological features—leave uncertain what bird in nature is represented. National Museum of the American Indian, Smithsonian Institution, 16-5232. Photo by NMAI Photo Services Staff.*

power, and endemic hostilities, the connection with powerful beings, including birds, is understandable. Indeed, many SECC artifacts, including those with avian associations, surely involved the expression of authority, rank, power, and religion.[16]

Some avian images are, as mentioned, naturalistic representations of birds. But others evoke other-than-avian or other-than-human beings. They are not all of a piece. They depict men with anthropoid hands or feet (or both), or talons in their place; sharply curved, beaked, avian noses; bird-masked faces; feathers hanging down backs; bird tails between and behind the legs; antlered heads; feathered-serpentine features; or avian features lacking human attributes.

Despite different styles and iterations, this imagery collectively is common in the South. But the debate over what these ornithanthropic and ornithoserpentine beings represent is inconclusive. The suggestions include bird-men; spirit-birds; serpent-birds; some other composite other-than-human being with avian attributes; men garbed and

FIGURE 90. Shell gorgets representing other-than-human combat. *On the left, an avian being (Cherokee* dhla:nuwa*?) combats an anomalous monster (underwater panther?); on the right, antlered, winged anthropoid beings with raptorial feet fight each other—both gorgets offering windows, however opaque, on the other-than-human (and ornithoanthropoid) worlds of southern Indians.* Left: *Bell County, Tex., ca.* AD *1200–1500, 5.9 in. diameter. National Museum of the American Indian, Smithsonian Institution, 22-7574. Photo by* NMAI *Photo Services Staff.* Right: *Hixon Site, Hamilton County, Tenn.,* AD *1300–1500, 4.5 in. diameter. Frank H. McClung Museum, University of Tennessee, Knoxville, 566/1Ha3. Photo © John Bigelow Taylor.*

performing as, or in association with the attributes of, birds. It is easier to pose the questions than agree with the logic underlying various answers.[17]

If based in part in nature, the strongly raptorial men or anthropoid raptor-beings point to raptors as models. The representations with strongly beaked (decurving upper mandibles) "nose-bills" and banded tails are convincingly raptorial. But these features are also common in raptors and do not really help determine which (if any single one) was the model (owls, hawks, eagles, kites, vultures, falcons, and the osprey and the caracara are all possibilities). One feature in many, however, stands out as nearly unique: the eye "forked" behind and below, which evokes the pronounced moustachial stripe of eastern forms of the peregrine falcon. The peregrine is a remarkable bird. The artist Alexander Wilson remarked on its reputation as "uncommonly bold and powerful," and how it "darts on its prey with astonishing velocity" and "strikes with its formidable feet." A renowned aerialist and hunter—it has been called "nature's perfect aerodynamic performer"—the peregrine is known to kill over 425 species of birds in North America, ranging in size from hummingbirds to the sandhill crane, often by stooping at breath-taking speed and then grabbing or striking a bird with talons splayed at impact and then balled into a fist.[18] Other raptors, of course, including the golden and bald

FIGURE 91. Drawings of raptorial birds and bird-men from shell-cup engravings, copper-repoussé plaques, shell gorgets, and other artifacts. *The Mississippian period produced a variety of depictions of birds and bird-men, from highly stylized raptorial birds, some seemingly in mortal combat, to winged and tailed bird-men whose hands and feet combined human and bird (taloned) characteristics, and who were accompanied by symbols of authority and power. Many of these objects were interred in graves.* Drawn from, left to right, top to bottom: *a shell cup, Spiro Okla. (AD 1200–1350),* Phillips and Brown, Pre-Columbian Shell Engravings, *vol. 2, plate 303; a limestone pipe, Moundville, Ala., AD 1250–1550, in Clarence Moore, "Moundville Revisited," fig. 86, John Hay Library at Brown University; a shell cup, Spiro, Okla., AD 1200–1350,* Phillips and Brown, Pre-Columbian Shell Engravings, *vol. 1, plate 88; two shell cups, Spiro, Okla., AD 1200–1350,* Phillips and Brown, Pre-Columbian Shell Engravings, *vol. 2, plates 203, 177; a shell gorget and an embossed copper artifact, Etowah, Ga., AD 1300–1375, two copper repoussé plaques, Dunklin County, Mo., AD 1200–1400, and a copper repoussé plaque, near Peoria, Ill., in* Moorehead, Etowah Papers I, *figs. 29, 9, 8a, 8b, 8c.*

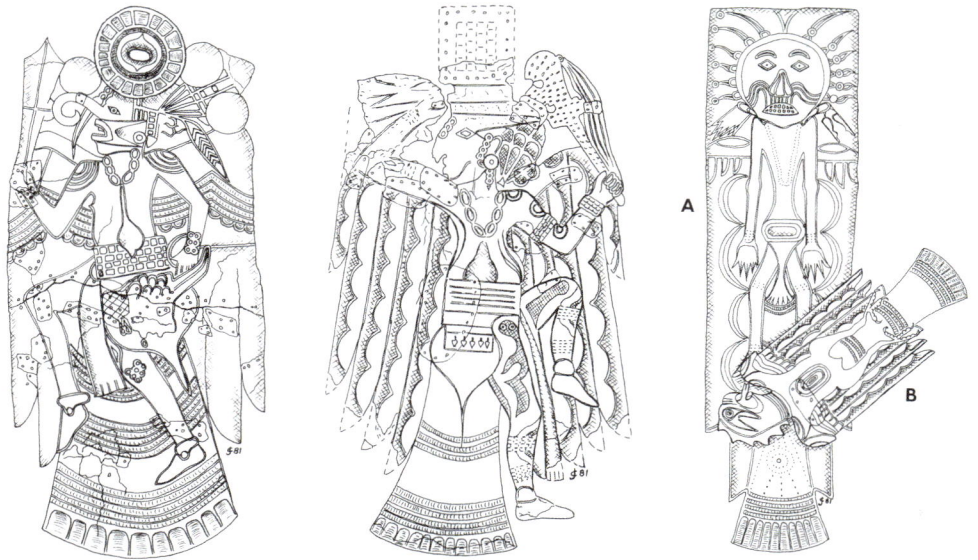

FIGURE 92. *(Top)* Copperplate images of warriors, dancers, raptors, and other-than-human beings. *Line drawings of repoussé sheet copperplates, Leon County, Fla., ca. AD 1240–1476, 21.3 in. long (left), 17.1 in. long (center), 22.4 in. long (right A). The dancers (left and center), or other-than-human beings, if that is what these burial breastplates represent, combine wings, tails, and other features of raptors with the characteristics of elite human warriors, such as maces, a trophy head, and signatures of office and status around the neck and above the head. The forked-eye falconid raptor (right B) with highly abstracted avian features, overlays an image of an other-than-human being (right A). The drawings of the plates at center and left fit the bellicose Mississippian climate. Jones, "Southern Cult Manifestations," figs. 6b (left), 7b (center), 8b (right). Courtesy of the Florida Division of Historical Resources.*

FIGURE 93. *(Bottom)* Copperplates depicting beings with human and bird attributes. *Repoussé sheet copper, Mound C, Etowah, Ga., AD 1300–1375, 14 in. high (left), 15.5 in. high (right). Representations of other-than-human beings or important men who have appropriated avian attributes, these individuals display a forked motif at the corner of the mouth and wear symbols of office and power around the neck and body, or on the head, or hold them and trophies in their hands. Department of Anthropology, Smithsonian Institution, A91117 (left), A91113 (right).*

Great-footed Hawk. FALCO PEREGRINUS. Gmel. Male 1 Female 2. Green-winged Teal and Godwit

eagles, also have prominent feet and claws that might well be referenced in the starkly powerful mica and copper talons dating from Woodland and Mississippian times.[19]

Like the wild turkey and the ivory-billed woodpecker, the peregrine falcon and other raptorial representations keep the focus on power, aggression, and war as subtexts for the avian imagery of copper plates, whelks, shell gorgets, and other objects. During bellicose Mississippian times, when warfare was endemic due to demographic, subsistence, and resource stress, and important centers like Moundville were firmly palisaded, it is easy to see why a bird like the peregrine (or another raptor) might be an important symbol of aerial (celestial) power. The Mississippian people who lived at Etowah entombed men of high status in feather costumes, with copper-plate headdresses displaying avian attributes. The link between birds, on the one hand — raptorial birds and other-than-avian beings — and status that flowed over into powerful social and religious networks, on the other, is transparent. It might not be too far-fetched to speculate that some representations echoed mythical giant raptorial birds akin to so-called Thunder Birds elsewhere that were capable of preying on human beings. The Creek, Seminole, Cherokee, and others believed in the existence of dangerous, large birds or spirit-birds (discussed elsewhere in greater detail), the Choctaw attributed thunder and lightening to giant male and female birds, but the Chickasaw, according to the ethnologist John Swanton, knew nothing about a Thunder Bird. Thus the evidence for a Thunder Bird in the South is quite mixed.[20]

FIGURE 94. Great-Footed Hawk (peregrine falcon). *Hand-colored engraving by Robert Havell from a painting by John James Audubon,* Birds of America, *vol. 1 (1827–30), plate 16. This powerful raptor was the most likely model for representations of beings with forked designs near the mouth and eye. Rare Books and Special Collections, Thomas Cooper Library, University of South Carolina.*

Imagery : : : 95

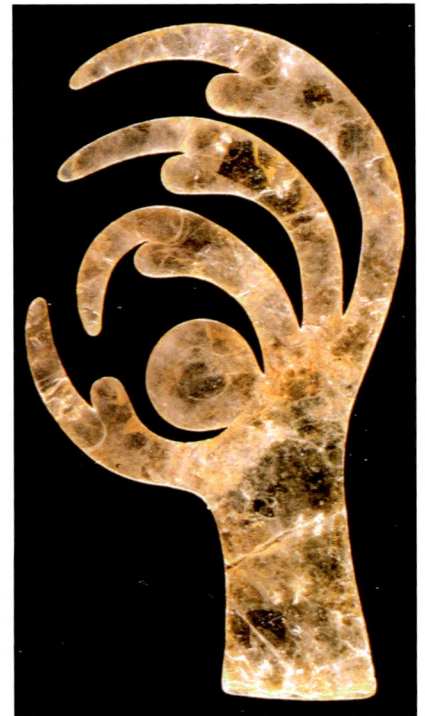

FIGURE 95. *(Left)* Mississippian raptor talons. *These Mississippian-era copper and flint artifacts reduce lethal and predatory raptors to their most devastating weapons: the hallux and other claws that constitute talons, a fitting symbol for elite authority and power among warlike people.* Left: *Repoussé sheet copper, Etowah, Bartow County, Ga., AD 1200–1400, 7.1 in. long. Georgia Department of Natural Resources, Antonio J. Waring Jr. Archaeological Laboratory at the University of West Georgia, UWG-1017/1146, burial 109.* Right: *Flint, Humphreys County, Tenn., AD 1200–1400, 5.85 in. long. Frank H. McClung Museum, University of Tennessee, Knoxville 1902/41. Photos courtesy of Susan Power.*

FIGURE 96. *(Right)* Mica raptor talon. *Hopewell, Ross County, Ohio, ca. 200 BC–AD 400, 11 in. high. Even though found outside the South, this exceptional Woodland-era mica talon signals the early interest in the strength of birds' claws, particularly the hallux or hind claw, in the eastern woodlands. Why there was such interest is the question; in the South one answer is that in time it flourished among mutually hostile people whose aggressive designs captured the essence of raptorial birds. Ohio Historical Society, OHS 10832.*

Although the precise meaning of this imagery remains elusive, indigenous people in the South fixed on birds, bird-spirits, or avian other-than-human beings as active inhabitants of their world long before Europeans arrived in the region. We therefore have a preliminary answer to the question posed at the beginning of this section: the avian world that we have just managed to glimpse resonated in far more interesting ways than the narrow, if indisputably important, utilitarian contexts relating to subsistence, clothing, and other ends. We might not always know which specific birds are represented, but what is striking is that if the imagery is based in nature we can then rule out many species — in fact most of the avian diversity in the region. What remains are owls with ears (great horned, long-eared, screech), vultures (black and turkey), other raptors (hawks, falcons, eagles, and allies), ducks, woodpeckers with crests, the wild turkey, ornithanthropic or ornithoserpentine other-than-human beings, and a few other birds. In some cases the species can be identified: the best cases can be made

Nahyápuw. The Grype. almost as bigg as an Eagle.

FIGURE 97. Bald Eagle. *Pen and ink with watercolor, associated with John White, ca. 1585–1600. Inscribed: "Nahyápuw. The Grype. almost as bigg as an Eagle." The artist gives formidable talons to this bald eagle; an interesting convergence with talon-shaped artifacts. "Grype" refers to a large, fabulous bird as well as to the white-headed Old World griffon vulture. The larger "Eagle" of the inscription must be the golden eagle. Sloane volume. © The Trustees of the British Museum, SL,5270.75.*

FIGURE 98. Shell gorgets representing crested woodpeckers and turkey cocks. *These and other gorgets, which, as implied in their name (and perforations) were worn suspended over the throat and upper chest, display two of the most powerful birds in the South: crested woodpeckers (presumably the ivory-billed) and the wild turkey. The woodpeckers are often arranged, bills pointed counterclockwise, at what seem to be cardinal points in a sacred geography surrounding a central sun or fire (bottom left); the turkeys often reveal their tails but some (upper right) are highly stylized.* Left: *Crested woodpecker gorgets: (top) Spiro Mound, Le Flore County, Okla., ca. AD 1300, 3.8 in. diameter, Sam Noble Oklahoma Museum of Natural History, University of Oklahoma, LfCrl/D14; (bottom) prob. Tennessee or northern Alabama, Mississippian, 4.25 in. diameter, Department of Anthropology, Smithsonian Institution, 30201.* Right: *Turkey-cock gorgets, Hixon Site, Tenn., AD 1200−1350, 2.5 in. diameter (top), ca. 2.25 in diameter (bottom), Frank H. McClung Museum, University of Tennessee, Knoxville, 567/1Ha3 (top), 508/1Ha3 (bottom).*

for birds like the wild turkey, wood duck, peregrine falcon, ivory-billed woodpecker, and several others. In nature each of the birds represented stands out in some way. Turkeys and raptors are aggressive. Ivory-billeds are dominant. Owls and others are anomalously nocturnal, while most birds are diurnal. Wood ducks are not just stunning in coloration but anomalously tree nesters among ducks. For whatever reasons, these birds attract notice.[21]

Inconclusive or cautious as these ruminations may seem, they, and the pre-Columbian representations on which they are based, nevertheless provide a foundation for the antiquity of avian interest in the South rooted in something other than narrow utilitarian grounds and open up further associations between birds and people that impinge upon social and political arrangements, war and peace, spiritual life, and other domains, to which we turn next.

FIGURE 100. That Which Outina Considers Military Order of March When He goes to War. *Engraving by Theodor de Bry (after Jacques Le Moyne de Morgues), 1591, in Hariot,* Der ander Theyl, *plate 14. This image of sixteenth-century might and military discipline along the Florida Atlantic coast depicts heavily plumed paramount leaders; one appears to wear the entire head and upper body of an eagle atop his own head. John Carter Brown Library at Brown University.*

Descent & Power

Reflecting on the life of Will West Long, a Cherokee elder and mentor, the anthropologist John Witthoft recalled Long's vast knowledge of natural history and eagerness to discuss the last uncommon bird or plant he had encountered. Like Long, Witthoft possessed a strong interest in birds. Thus it is not surprising that in his ethnography in the 1940s he provided insights on how birds influenced Eastern Cherokee culture, noting, for example, that one Cherokee town was named Birdtown, one of seven clans were "the bird people," and some Cherokees bore the surname of Owl, including Moses Owl and Sally Owl.[1]

Witthoft's work reveals that something had been lost in the translation from Cherokee to English names: in Cherokee, Moses Owl was Moses Barred Owl, and Sally Owl was Sally Screech Owl. This could not have been uncommon — neither the loss of a species name (e.g., screech-owl, golden eagle, turkey vulture) in translation, nor the substitution in English of a more inclusive vernacular name (e.g., owl, eagle, buzzard) for family or personal names.

Nor, for that matter, were bird names rare in the South. Through life, in naming ceremonies, at marriage, and on many other occasions, southern Indian men and women acquired different personal names. This process began with birth. Eighteenth- and nineteenth-century Creek infants, for example, were known by the names of the descent groups into which they were born. They kept these names until initiation, when they acquired new names. Since one descent group (one clan) was Bird, this was conceivably the name of many Creek children. Regardless of name, a southern Indian infant at birth became a lifetime member of a clan, some of which had bird names and associations like Bird, Eagle, or Turkey. Children sometimes acquired names according to their character; the Chickasaw, for instance, named their children according to appearance and temperament, sometimes choosing for daughters Mourning Dove (which did not stop them from killing this bird).

For some, names changed at adolescence or at other times during life. Lawson remarked that in the early eighteenth-century North Carolina Piedmont, Indian boys at age sixteen or seventeen took permanent names like Eagle or another "Wild-Fowl," animal, fish, or "wild Creature." Among southern Indians appeared names such as Red Bird, Pigeon Roost, Red Feather, Humming Bird, Red Eagle, Bird Tail, Little Turkey, Snipe, and Raven — the last a Cherokee name for one who had taken scalps (and a title referencing a certain number of scalps to one's credit).

Although the names were greatly variable, collectively many were avian, which allowed birds and their feathers (worn, as when a young eighteenth-century Creek man acquired a war name, on naming occasions) an arena as vast as society itself in which to figure visibly and meaningfully.[2]

KINSHIP AND DESCENT

At birth, each southern Indian joined a universe of lineal and collateral kin, acquiring first a mother and father, one or more siblings if not the firstborn, grandparents, and relatives in one's parents' and grandparents' generations as well as in one's own. In time, each person grafted new people onto his or her kinship network: younger siblings, children of one's own and of other relatives, grandchildren, outsiders adopted as kin, relatives through marriage, and so on. All were defined using the models and metaphors of kinship. Each person addressed or referred to others using terms reflecting the understandings of kinship, and because of the rights and obligations of kinship, each joined with others for common purpose in the economy, politics, feuding, warfare, marriage, religion, death, and other arenas essential to daily existence.

Despite its biological base, kinship was conceived in culturally specific ways. For example, with regard to the all-important link between an infant and his or her parents, southern Indians tended to emphasize the tie with the mother at the expense of the tie with the father, a principle of matrilineal descent on the basis of which one gained membership automatically at birth to categories that ranged from the family to the more-inclusive clan and moiety. The significance of matrilineal descent cannot be too strongly emphasized. Through it, southern Indians defined who was eligible (or not) for courtship and marriage; secured access to property, both real and intellectual; gained eligibility for positions of leadership; and knew who could be counted on as an ally or was likely to be an enemy. The clans bore names, many of which were animals such as Deer, Bear, Beaver, Panther, Raccoon, Wildcat, and Wolf. Clans were also named for birds. Most common was simply Bird, then Turkey, then, in declining order, Raven or Crow, Eagle, Buzzard, Pigeon or Dove, Blackbird, and Quail or Partridge.[3]

According to the Creek, who named forty different clans for animals, plants, natural phenomena, and artifacts, when their ancestors emerged on earth they determined whether they would be a bird, a beaver, a bear, or some other animal or thing, from which the clans drew their identities and names. The association was construed more as figurative and symbolic than as one of actual ancestry to an animal or a thing.[4]

No doubt there were many such stories about the origin of clans. A Chickasaw foundational myth about primordial relationships specifically concerned the Bird clan, which was never very large and for a long time had obscure origins. The Chickasaw relate,

> There were some people living on two neighboring hills, but for a long time it was not thought that these had inhabitants because other people did not see how they could get down from them to hunt. When they found that they actually were inhabited they thought that the inhabitants must have wings, and so they called them

Birds. They were people who were up and off before day. They did not have many peculiar customs. They were like real birds in that they would not bother anybody. They usually had many wives. . . . They kept to the ways of their ancestors. . . . The people of the clan have different minds just like there are different birds: Some have the minds of woodpeckers, others of crows, others of pigeons, eagles, chicken hawks, horned owls, common owls, buzzards, screech owls, day hawks, prairie hawks, field larks, red-tailed hawks, red birds, wrens, humming-birds, speckled woodpeckers, cranes, bluebirds, blackbirds, turkeys, chickens, quails, tcowe'cak (birds found only in winter and looking like martins), yellow hammers, whip-poor-wills, and like all other kinds of birds. Some have homes and some have not, as is the case with birds. It seems as though the best people of the Bird clan were wiser than any others. They do not work at all, but have an easy time going through life and go anywhere they want to. They have many offspring, as birds have. They do whatever they desire, and when anything happens to them they depend on persons of their own house group without calling in strangers.[5]

This text is important for distinguishing at least twenty-five different kinds of birds, each conceived of as categories of persons with different "minds." It also links birds (and humans) with traits like polygyny, fecundity, variable dwellings, harmlessness, ease of living, hard work, dependence on one's kind (clan), wisdom, and variation in thought and mind.[6]

As for the relationship between the members of a descent group and their eponymous species, it varied. A Yuchi who belonged to a clan associated with a bird (Turkey, Eagle, and Buzzard) felt a close relationship with the clan bird and was not supposed to harm it. A Creek Indian belonging to the Bird clan was said to be able to demand payment from a non–Bird clan hunter who killed birds — "You have killed my parents; you will have to pay me for it." But being a member of the Bird clan did not stop a person from killing birds. Regionally, lack of consistency seemed the rule.[7]

Clans were linked with other clans in the most inclusive set of categories that divided society into two halves, known as moieties. The Creek named the moieties "white people" and "people of a different speech." The clans belonging to the first were known as "white" or peace clans and to the second as "red" or war clans. The moieties became functional in ceremonies, funerals, and ball games within the town.

Although clans always belonged to a moiety, they were not necessarily related to others with which they shared a particular category of nature. That is, a clan named for a bird was not necessarily connected to other clans named for birds. For example, instead of being linked with the Eagle or the Turkey clan, the widespread Creek Bird clan, which was a white clan of peace and medicine symbolized by white bird feathers, was linked with the Beaver clan, and the Turkey clan with the Alligator clan, perhaps because beavers and some birds of the Bird clan were associated with water, and both turkeys and alligators produce eggs.

Nor did a particular clan always belong to the same moiety. Thus the Bird clan was almost always a white clan but in some towns was in the red moiety. In this way, people who might otherwise consistently be apart were instead linked in cross-cutting ways. Each town was led by a chief and a second man, and the Bird clan, among eight others, was a principal source of both. The Creek sometimes wore feathers in their hair that were symbolic of their moiety. The crane, heron, pelican, and "spring crane"—all associated with water or wetlands—lent white plumage to the Bird clan. In one Creek town, white moiety dancers bore whooping crane feathers, and red moiety dancers bore eagle and buzzard feathers. White and red, either a natural color in the feathers or applied to them, were of symbolic significance throughout the South in contexts relating not just to descent but to politics, war, and peace, to which we turn next.[8]

POWER

When the de Soto expedition reached northwestern Georgia, the chroniclers reported that the chief of Coosa welcomed them with "a crown of feathers on his head." In Alabama, the chief of Atahachi was more flamboyant, wearing "about his head a certain headdress like an *almaizar* [turban], worn like a Moor, which gave him an appearance of authority, and a *pelote* or blanket of feathers down to his feet, very authoritative, seated upon some high cushions, and many principals of his Indians with him."[9] The chroniclers drew on the imagery of orientalism to make sense of the symbols of power, but as important were their persistent references to Indians who killed "many kinds of birds" not just to eat but to "adorn their heads with the feathers, which they [wore] in showy, multicolored headdresses half a fathom tall." In this manner, suggested Garcilaso de la Vega, who was the most literary of the chroniclers of Hernando de Soto's expedition, "they distinguish[ed] the nobles from the plebians in time of peace, and the soldiers from those who [were] not such in time of war."[10]

Not merely ornamental, feathers were tightly linked to social position and power. Plumes adorned the chief as well as retainers and conveyances. On the Mississippi, the adventurer Elvas reported that the chief of Aquijo met the de Soto expedition with two hundred canoes "full of Indians with their bows and arrows, painted with red ocher and having great plumes of white and many colored feathers on either side [of the canoes]." These craft were "very large and well built; and together with the awnings, the plumes of feathers, the shields, and banners, and the many men in them, they had the appearance of a beautiful fleet of galleys."[11]

No doubt much of this was meant to, and did, impress. Strangers reported feathered Indians at political events and feasts from all over the region. On the sixteenth-century southern Atlantic coast, the Huguenot Ribault encountered Indians "trymed with newe pictures upon there faces, and fethers upon ther heddes"; and Laudonnière reported—ominously perhaps, given the association of the color with hostility—that one chief presented Ribault with "a plume of egret feathers, dyed red." Farther west, the Caddo prepared themselves for feasts with red-dyed swan or duck down in their hair;

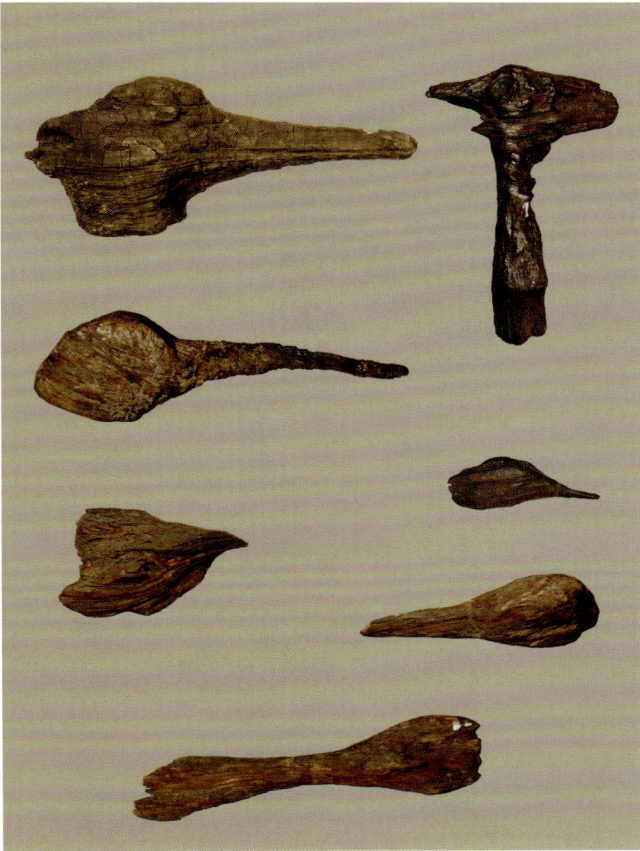

FIGURE 101.

Bird heads sculpted in wood. *Left to right, top to bottom: possibly a merganser, a woodpecker, a wading bird, a teal or other duck, an owl, a heron or other wading bird, and a roseate spoonbill. Birdlike, these heads reflect a level of intimacy with the species depicted. Each carving (and bird) was speculatively related to kinship, naming, or descent; to a personal spiritual relationship between an individual and a bird; or to ritual intended to influence a bird's availability or impact. The Fort Center carvings were erected over or alongside the dead on a mortuary platform and thus fit best the first two of these three categories. Top left: Belle Glade, Palm Beach, Fla., ca. AD 200 to Historic, ca. 9.8 in. long. Department of Anthropology, Smithsonian Institution, 383867. Others, in sequence as above: Fort Center, Glades County, Fla., ca. AD 200–800, 7.25 in. long., 9.25 in. long, 3.75 in. long, 4.75 in. long, 6 in. long, 8.75 in. long. Collections of the Florida Museum of Natural History, 98793, A15372, A15829, A16106, A15346, A15880. Photos by Jeff Gage.*

and another leader received "a most beautiful fly flap . . . made of showy birds' plumes of great value." East and west, retainers fanned their leaders: men attending the chief of the Taensa, in a procession for a redistribution and feast, waved "fans of white feathers" in front of him; the Timucua affixed plumes to the ends of poles in order to fan their chiefs; and much later in time, men seeing to his welfare fanned the chief of the Cherokee with turkey-feather fans.[12]

In the stratified native societies of eighteenth-century French Louisiana, feather crowns were a privilege of the political and religious elite, as could be seen in 1725, when a Natchez named the Tattooed Serpent died; he was the head war chief and the brother of the Great Sun, the chief. The Dutch planter Le Page du Pratz attended the funeral in this last of the great chiefdoms of the South and depicted the Tattooed Serpent dressed and decorated "as if for a journey." On his head he wore a "feather-crown" of white and red feathers, and circling his waist was a belt of red and black feathers — both, presumably, appropriate in this socially layered society of powerful rulers and retainers for one born into the noble class and of such close kinship with the paramount chief. The priest who officiated was described as painted entirely red on the upper half of his body, except the arms, and resplendent. He wore a "red-feathered crown, which half encircled his head," and a waist-to-knees skirt of "a fringe of feathers, the rows of which

FIGURE 102. The Pageantry with Which a Chosen Queen Is Brought to the King. *Engraving by Theodor de Bry (after Jacques Le Moyne de Morgues), 1591, in Hariot,* Der ander Theyl, *plate 37. Men wearing vertical plumed headdresses accompany the prospective bride and either shield or cool her with what appear to be large feathered fans. John Carter Brown Library at Brown University.*

were alternately white and red." In his hand he grasped "a red staff . . . in the form of a cross, at the end of which hung a garland of black feathers." Clearly, feathers pervaded this ritual.[13]

The Natchez associated crowns in particular with the Great Sun and his family. As Le Page reported, "The chief ornament of the sovereigns, is their crown of feathers; this crown is composed of a black bonnet of net work, which is fastened to a red diadem about two inches broad. The diadem is embroidered with white kernel-stones, and surmounted with white feathers, which in the fore-part are about eight inches long, and half as much behind." All this, Le Page ventured, made "a very pleasing appearance."[14] The eighteenth-century Caddo also kept in the storerooms of political or religious buildings, seemingly for later use, "rolls of ornamental feathers, crowns made of skins and feathers, [and] a bonnet of the same."[15]

In southern Indian societies marked by distinctions of wealth and class, access to which was at times ascribed by birth and at times gained by achievement, feathers evidently were especially connected to the upper classes. For example, in North Carolina, feathers seem to have been the province in particular of people in positions of

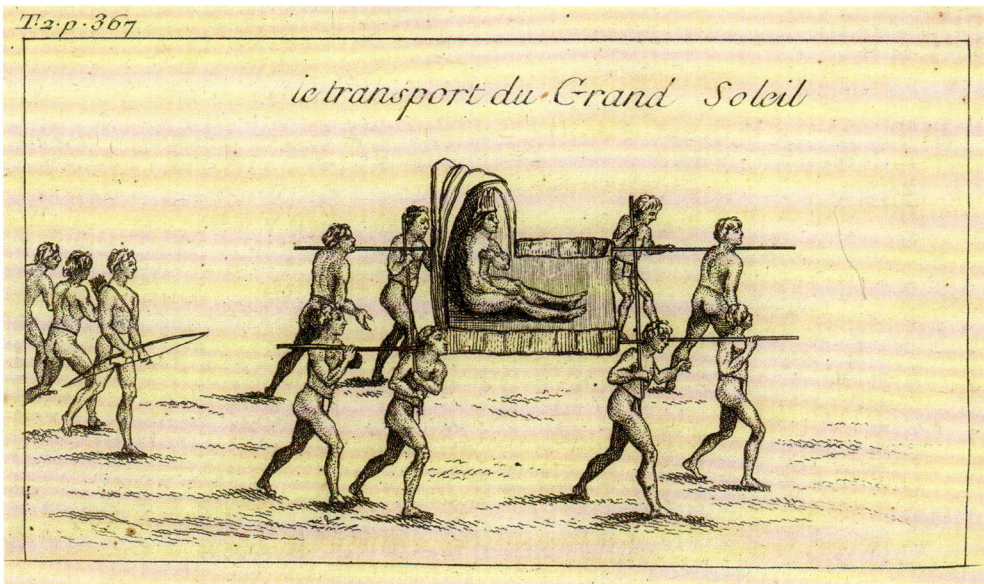

Tap 367

le transport du Grand Soleil

authority, with long feathers worn by secular leaders in their hair or roach as markers of status.[16] In Virginia, the Powhatan often decorated their hair with the feathers of birds and at times entire bird skins. The seventeenth-century elite — the rulers and their relatives — preferred pearls, copper, and other exotic objects to feathers in the display of wealth, but nevertheless evidently had greatest access to feathers worked by artisans into woven or netted fiber bases.[17] Reporting on one woman of high rank, who was carefully attended and elaborately dressed, William Strachey noted, "[She wore] a Mantell, which they call Puttawus, which is like a side cloak, made of blew feathers, so arteficially and thick sowed together, that yt showes like a deep purple Satten, and is very smooth and sleek."[18] One can only imagine the impact of a cloak such as this, fabricated perhaps from the feathers of little blue herons, blue jays, eastern bluebirds, blue grosbeaks, or indigo buntings.

EAGLES AND POLITY

In 1734, the Creek-Yamacraw chief Tomochichi and his nephew Tooanahowi joined a delegation that traveled from America to England to discuss the gun and alcohol trade and other aspects of commerce, as well as the prospect of attracting Christian missionaries to educate their people. Twice they were painted by the Flemish painter William Verelst; one oil, subsequently engraved, is a striking portrayal of the confidence and promise of birth and office in Tomochichi and his sister's son, the latter an inheritor of position and property in this matrilineal society. In both the painting and the engraving appear a bald eagle in full adult plumage. In the best-known portrait, Tooanahowi clutches it tightly in his arms.[19]

The golden eagle and the bald eagle are powerful birds in both nature and symbol. Historically, both lived in the American South. The golden eagle was primarily an Ap-

FIGURE 104. Tomo Chachi Mico or King of Yamacraw, and Tooanahowi, His Nephew Son to the Mico of the Etchitas. *Mezzotint engraving on paper by John Farber Sculpsit after an oil by William Verelst, about 1735. Both Tomochichi, the Creek-Yamacraw chief, and Tooanahowi, son of the chief of the Hitichi, accompanied Governor Oglethorpe of Georgia to England to further trade, diplomacy, and other matters. The bald eagle is a symbol of status, polity, and perhaps descent. John Carter Brown Library at Brown University, 31731.*

FIGURE 105. White-headed Eagle (bald eagle). *Hand-colored engraving by Alexander Lawson based on drawing by Alexander Wilson,* American Ornithology, *vol. 4, 1808–14, plate 36. A powerful bird in nature and the ethno-ornithology of the South. John Hay Library at Brown University.*

Tomo Chachi Mico or King of Yamacraw, and Tooanahowi his Nephew Son to the Mico of the Etchitas.

White-headed Eagle.

palachian and Piedmont bird, and the bald eagle could be found throughout the region but was especially abundant on the coastal plain. Both are impressive, strong, acrobatic flyers — the golden eagle especially so and fully capable of killing large birds such as cranes or young deer. In mock combat associated with courtship or real combat connected to defending territory, the golden eagle will unhesitatingly flip upside down, cartwheel, and display. If desired, it will lock massive talons with a mate's; if necessary, it locks talons with an intruder stooping on it from above, or will itself stoop, or dive steeply, on another with death-defying abandon. In 1925, the ornithologist William Brewster described the stoop of a golden eagle on a great blue heron in a canopy of trees: the eagle "swooped, apparently as straight and vertically as a heavy stone may fall, yet all the time revolving like a spinning rifle bullet, if more slowly, thereby showing us his (normally) upper and under parts alternately." As he stooped, "his wings, apparently set and almost closed, made a sound like that of a strong wind blowing through pine branches." This bird rarely failed to make an impression.[20]

Since antiquity, the golden eagle has held a distinguished and secure status in the Old World as an emblem of military might and national authority and as the king of bird society. In different religious contexts it is a divine bird or a symbol of resurrection. Although Europeans considered the golden eagle a noble bird in the abstract, they nevertheless did not place it above reproach when it preyed on domesticated flocks or exhibited other undesirable habits. In the New World, newcomers from Europe regarded North American eagles with the same set of contradictions in place. In fact, the relationship between people of European descent and eagles is marked by admiration, on the one hand, and death and destruction, on the other, especially from the nineteenth century on, when farmers, ranchers, and others widely viewed the birds as predators and killed as many as they could. When the bald eagle became the symbol of a fledgling America in 1782, it was over the objections of Benjamin Franklin, who denigrated it as a coward, a fish eater, and a scavenger; he preferred the wild turkey as the national bird, as did Audubon and others. In Franklin's view, the bald eagle lacked "moral" rectitude and was all style and no substance.[21]

Native people construed eagles in similarly complex ways in the American South. To start with, eagles were more closely bound up with polity than any other bird for people like the eighteenth-century Creek, Chickasaw, and Cherokee.[22] In some towns

FIGURE 106. Ring-tail Eagle (golden eagle). Sea Eagle (bald eagle). *Hand-colored engraving by J. Warnicke based on drawing by Alexander Wilson,* American Ornithology, *vol. 7, 1808–14, plate 55. Both eagles are immatures. The golden eagle was more highly esteemed than the bald eagle, the immature golden especially so for its feathers. Natives and nonnatives alike often gave different names to adult and juvenile raptors of the same species, a confusion that extended to early ornithologists. John Hay Library at Brown University.*

Aquila capite albo.
The White headed Eagle.

The size of the Eagles head

FIGURE 107.
The Bald Eagle.

FIGURE 107.
The Bald Eagle.
*Hand-colored etching
by Mark Catesby,*
Natural History *(1771),
plate 1. As depicted
here, the bald eagle
frequently steals the
osprey's catch. Like
John White, Catesby
distinguished the
"White headed Eagle"
of the inscription
from the golden eagle
familiar in the Old
World (and many
parts of the New).
John Carter Brown
Library at Brown
University.*

their importance was visible in public architecture, as when the Chickasaw displayed "a large carved eagle" on a pole at the peak of the roof of a circular communal wintertime "hot-house." It is not known which eagle was represented, but such prominence recalls an earlier and distant report of a temple in the town of Ozita on Tampa Bay in today's Florida atop which could be seen, according to the de Soto chroniclers, a wooden bird with gilded eyes. Like the powerfully taloned Woodland and Mississippian artifacts (displaying in particular the large hallux, or hind claw), these birds — these raptors or raptorial beings — were arguably based on, or analogized from, strong-beaked, large-headed eagles.[23]

The significance of eagles was also reflected in how men were said to spend time, one principal activity being "forming their . . . eagles tail or standard." That is, men dedicated energy to hunting and killing eagles, whose price as a commodity went up with increasing scarcity, especially of golden eagles.[24] The Chickasaw and the Creek so valued eagle feathers that a town paid two hundred deerskins to the man who killed a "large" eagle (and granted him honors equivalent to taking a scalp). If James Adair was correct in concluding that these Indians did "not esteem" the bald eagle, then this large eagle must have been the golden.[25]

Juvenile golden eagles were particularly valued because of their tail feathers. The naval officer Jean-Bernard Bossu told how Mobila Indians who accompanied him on the Tombigbee River in 1759 found the nest of a golden eagle in a tall tree, cut down the tree, and discovered "game of all sorts" in the nest, including fawns, rabbits, turkeys, quail, and passenger pigeons. They kept four immature eagles and killed the "furious" adults, who through their fearlessness deserved the title, so Bossu thought, of the "King of Birds." "Bullets," he remarked with irony, "did not spare their feathered majesties, who fell victim to paternal love."[26]

Eagle tails and feathers were symbols of office, and no tail was more highly esteemed than that of the immature golden eagle. Often carried by chiefs and headmen, eagle-tail feathers served to bring authority to, or confirm, speeches. For example, the eighteenth-century Cherokee greeted a visitor deemed distinguished in their town house, where they danced, sang songs, and "stroaked his Head and Body over with Eagles Tails." At the close of one formal address to a visitor from Europe, a Cherokee leader put feathers on the table and declared, "This is our Way of Talking, which is the same Thing to us, as your Letters in the Book are to you; and to you, beloved Men, we deliver these Feathers, in Confirmation of all that we have said."[27]

As suggested in the account of Tomochichi and Tooanahowi, eagles and their feathers also figured in trips made by native people from the South to Europe. In 1730, seven Cherokees who went to London on a political mission presented five eagles' tails, a feather headdress, and scalps to King George II. In return they received a large plume in friendship and peace; one of them remarked formally of their part of the exchange that "[i]t should be as good as the Bible to bind the contract with King George."[28] Eagles were as powerfully charged for the Cherokee as for other Indians in the South: they isolated eagle feathers from lesser objects, wrapping them in deerskin in their own feather house; a man who dreamed of an eagle had to sponsor a dance for it; and a hunter who killed an eagle was honored accordingly.[29] The boundary between sacred and secular was rarely clear (if in fact there was one) when it came to eagle feathers; for example, for the Caddo, eagle wings, sometimes "elaborately decorated," figured in prophecy and divination in multiple symbolic ways, as the bird "whose feathers they ha[d] in hand, ascend[ed] to heaven to consult with [God] for the coming events of the year" and returned to deliver the forecast to men and women below.[30]

When he had an audience with and presented eagle feathers to King George II, Tomochichi apparently hoped that King George would in turn send him two swans; evidently the swans — whether mute or not is unknown — were collected but never sent.[31] For Tomochichi, swans loomed large with eagles because they were of great significance to the Creek, who considered swan wings and eagle feathers as the "emblems of peace and war" and kept them with scalps and related paraphernalia in the rafters of houses positioned at the cardinal points around the sacred central squares of their towns.[32] Eagles' tails, half of each feather painted red and mounted on sticks, and swans' wings carried in the hand were prominent in social and political ceremony.[33] The

FIGURE 108. Mó-sho-la-túb-bee, He Who Puts Out and Kills, Chief of the Tribe. *Oil on canvas by George Catlin, near Fort Gibson, Indian Territory, 1834. Four years before this painting, Mushulatubbee, chief of the northeastern district of the Choctaw, cosigned a treaty ceding ten million acres—the last of their land east of the Mississippi—and agreed to removal west. In the ensuing period of sharp factionalization, Catlin painted him with a peace medal on his chest, feathers in his hair, and a feather fan in his hand—all insignia of office. Smithsonian American Art Museum, gift of Mrs. Joseph Harrison Jr., 1985.66.294.*

emblem of one early twentieth-century Creek town was "a wooden eagle marked like a spotted eagle and with blood dripping from its mouth," which was displayed facing east, in front of the chief's seat, during important meetings of the town's council.[34]

The eighteenth-century naturalist William Bartram provided a detailed account of the Creek "imperial standard, or eagle's tail curiously formed and displayed like an open fan on a scepter or staff." He saw it in the sanctuary of the council house in the Creek town of Atasi, along with other objects. The Creek, according to Bartram, called it "the eagle's tail," "constructed and ornamented [it] with great ingenuity," and held it "most sacred . . . on all occasions." They displayed it when at war or seeking peace. In war they "carried it with them . . . into battle" and "painted or tinged" the feathers with "vermilion" or "with a zone of red within the brown tips"; when displayed for peace, it was "as white and clean as possible" or "new, clean, and white."[35]

According to Bartram, the standard came from the king vulture. The assertion is both haunting and troubling, because, except for one detail, Bartram's description of this bird is accurate and the king vulture is otherwise unknown north of the lowland forests of Mexico. The only other "record," if it can be called that, is the amazingly suggestive vulture whose head and neck were sculpted on the outside of a stone bowl. The archaeologist Clarence B. Moore speculated—on the basis of an abstract "wattle" on the top of the head—that this bird resembled a king vulture. Even if the wattle had

FIGURE 109. McIntosh, a Creek Chief. *Colored lithograph. Raised among the Creek, William McIntosh (White Warrior), the son of a Creek mother and a Scottish father, gained both fame and notoriety during the chaos of war (including civil war), treaty making, and land cession in the early nineteenth century. A wealthy slave-owner, an ally of the United States, and a signatory to treaties ceding land for cash, McIntosh was executed by Creeks opposed to him in 1825. In this formal portrait, McIntosh's clothing and regalia of office reflect his paternal ancestry, and the headband and predominantly white color of the plume, his birth into the Creek Wind clan, which is usually part of the white moiety. McKenney and Hall,* History of the Indian Tribes, *vol. 1, opp. 129. John Carter Brown Library at Brown University.*

been adjacent to the bill, as it is in nature, what draws equal attention is the vulturine neck and striking eye — the latter as distinctive in the living bird as on the sculpture. As for Bartram's bird, the king vulture has a white body and white underwing and upper-wing coverts — it is unmistakable soaring or perched — but its flight and tail feathers are dark (the one detail), and they cannot possibly make the "standard" that he described. Even if he saw a king vulture — he said that they "seldom appear[ed]" except when there were prairie fires behind which they scavenged, except he does not seem to have observed this — Bartram nevertheless erred in identifying the feathers as from this bird. Far more likely they were from eagles: the immature golden eagle, which has white, brown-tipped tail feathers and some white-based flight feathers; the adult bald eagle, whose tail feathers are all white; or the immature bald eagle, whose flight feathers often show different degrees of white near the base.[36]

Feathers stood, then, for authority and power, as among the Creek, whose leaders held white feathers or wings in their hands when they were installed in their positions, white signifying peace and rule. Much later, when eagles and swans were harder to come by, the white wing of a domesticated turkey sufficed.[37]

FIGURE 110. *(Left)* Osceola, the Seminole Chief. *Pencil drawing by John Rogers Vinton, 1837–38. This early drawing of the Seminole war leader Osceola, who held out against removal until his capture in 1837 by General Joseph Hernandez (whose signature appears below the drawing) and death in 1838, shows him with exotic plumes inserted into his turban. National Museum of the American Indian, Smithsonian Institution, neg. 26048, print 18412. Photo by NMAI Photo Services Staff.*

FIGURE 111. *(Right)* Os-ce-o-lá, the Black Drink, a Warrior of Great Distinction. *Oil on canvas by George Catlin, 1838. A heroic painting of the famous leader of the Seminoles (whose name was linked to the purifying black drink), with his trademark black and white ostrich plumes arranged (unlike others at his time) at the back of his head. Catlin visited Osceola in prison in Fort Moultrie, S.C., and was greatly affected by him and his cause. Smithsonian American Art Museum, gift of Mrs. Joseph Harrison Jr., 1985.66.301.*

Feathers worn in conjunction with turbans and headbands could also indicate social and political position; by the nineteenth century they included plumes from exotic species like the ostrich. Most formal portraits of the Seminole leader Osceola, for instance, depict ostrich feathers in his turban — indeed, four black and two white ostrich plumes could be found among his effects after his death. The Seminole Billy Bowlegs also wore ostrich plumes in his turban; by his time in the nineteenth century the Seminole were exchanging egret plumes for ostrich plumes from traders. According to the artist George Catlin, the Seminole were "plain & vulgar" in daily dress, but on ceremonial

FIGURE 112. Billy Bowlegs. *Daguerreotype, unknown photographer, 1852. In this portrait, the Seminole chief (who became a leader of the Third Seminole War several years after this photograph and later moved to Indian Territory, where he fought for the Union) is shown during an interlude of peace with silver gorgets and a peace medal around his neck, and turbaned and plumed with black ostrich feathers—much as earlier Seminole leaders such as Osceola represented themselves. National Anthropological Archives, Smithsonian Institution, neg. 53887.*

FIGURE 113. Mikasuki Seminole men. *Black-and-white photoprint by Charles Barney Cory Sr., 1877. Like generations before them, these Mikasuki-speaking Seminole men (Tommy Jumper, or Kowakkocla, left; Billie Stewart, right) wear gorgets and feathered turbans on their heads. National Anthropological Archives, Smithsonian Institution, SPC Se Seminole BAE 4541, vol. 1 01819100.*

FIGURE 114. Chief Sam Blue (1873–1959), Catawba, with feather standard. *Photograph by Frank G. Speck, South Carolina, 1932. Chief Blue, standing with his grandson, holds a feathered staff, the symbol of office. University of Pennsylvania Museum, s4-143915.*

occasions, there were "certain peculiarities of costume which [were] seldom departed from," one of which consisted of "[t]he ostrich plumes which decorate[d] the heads of the Chiefs." There was variation in how men trimmed their heads and turbans with plumes; many wore feathers on the fronts of their heads, but Osceola "was peculiar for wearing his always on the opposite side and hanging off to the rear."[38]

Feathers continued to form the insignia of chiefs in the twentieth century, in some instances appearing on staffs held by chiefs. For the Catawba these were signs of peace carried on formal occasions: five-foot-long staffs attached to which were bunches of feathers of a bird deemed worthy — formerly eagles, then turkeys after eagles became scarce. The substitution of turkey feathers for the feathers of golden and bald eagles is of less importance than the persistence of an association of feathers with expressions of polity. In the end, the turkey possesses impressive qualities, and its feathers atop a standard signal continuity with an ancient avian political symbolism.[39]

FIGURE 115. A War Dance. *Watercolor by Philip Georg Friedrich von Reck, Georgia Territory, 1736. Yuchi men recount war deeds, dance, and perform with rattles and feather wands in their hands. Courtesy of Det Kongelige Bibliotek, Copenhagen,* NKS *565, 4to, 29r.*

War & Peace

At first glance, the Virginia colonists must have thought Nemattanew, an assertive and flamboyant Powhatan war leader, unpredictable and improbable, even bizarre. Calling him Jack of the Feathers, they said that he would "often dress himself up with Feathers after a fantastick Manner," covering himself, as the colonist George Percy remarked, "all . . . over with feathers and Swans wings fastened unto his showlders as thowghe he meante to fly." Thus feathered and slathered with a special ointment, Nemattanew claimed that he was impervious to bullets; the Powhatan believed him "immortall." An accomplished warrior, Nemattanew erred fatally by wearing the hat of an Englishman who had gone with him to trade but was killed by other Indians. Blamed for his death, Jack, as John Smith referred to him, was shot mortally in a scuffle with colonists. Wishing to perpetuate the belief in his invincibility, he asked the English before he died not to reveal the means of his death but to bury him among them. Whether or not word got out, the Powhatan shortly after took revenge for numerous humiliations and insults, including the murder of Nemattanew, and in a well-planned assault on the English on March 22, 1622, killed nearly 350 of some 1,250 colonists.[1]

As it turns out, Nemattanew's penchant for feathers was not odd, at least not in seventeenth-century Virginia, where native men, according to John Smith, William Strachey, and others painted their bodies black and yellow, oiled their bodies, and stuck in the grease "the soft downe of sondry Coloured birdes, of blew birdes, white herneshews, and the feathers of the Carnation byrd, which they call Ahshowcutteis, as if so many variety of laces were stiched to their skyns, which [made] a wonderous shew."[2]

Across the South, Indians like Nemattanew associated feathers with display, aggression, and hostility; with war and peace. If the link between falconid representations and endemic war in Mississippian times is correct, then this connection with birds is ancient. The first Europeans in the region soon realized that feathered Indians were potentially dangerous. De Soto's men quickly figured out that Indians carrying quivers and bows with faces painted red or black and plumes waving in their hair were dressed and painted for hostile action.[3] At one place they confronted 1,500 armed warriors "decked out with plumes"; at another, 5,000 men "well armed and adorned with large plumes" and bent on revenge; sometimes they saw only a solitary Indian with "a handsome plume on his head and . . . his bow in his hands and a quiver of arrows on his back" or others similarly armed and "decked out in long plumes."[4]

Sixteenth-century Indians bent on aggression, or simply taking a stand, feathered and colored not just their bodies but weapons, canoes, and other equipment used in

war. Elvas, one of the chroniclers of the de Soto expedition, took note of hostile Indians from Quigaltam who appeared in a fleet of canoes, some holding sixty to seventy men each and others transporting "the principal men with their awnings" and "white and colored plumes of feathers as a device."[5] The dugouts belonged to "the rich and powerful men" and reportedly were dyed inside and out "with a single color, as for example blue, or yellow, white, red, green, rose, violet, black, or some other color" according to "the blazon or the fancy of the captain or curaca or rich and powerful man to whom the canoe belonged." Paddles, canoes, and men "down to the plumes and the skeins of thread that they wound about their foreheads as a headdress, and even their bows and arrows, were all tinted with this one color."[6]

The association of feathers with war and aggression was widespread and witnessed not just in the sixteenth century by the de Soto expedition or would-be colonists on the Florida Atlantic coast, where native men went to war with their hair full of feathers, or in seventeenth-century Virginia, but across the region through time. In seventeenth- and eighteenth-century Caddo territory, for example, warriors wore skin caps adorned "with a diversity of plumage" and decorated the hilts of swords obtained from the Spaniards with feathers.[7] And in early eighteenth-century North Carolina, according to the naturalist John Lawson, "[Indians dress differently] in Peace and War . . . when they go to War, their Hair is comb'd out by the Woman, and done over very much with Bears Grease, and red Root; with Feathers, Wings, Rings, Copper, and *Peak*, or *Wampum* in their Ears."[8]

Later in the eighteenth century, the Choctaw, Chickasaw, Creek, Seminole, and Guale all incorporated feathers into personal preparation and dress for war. In the preliminaries to war, some sought to embrace the symbolism of powerful swans in the wings, feathers, and down from these birds. Bernard Romans, the eighteenth-century surveyor, reported that it was "no small diversion to see a Chactaw during this preparation act all his strange gestures, and the day before his departure painted scarlet and black almost naked and with swan wings to his arms run like a bacchant up and down through the place of his abode; not drunk neither, as rum [was] by them avoided like poison during this preparation." Following a successful campaign, the Choctaw danced wearing on their heads an otter skin with "as many broken white feathers as they have killed men in their lives" fastened to it; the symbolism of ruptured peace is transparent.[9] In 1765, the Chickasaw returned from war with scalps and bodies painted red and black, with "heads covered all over with swan-down" as well as a "tuft of long white feathers fixt to the crown of their heads."[10] One late eighteenth-century group of Seminoles seen by William Bartram on the path to war seemed little different, at least in their penchant for feathers: they were "dressed and painted with a singular elegance, and richly ornamented with silver plates, chains, &c. after the Siminole mode, with waving plumes of feathers on their crests."[11]

If Indians wearing feathers of a certain kind and color failed to unnerve people of European descent, it is quite possible that the sound of birds unseen did. Indians commonly used bird-calls to signal and maintain contact on a war expedition. Some mimicked the cry of certain birds either to maintain contact with one another or to cover inadvertent noise. Others approaching the enemy called like owls. Adair thought that they could imitate "the voice and sound of every quadruped and wild fowl through the American wood."[12]

BIRDS IN WAR AND PEACE

In 1776, John Stuart, superintendent of Indian affairs for the British in the colonial South, reported that the Creek and the Choctaw, seeking an end to their war, "halted about three hundred yards distance from each other their principal chiefs singing the Peace song and waving Eagles Tails and Swans wings over their heads."[13]

As implied on several occasions, no birds stand out more in connection with war and peace than swans and eagles. Because of cultural considerations stemming from the size and characteristics of the birds, as well as the colors of their feathers, swans' wings and eagles' tails figured time and again in war- and peacemaking contexts. Ordinary Creek warriors wore swan feathers, war leaders wore "war eagle" feathers, and a war chief was invested in a rite in which both red-painted eagles' tails and white swan or egret wings figured. For the eighteenth-century Creek, the eagle was paramount.[14] For the Cherokee also the golden, or "pretty-feathered," eagle was, as the anthropologist James Mooney remarked, "the great sacred bird" crucial in anything relating to peace and war. Killing an eagle involved extensive ritual both before and after the hunt to ensure that the bird was shown proper respect, including dance, the sacrifice of a deer, and deluding the eagle into thinking (by informing it) that a Spaniard, not a Cherokee, was responsible for its death.[15]

Another important bird in war was the wild turkey, which, as remarked earlier, lent well-known strength, speed, and aggressiveness to hostile action. For instance, in removing the scalp of an enemy, a Creek warrior evidently "whooped," perhaps to announce the act to his fellow warriors, winding down in "several tremulous throat tones in imitation of a turkey's gobble." The Caddo also linked bald-headed, bearded turkeys with scalps: their name for the scalp dance was the turkey dance because turkeys, they said, invented it and wear scalps around their necks (beards) when they dance among the trees.[16] Of interest in this context is the description of a large tomahawk found inside a ceremonial structure in seventeenth-century Virginia; attached to the outsized

FIGURE 117.
Tah-Chee, a Cherokee Chief. *Colored lithograph. Born in 1790, Tah-chee ("Dutch"), the son of a chief, gained great renown as a warrior in wars against the Osage, the Comanche, and other Indians following removal to the West. The colors of his exotic plume— overwhelmingly red but white at the base—seemingly evoke his substantial prowess in war as well as peace late in life. McKenney and Hall,* History of the Indian Tribes, *vol. 1, opp. 163. John Carter Brown Library at Brown University.*

FIGURE 118.
Láh-shee, the Licker,
called "Creek Billy."
*Oil on canvas by
George Catlin,
1838. Evidently
a distinguished
Seminole warrior,
Lahshee wears silver
or plate gorgets
around his neck
and an exotic red
plume — the color of
war — in the silver
headband about
his cloth-covered
head. Smithsonian
American Art Mu-
seum, gift of Mrs.
Joseph Harrison Jr.,
1985.66.305.*

weapon were "a Wild Turky's Beard painted red, and two of the longest Feathers of his Wings hung dangling."[17] What better bird than the turkey to recruit to war? Not only did it provide spurs for arrow points, literally killing the foe with its major weapon, but its strengths were nearly second to none in the avian world of the South.

Another bird that figured in war, at least for the Cherokee, is the red-headed woodpecker, said to be "the great war symbol." They invoked this same bird for aid when they played in the ball game, the surrogate for war when contested between different towns. Not coincidentally, this woodpecker has the reputation among naturalists for being the "most pugnacious of North American woodpeckers."[18]

Other birds, including raptors like the kestrel and vultures, and corvids like the crow, also figured in war. All appeared in contexts relating to power and war waged by the Creek. The crow, according to the anthropologist John Swanton's Creek informants, yielded "anciently the great feather . . . used principally in war." It was "conjured over . . . to put the enemy into a sound sleep," and if others sought to do the same to you they could be combated with blue-jay feathers. And the mid-eighteenth-century trader James Adair reported that one venerable Creek chief delivered a harangue with his "Head full of Turkey Buzzard Feathers." Why is less clear; perhaps he belonged to the Turkey Vulture clan, or was a curer, or could use the power of that bird to his own ends.[19]

RED AND WHITE

In 1560, the Tristan de Luna expedition encountered a group of warriors carrying a "mysterious" twelve-foot-high standard or banner with white plumes at the top. The men "insisted that they did not wish war with" other Indians on whom they advanced, only "to reduce them" to a former tutelary condition. Far from a mystery — unless it was a ruse — the white plumes proclaimed their peaceful intentions. On another occasion, a "sham" ambassador from the Indians tried to trick the Spaniards into joining them by carrying a standard topped with white feathers (appearing to be "heron," that is, egret, plumes) when their real intentions were anything but peaceful.[20] Later, some sent ahead a man painted white or holding a white swan's wing in his hand; or they "cover[ed] their heads with swan down," adorned their "temples . . . with the swan-feather-cap," or waved "large fans of eagles-tails" back and forth — all considered honorable tasks.[21]

Indians across the region communicated their intentions, peaceful or warlike, with the colors white and red. In the westernmost part of the region, Caddo Indians welcomed one Spanish official in the early eighteenth century by ornamenting themselves with feathers and him "carefully with white feathers plucked from the breasts of geese, which they placed on his head after their own fashion." They greeted another official with a tobacco-filled pipe "adorned with many white feathers as a sign of peace."[22]

White was the color of peace — peace was "the white road" and tobacco shared was a "white smoke in token of friendship" — and red the color of war; in Creek, *red* and *blood* were related words. In both war and peace, feathers and beads colored the appropriate hue, either naturally or artificially, figured in dress and ornamentation. The eighteenth-century Creek, for example, who considered the eagle "a great King" of birds, "carr[ied] its feathers when they [went] to War or [made] Peace; the red mean[t] War; the white, Peace. If an enemy approache[d] with white feathers and a white mouth, and crie[d] like an eagle, they dare[d] not kill him." In the eighteenth century, young Creek warriors displayed eagle tails and the priests swans' wings in a procession and dance. The white wings of swans, sometimes whitened further with white clay, and eagles' tails waved over the head and toward the sky were expressions of good will and friendship.[23]

TOBACCO AND FLIGHT

Thomas Nairne, a South Carolinian on a diplomatic mission in the early eighteenth-century South, remarked that in an act of "great congruity," the Creek, the Chickasaw, and other Indians on a "[d]esign of conquest," would fan the fires of war leaders with the wings of eagles, using the feathers of a bird successful (as they hoped to be) in its "[aerial] pillageings"; and that they smoked "the Eagle pipe" in order to cement friendship or alliance.[24]

Nairne's eagle pipe was known more widely from a French word for pipe, *calumet*. By 1700, ceremony involving the calumet was widespread in the South thanks probably

FIGURE 119. Desseins de Sauvages de Plusieurs Nations, Nlle. Orleans 1735 (Drawing of savages of several nations, New Orleans, 1735). *Watercolor by Alexandre de Batz, 1735. In addition to the probable (but peculiar) domestic turkey in the foreground, an Atakapa man (far right) holds a feathered calumet and an Illinois man (far left)—a visitor from up the Mississippi River—a crane, apparently alive, probably the whooping.* © 2006 Harvard University, Peabody Museum, 41-72-10/20.

to the French, who for many years had favored it as a symbol of peace in their dealings with native people along and west of the upper reaches of the Mississippi River.

The calumet might have been a recent introduction to the South, but the use of tobacco was ancient in the region. Eastern woodlands people had cultivated this plant for over two millennia and smoked it in stone pipes, many of which were sculpted as animals, including ducks, geese, owls and other raptors, the Carolina parakeet, the raven, and other birds. Pipe ceremonies involving elaborate meeting or peacemaking rituals also probably had considerable time depth in the region; as the archaeologist Robert Hall suggests, the presentation of a pipe to visitors, especially one with a long stem, mimics the presentation of arrows. In certain contexts, smoking was a ritual activity, but in others it was apparently recreational; Lawson, for example, noted that early eighteenth-century North Carolina Indians had teeth "yellow with Smoking Tobacco, which both Men and Women [were] much addicted to."

The tobacco smoked, *Nicotiana rustica*, was potent. Bursting with nicotine, it was often combined with a product such as dogwood or the inner bark of cedar trees or sumac or bearberry leaves, with the mixture known widely by its Algonquian name,

FIGURE 120.

Avian pipes. *Repre-
sented (top to bot-
tom, left to right)
are a raptor or the
Carolina parakeet, an
eagle or other raptor,
an owl with ear-tufts,
and a wood duck or
other duck (left) and
eared owl (right).
There is great range in
type and style, from
the naturalistic duck
and the raptor etched
onto the stone bowl,
to an owl abstractly
reduced to ear tufts,
hooked bill, and open
mouth. When using
a pipe, the smoker
would often have
been nose to bill with
the bird represented.
Top: Steatite, Coffee
County, Tenn., ca.
1200–1600, 7.25 in.
long. National Mu-
seum of the American
Indian, Smithsonian
Institution, 00-7757.
Photo by NMAI Photo
Services Staff. Center
left: Limestone, Tus-
caloosa County, Ala.,
in Clarence Moore,
"Moundville Revis-
ited," fig. 80. John
Hay Library at Brown
University. Center
right: Shell-tempered
ceramic, White
County, Ga., after AD
1000, 4.37 in. high.
National Museum of
the American Indian,
Smithsonian Institu-
tion 04-7919. Photo
by NMAI Photo Ser-
vices Staff. Bottom:
Stone, Scott County,
Va., 10 in. long. De-
partment of Anthro-
pology, Smithsonian
Institution, 211243.*

kinnikinnick. Uncut, *N. rustica* conceivably produced a mild psychoactive reaction; if swallowed, a stronger intoxication resulted. Thus smoking invited an altered mental and spiritual state believed presumably to enhance results in contexts ranging from religious and medical endeavors to alliance building and peacemaking.[25]

Avian imagery pervaded the key elements in the material culture of smoking — pipe bowls and stems — from the earliest bird-shaped stone pipes to calumet paraphernalia treated heavily with feathers and other bird products. The eighteenth- and nineteenth-century Cherokee and Creek hung feathers, wild turkey–cock spurs, and other objects from their long pipe stems. Choctaw pipes with from eight to ten black and white feathers pendant, as well as red feathers circling the stem, served both as a "war standard" and as a "seal in alliances." A Caddo pipe with white feathers along the length of the stem was presumably used in a rite of friendship and peace.[26]

In eighteenth-century French Louisiana, Le Page du Pratz remarked that Indians had calumets for peace decorated with eagle feathers and duck skins, and calumets for war decorated with flamingo feathers and vulture skin. If the vulture was the turkey vulture, then the bald-red skin did not merely resemble the head of a scalped victim but was also the color of war.[27]

Le Page described an elaborate but typical calumet used by Indians soliciting allies "by the pipe of peace, the stalk of which [was] about four feet and a half long, and [was] covered all over with the skin of a duck's neck, the feathers of which [were] glossy and of various colours." A similar calumet was painted by de Batz in his 1735 watercolor of Indians in New Orleans. Le Page called the duck that lent its neck to the pipe stem the "Perching-Duck," which describes where it is often found — in trees — or the "Carolina Summer-Duck," which was a common name for the wood duck, with its stunning white-spotted red breast, iridescent white and green neck, and multiple-hued head.

Fastened to the pipe, according to Le Page, was "a fan made of the feathers of white eagles, the ends of which [were] black, and [were] ornamented with a tuft dyed a beautiful red." Natives were said to "purchase at a great price the large feathers of his wings, with which they ornament[ed] the Calumet, or Symbol of Peace." The cost was due to the demand for feathers and that fact that the eagle was "very rare." This does not all add up. Le Page described the bird as entirely white with black wingtips, but no eagle fits this description, and he must have mistakenly identified the feathers pendant from the pipe as primary feathers from the wings. If instead they were tail feathers (retrices), they matched perfectly those from the immature golden eagle.[28]

The question remains, why might smoking paraphernalia have represented birds so heavily? One obvious possibility was the link between the unquestioned ability of birds to fly, at times high and powerfully, and the potential of uncut *N. rustica* to produce levity and even perhaps to simulate flight. The anthropologist Alexander von Gernet has reminded us of the intoxicating and dizzying power of tobacco for sixteenth-century Europeans and argued that American Indians were fixed on *N. rustica* at least in part because of the attraction of altered, dissociative states of consciousness induced when smoking the psychoactive plant at full strength.[29]

In the South, the smoker was literally nose to bill with the bird carved on a stone pipe or whose skin wrapped the stem of a calumet, which must have focused his attention on the being whose powers, including flight, he sought to emulate or control. In 1673, the Jesuit Father Jacques Marquette remarked that an Illinois Indian guiding a calumet ceremony related to the powerful sun "cause[d]" a calumet "ornamented with the heads and necks of various birds, whose plumage [was] very beautiful" to dance and "execute many differing figures." He "offer[ed] it to the sun, as if he wished the latter to smoke it . . . incline[d] it toward the earth . . . [and made] it spread its wings." In other words, as

birds fly, so does the feathered calumet — and so, by extension, do those who consume tobacco. They also fly metaphorically or, in their belief, literally.[30]

THE BALL GAME

Inasmuch as it could become a ritualized substitute for hostility and even warfare, the ball game, a widespread southern institution, is fundamentally related to war and peace. As it happens, birds also played a significant role in the game. Some are the same ones that figured in calumet ceremonialism and other conduct for war and peace, and others are new; a story told by the Cherokee and others sets the stage.

Once upon a time, the Cherokee say, the four-footed terrestrial animals, led by Bear, challenged the birds, with Eagle as captain, to a ball game. The birds got the better of the animals, winning, however, only after the animals rejected as laughably insignificant two among them, who immediately and successfully petitioned the birds to play on their side. The two were the flying squirrel and the bat, for whom the birds promptly made wings, and they proceeded to win the game for their feathered friends. Purple Martin helped to seal the victory, catching the ball when it had been dropped, and was awarded a gourd for his effort.[31]

Other versions of this myth are found among the Creek and the Seminole. One

FIGURE 121. That in which They Train their Youth. *Engraving by Theodor de Bry (after Jacques Le Moyne de Morgues), 1591, in Hariot,* Der ander Theyl, *plate 36. In what might be the earliest representation of the regional ball game, young men toss balls at a cage — a nest? — atop a goal post as others shoot arrows fletched with bird feathers and engage in other sporting pursuits.* John Carter Brown Library at Brown University.

FIGURE 122. Dibujo del juego de pelota (Drawing of the ball game). *This drawing of the goalpost for the ball game accompanies a description of the Apalachee ball game in 1676, written by Juan de Paiva, a Franciscan; at the top of the post is an effigy of what is identified as an eagle sitting on a nest, above (protected by?) bundles of sticks shaped like talons or war knives. Gobierno de España, Ministerio de Cultura, Archivo General de Indias, MP-Estampa 49.*

rendering ends the same way, with the birds besting the animals, but many details vary: the four-footed animals led by Alligator as chief challenged the birds with Eagle as chief; Alligator turned out to be at first unstoppable and the animals too large and strong until Eagle flew so high that he was nearly out of sight, plunged down on Alligator, and broke his nose; Turkey quickly grabbed the ball from inside Alligator's tooth-filled mouth, and the birds won.[32]

In the Creek version, the feathered, toothless birds challenged the four-footed, toothed animals to a game. Bat was rejected both by the animals, because he had wings, and by the birds, because he had teeth and was too small. So Bat returned to the animals and asked them again to let him join their team, and at last they consented. As the game progressed, the birds had the advantage as Crane and others kept the ball in the air, but in the end Bat swooped in, stole the ball from the slower and less agile Crane, and carried the day for the animals.[33]

Indians across the South — the Cherokee, Creek, Chickasaw, Choctaw, Seminole, and others — played the ball game (and some still do), each player, usually with two lacrosselike sticks, trying to throw a ball between two posts or at a single pole. The game was the preeminent regional institution pitting one town against another or one moiety against the other, and in the process revealed social arrangements and tensions. People regarded the game with great seriousness. They fought it hard and often violently in teams ranging in size from under one dozen players to over one hundred. Waged between different towns, the game was a substitute for war, albeit a violent and at times fatal one.[34]

The Choctaw were among many who dressed themselves with feathers when they played ball. Bernard Romans, the mid-eighteenth-century surveyor with a keen eye for indigenous custom, spoke of Choctaw ballplayers "being almost naked, painted and ornamented with feathers . . . during this violent diversion." Jean-Bernard Bossu, who was in Choctaw territory at virtually the same time, also took note of ballplayers naked save for painted bodies, a "tiger tail" fastened in the small of the back, and "feathers on their arms and heads which flutter[ed] as they [ran], giving a remarkable effect."[35]

Players were also feathered meaningfully in intratown games. For example, in one Natchez game pitting sides playing for the Great Sun and the Great War Chief against each other, the Great Sun's players wore white feathers on their heads against the Great War Chief's red.[36] Among the Creek, players for the White moiety dressed themselves in (white) crane feathers and players for the other moiety, the People of a Different Speech, accessorized with eagle feathers. Some apparently also wore the feathers of the

FIGURE 123.
Ball Players. *Hand-colored lithograph on paper by George Catlin, ca. 1834. These Choctaw men in Indian Territory are stripped down and pigmented, feathered, roached, and otherwise accessorized. Sticks in hand, they are prepared for a competitive and violent game in which certain birds whose feathers adorn them, like those of the golden eagle that trail down the backs of two men at right, figure meaningfully. Smithsonian American Art Museum, gift of Mrs. Joseph Harrison Jr., 1966.48.68.*

kestrel, said to be a "masterful animal." In what appeared to be an attempt to neutralize the bird-spirit helpers of one's opponents, one ball used in the game held a measuring worm inside that was supposedly invisible to a bird and therefore to bird helpers that might prevent it from scoring.[37]

Eagles, carved or stuffed, could be found atop the ball-game posts of the Creek, Apalachee, and Timucua; by the early eighteenth century, the ball games of the latter two had disappeared along with most of the people. The Apalachee and the Timucua, who used their feet to propel the ball, placed a stuffed eagle in a nest on top of their goalposts, and one thirty-foot-high Creek ball post had a wooden eagle on the top. In 1912, the Creek, mindful perhaps of the symbolism of the eagle for American citizens, remarked that this bird was used because it is "emblematic of the United States."[38]

Birds and feathers figured more widely in the ball game. Prior to a game, the Cherokee danced "painted and ornamented," with "high waving plumes in their diadems." The players bled themselves ritually with a scratching instrument made of knife-edge-sharp splintered turkey-leg bones; wore eagle feathers in their hair; and decorated their sticks with the feathers of great crested flycatchers and purple martins, hoping perhaps either that the birds would help or that their skills would transfer to them. The night before the game, one player called *dalala* (red-headed woodpecker) sought magically to influence the outcome of the game by yelling at the opposition in another town. The Cherokee invoked birds noted for qualities conducive to success in the contest: the eagle was strong and keen in sight; the red-headed woodpecker was supreme in war; great crested flycatchers and purple martins were both strong, swift, and agile aerialists

FIGURE 124. Ceremony before the ball game. *Black-and-white gelatin-glass negative by James Mooney, Qualla reservation, North Carolina, 1888. Feathered players (right) and clanswomen behind the dance leader (left) participate in a lengthy ceremony prior to a ball game between two Cherokee towns. National Anthropological Archives, Smithsonian Institution, 01044b 06218300.*

with well-deserved reputations. Audubon spoke of the great crested flycatcher's "unrelenting fierceness almost amounting to barbarity," attacking small birds and sometimes plucking a vanquished rival, and remarked that purple martins were "extremely courageous, persevering, and tenacious of what they consider their right," unhesitatingly and "indiscriminately" going after "every species of Hawk, Crow, or Vulture." Players sought influence over the outcome of the contest through the time-honored principle of contact or contagion, through the belief that the feathers that brought desired qualities to specific birds would now work on behalf of them and against the opposition to influence the game in their favor.[39]

From Nemattanew to the ball game, contexts relating to war and peace in the South invariably linked to the avian world. Some birds, such as turkeys, eagles, swans, and red-headed woodpeckers, were conspicuous for well-known qualities of strength or aggression; several of these appeared in more than one context. In other cases — calumet ceremonialism or smoking in general and the ball game — the list of birds lengthens

FIGURE 125. *(Left)* The Red headed Wood-pecker. *Hand-colored etching by Mark Catesby,* Natural History *(1731–43), plate 20. This aggressive woodpecker figured significantly in the Cherokee ball game. John Carter Brown Library at Brown University.*

FIGURE 126. *(Right)* The Crested Fly-Catcher (great crested flycatcher). *Hand-colored etching by Mark Catesby,* Natural History *(1731–43), plate 52. Like the red-headed woodpecker, this was another bold and important bird in the Cherokee ball game. John Carter Brown Library at Brown University.*

to include ones connected, for example, through color to war (vultures and flamingo feathers); by sculpture, via tobacco, to flight (many birds); or by their role in a foundational myth to the ball game (the swift, agile purple martin and the aggressive great crested flycatcher). When we take up spirituality, spirit-birds, and narrative, this broadening of species linked to humankind becomes even more noticeable.

FIGURE 127.
A medicine man.
*Watercolor over black
lead by John White,
ca. 1585. Inscribed,
"The flyer," this
medicine man wore
a small black bird—a
rusty blackbird?—on
the right side of
his head. As it once
(and perhaps still,
figuratively) flew, so
did he, perhaps with
the aid of tobacco in
the pouch at his belt.
© The Trustees of
the British Museum,
1906,0509.1.16.*

The flyer.

Spirituality

In one of his remarkable watercolors of coastal Algonquian people in North Carolina in the 1580s, John White, the artist and governor of Roanoke colony, painted "The flyer," or, as the title became in the subsequent engraving, "Indian Conjurer," a man with both arms upraised and a bird with wings spread, presumably dead, conspicuously in his hair above one ear. As Thomas Harriot explained in the text accompanying the engraving, "[Shamans] shave all their heads savinge their crests which they weare as other doe, and fasten a small black birde above one of their ears as a badge of their office." Many colonists remarked on the association between birds and coastal Algonquian men in sixteenth- and seventeenth-century North Carolina and Virginia and noted furthermore the special link between birds and religious specialists such as priests, shamans, and curers, especially in feathered regalia like mantles and feathers in the hair. White's "Flyer" and Harriot's comments pertained to medicine men or shamans; in Virginia early in the next century, William Strachey and John Smith remarked on priests, Strachey commenting that a Powhatan head priest wore a "middle seised Cloke of feathers" and a "Crownet (as yt were) of feathers," and Smith agreeing about the "Crownet of feathers on his head."[1]

In 1705, Robert Beverley, born in Virginia, struggled to comprehend a medicine man like the one imaged by White with "a black Bird with expanded Wings fasten'd to his Ear." For insight, Beverley reached comparatively to Islam and decided that it differed "in nothing but colour, from *Mahomet*'s Pidgeon." What Beverley meant is not clear: perhaps that as the Holy Spirit spoke through a pigeon into the prophet Muhammad's ear, so too was there a spiritual connection between a blackbird and a shaman in Virginia; or (more skeptically) that as Muhammad deluded others into thinking that he received divine inspiration when in fact he had trained a pigeon to eat peas (or wheat) from his ear, so too did shamans in Virginia falsely claim similar inspiration from blackbirds in their hair.[2]

Whatever Beverley intended, birds and religion were linked tightly throughout the South in perception and reality. Religious specialists across the region incorporated birds or feathers into their dress or ritual. They were often distinguished by richness of dress; an early eighteenth-century Santee "chief Doctor or Physician" was "warmly and neatly clad with a Match-Coat, made of Turkies Feathers, which [made] a pretty Shew, seeming as if it was a Garment of the deepest silk Shag."[3] As part of his regalia, a mid-eighteenth-century Chickasaw priest wore around his forehead "either a wreath of swan-feathers, or a long piece of swan-skin doubled, so as only the fine snowy feathers appear[ed] on each side." On the top of his head he wore "a tuft of white feathers which they call[ed] *Yatera*," and on the top of his moccasins, near the toes, he "fasten[ed] a tuft of blunted wild Turkey cock-spurs."[4] Early nineteenth-century Creek prophets were said to "cover their body with feathers."[5]

Farther west, Le Page du Pratz reported from French Louisiana that during ceremonies a Natchez priest wore "a crown which [had] feathers only in front and [was] thus a half crown," and held a staff attached to which were red or white feathers according to the context of the ceremony. Caddo medicine men wore clothing "decorated with big bunches of feathers" and, reportedly, the skins of coral snakes, accessorized with "particular insignia or feathers" in their hair, and used turkey-tail fans in healing rituals. Feathers and birds seemed especially prevalent in Caddo religious contexts: carvings of birds appeared at the entrances to their temples, and priests kept within boxes small vessels or platters representing ducks, as well as "many feathers of various shapes and colors, handfuls of feathers of wild birds . . . rolls of ornamental feathers, crowns made of skins and feathers, a bonnet of the same, [and] many little carved crane bones which serve[d] them as flutes or fifes."[6]

Southern Indians widely linked birds and feathers with religion, ritual, curing, and religious specialists and structures. It is not always possible to tell which species were involved, merely that birds were, and as a consequence the precise meanings of the associations are inscrutable. Yet when the Catawba or the Cherokee purified the hearth, house premises, or other spaces by sweeping them with a fan of turkey-, goose-, heron-, or hawk-wing feathers, then the association between birds and the spiritual world was quite fundamental. On the most basic level, birds belong to the sky and move in the same medium of the cosmos as powerful beings. It takes no stretch of the imagination to extend links with birds — powerful avian beings — to spirits of transcendent importance in the welfare of human beings: the Sun, Thunder, Lightning, and Fire, all of which were essential to life as southern Indians understood it. The strongest birds, such as eagles, could transport thoughts to spirits above who made things happen. Something as partial as an eagle's wing or another bird's plumes were symbolic of this process; something as simple as a feather could be charged with power, positively or negatively depending on circumstance. In the end, as written on John White's watercolor, the shaman flew.[7]

TEMPLES AND MORTUARIES

The association between birds and the other-than-human world is also evident in religious structures such as mortuaries and temples; these were sometimes one and the same: a mound atop which was a temple, with interment in both. Some Mississippian-era burials contain the remains of birds or feathers (or the imagery of birds), for instance, the burials of the elite in the stratified societies of Moundville and Etowah. The human-bird connection in mortuaries and death is ancient: at one 1,500 – 2,000-year-old site in central Florida, people had excavated a pond, erected a platform in the center, placed some three hundred burials on it, and proceeded to ornament this mortu-

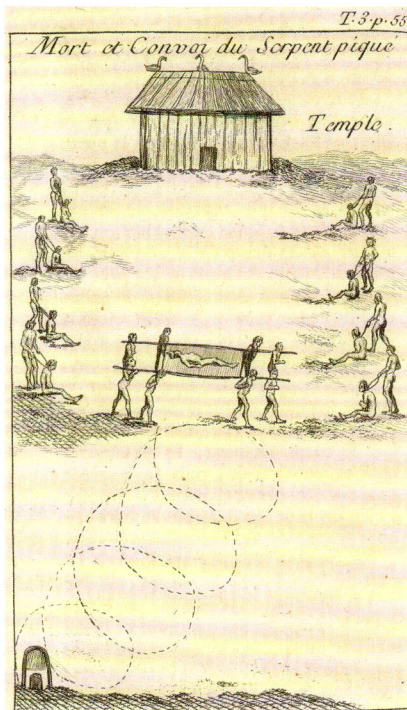

FIGURE 128.
(Left) Temple des Sauvages . . . Cabane du chef . . . (Temple of the savages . . . cabin of the chief), Acolapissa. Pen and ink drawing by Alexandre de Batz, 1732. According to de Batz's text, atop the temple are three birds that resemble both eagles and turkeys in various parts of their bodies, linking the Acolapissa with others who topped their religious structures with important birds. © 2006 Harvard University, Peabody Museum, 41-72-10/16.

FIGURE 129.
(Right) Mort et Convoi du Serpent Pique (The death and funeral procession of the Tattooed Serpent). Woodcut in Le Page du Pratz, History of Louisiana, vol. 3, opp. 55. Atop the Natchez temple in the background are three birds that Le Page compared to geese, but twice as large and fantastically colored. John Carter Brown Library at Brown University.

ary structure, as well as the tops of socketed poles driven into the muck nearby, with wooden sculptures of animals including waterfowl, large wading birds, raptors, and other birds probably associated with particular descent groups.[8]

Nearer in time to today, de Soto's expedition described mortuary/temple structures twice, once in Florida, where atop the structure was "a wooden bird with its eyes gilded," and a second time, when the building was decorated with shells, pearls, and "large plumes of multicolored feathers."[9] Farther west in the eighteenth century were similar representations, including one of "three great birds [carved] on flat pieces of wood" on top of the ridge pole of a Natchez temple. Le Page compared them to geese ("twice as large," shorter necks, ungooselike heads) and said that they lacked feet, had white and "beautiful red" feathers including "large and very distinct" wing feathers, and faced eastward.[10] Imitating perhaps the Natchez structure, an Acolapissa oval "temple" had atop it three wooden birds with eaglelike heads and turkeylike bodies and tails.[11] Carved wooden images on both Taensa and Natchez temples are often referred to as eagles.[12] In contrast, an eighteenth-century Choctaw mortuary had on its peak what was described as "the carved image of a dove, with its wings stretched out, and its head inclining down, as if earnestly viewing or watching over the bones of the dead."[13]

It is not known what these birds were precisely — eagles, doves, turkeys, spirit-birds, or something else — or what they signified. But certain birds, as described earlier, including raptors, resonated symbolically in a range of contexts and were of significance either to society at large or to members of descent groups whose bodies ended up in

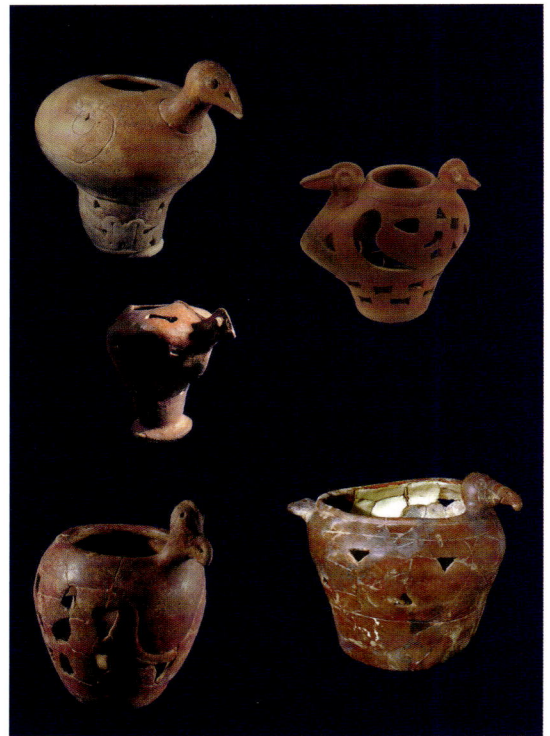

FIGURE 130. Bird effigy mortuary pottery. Weeden Island, ca. AD 250–700, left, top to bottom: Liberty Co., Fla., 8.7 in. high; Taylor County, Fla., 6.7 in. high; Calhoun County, Fla., 9.25 in. high; right, top to bottom: Burnt Mill Creek Site, Fla., 7.5 in. high; Columbia County, Fla., 8.7 in. high. Perforated pots, each with the head of a bird (or two) on the rim; left, top to bottom, and right, top to bottom, perhaps: a turkey, unknown, vulture, unknown, and vulture. These mortuary pots might have functioned as incense burners; some perforations correspond to bird anatomical or morphological features. Left, top to bottom: National Museum of the American Indian, Smithsonian Institution, 17-4905; private collection; National Museum of the American Indian, Smithsonian Institution, 17/3955. Photos by Roy C. Craven Jr., courtesy of Barbara A. Purdy and the University Press of Florida. Right, top to bottom: National Museum of the American Indian, Smithsonian Institution, 17/4875, photo by NMAI Photo Services Staff; Collections of the Florida Museum of Natural History, A20086, photo by Jeff Gage.

mortuaries or temples. As such, they stood to influence, in ways suggested earlier, people after death as well as the essential beings who, like them, moved through and dwelled in the sky above.

VULTURES

How the body was treated after death varied culturally and according to one's position within society; in some Mississippian-era societies, the elite, as we have seen, were destined for mound interment. Often an individual's personal possessions were buried alongside the body or displayed about the grave. Birds and feathers were widely included: the Santee hung feathers about the grave; the Powhatan, for whom the afterlife was plentifully supplied with food, feathers, and other commodities, placed the body of a leader on a scaffold with various possessions and goods, including turkey flesh; the Natchez ornamented a man's body with plumes; the Alabama buried movable property with the deceased, including a large knife to fight off a "great eagle"; and the Caddo buried men with "all of their feathers and beads."[14]

In some southern societies, men or women defleshed the bones of the deceased as part of the ritual treatment of the dead, usually following an interval of interment (a custom that under missionary influence was on the wane by the early nineteenth century, if not earlier). Some of the names for these flesh strippers are revealing: for example, the Chitimacha called them "turkey-vulture men," and the Choctaw used labels whose English versions were "turkey vulture," "vulture," or "buzzard" for the men or women who performed this task.[15]

FIGURE 131. *(Left)* Turkey Buzzard (turkey vulture). Black Vulture. Raven (common raven). *Hand-colored engraving by Alexander Lawson based on drawing by Alexander Wilson, 1808–14,* American Ornithology, *vol. 9, plate 75. All three birds figure in the ethno-ornithology of the South, the widely distributed turkey vulture and black vulture most often simply as "buzzard." John Hay Library at Brown University.*

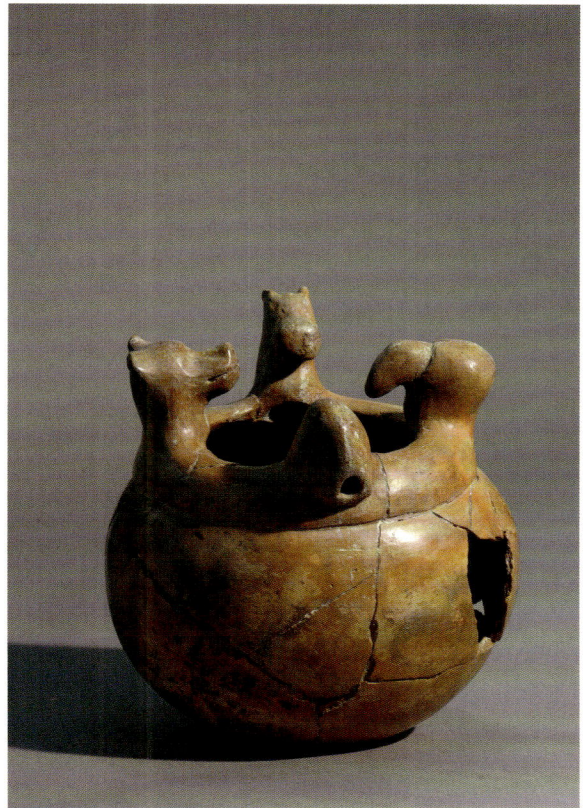

FIGURE 132. *(Right)* Ceramic bowl with vulture and mammal heads on the rim. McKeithen Site, Columbia County, *Fla., AD 250–700, 5.5 in. diameter. The animals on the rim of a bowl holed and displayed in a mortuary context seem blinded or extinguished in death. The birds are vultures, common in mortuary contexts; the mammals include a bear with a typically robust snout. Collections of the Florida Museum of Natural History, A-10952.*

Given their role as scavengers, it is not surprising that vultures might have been especially linked with death (and mortuaries). Two kinds of vultures exist in nature in the South: the turkey vulture and the black vulture. It is rarely apparent which is meant (or if both are) by the label "vulture" or "buzzard." When soaring high overhead, the two look much the same to the untutored eye, but they are quite different in behavior and ability. The turkey vulture is rather passive and locates carrion largely through scent. Alexander Wilson, the ornithologist and painter, considered it "gregarious, peaceable and harmless," with an "astonishingly exquisite" sense of smell. The black vulture, in contrast, is highly aggressive and has a poorly developed sense of smell. It often watches turkey vultures, descends on them and takes their carrion, or sometimes, predator as much as scavenger, catches and kills young birds and small prey.[16]

Jean-Bernard Bossu, who called black vultures carrion crows (an Old World corvid), remarked that they were "impatient" and would "avidly eat anything," including

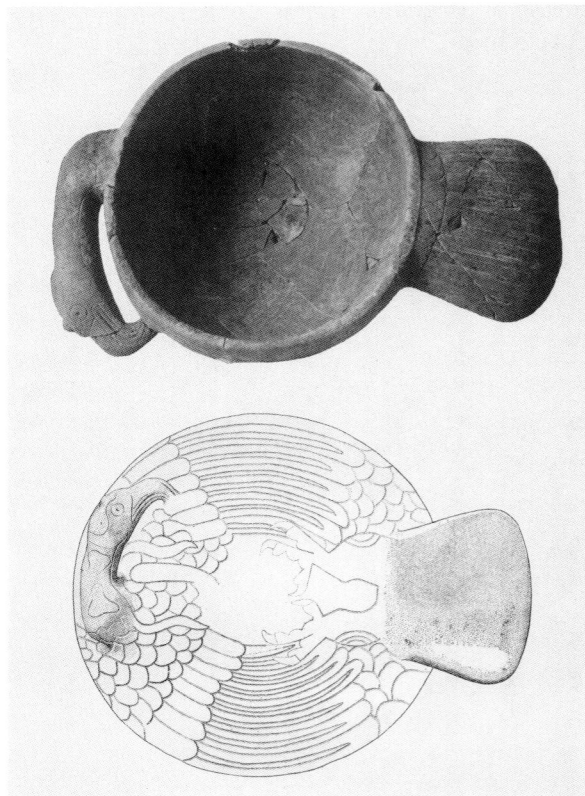

FIGURE 133. Limestone vulture-effigy bowl. *Tuscaloosa County, Ala., ca. AD 1250–1550, bowl 13.75 in. max. diameter. If based in nature, the bird represented in this noteworthy bowl (photograph, top; drawing, bottom) from a Moundville burial resembles foremost— in its bill, neck, talons, and nails—a vulture; most likely, the turkey vulture, although (as discussed in the text) Moore proposed the king vulture. Given the association of vultures with death, immunity from smallpox, and healing gunshot wounds, among other matters, one can imagine the use of this bowl and the liquid therein for prophylactic, curative, or other purposes. The bird also possesses characteristics of the wild turkey: a possible snood in the small (but misplaced) knob on the head (top), and what might be a beard in the decorative elements on the underside (bottom). Clarence Moore, "Moundville Revisited," figs. 77 (top) and 79 (bottom). John Hay Library at Brown University.*

"human corpses whenever they [could] find them." Wilson agreed. In Charlestown, Savannah, and other towns, black vultures commonly "saunter[ed] about the streets" or on rooftops and might "be said to be completely domesticated, being as common as the domestic poultry, and equally familiar." Aggressive birds, they sought advantage tearing at dead animals by hissing, striking out, or grabbing others by the head with their talons. There were reports of them "attack[ing] young pigs, and eat[ing] off their ears and tails," as well as "assaulting feeble calves and picking out their eyes." Wilson commented that even though Americans regarded vultures as "filthy," they respected them "for their usefulness" in removing offal and waste and protected them by law.[17]

In seventeenth-century Virginia, turkey-vulture fat was said to be useful in the treatment of "old Aches and Sciatica Pains," although whether by Indians or the English is unclear. But the Cherokee definitely linked the vulture to curing, regarding it as "a doctor among birds." They thought it immune from sickness and believed that consuming its flesh would bring them immunity against smallpox. For them, vultures played important roles in contexts relating to curing and death. A medicine man or curer placed vulture down and other soft vulture feathers in a gunshot wound, used vulture feathers to clean other types of wounds, and blew powdered medicine through a vulture quill cut at both ends. He displayed a vulture feather as a sign that he could cure gunshot wounds. Like the Cherokee, the Creek also linked this bird to medicine and curing, and a Creek priest who cured wounds signaled this ability by wearing a vulture feather.[18]

OMENS

Many birds were probably augural; that is, their presence, calls, or behavior foretold events, from important to trivial. This was especially true of vocalizing birds: a chattering blue jay, or birds calling around the door of the house, meant that a visitor was en route; a cawing crow forecast good weather; a screech-owl calling left or right of a path to war was a sign of victory, but one that called persistently ahead or behind was a sign of defeat; a nighthawk or a whip-poor-will calling near a house, or a screech-owl calling in town, meant sickness or death for a resident; and roosters crowing at odd times meant that bad weather or trouble, either among women or in the family, was on the way. Other omens included failing to be quiet after seeing a woodpecker, which was believed to bring on a nosebleed; the sapsucker, regarded as a harbinger of news; a cardinal that flew up suddenly, which foretold the arrival of a visitor; a wild goose shot with a gun, believed to ruin the gun; and a grouse wandering through the yard, or a sick man approached by a screech-owl, either of which foretold death.[19]

FIGURE 134. The Blew Jay (blue jay). *Hand-colored etching by Mark Catesby,* Natural History *(1771), plate 15. Inscribed "The crested Jay." For some, an augur announcing an impending visitor.* John Carter Brown Library at Brown University.

Smilax lævis Lauri folio non Serrato, baccis nigris

Pica cristata cærulea
The crested Jay

FIGURE 135.
The Red Bird
(northern cardinal).
*Hand-colored etching
by Mark Catesby,
Natural History
(1731–43), plate
38. Some southern
Indians believed
that its sudden flight
foretold the arrival of
a caller. John Carter
Brown Library at
Brown University.*

For the Choctaw, one object of divination was a taxidermied owl. According to the eighteenth-century surveyor Bernard Romans, when the Choctaw went on the warpath they carried with them "the genius of the party," which he described as "the stuffed skin of an owl of a large kind." Romans noted, "[T]hey are very careful of him, keep a guard over him, and offer him a part of their meat; should he fall, or any other ways be disordered in position, the expedition is frustrated; they always set him with his head towards the place of destination, and if he should be provided to be turned directly contrary, they consider this as portending some very bad omen, and an absolute order to return; should therefore any one's heart fail him, he needs only watch his opportunity to do this to save his character of a brave or true man."[20]

The naturalist William Bartram also spoke about "a great owl skin cased and stuffed very ingeniously" in the possession of "junior priests" that was "so well executed, as almost to represent the living bird, having large sparkling glass beads, or buttons, fixed in the head for eyes; this insigne of wisdom and divination, they [wore] sometimes as a crest on the top of the head, at other times the image [sat] on the arm, or [was] borne on the hand."[21] Creek priests had the right (or power) to wear horned-owl feathers in their headdress, carry owl skins as symbols of their office, and use them in divination.[22] Farther west, the Taensa also were said to keep "stuffed owls" in their temples, perhaps to the same end.[23] As discussed below, of the two large owls in the South, the great horned and the barred, the former was the more powerful in conception and more likely to possess the potential to prophesy or cause harm.

"A SPECIES OF *MOTACILLA*"

In 1775, James Adair and Bernard Romans, both competent observers, independently identified as an omen a small bird that affected warriors on the warpath. According to Adair, the Creek were "intimidated at the voice of a small uncommon bird, when it pitched, and chirped on a tree over their war camp." They regarded this "kind ill messenger," he continued, as a "true oracle of bad ways." Romans told a similar story about Choctaw warriors, who evidently possessed a belief about "a species of *Motacilla* (which [he] often endeavored to catch, in vain) whose chirping near the camp, [would] occasion their immediate return."[24]

What was this bird? Answering this simple question illustrates the great difficulty in arriving at ironclad conclusions on the identity of many birds from this time. In the seventeenth and early eighteenth centuries, as well as today, *motacillas* were wagtails: small, active, tail-wagging insectivorous birds that forage on the ground. Predominantly Old World species, they are unknown in the American South. In the time of Romans and Adair, however, naturalists and others extended the category *motacilla* to other birds. Linnaeus (Carl von Linné), for example, the influential founder of binomial nomenclature and advocate of hierarchy in taxonomy, applied *motacilla* to wagtails as well as eight other categories including warblers, chats, and the wren, nightingale, goldcrest, and others; a Danish ornithologist named Morten Thrane Brunnich closely followed suit.[25]

Romans is unfortunately mute on which *motacilla* he might have had in mind. If he had been thinking of a wagtail-like bird, then the nearest relative in the American South was the American pipit. Small, streaked, sparrowlike birds, these pipits "suffer their tails to vibrate," Audubon remarked, "whenever they stop running." Widespread in winter, they tend to keep to the ground, have thin, high calls, and sing mainly in flight. These traits would seem to leave them lacking as candidates for Romans's *motacilla*.[26]

A better possibility might be a waterthrush, which is a warbler and therefore, by extension from its Old World relatives, part of Linnaeus's inclusive *motacilla* category. Two species, Louisiana and northern, migrate through the South in spring; the Louisiana stays to breed, but the northern keeps going. The two are difficult to tell apart except in voice and confused early ornithologists. They also bob their bodies or wag their tails, action enshrined in the species name for the Louisiana waterthrush (*Seiurus motacilla*), which means "little mover" or "tail mover." Both waterthrushes favor wet ground but are found at different levels, including trees overhead during migration. Both have distinctive, strong voices, the Louisiana a striking slurring call, and the northern a vigorous series of descending notes. The most "uncommon" — Adair's word — during the prime seasons for war, from late spring to fall, was the northern waterthrush. But the case for either is inconclusive.[27]

The Choctaw and the Creek were not the only southern Indians to consider small birds augural; if we take up the others briefly, we might gain useful insights. The Caddo, for example, thought that the appearance of small birds called *banit* meant that buffalos or enemies (whichever they sought) were near; the identity of this bird is unfortunately obscure.[28] And the Cherokee, according to Alexander Long, a trader among them in 1710–25, noticed a "small bird" called *ihigelelie*, whose singing, they remarked, signified the approach of enemies on the trail or near town. Long identified the bird as a wren, but he was surely mistaken. According to the anthropologist Arlene Fradkin, it was the Carolina chickadee (*jigilili*), a truth-teller in both Cherokee myth and life (as explained in the next chapter).[29]

Even if Long's wren was a chickadee and an augur for the Cherokee, this does not solve the problem for Adair's "uncommon bird" or Romans's *motacilla*. Neither was the chickadee uncommon, nor did Linneaus and others include the chickadee's obvious Old World relatives, European tits, in the broader *motacilla* category.

FIGURE 136. Brown Creeper. Golden-crested Wren (golden-crowned kinglet). House Wren. Black-capt Titmouse (black-capped chickadee). Crested Titmouse (tufted titmouse). Winter Wren. *Hand-colored engraving by Alexander Lawson based on drawing by Alexander Wilson*, American Ornithology, *vol. 1, 1808–14, plate 8. Several of these birds — the winter wren, the chickadee, and the titmouse — were either omens or good candidates for augury. John Hay Library at Brown University.*

FIGURE 137.
Bachman's Sparrow
and Carolina Wren.
*Drawing by William
Bartram. To the
Chitimacha, the
common Carolina
wren was an omen
when singing; the
Bachman's sparrow
was also common
but seemed not to
register. Botanical
and zoological
drawings, 1756–88,
the Botany Library,
no. 53 (Ewan upper
16), © Natural History
Museum, London.*

It is possible that like Long, Adair and Romans had wrens in mind. In its favor is that European taxonomists placed the common European wren in the larger *motacilla* category. Six species of wrens occur in the South — Carolina, Bewick's, house, winter, marsh, and sedge — one of which, the winter wren, a resident of the Appalachians, is conspecific with the wren of Europe. (As for the others, the Carolina wren is familiar everywhere, the marsh wren is common along the coast, Bewick's is very rare, and the others occur mainly in winter. All are active, cock their tails, and have noticeable chattering or tinkling trills — or, in the case of the Carolina wren, an extremely loud three-syllable call.)[30]

Moreover, at least one Indian people considered a wren to be an augur: the Chitimacha, who lived along coastal Louisiana west of the Mississippi delta, regarded singing Carolina wrens as omens; perched above, they announced (in different calls) the imminent arrival of a visitor, danger, or good luck.[31]

But these Indians were unrelated linguistically (and in other ways) to the Creek and the Choctaw, so there is no reason for the latter to have followed suit. Yet another wren might have been a better candidate: the winter wren — a *motacilla* familiar to someone like Romans. This wren departs from the others in being miniscule and dark, a forager in tangles and under leaves, often jerking its minute tail or raising it to a vertical position and sometimes, in winter, chattering harshly. It often appears anomalous as a bird, more mouse than bird.

Some years ago, the anthropologist Mary Douglas suggested that anomalies, which by definition do not fit into the class in which they belong, are often marked, auspiciously or inauspiciously, for special consideration. Perched overhead, singing harshly (or at breeding elevations and in season, breathlessly and at length), a mouselike winter wren, which is resident in northern Creek territory and a winter visitor to Choctaw territory, might well have been a candidate for augury. The problem (the same one that complicates an explanation for food taboos), however, is that anomaly derives not unmediated from nature alone but from its intersection with culture and society, from what people perceive as normal or abnormal. Unfortunately, in this as in many other cases of events that unfolded deep in the past among people whose knowledge, like that of all people, changes constantly and in part unpredictably, knowing what was perceived as anomalous or how anomaly was noted is elusive.[32]

WHIP-POOR-WILL

In the early eighteenth century, the Virginian Robert Beverley reported that the Powhatan had "great Reverence" for a "small Bird that uses the Woods" and "flys alone, and is only heard in the twilight." They venerated it and "wou'd not hurt it for the World,"

PLATE. LXXXII

Whip-poor-will, CAPRIMULGUS VOCIFERUS, Wils. Male, 1 Female, 2, 3, Black Oak or Quercitron, Quercus tinctoria.

FIGURE 138. Whip-poor-will. *Hand-colored engraving by Robert Havell from a painting by John James Audubon,* Birds of America, *vol. 1 (1827–30), plate 82. This nocturnal bird was an ill omen for many southern Indians. Rare Books and Special Collections, Thomas Cooper Library, University of South Carolina.*

FIGURE 139. Great Horned Owl. *Hand-colored engraving by Robert Havell from a painting by John James Audubon,* Birds of America, *vol. 1 (1827–30), plate 61. A powerful bird: an augur for some but member of the malevolent other-than-human world (a witch, for example) for many others. Rare Books and Special Collections, Thomas Cooper Library, University of South Carolina.*

FIGURE 140. Large sculpted owl with ear-tufts. *Volusia County, Fla., ca. AD 1200–1300 (now at Fort Caroline National Memorial), carved portion: 6 ft. 3 in. long. This massive wooden sculpture of a great horned or eastern screech-owl, found in the muck of the St. Johns River, had originally been placed upright in the ground. Its function and cultural meaning are unknown, although other wooden sculptures of birds were erected in mortuary contexts. Many southern Indians regarded great horned and eastern screech-owls as malevolent, and themselves as in need of protection against them; some thought of the great horned owl as a diviner. Photo Collections of the Florida Museum of Natural History, PN2000.5.1.*

believing it to be "the Soul of one of their Princes." One man who had been bribed to kill one of these birds later disappeared — not, it was believed, coincidentally. The Powhatan called this bird Pawcorance, which "in their note continually sound[ed] that name." This onomatope and the description of the bird as active at dusk makes one think of the whip-poor-will, with its three-syllable call.[33] In what is conceivably a reference to the English assault on native people in Virginia in revenge for the 1622 massacre, the artist and naturalist Mark Catesby heard that whip-poor-wills, according to native people, were "never known till a great massacre was made of their countryfolks by the English, and that they [were] the souls or departed spirits of the massacred Indians."[34] As remarked elsewhere, southern Indians regarded the whip-poor-will with ambivalence, if not fear; and some newcomers from Europe conceivably regarded this New World goatsucker as they had its Old World relative, the nightjar: as a bird that could cause disease in domesticated stock, suck goats dry of their milk at night, or be connected to death.

OWLS

Owls were without doubt the most dreaded and dangerous birds in the South. Most Indians feared them intensely, perceiving them not simply as ill omens but, more terrifyingly, as witches and spirits bent on malevolence. Yet owls were not universally destructive; they were also capable of a moderating and even beneficial influence. Some people knew how to marshal their powers; some, as we have seen, considered an owl in a taxidermied state to be a powerful diviner. Thus a basic ambivalence tempered ever so slightly the overwhelmingly negative relationship between southern Indians and owls.

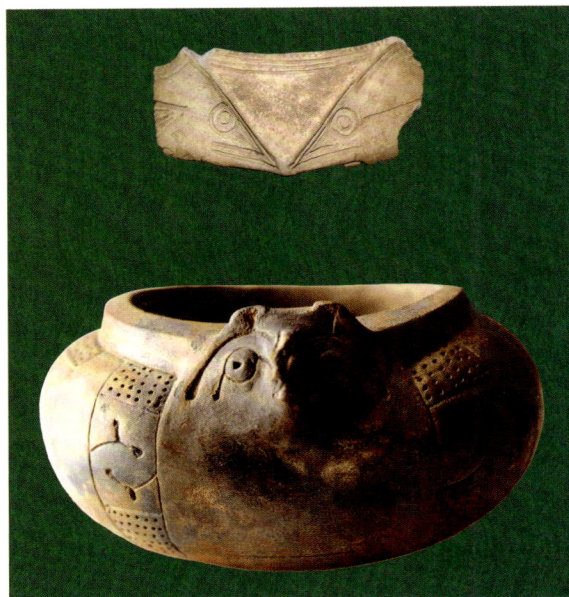

FIGURE 141. *(Left)* The Little Owl (eastern screech-owl). *Hand-colored etching by Mark Catesby*, Natural History *(1771), plate 7. Another unsettling nocturnal bird linked by some southern Indians to witches or ghosts. John Carter Brown Library at Brown University.*

FIGURE 142. *(Right)* Owl effigy bowl and shard. *Top: ceramic owl-head shard, Choctawhatchee Beach Cemetery Site, Walton County, Fla., AD 1350–1500, 2.7 in. high; bottom: ceramic owl effigy bowl, Spring Warrior Mound, Taylor County, Fla., AD 400–1000, 5.17 in. high. Owls are frequently represented in the material record in the South, from Archaic times onward.* Top: *Courtesy of the Indian Temple Mound Museum Collection, City of Fort Walton Beach Heritage Park and Cultural Center, Fla., 1415.* Bottom: *Museum of Science and History, Jacksonville, 76441. Photo courtesy of Susan Power.*

The nineteenth-century Creek, according to the anthropologist J. N. B. Hewitt, regarded all owls with fear and the great horned owl in particular with "great terror." They connected owls powerfully to witchcraft, believing that a witch or sorcerer, after taking out his intestines, could morph into an owl — probably the great horned — and fly about and do ill (they also believed that the shape-shifting could be to a northern flicker or some other bird). During the early nineteenth century, the Creek were on the verge of civil war, and witches were said to be especially troublesome, "flying about to do mischief" at twilight. The Chickasaw also thought that witches could shift shape and become owls or nighthawks, and that the sound of a screech-owl signaled a witch nearby. Many Creek Indians also connected screech-owls and great horned owls with ghosts or wandering souls — spirits of the dead with potential to kill any who heard them wail or hoot.

But the relationship of Creek Indians with owls was not uniformly negative: they also believed that a person who understood the powers of medicine could transform a man into an owl so that he might discover the enemy's intentions. Because they often doubled as curers and possessed supernatural abilities, prophets were believed to transform themselves into owls, foxes, or other animals and scout the enemy, presumably for the benefit of the people of their villages.[35]

FIGURE 143.
Owl-head and owl-
body ceramic bottles.
*Left: owl-head bottle,
near Nashville, Tenn.,
Mississippian; center:
owl-body bottle,
Monroe County,
Tenn., Mississippian,
ca. 9 in. high; right:
owl-head bottle,
Monroe County,
Tenn., AD 1300–1500,
ca. 12 in. high. Al-
though they all
have short ear-tufts,
these three owls are
envisioned quite
differently, from an
abstracted face—
and rattlesnake
design—(right) to
a thick (feathered?)-
legged full-body
effigy (center). Why
owls is the difficult
question, except that
they were power-
fully charged, usually
negatively, and there-
fore in need of careful
thought and monitor-
ing, perhaps through
imbibing liquids con-
tained in the bottle.
Left: Thruston Col-
lection, Department
of Anthropology,
Vanderbilt University,
courtesy of William
R. Fowler, photo by
Hunter Darrouzet.
Center: Department
of Anthropology,
Smithsonian Institu-
tion, A115559. Right:
Frank H. McClung
Museum, University
of Tennessee, Knox-
ville, 211-4/40MR6.*

The Choctaw presented a similar picture on owls as the Creek — at least on the negative side. Like the Creek they believed that owls were connected with the dead. After death, they said, an interior soul, or ghost, went to the land of the dead, but an exterior soul wandered the land at night and took the form of an owl or a fox, revealing itself in a screech or a bark that went unanswered. Like others, the Choctaw associated great horned owls (*ishkitini*) with witchcraft; they also believed in a supernatural horned owl, *Ishkitini*, an other-than-human person who undertook lethal nighttime forays against humans and animals. They assumed that the call of a great horned owl meant sudden death somewhere, that a screech-owl's wail portended the death of a child in the family, and that the hoots of the "common owl (*ōpa*)," which was either the barred or the short-eared owl, prophesied the death of a relative.[36]

Like the Creek, the Chickasaw, and the Choctaw, the Cherokee linked owls with impending death or dire misfortune. Their owls, especially the great horned, screech-, barred-, and long-eared owls, were overwhelmingly malevolent. They feared in particular the long-eared, which they would not kill or eat. Their dread came partly from the association of owls with ghosts but mainly from their connection with witches — the link to which was transparent in language, the same word being used for the long-eared owl, the great horned owl, and witch. Witches were slippery and could morph into any bird but were likely to take the form of an owl, a whip-poor-will, a common nighthawk, a hawk, or a wolf. The Cherokee also thought that the screech-owl forecast and brought death, sometimes spoiling medicine given to a patient; if they caught one, they gave it "no quarter" and cut it "to pieces."[37]

Even though the Catawba apparently regarded the dueting of a great horned and a barred owl as a sign of good news, they more strongly regarded owls as witches in disguise and tried to make the especially malevolent screech-owl go away by putting a scrap of iron in the fire. This belief in owls and witchcraft persisted into the early twentieth century: in one Catawba story, an owl in the rafters of a Cherokee man's house turned out to be his wife, a witch; in another, an old woman who was a witch sat next to the fire one night, disappeared up the chimney, became a great horned owl, and went out to steal chickens.[38]

The Caddo regarded screech-owls as did others in the region, with fear and loathing, because they believed that witches could transform themselves into screech-owls or derive power from partnerships with owls and harm people. For this reason they would try to kill an owl near a house (although they were not sure that it was possible to do so). Yet like the Catawba, the Caddo also regarded owls with ambivalence, connecting them not just with witches but with curing. They thought that people named Bidai, who lived between them and the Gulf of Mexico, possessed the power to make them sick and, "in the shape of owls," well. The Caddo therefore sought Bidai medicine men to cure them of their ailments. Isidro Espinosa, an eighteenth-century Franciscan friar, remarked, "[T]here are three kinds of owls on earth and when the Indians hear the sound of the hoot of an owl they raise a shout of joy as if they had won a victory." For the Caddo, then, owls could be either malevolent witches or benevolent curers.[39]

In many of these accounts it is not always possible to tell which of the seven species of owls in the South was meant when people connected an "owl" to events. Not all owls were equally common in the region, however: barn, great horned, barred, and screech-owls were widespread, year-round residents; the long-eared owl was a winter resident throughout and widespread at other seasons (today it is restricted to the Appalachians year-round); and the short-eared owl and the diminutive saw-whet owl were present only in winter. It seems that great horned, screech-, and long-eared owls loom larger than the others. Aside from the fact that the first two of these are widespread residents, it is easy to understand why they might be startling. For example, the long-eared owl, which the Cherokee perceived as especially alarming, hoots up to two hundred times when advertising itself, each hoot several seconds apart; when disturbed, it barks and shrieks. In 1925, the ornithologist William Brewster remarked that a large female shrieked at him, flew to the ground, erected her feathers, and rotated and cupped her wings menacingly, swaying her head back and forth. When alert, long-eared owls are also well known for standing rigidly upright; in wintertime groups, their bodies compressed vertically, horns erect, and piercing yellow eyes fixing the source of their interest, they are unsettling in appearance.[40]

Despite the occasional ambivalence, it is interesting that birds perceived as dangerous and malevolent by southern Indians were to a degree regarded in the same way by newcomers of European and African descent. Since antiquity, Europeans had regarded owls as wise or as ominously connected with evil and death; despite the great difficulty of translation, eight of the twenty unclean birds mentioned in Leviticus and Deuteronomy might have been owls. Through time the malevolent associations prevailed. In England, the call of a tawny or a barn owl was "a sign of death," and southerners of European descent shared the basic belief that owls, as birds of "witchcraft, death and doom," were negative forces. So, apparently, did at least some Americans of African descent. Why this might be, and why it was shared with native southerners, can surely

FIGURE 144.
Long-eared Owl.
*Hand-colored
engraving by
Robert Havell from
a painting by John
James Audubon,*
Birds of America,
*vol. 4 (1835–38),
plate 333. A very
dangerous owl (and
transformed witch)
for the Cherokee. Rare
Books and Special
Collections, Thomas
Cooper Library,
University of South
Carolina.*

be traced to the birds themselves: their nocturnal habits; their silence in flight; their incredible lightness for their size; their enormous external ear openings (the "ears" of a great-horned or a long-eared owl have to do not with hearing but perhaps with display); their ability to swivel their heads to gaze behind with large and in some cases strikingly yellow eyes; and their vocal repertory of hoots, moans, whinnies, hisses, and other

PLATE XCVII.

Little Screech Owl. STRIX ASIO. *Lton. Adult 1, Young 2.3. Jersey Pine Pinus inops.*

FIGURE 145. Little Screech Owl (eastern screech-owl). *Hand-colored engraving by Robert Havell from a painting by John James Audubon,* Birds of America, *vol. 1 (1827–30), plate 97. Another bird with weird calls and nocturnal habits widely perceived as dangerous. Rare Books and Special Collections, Thomas Cooper Library, University of South Carolina.*

weird calls, as well as snapping, on occasion, the upper and lower bills. The barn owl, for example, known colloquially in English as the monkey-face owl, utters a variety of rattles and screams that many find disconcerting. These traits, most of which do not fit neatly within the category to which other "birds" belong, make them prime candidates for fear, augury, magic, taboo, or other special consideration.[41]

CEREMONY AND PERFORMANCE

As the green corn matured in July 1905, the anthropologist Frank Speck noted that over one hundred Yuchis assembled in the town square for ceremonies that continued intermittently, with time out for ordinary household tasks, over a period of seven days. The rites included dances, renewal of the town fire, fasting, drinking an emetic, and scarification. One dance was eye-catching by any stretch of the imagination. In it the performers waved their arms as if they were wings, sometimes moving their arms quickly and sometimes slowly, with palms down. Five times, as if they were performing refrains, the dancers, Speck said, "all bent over, spat and hissed like buzzards disgorging food," a sign of bad taste in the mouth and bad breath.[42]

This dance for the buzzard or vulture was one of many performed by the Yuchi for a range of animate and inanimate things, ancient and new, including birds like the northern bobwhite, wild turkey, owl, chicken, and duck. They danced for clan animals like the buzzard, animals useful in subsistence, the spirits of animals that could cause sickness unless placated, and for pleasure. Each dance was expressive and highly suggestive. The duck dance, which was intended to influence the availability of ducks, ended in cries imitative of these birds, including a nasalized "hank" repeated rapidly. In the chicken dance, men and women held hands, and men, like cocks, "were allowed liberties" with their partners. There was little difficulty knowing what bird (or other animal) a particular dance was for, since the performers gestured or cried out in a manner imitative of it.[43]

Throughout the South, birds figured often in performance and ceremony, often through their feathers; many Indians adorned themselves with feathers, such as the seventeenth-century Powhatan, who wore long feathers in their hair, or the eighteenth-century Carolina Siouan men, who "dress'd up with Feathers" for a dance of welcome.[44] Like the Yuchi, Indians across the region danced, often in connection with the green corn ceremony, in order to appease animals deemed potentially dangerous or to mark others considered important, naming the dances for the animals. The dances ranged widely in time, from the seventeenth through twentieth centuries (some continue today), as well as in place, being widely spread throughout the region. For example, each fall the Alabama danced to the "horned" (presumably great horned) owl; the Catawba performed nighttime dances, including one in fall for wild geese; the Choctaw often ornamented themselves with plumes and danced for the duck, the quail, the owl, and (each holding an eagle wing in his hand) the eagle; and the Chickasaw performed clan

FIGURE 146. Turkey Buzzard (turkey vulture). *Hand-colored engraving by Robert Havell from a painting by John James Audubon,* Birds of America, *vol. 2 (1831–34), plate 151. An important bird for many Indians in the region, from myth to medicine. Rare Books and Special Collections, Thomas Cooper Library, University of South Carolina.*

and other dances for the crow, the duck, the quail, the turkey, and the chicken. When they danced, the performers often accessorized with feathers: white egret feathers attached to their hats and trimmed so they trembled; multicolored bunches of feathers in hatbands; turkey-, vulture-, or eagle-tail fans in their hands; or feathers at the top of long thin poles.[45]

Like others in the South, the Creek danced. Their creator and most important deity, the Master of Breath, often identified with the Sun, was responsible for dances and therefore for the propitiation of animals and the continued well-being of the people. In the early nineteenth century, the Creek accessorized with or used feathers not only when they performed certain dances but when they witnessed them, dressed in turbans or, in the case of a chief, a tall black hat, both feathered with ostrich plumes, eagle feathers, or black feathers. Performers danced chicken and duck dances in thanks for these birds' support of human life; they danced to the long-eared and the great horned owls (both possible human ghosts) in order to placate and prevent them from causing death; and they danced for the turkey vulture, because it is a clan animal, in Yuchi fashion circling and waving or, rather, flapping their arms and bending over at intervals to hiss and spit and feign disgorging food. Other dances related to birds were the quail, turkey, long-eared owl, and feather dances. In each dance they sang songs that evoked the bird, rapidly quacking the duck dance to a close, for example, or hooting the long-eared owl dance to its end.[46]

Feathers pervaded the widespread green corn ceremony, or what was known in English as the busk (from the Creek *puskita*, "fast"). Many Indians, like the Chickasaw, favored white feathers because they stood for peace and purity and wore white swan skins and tufts of white feathers on their heads. For the Creek, the ceremony marked a period of peace, a "white" day when one wore white feathers, produced white smoke, and drank the black drink conceived as "white" from a beloved tree — all in a "yard of peace." Creek men and women stuck their hair "full of Feathers" when they danced, and in the important feather dance honoring the feather for its power to shield people from the aggression of human and other-than-human enemies, the leaders carried tomahawk-shaped boards ornamented with black and white feathers, and dancers carried poles with white (alternatively red) or red (alternatively black) feathers, depending on clan membership. The feathers were those of *wagohatki* (*hatki* means white), said to be "white egrets, snowy herons, or wood ibis," and the Creek Indians who lived in the town of Taskigi were said never to have "molested or handled this bird for any other purpose."

Everywhere this ceremony represented the height of community ritual, a moment to celebrate agricultural fertility, propitiation of spirits, forgiveness, peace, social solidarity, and other values through fasting, purification, dancing, and social events such as the ball game. The events took place in rectangular public grounds where people erected a pole at the top of which could be found a sculpted figure; as described at the

Creek town of Kashita in 1820, "a high pole, like [the English] may-poles, with a bird at the top, round which" the green corn dance unfolded.[47]

The feather dance, remarked the anthropologist Frank Speck, was "rather spectacular":

> Picture the town square with its four brush covered arbors filled with interested spectators. . . . The dancers clad in their calico finery, with ostrich and other highly colored plumes in their head bands and their fluttering wands, start circling in a single file behind the leader, the drum and hand rattle beating time. At the end of the second song they group together in a squad, elevate their wands and rush whooping toward the west arbor. . . . Bringing themselves suddenly to a halt, they raise the wands high, then drive them into the earth before the arbor.

They then repeated the performance at the three other arbors.[48]

In 1944, Speck recalled an earlier visit to the Rappahannock of tidewater Virginia, whose chief taught the ditty,

> Is Jerry dead
> Oh yes
> Is Jerry dead
> Oh yes
> Is his eyes out
> Oh no
> Is his eyes out
> Oh no
> Plinka, plinka mo' meat
> Plinka, plinka mo' meat
> Plinka, plinka mo' meat
> S-s-s-s-s-sock 'im, S-s-s-s-s-sock 'im.

Like many tales and songs in the South, this one betrays a narrative link with people of African descent. The Rappahannock used to sing this song, a dialogue between old buzzards about pecking the eyes out of a supposedly dead mule named Jerry. While singing the song, the chief bent over, shuffled, and flapped his arms up and down like a turkey vulture. In 1944, Nanticokes on the eastern shore of the Chesapeake Bay laughed at a rendition of this performance. They had their own story about Buzzard and Crow, and a dog that was not quite dead, as well as their own taboo on harming vultures. In fact the vulture's role as a scavenger, which helped control the spread of disease, was considered so important that the Nanticokes placed carrion in convenient, safe places for them to eat.[49]

On the one hand, humorous, on the other, spiritual; on the one hand, ancient, on the other, a product inseparable from newer immigrants to the South: this tale takes us all the way back to John White's "Flyer" and the widespread if not universal belief among southern Indians of birds — numerous and different birds — as animate beings intersecting with people's lives, for better or worse, as omens, as diviners, as harmful, as helpful, as witches, as healers, in need of propitiation, requiring thanks, connected always with life and death.

FIGURE 147.
Blue Jay. *Pen and ink with watercolor, associated with John White, ca. 1585–1600. Inscribed: "Artamóckes. The linguist. A birde that imitateth and useth the sounde and tunes almost of all the birdes in the countrie. As bigg as a Pigeon." A confused inscription: the linguist and imitator refer to the northern mockingbird, not the blue jay. Sloane volume.* © The Trustees of the British Museum, sl,5270.94.

Bird Spirits & Spirit-Birds

When he or she became ill, a Creek Indian often brought in a specialist to figure out why. This was not a simple matter, because any number of possible agents or processes, singly or in combination, affected a person, including one's own transgressions; the loss of the soul; the sun; a witch, sorcerer, or ghost; fire; thunder; a rainbow; or an array of other spiritual beings — including spirits of birds such as the buzzard, the turkey, the owl, or the eagle. If specific, the symptoms helped pinpoint the cause and suggest a therapy. If a person was afflicted with diarrhea or nausea, for example, a bird spirit was responsible, and to effect a cure a medicine man took a bird's nest, steeped it in water, and before the patient drank the infusion, sang the following song:

> They chatter, they chatter, they chatter, they chatter,
> they chatter and flitter about,
> they chatter, they chatter, they chatter, they chatter,
> their settlement is here
> gathering together they make a fluttering noise
> martin
> tins tins [blue jay's cry].[1]

Southern Indians widely believed that bird spirits caused and cured sickness. Like the Creek, the Chickasaw sought the cause of sickness in an animal spirit or sorcerer. If they had a severe headache, they thought that an eagle must be responsible; if they were sleepy, then an owl was the cause; if their eyes were itchy and watery, then a screech-owl was up to no good. Medicine men, according to the eighteenth-century trader James Adair, tried to transfer sickness from their patient to owls or eagles, using the feathers of these birds. They invoked the raven, "mimic[king] his croaking voice." They "solicit[ed]" the eagle "as he soar[ed] in the heavens" because of its "supposed communicative virtues" and because, Adair ventured (with his consuming interest in parallels between American Indians and Israelites and, no doubt, knowledge of relevant passages in Exodus and Deuteronomy), it was "according to its Indian name, a cherubimical emblem, and the king of birds, of prodigious strength, swiftness of wing, majestic stature, and loving its young ones so tenderly, as to carry them on its back, and teach them to fly."[2] Indians throughout the South not only called upon the spirits of birds for cures but used bird products in curing, from the Pampticough Indians in the Carolinas, who employed "the soft Down growing on a Turkey's Rump" (and rotted grains of corn) to dry an open ulcer on someone's leg, to the Caddo, who deployed feathers and bird-bone flutes in curing rituals.[3]

FIGURE 148.
The blue Linnet (indigo bunting). *Hand-colored etching by Mark Catesby, Natural History (1731–43), plate 45. A bird invoked by the Cherokee to control wind. John Carter Brown Library at Brown University.*

Many of the deeper and more nuanced meanings of birds, as well as the traditional cultural contexts in which birds figured, sadly remain opaque or elusive. A hint of what they must have entailed is, however, contained in impressively detailed information on the Eastern and the Oklahoma Cherokee collected from 1890 on by a succession of ethnographers and Cherokees, including James Mooney and Swimmer, John Witthoft and Will West Long, Raymond D. Fogelson, and Jack, Anna, and Alan Kilpatrick.[4]

Birds figured fully in Cherokee magical formulas, songs, and incantations designed to influence the course of love, hunting, illness, and other human affairs. The Cherokee called the formulas *idi:gawé:sdi* — the singular form, *i:gawé:sdi*, means "something that one says (or merely thinks) or sings" — and individuals and medicine men used them to ensure optimum conditions and results in love, hunting, witchcraft, and many other endeavors.[5] They frequently invoked not just bird spirits but spirit-birds to bring about desired ends.[6] Spirit-birds, which live "on high" where they can intercede in the affairs of humankind, include a mythical gigantic, human-eating, raptorial bird named Dhla:nuwa; Tsugv:tsala:la, which resembles a northern bobwhite; and Di:sdi, a very small, blue bird. The first of these is rather frightening, but the latter two are beautiful and invoked in affairs relating to love.[7] Bird spirits and spirit-birds are often colored meaningfully, for example, red purple martin, white bluebird, black yellow-breasted chat, red Tsugv:tsala:la. In Cherokee culture, red stands for power or victory; white for serenity, happiness, and peace; black for death; blue and yellow for loneliness, weakness, misfortune, and death; purple for witchcraft and evil; and brown for normality. As goes the color, so goes the bird or spirit-bird.[8]

The birds mentioned in the formulas are remarkably varied. The Cherokee invoked the osprey, kingfisher, and eagle to ensure success in fishing, the indigo bunting and bluebird to control wind, the ruby-throated hummingbird to shorten the way home, and the Dhla:nuwa, eastern wood-pewee, great crested flycatcher, purple martin, and chimney swift for success in the ball game. From the standpoint of natural history, a lot of this "makes sense," in that ospreys, kingfishers, and eagles are good fishers, hummingbirds fly fast and directly (and are, as Audubon put it, "courageous"), purple martins and chimney swifts are swift and agile in flight, and martins and great crested flycatchers fiercely defend themselves and their territories. Moreover, from the standpoint of Cherokee culture, the purple martin played a role in the mythical ball game between the birds and the animals.[9]

The list of birds invoked in spells used by men to win over women is long, including the white-fronted goose, gull, common raven, long-eared owl, eagle, kestrel, osprey,

FIGURE 149.
The Purple Martin.
*Hand-colored etching
by Mark Catesby,*
Natural History
*(1731–43), plate 51. An
important territorial
bird and strong flyer
that the Cherokee
attracted to gourds
hollowed out as
nests above their
gardens and invoked
for success in the ball
game. John Carter
Brown Library at
Brown University.*

red-headed woodpecker, Carolina wren, great crested flycatcher, purple martin, eastern kingbird, northern cardinal, eastern bluebird, loggerhead shrike, ruby-throated hummingbird, mourning dove, yellow-breasted chat, scarlet tanager, eastern meadowlark, and others.[10]

Some spells were aggressive and others less so. One designed to get a woman invoked the spirits of powerful birds:

Wa-hi! Wa-hi! Wa-hi! Wa-hi!

I, I am a Wizard.
I just took your heart away from you.
Already I have just taken it away from you. . . .

I, I am a Wizard.
I just took your heart away from you.
Throughout the night your soul will be lonely.
Already I have taken it away from you. . . .

I, I am a Wizard.
Your heart was just taken by me.
Throughout the night your soul will be lonely.

Wa-hi! Wa-hi! Wa-hi! Wa-hi!

Your heart! Your heart!
Dhla:nuwa!
Gigi! Gigi!
He just took your heart away from you.
Already He has taken it away from you. . . .

The *Dhla:nuwa* just carried it away.
He just took your heart away from you.
Throughout the night your soul will be lonely.
Already He has taken it away from you. . . .

· · · · · · · · · · · ·

The Eagle just took it away from you.
Throughout the night your soul will be lonely.
Already He has taken it away from you
He just took your heart away from you.
The Eagle just took it away from you.

· · · · · · · · · · ·

The Long-eared Owl just took it away from you.
Throughout the night your soul will be lonely.
Already He has taken it away from you.
He just took your heart away from you.
The Long-Eared Owl just took it away from you.

· · · · · · · · · · · ·

The Barred Owl just took it away from you.
Throughout the night your soul will be lonely.
Already He has taken it away from you.
He just took your heart away from you.
The Barred Owl just took it away from you.

These birds or, in the case of Dhla:nuwa, spirit-bird, are all strong, and the owls, as we have seen, have "sinister reputations."[11]

Cherokee men also used positive spells to attract women, including the following about the "redbird," or northern cardinal:

I am dressed as well as the Redbird
I am as handsome as the Redbird
I am as masculine as the Redbird
I can do as much as the Redbird
I can say as much as the Redbird:
Dho:tsu! Dho:tsu:hwi![12]

And another:

Now! Listen! *Ha!* I, who am as beautiful as the Red
   Tsugv:tsala:la, speak.
I, who am as beautiful as the Shrike, speak.
I, who am as beautiful as the Bluebird, speak.
I, who am as beautiful as the *Di:sdi*, speak.
Now! Listen! Yellow Mockingbird, I have a nest.
Then all you women, the Bluebird has just come by:
It was my body![13]

The "yellow mockingbird" is the yellow-breasted chat, which
is invoked here and in other love incantations perhaps because of
its acrobatic aerial courtship displays and extensive mimicking
vocal repertoire.

The Cherokee attributed many ailments to animal spirits and
dreams, either of which might involve birds. The yellow-breasted
chat, for example, was believed to cause urinary-tract infection
(on the basis of a principle of similarity or imitation, intensely
yellow urine is caused by a bird whose underparts are intensely
yellow). They tabooed certain birds for consumption because
they were powerful; vultures, for example, although one could eat them as a hedge
against smallpox. They prohibited the consumption of others because they were linked
to certain ailments: chickens to diarrhea (because they ate feces); turkey necks to
goiter (because of that bird's caruncles, or "kernels"). If they thought that birds caused
a particular illness, the Cherokee avoided the shadows of flying birds in the belief that
they made it worse.[14]

The Cherokee also believed that bird spirits cured ailments — the bittern, goose,
snipe, swan, and sandpiper all healed worms; the eagle, osprey, killdeer, and kingfisher
took care of pain in various places and "yellow" navel; the raven could eliminate sharp
pains, and birds naturally yellow like the goldfinch or colored yellow like the yellow
passenger pigeon were called upon to rid the body of biliac disorders with yellow symptoms. Incantations involving them were used to effect cures. If the Cherokee thought
that a fish had made them sick, they invoked the osprey, a heron, or another fish-eating
bird to bring them relief; if an insect, then an insectivorous bird; if a flock of northern
cardinals or the shadow of a bird, then the kestrel; if the rabbit, then the red-shouldered
hawk. The raven, the eagle, and the vulture were regarded as especially potent in com-
bating or curing pains and other ailments, and the vulture was also prophylactic when
its feathers were hung in the entrance or a carcass hung up in a room and allowed to
decay in the belief that it would keep disease at bay.[15]

Consider the following incantation, intended to cure toothache:

FIGURE 150.
Tyrant Fly-catcher
(eastern kingbird).
*Hand-colored
engraving by
Robert Havell from
a painting by John
James Audubon,
Birds of America,
vol. 1 (1827–30),
plate 79. One of
many birds invoked
by Cherokee men in
their incantations
designed to woo
women. Rare
Books and Special
Collections, Thomas
Cooper Library,
University of South
Carolina.*

FIGURE 151.
(Left) Northern Cardinal. *Pen and ink with watercolor, associated with John White, ca. 1585–1600. Inscribed: "Meesquouns. Almost as bigg as a Parratt." The Carolina parakeet was in fact half the size of the northern cardinal. Sloane volume. © The Trustees of the British Museum, SL,5270.92.*

FIGURE 152.
(Right) Yellow-breasted Chat. *Hand-colored engraving by Robert Havell from a painting by John James Audubon,* Birds of America, *vol. 2 (1831–34), plate 137. A warbler with a spectacular courtship display, this chat, known colloquially as the yellow mockingbird, not surprisingly figured in Cherokee men's formulas intended to win over women. Rare Books and Special Collections, Thomas Cooper Library, University of South Carolina.*

Pileated Woodpecker, very quickly You have just come to make it resound.

You have just come by to get out the White "Insect."

Hairy Woodpecker, very quickly You have just come to make it resound.

You have just come by to get out the White "Insect."

Great Crested Flycatcher, — Ha! — very quickly You have just come to make it resound.

You have just come by to get out the Red "Insect."

Red-Headed Woodpecker, — Ha! — very quickly You have just come to make it resound.

You have just come by to get out the Red "Insect."

To relieve toothache, the Cherokee invoked insect-eating birds, including, in this particular formula, the great crested flycatcher, whose reputation for being aggressive was well deserved, and woodpeckers. Given their foraging behavior and rapping and drilling, what species could be better than woodpeckers to eliminate tooth pain?[16]

Like other southern Indians, the Cherokee were deeply ambivalent about and fearful of nocturnal birds. Even the northern mockingbird, which kept hours around the clock, was suspect if it sang at night near the bed of someone ill. They imagined fire (the sacred fire) as an old woman who, if neglected in the offerings she should receive to placate her, might take vengeance in the guise of an owl or a whip-poor-will. These people, we have seen, regarded owls as ill omens that forecast misfortune or death; used the same word for witch, great horned owl, and the especially dreaded long-eared owl; and believed that any owl might be a morphed witch.[17]

The Cherokee invoked owls and other nocturnal birds in their incantations; the screech-owl, for example, was invoked in one about apprehending criminals. Two others that involve nocturnal birds follow. In one, the whip-poor-will is called upon to make a woman restless and to protect against evil thought.

> Now! The Whippoorwill knows that I have just struck you, [name], you woman.
> I just turned over your soul.
> Sleepless, you will be unable to think of anything else!

In the other, the long-eared or the great horned owl is deployed in the search for the souls of one's enemies. The chilling incantation reads in free translation:

> Bring me your soul.
> I am a black owl of the night.
> Your name is Night.
> It [the owl] hunts your heart.
> Bring me your soul.
> I am a brown owl of the night.
> Your name is Night.
> It hunts your heart.
> Bring me your soul.
> I am a yellow owl of the night.
> Your name is Night.
> It hunts your heart.
> Bring me your soul.
> I am a white owl of the night.
> Your name is Night.
> It hunts your heart.[18]

Another greatly feared spiritual being took on attributes of a bird: the so-called Raven Mocker, who flew, the Cherokee said, with arms outstretched like wings, cawing like a raven in free fall, trailing sparks behind, and tormenting the sick. The Raven Mocker had the capacity to take life. Many assumed that it was a witch transformed into a raven, for witches had the ability to metamorphose into this bird or owls, eagles, moles, or other beings.[19]

These magical formulas and incantations reveal that in the past, birds were never far from Cherokee minds. Their avian world was full and rich. They distinguished by name many birds that figured meaningfully in cultural contexts bearing on sickness, well-being, emotions like love, and aesthetics. Apparently they slighted or ignored other birds. If it were not for the vagaries of cultural memory, we might know far more. One

FIGURE 153. *(Left)* The American Goldfinch. *Hand-colored etching by Mark Catesby, Natural History (1731–43), plate 43. One of many yellow birds named by the Cherokee in formulas whose goal was the elimination of disorders with yellow symptoms. John Carter Brown Library at Brown University.*

FIGURE 154. *(Above)* The Fishing Hawk (osprey). *Hand-colored etching by Mark Catesby, Natural History (1771), plate 2. This expert "fishing hawk," as it was colloquially known, was invoked by the Cherokee for well-being, if they thought that a fish had made them sick, or for success in fishing, but otherwise this widespread raptor seems not to have been especially common in the ethno-ornithology of the South. John Carter Brown Library at Brown University.*

Oklahoma Cherokee lamented in the mid-twentieth century that "the things" that people "told long ago are very interesting to hear," but "one can only remember only a small amount of it," and "many people do not tell the stories right: they get them all mixed up. That is the reason why these stories sometimes vary. Some people know more of the stories, some less." Another bemoaned, "It is amazing, the number of things they used to tell in comparison to what they tell today. It is very difficult to find someone who can tell these stories, someone who can recall them." In these instances, time itself has been an enemy to the process of storytelling as well as individual and collective memory. Another contributing factor was enforced relocation from homelands in the South to Oklahoma, where new environmental circumstances (and different birds) presented themselves.[20]

Forgetting, or never knowing, is one kind of problem. Another is that while the system invoked by the formulas might remain intact on the surface, the assumptions underlying it as well as its specific meanings can change or disappear. In 1958, the anthropologist Raymond Fogelson elicited from a Cherokee consultant a formula that was identical to one collected by James Mooney sixty years before. In Mooney's time, the Cherokee used the formula to help frightened children, who were being eaten, they

FIGURE 155. Raven (northern raven). *Hand-colored engraving by Robert Havell from a painting by John James Audubon,* Birds of America 2 *(1831–34), plate 101. A potent bird linked by some to war and scalps, by others to success in curing and the courtship of women, the raven was also sculpted in stone tobacco pipes and associated with the fearsome Cherokee other-than-human being, the Raven Mocker, and with witches. Rare Books and Special Collections, Thomas Cooper Library, University of South Carolina.*

believed, by four disease spirits, including a screech-owl and a "hoot" owl. In 1958, the Cherokee ascribed the children's symptoms to high blood pressure or a weak heart (the disease theory of Americans of European descent), and as spirits to banish they selected ones merely because they were perceived as frightening. Nothing remained of the idea of evil disease spirits.[21]

FIGURE 156.
The King-Fisher
(belted kingfisher).
*Hand-colored etching
by Mark Catesby,*
Natural History
*(1771), plate 69. A bird
important enough
to be a person in
the mythical corpus
of several Indian
cultures in the
South, Kingfisher,
the Cherokee say,
received his bill in
thanks for having
killed Blacksnake
after he ate young
flickers. John Carter
Brown Library at
Brown University.*

Sacred & Secular Narratives

Through time, southern Indians have told a variety of stories about their past, some rooted deeply in the sacredness of genesis and myth, others nearer in time to immediate ancestors and today and of a more secular cast. They embrace narratives ranging widely from those recounting the beginning of life and human society, and the origin of corn, to accounts of the adventures of supernatural beings, heroes, and tricksters and of recent history. Birds figure in many, their roles ranging from protagonist to minor character.[1]

In one Chitimacha origin myth, for example, a group of young men walk north to the edge of the sky, where the rim crushes several, but six continue to the zenith, the home of a supreme being named *kutnehin*, said by some to be the sun and by many to be a trickster. Here they remain until they wish to return to earth, but to do so they must morph into other forms. Three who change into animals fall to their death. A fourth succeeds as a spider, bringing shamanism to people, and the remaining two descend to earth in the form of a dove and an eagle, transporting corn and the knowledge of fishing, respectively. A second myth nearer in time to today, but still in the distant past, relates that a great flood had covered the world except for two people who live in an earthen pot; a red-headed woodpecker, who clings to the sky above the water except for the base of its tail; and a dove, who flies to the sky. The leader of the earthen-pot people sends the woodpecker to find land, to no avail, and then sends the dove, who returns with a grain of sand that becomes dry land.[2]

In another story of events that took place long ago, a mad man wants to set fire to the world, and a small bird, presumably black in color, makes fun of him, so the man throws a shell at it, hitting it in the shoulder and giving it, the red-winged blackbird, red epaulets.[3]

These are typical tales in a region where, not surprisingly, the intersections of birds and people are reflected in myth and folktale. In them the boundaries between birds, men, and other beings are amorphous and easily transgressed — as in North America generally. Characters, including birds, are often personified — Buzzard, not buzzard; Chickadee, not chickadee — and, with humans, undergo metamorphosis or transformation: blackbirds and crows are the transformed ashes of a cannibal-being; humans change themselves, or are changed by another agency, into a duck, a crow, a flying feather, a puff of down, a quail (northern bobwhite), or a Cooper's hawk, and change back again. Humans and birds converse, court, marry, kill, and eat each other. And at times birds are just birds, doing things appropriate to their kind, often, as in real life, being eaten by others.[4]

FIGURE 157.
The crested Titmouse (tufted titmouse). *Hand-colored etching by Mark Catesby,* Natural History *(1731–43), plate 57. The tufted titmouse figures in one of the most important Cherokee myths, inadvertently misleading people seeking to kill a fearsome cannibal stone-being and being punished by them for their false conclusion about what Titmouse had voiced. John Carter Brown Library at Brown University.*

GENESIS AND COSMOS

In general, birds play relatively minor and ambivalent roles in narratives of genesis. There are, however, exceptions. Both the Tunica and the Cherokee link birds to the important deity the Sun: the Tunica because a girl married to Kingfisher ate only minnows and, ashamed, danced into the sky to become the Sun; the Cherokee through Cardinal, the daughter of the Sun who died and was brought back to life and kept in a box, from which she escaped. The Cherokee also believe that Thunder appointed Eagle as "Ruler," with the ability to mold animals and birds; that he subsequently refused Quail's selfish request to kill people when they saw him fly, leaving him instead to frighten them with the explosive sound of his flying; and that he made Chickadee the fortune-teller, gave Redbird or Cardinal the power to sing when rain is on the way, and turned Shrike into a dance caller. At times birds fall short in performing tasks, as in a Cherokee tale in which Raven, Screech Owl, Barred Owl, and Great Horned Owl all failed (where Water Spider succeeded) to obtain fire for animals. Or when Snipe (in a Koasati story) claimed that he could fly to the very zenith of the universe: given the important task of taking sickness there in a bottle, he failed to fly high enough and dropped the bottle on the descent; it burst disastrously, releasing sickness everywhere.[5]

Chickadee plays one of the most important foundational roles when the Cherokee invoke him and Tufted Titmouse to rid them of a horrible stone-being with a taste for human liver. According to the story, Titmouse's calls unfortunately mimic the word for heart, which misleads people to aim at the stone-being's chest with their weapons. When they fail to harm the beast, who resumes his terrible ways, the people conclude that Titmouse has lied and so they cut out his tongue. Then Chickadee reveals the vital spot in the stone-being's hand, and the people aim there and at last kill this dreadful being. From this time on, Chickadee was deemed the truth-teller, as well as a fortune-teller able to divine the arrival of visitors and other events, while Titmouse was ever after a liar.[6]

BUZZARD

Buzzard also presents an exception to the general statement that the role of birds is relatively minor in narratives of genesis and early times. Buzzard created landscape across the South, making, according to the Creek, the Yuchi, and the Cherokee, the mountains and valleys. The Yuchi maintain that Buzzard's task had actually been to level the earth, but when he stretched his wings, he tired, wavered, and produced the ridges seen in today's countryside. The Cherokee say that this Buzzard was a great one in size and the father of known vultures.[7]

Buzzard figures in other myths, including a Choctaw tale in which he transports men who are brothers from the Sun to their own land; this was at a time when giant female and male birds made thunder and lightning — the noise of thunder representing egg laying in the clouds.[8] In an Alabama story, an old woman keeps the sun hidden from others until Rabbit obtains it by tricking her and then asks Buzzard and a bird named Tciktcikano — said to be "like a wren"; house wren is *cehcekwuce* in Creek — to fly it back to the sky. In return, Buzzard is granted exclusive access to carrion, and Tciktcikano, after regular morning bathing in cold water, is assured of good health.[9]

Consistent with other aspects of the relationship between men and vultures, the Cherokee, Creek, Hitichi, and Koasati all represent Buzzard in their tales as a healer. In one story, Buzzard uses his down and one of his feathers to mend Pigeon Hawk, who had managed to split a dangerous piece of iron and almost kill himself in the process. Like a medicine man, Buzzard was not above trickery or malice: in a widely distributed tale, Bear tricks Rabbit into stabbing himself in his side, and when blood gushes from the wound, Rabbit's wife calls in "the doctor," Turkey Buzzard, who eats Rabbit on the sly. In one version of this tale, the animals subsequently shoot Buzzard through his bill with their arrows, shaping the nostrils as they are today and making it, as Buzzard remarks, "good for me to breathe through," and indeed, as turkey vultures do today, good to locate carrion through renowned powers of smell alone.[10]

FLOOD BIRDS

Like many North American Indians, southern Indians hold that a flood once covered the earth; the idea is indigenous even if missionaries of various denominations influenced the forms it has taken. Woodpeckers figure in many southern Indian deluge tales. The Creek, Chitimacha, and Alabama all have stories about a red-headed woodpecker that, during the deluge, clings to the sky except for its tail, which dips into the water and becomes discolored.[11] According to the Creek, water covered the earth in the beginning, but one or two woodpeckers clung above its surface to the vault of the sky, and, again, only their tails got wet and muddy. In different Creek and Alabama versions, the woodpecker is the northern flicker, the red-headed woodpecker, or a larger woodpecker the Alabama called *titka*, which is perhaps the ivory-billed (in Creek, *tetkv* is a large black woodpecker). In the Creek version, the animals gather in a council to discuss whether there will continue to be water or land on earth. Eagle, who is the chief, decides that there will be land. Dove volunteers to find it and flies off but returns unsuccessful; then Crawfish dives deeply and succeeds in bringing up the makings of land. In an Alabama version of this story, two pigeons, after a failed attempt in which they find only worm leavings, discover a blade of grass, and the waters recede.[12]

In yet another variation, the Choctaw Noah gathers all birds except the yellow-breasted sapsucker (*biskinik*), the northern flicker (*fitukhak*), and a "large red-headed woodpecker" (*bakbak*), which eludes him by using strong, sharp claws to hop from one to the other side of trees (as woodpeckers often do when displaying), flies high to escape the rising waters, and finally clings to the sky — but their tails become wet, forked, and notched (which they still are today). The Great Spirit rewards them for their skill by making them guardians of the Choctaw, in which role they appear on the eve of the ball game and also warn war parties of approaching enemies with constant flitting about and calling. (In a clearly related Koasati story, a woodpecker warns an orphan, who rubs red paint on the bird's head, that a cannibal-being is pursuing him.)[13]

Other southern Indians believe that the creator brought the deluge because of his displeasure with humankind. In these tales, birds figure in life after the deluge, either finding land or discovering corn. Thus the Caddo keep a bird (*o-wah*) captive during the flood but after a month set it free, and when it returns with straw, they retrace its path to land. According to the Choctaw (and with clear parallels to the story in Genesis of how Noah found land after the deluge), a dove successfully discovers grass beyond the waters or disappears in the direction of land, after a large black bird — a raven of ill omen or more neutrally charged crow — either denies a call for assistance or flies off and never returns. In some versions the bird that succeeds is described as bluish with red eyes or bluish with red eyes and a red bill, and it is called Puchi Yushubah (Lost Pigeon). If based in nature, the first description evokes the passenger pigeon and the second the red-billed pigeon, a bird unknown in the South today. As for corn (maize), some Choctaws state that a crow brings a grain from beyond flood waters and in this way discovers it; according to the Chickasaw the bird is a raven, according to the Chitimacha and the Catawba, a dove.[14]

In a related story about woodpeckers and water, the Alabama tell how a man gambles away all the water in the world until Bicici'hka, a "small speckled woodpecker with a red head," lands on a tree-size stalk of cane, hears a noise within, and pecks its way to water, which, when released, fills the creeks and rivers to the delight of all.[15]

OWLS

Not surprisingly, owls figure widely in tales. Collectively the meanings are ambivalent, ranging from malevolent to harmless, and from significant to insignificant. Owl rarely plays a foundational role; one exception — a negative one — is when the Alabama emerged on the surface of the earth and heard hooting; scared, most people returned underground, accounting, the Alabama say, for their low population.[16]

Some Alabama and Koasati stories about Owl explore this negative or dangerous side. In one, Owl reveals the location of a bear to an orphan boy tending a hunting party and then divines adultery in one of the hunter's wives. In another, Horned Owl tries to convince a man to throw him Hawk by promising him that he will henceforth see at night. But Hawk represents Horned Owl as "very bad" and a wizard and eventually decapitates Horned Owl after the man refuses to give him up. In gratitude, Hawk gives the man a wing feather with which he can kill "anything." In another version of this story, Pigeon Hawk grants the man good fortune in hunting. In yet another tale about a "bead-spitter" who magically makes beads, Owl (called Night Owl) is revealed as a malevolent person who kills the bead maker, dances with entrails around his neck, and has designs on and beats women, and must be killed or left alone. In other stories, the Caddo represent Medicine-Screech-Owl as having "more powers" than the all-powerful Moon, and the Alabama tell about Horned Owl-Crawfish, a large, hooting, vaguely threatening ghost or other supernatural being.

Other tales about owls told by the Creek, Koasati, Hitichi, and Natchez are less substantial. In one, Owl tries to push over a house and instead bangs his head and fails, making himself "humpshouldered." In another, Alligator or Wolf chases Rabbit to a hollow tree and leaves Owl on guard while he gets an axe, but Rabbit tricks Owl into releasing him (in one version, Wolf clubs Owl, giving him his hooting voice). In a third, Owl fights and scratches a man who has yearned, Owl thinks, for Owl's wife. In several tales, Owl is outdone by other animals, like lowly Perch; small, yellow Mouse, who slanders Owl; and Turkey, who bests Owl in an exchange of calls.[17]

DANGEROUS SPIRIT-BIRDS

Southern Indians tell myths and stories about several kinds of extremely dangerous other-than-natural avian beings. Paramount among them are several large birds. One is a giant, swift, long-tailed blue bird that the Creek call the King of Birds, which ate people during the period when they wandered on the surface of the land. Ultimately, people in league with its son, a red rat, vanquished it.[18] This was akin to the large and powerful bird, somewhat like a giant eagle, that took an Alabama Indian away as food for the young in its nest. But the captive hid in a hollow log until he was able to return to earth on the back of a young bird. Other examples are "Big-crow," who took the Hitichi away in similar fashion, and a giant Turkey, regarded by the Seminole as the king of the birds, who swooped down and grabbed them and the Hitichi and carried them up to the sky. This same Turkey took and displayed Seminole and Biloxi scalps and fingernails as a necklace or decoratively around his legs. Finally a dog killed him. The final example is Dhla:nuwa, the giant raptorial, human-eating bird that preyed on the Cherokee. Eventually a medicine man defeated two of them by tumbling their young from their nest into the waiting jaws of an ornithoserpentine being below, and the parent raptors disappeared forever into the sky.[19]

HOW BIRDS GOT THEIR SPOTS AND OTHER STORIES

Other contexts for birds, including those in which they are linked to more important deities, seem less momentous. People everywhere tell tales about how birds came to look and behave. The Catawba, for example, attribute Flicker's white rump and pale yellow underwings to its having carried a pack in a white sheet that rubbed against its rump and wings, and Robin's red breast to having been burned in a brush fire. Ac-

FIGURE 158. Ceramic bottle with incised raptor head. *Moundville, Tuscaloosa County, Ala., AD 1400–1550, 5.9 in. high. One of many Moundville vessels decorated with an avian motif — here and elsewhere, a raptor. At times the bird has ornithoserpentine (often rattlesnake) features or is associated with hands, eyes, crosses, and other designs. Stolen from Mound State Monument, University of Alabama Museum of Natural History, NE80. Photo courtesy of Vincas Steponaitis.*

cording to the Caddo, Buzzards were at first powerful people who kept buffaloes locked up in a cave and hoarded meat until Coyote removed a rock blocking the entrance, from which time they turned themselves into birds and ate dead things. The Cherokee say that Turkey Vulture once had beautiful crested feathers on his head and vainly refused to dirty himself scavenging carrion, so the other birds punished him by getting a buffalo — in later versions, a cow — to feign death and tighten his sphincter around Turkey Vulture's head when he came to feed, not releasing it until it was bare.

The Cherokee also remark that Kingfisher was supposed to be a water bird but lacked an appropriate bill until other-than-human beings known as Little People gave him a long bill in thanks for his having killed Blacksnake, who ate defenseless young flickers in a nest. The Cherokee also tell tales about Turkey, who swiped a scalp from Terrapin and made it his beard; Quail, who obtained his distinctive call by stealing it from Terrapin; Hummingbird — in one version he was a morphed medicine man — who obtained tobacco seeds stolen by geese; and Owl and Yellow-breasted Chat, who deceived an old woman by transforming themselves into men and marrying her daughter.[20]

There are many such stories. Some involve one animal fooling or besting another. In one widespread tale, Hummingbird and Crane (sometimes Heron) race each other, usually for the affection or hand of a woman. Crane wins because he flies at night. For some, this tale explains why ruby-throated hummingbirds eat nectar, and sandhill cranes or herons consume what is in the water; for others how being plain and steady (the crane or the heron) wins over flash and dash (the hummingbird). In a related tale, Crane bests others by whistling Panther into distraction and tricking a cannibal-being.[21]

Some birds, including cardinals ("redbirds"), blue jays, and Carolina parakeets, lend feathers and even their entire living beings to headdresses, as do jays in one tale about an orphan boy and the origin of corn, or on occasion they sing atop or next to headdresses.[22]

BIRDS AS BIRDS

In many tales birds perform as they do in nature, their roles related to their perceived strengths — but often with a twist. Kingfishers dive at fish but then turn a big one to shore so that it can be caught and cut open to release the singing head of a man. Ducks collectively pull a cannibal being to the sky. Woodpeckers open up a tree into which a cannibal has fallen. The trickster Rabbit recruits Woodpecker to peck around a tree, leaving it so thin that Rabbit cuts it down with a single blow from his axe, thereby obtaining a girl for a wife. Crane, Goose, Pelican, and Quail (in another version, ducks, geese, sandhill cranes, and quail) are delegated to watch on behalf of several brothers for the arrival of their angry father, Crane farthest away and Quail closest, because of the relative power of their calls or noise. Northern bobwhites (quail), of course, make an explosive sound with their wings when they launch themselves into the air.[23]

Turkeys and other birds, such as blackbirds, ducks, geese, quail, and parakeets, often seem merely destined for the pot, to be consumed by animal beings such as Rabbit, the region's trickster; Wildcat; or humankind.[24] The stories often take an unexpected turn: Rabbit fools turkeys to get Wildcat to consume them, not Rabbit's young, but turkeys retaliate by biting off Rabbit's tail. Or they contain a lesson: a hunter who lies still can kill turkeys just like Wildcat.[25] As implied in Seminole and Hitichi tales about being transported skyward and scalped, Turkey on occasion plays an important role. The Creek say that turkeys acquired beards when, long ago, the animals deemed Man dangerous. Rattlesnake struck and sank his fangs into Man, killing him, Turtle bit off his scalp lock, and Turkey ran away with it — but accidentally swallowed it, at which point it became the beard on his breast.[26]

These stories reveal a range both in cultural sentiments attached to birds in general and in narrative interest in particular species. Yet the birds that appear in tales are limited in kind compared to the many that lived in or migrated through the South. In the original texts as well as in the translations, their names often reveal their species, for example, (belted) kingfisher, red-headed woodpecker, quail (northern bobwhite), (Wilson's) snipe, turkey buzzard (turkey vulture), red-tailed hawk, (Carolina) parakeet, (ruby-throated) hummingbird, blue jay, yellow-breasted chat, (wild) turkey, and (American) crow. But just as often, they can be placed only in a genus, a family, or some other more inclusive category: pelican, duck, goose, hawk, owl, eagle, buzzard, woodpecker, blackbird, or bird-that-sits-on-deer. Several are confounding. Most birds in the region, including some of the most common and noteworthy, remain invisible, an absence to which we shall return.[27]

FIGURE 159. Blue Jay. Yellow-Bird or Goldfinch (American goldfinch). Baltimore Bird (Baltimore oriole). *Hand-colored engraving by Alexander Lawson based on drawing by Alexander Wilson,* American Ornithology, *vol. 1, 1808–14, plate 1. The oriole is curiously invisible in the ethno-ornithology of the South, but some native people consumed the blue jay and others used its feathers and invoked the bird to counter the ill effects of raven feathers used aggressively. John Hay Library at Brown University.*

FIGURE 160.
Great Carolina
Wren (Carolina
wren). *Hand-colored
engraving by
Robert Havell from
a painting by John
James Audubon,*
Birds of America, *vol.
1 (1827–30), plate
78. A very common
bird in the South in
Audubon's day and,
for some, an augur.
Rare Books and
Special Collections,
Thomas Cooper
Library, University of
South Carolina.*

Human Impact on Birds

Birds, we have seen, pervaded the lives and minds of southern Indians, from subsistence and clothing to adornment, and from social arrangements and displays of political authority to religion and spirituality, sickness and health, and narrative. That much seems certain.

But if birds impinged upon people in the South, did the opposite also occur? Did native people affect birds, shape their populations, extirpate them from the region, or cause their extinction? Such questions invite speculation on the impact on birds of hunting, burning and deforestation, the domestication of corn and other plants, and other human activity. The increase over time in human population and social complexity affected subsistence and consumer demand and conceivably shaped the use of birds in many arenas, including tribute. Maintaining habitats through periodic fire favored not just targeted species such as white-tailed deer but also birds that thrived on an open understory in longleaf-pine forests. Increasing the supply of domesticated plants for human consumption no doubt also increased food for grain-favoring birds. And new immigrants from Europe not only caused the indigenous human population to crash, through disease, war, and slavery, in theory lessening the human pressure on animals, including birds, but as quickly introduced new people, animals (including birds), and desires to the mix, reversing what must in retrospect have been only a temporary reprieve.

As to whether southern Indians extirpated birds from the region or caused the extinction of species, it bears notice that indigenous people in other parts of the world have shown themselves fully capable of doing so both prior to and following the arrival of Europeans. Perhaps the most extreme cases unfolded in the Pacific, where newly arriving native people set off chain reactions that spelled doom for thousands of species of birds. In Hawaii, Polynesian settlers transformed the land with fire and ambitious agricultural projects, introduced rats with enormous appetites for plant and animal food, and demanded brilliantly plumaged birds for feather capes and cloaks. There and elsewhere in the Pacific, on islands large and small, thousands of species of birds disappeared. Large islands did not escape: not New Ireland, where native colonists exterminated many birds; not New Zealand, where the late-arriving ancestors of the Maori killed off some 160,000 flightless, ostrichlike birds called moas. These slow-reproducing birds, one dozen species in all, first the largest and last the smallest, became the victims of the gustatory tastes of opportunist predators and of extravagant waste. Prior to European expansion to the Pacific, native people eliminated an estimated 40 percent of avifaunal diversity.[1]

Extinction claims victims disproportionately on islands, even large ones. So it is normal to wonder if anything comparable happened with respect to birds on an entire continent like North America, or part of one like the American South. American Indians did have an adverse impact on animals such as white-tailed deer, beaver, and buffalo, extirpating local and regional populations, but these cases unfolded in a post-European context of intense commodification, none resulted in extinction, and none involved birds.[2]

In North America, the most famous extinctions overlapping with humankind occurred at the end of the Pleistocene, but there is no agreement on the extent to which humans — Paleo-Indians, the earliest Indians to migrate from northeastern Asia to the Americas — were primarily responsible rather than climate and habitat change. The bird extinctions do not help settle this debate: ten or eleven genera of birds went extinct, a number proportionate to the mammal extinctions, yet many were in some way associated with the large mammals that also disappeared, either because they were commensal with or scavenged on them.[3]

Closer in time to today, the comprehensive reanalysis by the archaeologist Jack Broughton of thousands of bird bones deposited in a midden on the edge of San Francisco Bay over a period of nearly two thousand years (600 BC to AD 1300) suggests significant reductions in birds widely defined as edible (and that are in fact significant sources of protein), by size and proximity to human settlement. The first species depleted tended to be the largest and closest, and the last the smallest and most distant. This is a classic case of opportunistic rather than prudent predation, showing no hint of restraint.[4]

TEEMING NUMBERS

Prior to the nineteenth century, there are few signs of decline in bird populations in the American South. This is striking. Almost without exception, explorers, naturalists, and others noted rich and abundant avian resources from the sixteenth through the early nineteenth century.[5] Some birds seemed incredibly abundant: through time, passenger pigeons, wading birds, resident winter waterfowl, and others maintained robust populations. At the beginning of the nineteenth century, Benjamin Hawkins, United States agent to the Creek Nation, commented about ponds "abounding with ducks and geese" in midwinter, a typical remark for his day and for preceding times.[6]

Even in Audubon's day, which was slightly later than Hawkins's, abundance ruled — again with several exceptions that will be discussed. Audubon was not just a skilled artist but left a record of observations and anecdotes drawing on deep knowledge of birds. In the 1820s–1830s, he expressed amazement at the sheer avian bounty along the Mississippi River, on Florida's St. John's River, and in the Florida Keys. Here and elsewhere in the South, he remarked on myriad pelicans, cormorants, gulls, ibises, godwits, crows, grackles, swallows, and other birds. Going down the Mississippi, he encountered woods "literally filled with Parokeets"; heard "the constant cry" of ivory-billed woodpeckers; saw blackbirds in "immense flocks," countless crows, turkeys, and teal, and "millions" of geese; and recounted "astonishing" quantities of robins killed for the marketplace.

In Natchez in 1820, Audubon spoke about "vultures unnumbered," which flew near the ground, of an "immense number of Vultures that strode along the streets or slumbered on the roofs," feeding on refuse and anything else that struck their fancy. In the southern winter were "myriads of sparrows of different kinds"; swamp sparrow numbers, he remarked, were "immense" in winter. In Louisiana, common grackles were present in "immense numbers," and yellow-throated warblers threw "themselves by thousands onto all the cypress woods and cane-brakes." Barred owls were encountered every third mile. Carolina wrens could be heard from "all parts of the plantations, the deep woods, the swamps, the sides of creeks and rivers, as well as from the barns, the stables and piles of wood, within a few yards of the house." Blue jays abounded in winter, "few birds [were] more common" in winter than the chipping sparrow, and wood storks could be seen in "immense flocks."

FIGURE 161. Common Grackle. *Pen and ink with watercolor, associated with John White, ca. 1585–1600. Inscribed: "Tummaihumenes. Of this bigness."* Audubon remarked on their countless numbers. Sloane volume. © The Trustees of the British Museum, SL,5270.85.

The numbers and movements of birds as the seasons turned astonished Audubon. In late fall in Georgia and the Carolinas, mallards "pour[ed] into the rice fields by thousands from the interior" and were seen at times in Florida "in such multitudes as to darken the air." During migration, "the shores of our eastern rivers [were] swarming with myriads of Rice Buntings, Red-wings, Soras, and other migratory birds." At any time, he imagined, a predatory bird such as a falcon had "constantly" within its view "millions of birds on their way to the south, and which in the evenings [fell] thick as the drops of a hail-shower on the bordering marshes." Audubon shot birds, both to learn about and paint them and to eat them, and after one shoot on the incoming tide, he and others had at their feet a "mass of birds of different kinds" that "looked not unlike a haycock." In the Florida Keys, he noted, the flocks "so astonished us that we could for a while scarcely believe our eyes."[7]

From today's vantage point nearly two hundred years later, the numbers are phenomenal. Species common today were abundant in Audubon's day, and ones uncommon, rare, or threatened now were common then.

RESTRICTIONS ON KILLING BIRDS?

Why were bird numbers so great? There was certainly no lack of human demand for many of them. As we have seen, southern Indians ate and used birds in myriad ways, including as commodities and tribute. Some birds ended up far from the habitats they have been associated with in more recent times, for example, ivory-billed woodpecker bills and skins far from mature southern forests, and a roseate spoonbill skeleton, minus its skull (and spatulate bill), in a grave in Illinois adjacent to the remains of a five-year-old native boy.[8] Birds and feathers clearly counted as tribute. Powhatan tribute took the form of "skinnes, beades, copper, pearle, deare, turkies, wild beasts, and corne," and Powhatan himself revealed the currency of turkeys when he exchanged them, one for one, for swords from the English, and when he tried to induce the English to do his bidding with a gift of turkeys.[9] Throughout the region, native people presented feathers as gifts or traded them to others, including newcomers like the English.[10] Later, they also apparently traded mockingbirds to Cuba, presumably for their remarkable vocal repertoires as cage birds.[11]

There are several possible explanations for the continued abundance of birds. The most parsimonious is that the demand, no matter how high, never exceeded supply. A second is that cultural prohibitions on killing excessive numbers of birds checked demand. And a third is that diseases brought by Europeans killed so many native people that whatever pressure birds had been under lessened because hunting pressure declined; if they had been stressed, avian populations then recovered. No doubt there are other possibilities, but little concrete evidence bears on any of them — except for the great numbers of many different kinds of birds, which would support the notion, in the South at least, of the possibility of a sustainable harvest.

Some evidence relates to the role of prohibitions against overkill. In seventeenth-century Virginia, there were seemingly few, if any, significant restrictions on killing birds, except, as mentioned earlier, for a taboo on killing the whip-poor-will. At the time, Powhatan villages possessed their own "meeres and lymitts to fish, fowle, or hunt in," that is, fishing and hunting territories, in which restraints against hunting (except perhaps on outsiders lacking permission) seemed largely, if not entirely, lacking. According to John Smith, "Hares, Partridges, Turkies, or Egges, fat or leane, young or old, they devoure all they can catch in their power." Smith thought that if the population of native people declined then "the Deere, Turkies, and other Beasts and Fowles [would] exceedingly increase" because "at all times of the yeare they never spare[d] Male nor Female, old nor young, egges nor birds, fat nor leane, in season or out of season with them, all is one."[12]

Even though Smith's proposition about what would happen if the native population declined was forever complicated by the arrival of newcomers from Europe, his comment on a lack of taboos against overkill is of a piece with how southern Indians regarded white-tailed deer. Propelled by the desire for manufactured commodities, southern Indians who hunted deer for their hides believed that if they killed and treated deer properly, then deer would undergo reincarnation. Whatever prohibitions or taboos pertained to thinking about, hunting, killing, and treating deer, none pertained to killing too many — and, given their beliefs, it was not possible for them to kill too many. It seems that some, at least, made sense of birds in the same way. That is, no matter how many birds they killed, they could not kill too many.[13]

AN EXCEPTION: THE WILD TURKEY

The major exception to the picture of avian abundance through time pertains to wild turkeys living near human settlement. Like the white-tailed deer and other game, the wild turkey came under growing pressure as a valued commodity — for gustatory reasons, as detailed earlier, in expanding European-American settlements. In eighteenth-century Virginia and Maryland, for example, observers remarked widely that turkeys had become scarce: "It was strange," one observer commented, "we met with no wild turkeys . . . this being the season in which great numbers of them used to be seen." Another stated, "[T]he wild Turkeys which used to be so abundant . . . are now rarely seen." Farther afield, the mid-eighteenth-century surveyor Bernard Romans commented that game was "so scarce" among the Choctaw that "near one half of the men ha[d] never killed a deer or turkey during their lives"; perhaps this was an exaggeration, but by the turn of the nineteenth century some Choctaw were required to travel great distances to find deer plentiful enough to hunt.[14]

By the nineteenth century turkeys also had become scarce in many parts of the South. Audubon remarked that they had been very abundant in Kentucky at the turn of the nineteenth century, when they sold for three pence each, a price "not equal to that of a common barn-fowl" then, but at the time he wrote, three decades later, they were much scarcer and far more expensive.[15]

That turkey numbers declined was in part a function of immigrant demography. In 1685, one quarter of a million people lived in the South, of which 80 percent (200,000) was indigenous. By 1790, nearly 1.7 million people lived in the region, most of them newcomers, as native numbers plunged to nearly 56,000, or 3 percent of the total. The new majority of agrarian, land-hungry, slave-holding immigrants from Europe set in motion processes like forest clearance, exerted pressure on resources to meet their own subsistence and consumption needs, and commodified nearly everything in sight.[16] It is little wonder, then, that wild turkeys came under pressure. But immigrant settlers weren't the only ones responsible. There is ample evidence that native people (under no restraint) took advantage of the rapidly expanding market and joined in killing and trading turkeys to the new immigrants across the region from the moment they arrived, much as native people elsewhere engaged in other commodities trades.

Other clouds loomed on the horizon for the region's food birds. In 1838, Audubon sensed them among the highly esteemed canvasback, whose numbers in the Chesapeake along with other "fowl" had been cut in half in fifteen years, presumably because of hunting and market pressures.[17]

FIGURE 162. Wild Turkey. *Hand-colored engraving by William Lizars from a painting by John James Audubon,* Birds of America, *vol. 1 (1827–30), plate 1. Through time, a bird subject to great hunting pressure and locally extirpated. Rare Books and Special Collections, Thomas Cooper Library, University of South Carolina.*

EXTIRPATIONS

In time, certain birds were entirely extirpated from the region, such as the greater prairie-chicken and (perhaps) the king vulture, even if they continued to thrive elsewhere in viable populations. The greater prairie-chicken, also known as the heath hen, was confined mainly to prairies in the northeastern and southwestern parts of the region, which were habitats produced and maintained by Indian-set fires, and the king vulture, whose habitats closest to the American South today are lowland forests of Mexico, is known from Bartram's unique description.[18] Both birds, it should be noted, were associated with prairies whose existence depended on fires set by indigenous people.

Two other birds that declined in the South, for cultural, not gustatory reasons, are the golden eagle and the bald eagle. How many eagles lived in the South when Europeans arrived is unknown, but the bald eagle was widespread, and the golden eagle was apparently restricted to the uplands. Early on, the less-common golden eagle was virtually extirpated from the region, probably because of native demand for its feathers and its status as a pest among agrarian immigrants from Europe. Bald eagles, in contrast, were quite common and even abundant in certain parts of the South; an estimated 500,000 could be found in North America, and there were plenty along the eastern coastlines and waterways, where breeding and wintering densities could be extremely high. They had never been extirpated from a region. Yet Audubon and others

FIGURE 163.
Pinnated Grous (greater prairie chicken). *Hand-colored engraving by Robert Havell from a painting by John James Audubon,* Birds of America, *vol. 2 (1831–34), plate 186. A prairie bird that became extirpated from the South. Rare Books and Special Collections, Thomas Cooper Library, University of South Carolina.*

made note of the great decline in this bird's population in the early to mid-nineteenth century — even if in places like Florida they continued to be common until the early twentieth century.

All over North America, eagle populations went into free fall from the late nineteenth through the late twentieth century. Americans defined them as predators and shot them, first from the ground and then from small planes, eliminated their food supply, disturbed their nests, destroyed their habitats, and poisoned them with strychnine and, much later, DDT. Protective legislation was enacted for the bald eagle in 1940 and for the golden eagle in 1963. In 1978, the bald eagle was formally listed as endangered, which, together with the ban on DDT in 1962, allowed its population to recover to the point where it has formally been delisted.[19]

EXTINCTIONS

Today, the passenger pigeon, the Carolina parakeet, and Bachman's warbler are extinct, and the ivory-billed woodpecker is evidently hanging on by a thread. The first and the last — the passenger pigeon and the ivory-billed woodpecker — serve as poster birds for extinction (or, for the latter, an apparent near-death experience).[20]

Did native people play a role in their demise? For the Bachman's warbler, the answer seems to be no. An uncommon migratory bird of canebrakes whose population dynamics were never well understood, this warbler disappeared along with the eradication of bottomland hardwood forests in the nineteenth and twentieth centuries; the destruction of these forests and especially canebrakes, this warbler's preferred habitat and a very narrow ecological niche, had little, if anything, to do with native people.[21]

The issues are more complex with regard to the other three. At the height of its numbers, the passenger pigeon might have totaled some three to five billion birds and could be found in eastern woodlands wherever there was a supply of beechnuts, acorns, and other nuts, its principal food.[22] As already described in some detail, Indians clearly desired these birds; among avian remains in archaeological sites, theirs are second in frequency to those of the wild turkey.[23] Indians hunted them in roosts and rookeries and wherever else it was convenient. They loved the young squabs, eating them fresh or preserving their oil for later consumption as trail food.[24] Lawson's description of the winter hunt in North Carolina, quoted at length earlier, famously details both the carnage — the efficient bludgeoning of thousands of birds — and the importance of passenger pigeon oil to some southern Indians for winter subsistence. Lawson is not alone in suggesting that native people were capable of high kills at pigeon roosts.[25] But pigeon populations not only seemed inexhaustible, they *were* at the time southern Indians hunted them intensively. Moreover, as competent as native hunters were, they didn't hold a candle to nonnative market hunters, who, responding to the demands of the rapidly expanding American market and with ever efficient transportation at their disposal, can rightly be held responsible for the demise of this bird.[26]

The Carolina parakeet, which probably went extinct in the 1920s, could be found in substantial numbers in the South, especially in the cypress swamps and bottomlands — wherever it could find sandspurs and cockleburs and satisfy an eclectic need for fruits, seeds, and buds.[27] Its range was vast: from New York in the northeast; to Wisconsin, Michigan, South Dakota, and eastern Colorado in the northwest; then down the Mississippi, Missouri, and other major rivers to the Gulf Coast and southern Texas; and finally to Florida in the southeast.

Carolina parakeet bones show up in archaeological refuse heaps, and their likeness appears from time to time sculpted in stone or incised in ceramic or shell, but other intersections with native people remain largely speculative. They seem not to have risen to the level of focus of the passenger pigeon or the ivory-billed woodpecker. But maize was high on the list of preferred foods of the Carolina parakeet, and it is tempting to speculate that Indian boys were kept busy fending them away from agricultural fields when this crop was ripening. These parakeets also consumed fruit of all kinds, which brought them into conflict with cultivators of apple, peach and other fruit trees. Catesby, Wilson, and Audubon all remarked on parakeets' depredations of crops — ones grown by colonists and settlers of European extraction, not Indians. Catesby spoke of "numerous flights" that took to orchards in fall, "where they [made] great destruction for their kernels only," and Wilson about parakeets twisting off and scattering uneaten apples, one by one, from trees. Both Wilson and Audubon evoked

FIGURE 165. Passenger Pigeon. *Hand-colored engraving by Robert Havell from a painting by John James Audubon,* Birds of America, *vol. 1 (1827–30), plate 62. Native and nonnative people alike commodified, pursued, and consumed the passenger pigeon; a poster bird for extinction, it was gone by 1914. Rare Books and Special Collections, Thomas Cooper Library, University of South Carolina.*

FIGURE 166.
Carolina Parrot
(Carolina parakeet).
*Hand-colored
engraving by
Robert Havell from
a painting by John
James Audubon,
Birds of America,
vol. 1 (1827–30),
plate 26. This
multihued, raucous,
and gregarious
bird was branded
a pest in orchards
and cornfields and
probably extinct by
the end of the 1920s.*
Rare Books and
Special Collections,
Thomas Cooper
Library, University
of South Carolina.

the image of a carpet to depict these birds, "a carpet of the richest green, orange, and yellow" on the ground, thought Wilson, or a "brilliantly covered carpet" over stacks of grain, remarked Audubon.[28]

As for the ivory-billed woodpecker, the story is again different. This woodpecker ranged throughout old-growth forests in Florida, coastal Georgia, coastal South Carolina, part of North Carolina, and up the Mississippi and Ohio rivers into eastern Oklahoma and southern Illinois, but its population was apparently never great.[29]

FIGURE 167.
Ivory-billed Wood-
pecker. *Hand-colored
engraving by Robert
Havell from a paint-
ing by John James
Audubon,* Birds
of America, *vol. 1
(1827–30), plate 66.
Audubon captured
these ivory-billeds in
poses and at angles
faithful to life that
would be uncannily
mirrored in photo-
graphs in the 1940s.
Rare Books and
Special Collections,
Thomas Cooper
Library, University
of South Carolina.*

Compared to passenger pigeons and Carolina parakeets, large crested woodpeckers were abundantly represented in shell, ceramic, wood, and silver. They were probably ivory-billeds. The remains of these birds have shown up in archaeological contexts both in the heart of the South and far outside their range and the region. In the South, ivory-billed carpometacarpals (the major structural skeletal support for primary flight feathers) have been found in a burial mound at Etowah in Georgia; bill sections in a midden in West Virginia; and other remains in northern Alabama. Farther afield, ivory-billed tarsometatarsals (the fused bones of the foot to which the toes, or digits, are attached) and a maxilla (upper bill) were discovered in burial contexts and middens in Ohio and Illinois, other maxillae in an Omaha grave in Nebraska, another bill in a Cheyenne or Arapahoe grave in Colorado, and bills and portions of adjacent throats on a pipe stem from the western Great Lakes.[30]

The focus on bills and wings in these archaeological contexts finds support in anecdotal information provided by Catesby, Wilson, and Audubon. Catesby remarked, "[T]he bills of these birds are much valued by the Canada Indians, who make coronets of them for their princes and great warriors, by fixing them around a wreath, with their points outward. The northern Indians having none of these birds in their cold country, purchase them of the southern people at the price of two, and sometimes three buckskins a bill."[31]

Wilson, who claimed to have seen "a coat made of the skins, heads and claws of the raven; [and] caps stuck round with heads of Butcher-birds [shrikes], Hawks and Eagles," remarked, "[T]he head and bill [of the ivory-billed woodpecker] is in great esteem among the southern Indians, who wear them by way of amulet or charm, as well as ornament; and it is said, dispose of them to the northern tribes at considerable prices." Wilson opined, "An Indian believes that the head, skin, or even feathers of certain birds confer on the wearer all the virtues or excellencies of those birds," and "the disposition and courage of the Ivory-billed Woodpecker are well known to the savages, no wonder they should attach great value to it, having both beauty, and, in their estimation, distinguished merit to recommend it."[32]

Still fresh in Wilson's mind was an encounter with an ivory-billed. Both he and Audubon regularly shot the birds they sketched and painted but managed only to cripple some, whose behavior they then observed. Audubon, for example, said that a whooping crane was aggressive and struck convincingly at its captor; that a great blue heron aimed at the eye and could produce a "severe wound"; and that a pileated woodpecker caused a "severe wound if incautiously seized." The ivory-billed might have been in a class of its own: this bird will "strike with great violence, and inflict very severe wounds with [its] bill as well as claws, which are extremely sharp and strong."[33]

As for Wilson's encounter, he shot and wounded an ivory-billed in North Carolina, placed it in a sack, and headed on horseback for nearby Wilmington — a perilous trip because the cries of the bird "terrified" his horse. There he found an inn, left his gear and the ivory-billed in his room, and went to tend to his horse. He returned less than an hour later to discover that the bird, desperate to escape, "had mounted along the side of the window, nearly as high as the ceiling, a little below which he had begun to break through. The bed was covered with large pieces of plaster; the lath was exposed for at least fifteen inches square, and a hole, large enough to admit the fist, opened to the weather-boards; so that in less than another hour he would certainly have suc-

FIGURE 168.
The Blue Heron
(little blue heron).
*Hand-colored etching
by Mark Catesby,*
Natural History
*(1731–43), plate 76.
Esteemed for its
plumes.* John Carter
Brown Library at
Brown University.

ceeded in making his way through." Wilson next tied the bird by a string to the table and went out to look for something that the bird could eat. When he returned, he "heard him again hard at work" and discovered that "he had almost entirely ruined the mahogany table." Wilson sketched him; he remarked, "[The bird] cut me severely in several places, and on the whole, displayed such a noble and unconquerable spirit that I was frequently tempted to restore him to his native woods." The ivory-billed refused to eat and died within three days.[34]

The ivory-billed woodpecker diet has apparently always been broad, ranging from the larvae of large long-horned and hardwood stump-borer beetles to seeds, nuts, fruits, and berries. But this bird evidently has always preferred large beetle larvae, and it is doubtful whether Wilson found any for his wounded bird. The specialized food preferences, the bird's tendency to flee from human disturbance, and its uncertain breeding success all narrowed the ivory-billed's adaptation. Human beings commodified this bird, first American Indians and then people of European extraction, but their impact could not have measured up to the destructive desire of mercantilists and industrialists for the trees and forests needed by the ivory-billed. Always going against the ivory-billed has been its need for a large territory in mature bottomland forests.[35]

In the end, no matter how many they killed for their own purposes, indigenous people played a minor role in the demise of the big three — the passenger pigeon, the Carolina parakeet, and the ivory-billed. This is not to say that they lacked interest in them or failed to commodify them. Far from it. Yet in all three cases, the primary reasons for the loss of these birds can be traced, first and most importantly, to forest clearance and habitat destruction. This was especially true of the ivory-billed, and if it is to survive (assuming it is still with us), it will be because sufficient undisturbed habitat is set aside for it. As for the other two, passenger pigeons were also subjected to intensive market hunting and the fatal disturbance of their nesting colonies; and Carolina parakeets not only were labeled an agricultural pest and taken for the millinery and cage-bird trade but also lost nesting sites in large hollow trees through forest clearance and perhaps European honeybee competition.[36]

PLUME HUNTERS

A later wave of bird commodification and decimation took place during the nineteenth- and early twentieth-century plume trade and partly implicated native people. In two sorties in Manhattan in 1886, the ornithologist Frank Chapman spotted the feathers, or carcasses, of birds on over 550 women's hats in Manhattan; over forty different native species were represented. Many were the feathery breeding plumes of egrets and herons, which had become the latest rage in fashion. The suppliers were plume hunters, who destroyed phenomenal numbers of snowy egrets, great egrets, roseate spoonbills, herons, curlews, and other wading birds, as well as terns and some of the last remaining Carolina parakeets, mainly for their feathers and other uses in the millinery trade.[37]

The hunt for these birds was especially intense during the last three decades of the nineteenth century and the first two decades of the twentieth, when it was focused on breeding populations in Florida. Millions were killed for fashion. At first the hunters were Seminole; in the 1870s–1880s, the trade was said to be "most profitable" to them, with each plume worth thirty-five cents to the hunter. Beginning in the 1890s, efficient and systematic professional nonnative hunters led the way to the near-total destruction of rookeries. They and the Seminole killed many birds in the months of March and April, when wading birds were in full breeding plumage. The carnage was horrific, and in many places "it did not take the white and Indian plume hunters long to wipe out the rookeries" by killing the adults and leaving young birds defenseless against predators and starvation. But according to one contemporary account, albeit second- or thirdhand, at least some Indians were said to leave "enough of the old birds to feed the young of the rookery" — although whether adult birds fed young that were not theirs is an open question — while "the white man kill[ed] the last plume bird he [could] find."

Opposition to the plume hunt grew in the last quarter of the nineteenth century. The Florida legislature passed an egret protection act in 1877, and then in the 1880s the nascent Audubon Society voiced its disapproval. Congress then weighed in with a series of acts culminating in the Migratory Bird Treaty Act (1918), each of which brought a measure of protection. But none of the laws was rigorously enforced, and business continued as usual at many rookeries. After the turn of the century, the Seminole were selling egrets directly to tourists at twenty times the price they had been getting twenty to thirty years earlier. By 1909, with the trade flourishing, plume birds were said to be "practically extinct" in one part of Seminole country. At last, fashion tastes in the 1920s moved away from feathers and birds, conservationists established preserves, and game wardens finally enforced laws on the books.[38]

The populations of most birds killed for their plumes or skins recovered, but none to its previous level, and some species like the roseate spoonbill and the gull-billed tern were shattered. But none went extinct, nor is any today on the brink of extinction.

FIGURE 169. The crested Bittern (yellow-crowned night-heron). *Hand-colored etching by Mark Catesby,* Natural History *(1731–43), plate 79. A lovely wading bird, this common night-heron does not figure in the ethno-ornithology of the South. John Carter Brown Library at Brown University.*

FIGURE 170.
Red-tailed Hawk.
*Hand-colored
engraving by
Robert Havell from
a painting by John
James Audubon,*
Birds of America, *vol.
1 (1827–30), plate
51. Native people
distinguished this
common hawk in
language—the
Cherokee called it
"love sick" from their
perception of its
call—and in tales
about birds and
people in the South,
and its presence in
middens meant that
some consumed
it.* Rare Books and
Special Collections,
Thomas Cooper
Library, University of
South Carolina.

Visible & Invisible Birds

We should now be able to appreciate the range of intersections of birds and native people in this region, even if the data at times limit us to scratching the surface of contexts in which birds appeared. Methodological challenges are constant, not least the poor evidence (despite rich material culture) and rife speculation for the eras farthest removed in time, or the need to separate European from indigenous cultural meanings of birds after people of European descent arrived on the scene. As far as the latter is concerned, for example, Europeans and European Americans considered accessorizing with feathers as associated with royalty and the military; the eagle as the king of birds and a symbol of polity; the raven as both ominous and praiseworthy; owls as prophets of doom more than symbols of wisdom; the whip-poor-will and the chuck-will's-widow as goat-sucking kin of the nightjar; vultures as scavengers unfit for food; numerous small "dicky birds" as barely worthy of note; and so on. Many of these popular ideas started to give way to a science-based natural history in the late eighteenth and early nineteenth centuries, but nevertheless proved remarkably resilient, and it is a constant challenge in a wide-ranging historical work like this to be alert to the possibility that nonnative observers of indigenous life projected them onto native people as indigenous beliefs.[1]

As for the importance of birds themselves to southern Indians, to start with, through time native people ate many birds: wild turkeys, passenger pigeons, and ducks, geese, swans and other waterfowl especially, but also hawks, herons, northern bobwhites, and a variety of other land and water birds, dozens and dozens of species, from large to small. They clearly relished passenger pigeons, turkeys, and waterfowl, expending energy on them at the times of year they were available and in good condition. As time went on, most added the exotic chicken to the inventory.

As we have seen, native people found birds useful not only for subsistence but also for the artifacts they could manufacture from feathers, bones, and other body parts. They used turkey, duck, and swan feathers for clothing and robes. They fabricated headdresses, crowns, and a variety of decorations from the plumes and feathers of sandhill and whooping cranes, herons and egrets, tundra and trumpeter swans, raptors of various kinds, and other birds. They used turkey spurs for arrow points, and raptor claws, feathers, and skins to ornament their clothing, hair, and bodies. They fletched arrows with turkey and hawk feathers and made fans of turkey and eagle feathers. Many selected the same birds — swans, egrets, turkeys, and eagles and other raptors were among the top choices — in part for natural characteristics such as the size and color of plumage (if not just the right color, it could be pigmented) and in part for cultural

associations between particular birds and peace, hostility, aggression, flight, and other states.

A substantial number of different birds were valuable in subsistence and material culture, but an even wider variety was significant in more esoteric contexts that were religious, curative, narrative, political, or social, or a combination of these, in nature. Again, some birds stood out. For example, eagles were positively charged, with the golden eagle, where it could be found and prior to its extirpation, seemingly the bird of choice. Eagle feathers signaled accomplishment, authority (sacred and secular), and power. People used eagle-feather fans in ceremony and wore eagle claws on breech-clouts. They widely contrasted other birds in negative terms, relating some, like vultures (commonly known as buzzards), to death and construing others — owls especially — as malevolent night birds. As widespread as these beliefs might have been, they were nevertheless neither universal nor straightforward in the region. Indeed, as has been shown, the vulture played a productive role in the formation of mountains and valleys and a beneficial part in curing. Moreover, not all owls were automatically

FIGURE 172.
Long-eared Owl.
Marsh Hawk.
Swallow-tailed Hawk
(swallow-tailed
kite). *Hand-colored
engraving by
J. Warnicke based on
drawing by Alexander
Wilson,* American
Ornithology, *vol. 6,
1808–14, plate 51. The
long-eared owl is the
Cherokee witch —
and the marsh
hawk, although
distinguished by
name, is curiously
invisible, the swallow-
tailed kite more so.
John Hay Library at
Brown University.*

or equally evil, and not all kinds were construed in the same way. These birds appeared often in the material culture of the region — sculpted in and on small figurines, ceramic jars, pipes, and massive wooden images — and figured in contexts ranging from malevolent to benevolent, diviner to witch, inauspicious augur to protector, often, if not always, the occasion of heightened attention. In addition to these highly visible birds, a variety of others appeared — how widely is poorly understood — in a range of contexts meaningful to individuals from before birth to after death.

Despite the difficulty of arriving at ironclad conclusions about the identity of many specific prominent species, it is safe to conclude that from Woodland times onward,

FIGURE 173. Chuck will's Widow. *Hand-colored engraving by Robert Havell from a painting by John James Audubon,* Birds of America, *vol. 1 (1827–30), plate 52. This bird should probably figure more than it does but many confuse it with the whip-poor-will and some with the nighthawk; night birds in general, and nightjars like the chuck-will's-widow, are usually negatively construed. Rare Books and Special Collections, Thomas Cooper Library, University of South Carolina.*

that is, for the last 2,700 years, native people in the South have shown a strong interest in certain categories of birds that can today be identified at the level of the biological order or family. First were hawks, eagles, owls, falcons, vultures, and other raptors (and raptorial spirit-birds), which were sculpted, stamped, incised, woven, and tattooed in or on wood, stone, shell, ceramic, and other media. In some instances no more then a copper or stone talon was necessary to signal the importance of the category raptor. Second were big woodpeckers with prominent crests (there were only two species, each in its own genus, the pileated and the ivory-billed), and third was the wild turkey (one species). Fourth were the wood duck and other waterfowl. Others that are recognizable yet far less common include mergansers, pelicans, and the roseate spoonbill. The identity

FIGURE 174.
Summer or Wood
Duck. *Hand-colored
engraving by
Robert Havell from
a painting by John
James Audubon,*
Birds of America,
*vol. 3 (1834–35),
plate 206. Even
though other ducks
nest in trees, this
so-called "summer
duck" was common,
eye-catching, and
significant in the
native cultures in the
South. Rare Books and
Special Collections,
Thomas Cooper
Library, University
of South Carolina.*

of all is reasonable at the level of the order or the family; in some instances the genus and even the species is quite clear. Reasons for interest in some of these specific birds were sought in the link between the characteristics of societies prior to European arrival times, especially those in the Mississippian era, when war was endemic and birds with notable strengths and aggressive tendencies were associated with the elite in these societies; in the anomalous characteristics of a bird like the wood duck, which is not only spectacularly plumaged but nests, unlike most ducks, in trees; in the association between specific descent groups and specific animals, including birds; and in the need to influence beings, including owls and other birds, that, as animate other-than-human persons, could make one ill (or worse) in the absence of attention or propitiation.

FIGURE 175.
Northern Mocking-
bird. *Hand-colored
engraving by
Robert Havell from
a painting by John
James Audubon,* Birds
of America, *vol. 1
(1827–30), plate 21.
It is curious why this
bird, which is highly
visible in nature,
does not figure more
significantly in the
ethno-ornithology
of the South. Rare
Books and Special
Collections, Thomas
Cooper Library,
University of South
Carolina.*

Yet as important as it is to identify these birds and tease out the meanings associated with them, we cannot repeat this exercise for most species of birds that lived in or migrated through the South, for the simple reason that most don't seem to have loomed large for native (or nonnative) people. For whatever reasons, they remain invisible through time. The list of species is long. In some instances, it is also surprising.

Consider, for example, the northern mockingbird. In its own right this familiar bird is quite remarkable. People of European descent unfailingly remarked on it — usually, like John Lawson's "greatest diversity of notes" possible in a bird, on its voice. Alexander Wilson spoke about the caged mockingbird: "[It] whistles for the dog; Caesar starts up, wags his tail, and runs to meet his master." The bird next "squeaks out like a hurt chicken, and the hen hurries about with hanging wings." Then, "the barking of the dog, the mewing of the cat, the creaking of a passing wheelbarrow, follow, with great truth and rapidity."[2]

The storied mockingbird is also quite able to take care of itself; aggressive, it will kill other birds, toy with domesticated chickens, and is capable of pecking out the eyes of a snake (one five-foot diamond-backed rattlesnake hindered in this way struck out blindly, sinking its fangs into itself). But foremost an extraordinary vocalist and mimic, the northern mockingbird will sing all night long (and as active during the night as well as the day, joins the category of oft-dangerous nocturnal birds without, evidently, being similarly construed negatively). In native languages, the names for the northern mockingbird emphasize its vocal qualities and are weighty enough to establish a firm interest in this bird: in Choctaw it is *hushi balbaha*, "one that talks in a foreign language"; in Creek, *fus-svhayv*, from *svhayetv*, "to imitate"; in Chickasaw *fosh-ato'chi*, "mortgage-bird," or *foshi' taloowa'*, "singer-bird"; and in Cherokee, "head eating," from the idea that to eat the head of this bird will increase one's intelligence. Yet despite all this, the northern mockingbird seldom looms large.[3]

The many birds that remain even less visible in language and culture present more of a puzzle. Many seem not to have figured much, if at all, in the lives of people. Granted, some were killed and eaten, especially by "bird-brushing" people in winter, but the quantities are unknown and their bones were too fragile or small to leave traces in the archaeological record. They seem not to have ended up as ornamentation or in material culture, or to have been useful in ritual or medicine, polity or war, or kinship and descent, or to have played significant roles in myth and other narrative.

Entire families of birds seem left out. Where are the many ducks, gulls, terns, rails, shorebirds, flycatchers, vireos, thrushes, wood warblers, buntings, sparrows, and others? Did native people not take notice of or name them? Were some migrants that spent

FIGURE 176.
Wood Ibis (wood stork). Scarlet I(bis). Flamingo (greater flamingo). White Ibis. *Hand-colored engraving by J. Warnicke based on drawing by Alexander Wilson,* American Ornithology, *vol. 8, 1808–14, plate 66. These wading birds ranged from common to rare and largely escaped notice. John Hay Library at Brown University.*

FIGURE 177.
American Sparrow Hawk (American kestrel). Field Sparrow. Tree Sp(arrow). Song Sp(arrow). Chipping Sp(arrow). Snow Bird (dark-eyed junco). *Hand-colored engraving by Alexander Lawson based on drawing by Alexander Wilson,* American Ornithology, *vol. 2, 1808–14, plate 16. Although common in the South in winter, the kestrel, whose diet consists largely of insects and small rodents, is overwhelmed in numbers by small sparrows and the dark-eyed junco, which native people hunted and consumed. John Hay Library at Brown University.*

little time in the South? Did others winter silently or in drab plumage in the region? Were their ranges restricted by habitat and geography? Or did most explorers, mercantilists, missionaries, ethnographers, linguists, and others who recorded their observations fail to notice most birds from lack of knowledge or curiosity?

As has been suggested, many of the invisible ones were the "little brown jobs" that also remain elusive in the record of Europeans who took notice of the natural world. Perhaps, as explored here with the Cherokee, some went unnamed except as undifferentiated members of a category of "shorebirds," "blackbirds," "sparrows," or small flycatchers. After all, these are some of the same categories of birds — small shorebirds or passerines like diminutive flycatchers and drab fall warblers — that bedevil Western naturalists and ornithologists with interests in identification or taxonomy.

But as the detailed information available for the Cherokee suggests, the picture is probably more complicated, and we might simply lack the data bearing on these birds. For the Cherokee, this information enables a quite full appreciation of the many species of birds distinguished and named and the expansive range of contexts in which

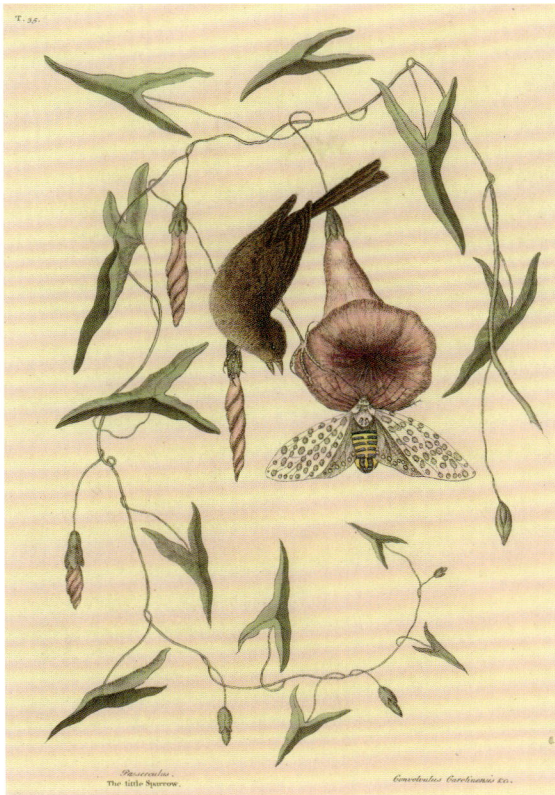

FIGURE 179.

The Little Sparrow. *Hand-colored etching by Mark Catesby*, Natural History *(1731–43), plate 35. Resident in Virginia and the Carolinas, this sparrow apparently frequented human habitation; with few distinguishing marks, it is the classic "little brown job" or "dicky bird." John Carter Brown Library at Brown University.*

birds appeared, while for other native people we need to extrapolate. If we can extrapolate from them to the South, then it is reasonable to conclude that avian beings have long captured the human imagination in this region, avian metaphors have long infused indigenous cultures in rich and complex ways, and over time the bond between people and birds has figured in nearly every cultural and social domain, from satisfying basic human requirements to myriad architectural, religious, social, political, and representational contexts. Whatever else we might conclude from this journey through the intersections of birds and native people, for an environmental history of the South, birds matter.

One hope is that the regionwide analysis presented in these pages will encourage fine-grained work on and with specific native people, even if gaining access to the subtler meanings of bird-human intersections in former times is difficult — because some native people tend to guard esoteric information closely, and, as the anthropologist Ray Fogelson has remarked with respect to hunting and fishing lore (and native people themselves admit), many have forgotten much. Nevertheless, the growing interest of scholars in the relationship between birds and people and various aspects of ethno-ornithology and the recent surge of public interest in birds leave one hopeful that the record of human-bird relations in this important region, past and present, will become even fuller and richer with time.[4]

Afterword

In the 1990s, Joshua Squirrel, a member of the Eastern Band Cherokee tribe in North Carolina, spoke with Diane Bernstein and Don Contreras about the powwows that he celebrated. "I am Bird Clan," said Squirrel. "I created my regalia. It's hawk and eagle feathers. The colors are symbolic to my tribe. These colors, the black, red, yellow, and white, are in our sacred hoop which is known as the medicine wheel and which represents the four directions. The gunstock that I carry was used in battle. The shield has a turtle for Mother Earth. The shield feather is redtail hawk." Jim Sawgrass, a member of the Florida Creek tribe and on the powwow circuit in the South at the time, commented on his own very different powwow clothing, including a turban in which were egret and ostrich feathers. "The ostrich plumes," said Sawgrass, "were traded because they were popular with soldiers and for ladies' hats. Each feather has different meanings. The war bird in our tribe was the woodpecker because of its colors, red and black."[1]

Today, the idea that southern Indians might not have had some relationship with birds in the past is inconceivable to anyone who has participated in or witnessed powwows. That is because powwows are overwhelmingly *avian*. Dancers envelop themselves in feathered worlds. Bird feathers, bird wings, and even the occasional taxidermied bird adorn hair and headpieces, are transformed into bustles, or grace accessories such as fans cradled in the hand. The feathers and birds are overwhelmingly raptorial.

In the South the powwow schedule is crowded. In a four-month period in the late summer and fall of 2005, one could attend powwows in Danville and Richmond, Virginia; Barboursville and Fairmont, West Virginia; Greensboro, Fayetteville, Manteo, and North Lumberton, North Carolina; Altoona, Florida; Tupelo, Mississippi; Robert, Louisiana; Athens, Alabama; and Euharlee, Atlanta, Rome, and Whigham, Georgia. Over fifty powwows are celebrated annually in the Carolinas and Virginia alone. Between once and twice a week, and perhaps more, southern Indians assemble somewhere in the region, in towns large and small or in the countryside, to dance and witness powwows.

People dance for many reasons, from sacred to profane. In powwows they express their identity as members of particular Indian groups and cement their ethnic solidarity with other native people. Some travel to powwows far and wide to compete for prize money, others to visit with relatives and friends, show ethnic solidarity, or bear witness to significant events, like the opening of the National Museum of the American Indian in Washington, D.C., in September 2004.

FIGURE 181.
Joshua Squirrel
(Eastern Band
Cherokee). *North
Carolina, 1995.
Plains-derived
regalia. Photo by
Don Contreras.*

Sometimes the connection with the avian world takes over the entire celebration. In August 2005, a notice was posted of an upcoming powwow in Fairmont, West Virginia, that would be entirely dedicated to birds: the Sixth Annual Honoring the Winged Ones Powwow Celebration, whose proceeds were earmarked for a new West Virginia Raptor Rehabilitation Center. The invitation promised a grand entry featuring Thunder the American Bald Eagle, Annie the Red Tailed Hawk, Snow the White Red Tailed Hawk, and Orion the Broad Winged Hawk.[2]

Today's powwow developed not among southern Indians but in the West, among American Indians on the Great Plains, spreading from there in all directions. Southern Indians, the descendants of those relocated in the nineteenth century, encountered the powwow in the West and in Chicago in the 1960s, and imported it to the South as an expression of Indian identity and in hope of cultural revival. Today's robust powwow circuit in the South is a result of decades of growth in interest and patronage, a regional manifestation of a pan-Indian phenomenon domesticated, or made cultural, in different ways by different Indian people.[3]

Joshua Squirrel's and Jim Sawgrass's regalia reflect the complex, if short, history of the powwow in the South. When first introduced to the powwow, participants in the

South imported Plains Indian powwow practices and regalia. They continue to do so, and many, indeed most, share with Squirrel a preference for Plains-derived regalia, singing, and dancing.

But southern Indians had their own distinctive ways of dressing and dancing, many of which fell away in the South after the forced removal to Oklahoma. As the powwow grew in popularity in the South, some southern Indians wished to revive and incorporate the obsolete ways. The tension between the originally exotic Plains and the newly endemic South plays out today as some southern Indians like Sawgrass promote regionally and culturally appropriate forms of expression, whether "authentic" clothing, the regional ball game, or animal-named stomp dances. For some, an awareness of the clothing came first from historical paintings and lithographs or from film dramatizations of Indian removal and other nineteenth-century events. As for traditional dance forms, in recent years southern Indians have invited their Oklahoma kin to their powwows to demonstrate dances that persist in the lands to which their relatives had been removed.[4]

With the caveat that it originated in the West among people whose roots were there rather than in the South, today's southern powwow and its feathered or plumed participants are nevertheless visible reminders of the strong, ancient ties between Indians and birds in this region.

BIRDS AND AMERICAN INDIANS

1. Krech, "Dodo."

2. The rediscovery of the ivory-billed woodpecker is based on observations, sound recordings, and a short video; discussion is intense. See, for example, Fitzpatrick et al., "Ivory-billed Woodpecker"; Fitzpatrick et al., "Response to Comment"; Jerome A. Jackson, "Ivory-billed Woodpecker"; Hill et al., "Evidence."

3. Jerome Jackson, *In Search*; Hoose, *Race*; Weidensaul, *Ghost with Trembling Wings*; Gallagher, *Grail Bird*.

4. Culture-area classification is the fundamental framework for organizing social and cultural diversity in native North America. Since the 1890s, anthropologists have partitioned North America into nine to twelve culture areas, one of which is usually the South or Southeast. The most influential classification was Clark Wissler's, nearly a century ago. For him and others, culture areas possess an environmental foundation and correspond to major geographical and biological regions (biomes). Wissler reduced the areas further to food areas based on the consumption of caribou, salmon, bison, wild seeds, and maize or other domesticated crops, again tied tightly to the environment. He gave lip service to birds (including turkeys in the East) but no more; others followed, and the upshot is that the biological class Aves is largely invisible over a century of classification (Wissler, *American Indian*; Kroeber, review of *The American Indian*; Krech, "On Feathered America").

5. Charles Reagan Wilson and Ferris, *Encyclopedia of Southern Culture*, xv; Reed, "South."

6. I could say that the interest here is in traditional uses of birds and forms of expression except that tradition is a vexed concept because of its numerous inventions. When "tradition" or "traditional" are used in this book, it signals merely a historical temporal interest, especially pre-twentieth century, in the relationship between birds and people.

7. David G. Anderson and Sassaman, "Early and Middle Holocene Periods"; Sassaman and Anderson, "Late Holocene Period"; Bruce D. Smith, "Origins of Agriculture."

8. Jeffries, "Regional Cultures." For post-AD 1000, see essays by Jerald T. Milanich, David J. Hally and Robert C. Mainfort, Martha Ann Rolingson, Tristram R. Kidder, Ann Early, and Ian Brown in Fogelson, *Handbook of North American Indians*.

9. In the pages that follow, my debt is apparent to John Swanton, James Mooney, Frank Speck, and Charles Hudson, as well as many contemporary anthropologists and historians whose works make the South unrivaled as a region in recent research on indigenous culture and history in North America. On the historical sketch here, see Hudson, *Southeastern Indians*; Hudson, *Juan Pardo Expeditions*; David Hurst Thomas, *Columbian Consequences*; Hudson and Tesser, *Forgotten Centuries*; Weber, *Spanish Frontier in North America*; Galloway, *Choctaw Genesis*; Scarry, *Political Structure*; Hudson, *Knights of Spain*; Knight and Steponaitis, *Archaeology of the Moundville Chiefdom*; Perdue and Green, *Columbia Guide*; Ethridge, *Creek Country*; Fogelson, *Handbook of North American Indians*. The major language families and speakers in the south are Muskogean (Alabama, Apalachee, Chickasaw, Choctaw, Creek, Hitichi-Mikasuki, Koasati), Iroquoian (Cherokee, Tuscarora, Nottoway), Siouan-Catawba (Biloxi, Catawban, Ofo, Tutelo-Saponi, Woccon), Algonquian (Powhatan, Rappahannock, and others), Caddoan (Caddo), and Timucuan (Tawasa, Timucua); isolates include Atakapa, Chitimacha, Natchez, Tunica, and Yuchi; Calusa, Cusabo, Eno, Guale, and others are poorly documented.

THE BIRDS

1. Lyon, "Canete Fragment," 309 ("all parts"). On orthography: the idiosyncratic spelling, punctuation, and syntax in original sources have been retained with the exception of the characters *s/f* and *u/v*, whose typographic representation and spelling have been modernized for the sake of readability (e.g., "numberless," not "numberlefs"; "swans," not "fwans"; "diverse," not "diuerse"; "have," not "haue"; "using," not "vsing"; "untruith," not "vntruith").

2. On nomenclature, I follow the AOU (American Ornithologists' Union, *Checklist of North American Birds*) except in using lower case for all but proper names (e.g., pileated woodpecker, Carolina wren, Bachman's warbler). An exception is made for names of clans (Turkey clan, Eagle clan) and persons in narratives (Buzzard). Goatsucker is the name for the family that includes whip-poor-will, nighthawks, chuck-will's-widow, and poorwill in North America. An ancient term, it was first applied to the European nightjar, which was believed to suck goats dry and gulp insects on nocturnal foraging flights (e.g., Feduccia, *Catesby's Birds*, 73).

3. Silver, *New Face on the Countryside*, 1; Melosi, "Environment," 315–21.

4. Robertson, "Account," 170 ("many wild fowl"). On debates over veracity in accounts of the de Soto expedition, see Young and Hoffman, *Expedition of Hernando de Soto*; Hudson, *Knights of Spain*,

441 – 81; Galloway, *Hernando de Soto Expedition*; Hann, "Hernando de Soto in Apalachee"; Patricia Galloway, personal communication, February 9, 2004.

5. Biggar, *Jean Ribaut*, 72. The correct spelling is Ribault. Today's states (e.g., Georgia), usually lacking the qualifier "today," are mentioned throughout the text as a geographical aid.

6. Biggar, *Ribaut*, 92.

7. Laudonnière, *Three Voyages*, 9.

8. John Smith, "Map of Virginia," 349 – 50, 387; John Smith, "True Relation," 177, 179; John Smith, "The Generall Historie of Virginia," in Barbour, *Complete Works*, 2:111. See also Strachey, *Historie of Travell*, 126 – 27. Barbour (*Jamestown Voyages*, 2:321 – 26), Rountree (*Powhatan Indians of Virginia*, 3 – 6), and others rightly caution that Strachey and Smith must be read critically. Rountree notes that Smith's egotism left him unreliable; Strachey often copied Smith; Henry Spelman's valuable account is marred by youth and poor writing; George Percy sought to rebut Smith and had little interest in Indians; Gabriel Archer and John Banister had useful things to say, as did Robert Beverley when he was not plagiarizing Banister; and Samuel Purchas, who never went to Virginia, managed to say some unique things about religion based on conversation with Smith and an Indian priest.

9. Quinn, "First Colony: Thomas Hariot," 358 – 59; on the spelling of Harriot, I follow many, including Kupperman, *Indians and English*.

10. Quinn, "Arthur Barlowe's Discourse," 1:91 – 117 ("full of Deere"); Magnel, "Francis Magnel's Relation," 153 ("infinite number"); Archer, "Relation," 82; Ewan and Ewan, *John Banister*, 335, 366 ("covered with swans"); Beverley, *History and Present State*, 153 ("such a Multitude"; "Plenty of"; etc. [copied from yet also expanded on Banister]); Strachey, *Historie of Travell*, 126 ("aboundaunce as I dare").

11. Many raptor names came from falconry: "falcon" is the peregrine falcon; "falcon-gentle" the female peregrine;

"tiercel-gentle" (or a variation) the male peregrine; "fishing hawk" or "fishing eagle" the osprey; "goshawk" the female goshawk; "tercel" the male goshawk; "gyrfalcon" the female gyrfalcon; "jerkin" the male gyrfalcon; "hobby" the female hobby, hen harrier, or merlin; "jack" or "robin" the male hobby or male merlin; "ring-tailed eagle" the golden eagle (Swann, *Dictionary of English and Folk-Names*, 84, 87, 101, 116, 123, 130, 156, 177, 197, 227, 237 – 38; see also Lockwood, *Oxford Dictionary*, passim.

12. Swann, *Dictionary of English and Folk-Names*, passim; Lockwood, *Oxford Dictionary*; "Ox-eye" and "Dotterel," in *Oxford English Dictionary Online* (accessed February 13, 2004). Ox-eye was used for three very different birds — dunlin, Carolina chickadee, and tufted titmouse — but probably referred to the first, given its position in the list as well as other birds noted. In these early lists, ed-ertes is obscure; guinea fowl was probably the wild turkey; Indian chickens were either turkeys, rails, or herons.

13. Percy, "George Percy's Discourse," 138. See also McAtee, "North American Bird Records"; McAtee, "North American Birds of Virginia Chroniclers."

14. Swanton, *Early History*, 63 (William Hilton and others).

15. Lawson, *New Voyage to Carolina*, 16, 52, 73 – 74. "Conies" are rabbits.

16. Lawson, *New Voyage to Carolina*, 150.

17. Lawson, *New Voyage to Carolina*, 150. Debate has raged over the former range of the trumpeter swan ever since the proposal to reintroduce the species to its original area. See Banko and Schorger, "Trumpeter Swan"; Mitchell, *Trumpeter Swan*; Johnsgard, "Triumphant Trumpeter"; Philip M. Rogers and Hammer, "Ancestral Breeding"; Houston and Houston, "19th Century Trade." For the debate over breeding and wintering ranges, see http://www.acsu.buffalo.edu/~insrisg/nature/swans.html (accessed November 15, 2005).

18. Lawson, *New Voyage to Carolina*, 23, 31 – 33, 35, 74, 79, 153.

19. Adair, *History*, 360 – 61, 405.

20. Swanton, *Indians*, 284 (Timberlake).

21. Harper, *Travels of William Bartram*, 157, 274.

22. Swanton, *Source Material . . . Caddo*, 135.

23. Tregle, *History of Louisiana*, 69, 142 ("hideous"), 153, 161, 273. For flamingo, see discussion of clothing in "Material Culture." I follow Gordon Sayre in using "Le Page," his manuscript signature, as an alternative to Le Page du Pratz (Le Page du Pratz, *History of Louisiana*, http://darkwing.uoregon.edu/~gsayre/LPDP.html (accessed March 7, 2006).

24. Feiler, *Jean-Bernard Bossu's Travels*, 61, 202 – 5; Dickinson, *New Travels*, 44 ("[t]oward the end of autumn").

25. Swanton, *Source Material . . . Caddo*, 135.

26. Laudonnière, *Three Voyages*, 114. For confusion in names of doves and pigeons, see "ring-dove" (the wood pigeon) and "wood pigeon," "stock pigeon," and "stock dove" (all the stock dove) in Swann, *Dictionary of English and Folk-Names*, 196, 227.

27. Feduccia, *Catesby's Birds*, 62 – 63; Schorger, *Passenger Pigeon*, 123 – 24.

28. Strachey, *Historie of Travell*, 127.

29. Ewan and Ewan, *John Banister*, 355, 366 – 67 (cf. Beverley's account).

30. Lawson, *New Voyage to Carolina*, 145 – 46.

31. Feduccia, *Catesby's Birds*, 61.

32. De Vorsey, *De Brahm's Report*, 239.

33. Tregle, *History of Louisiana*, 278 – 79.

34. Alexander Wilson, *American Ornithology*, 5:103 – 4.

35. Dickinson, *New Travels*, 47; De Vorsey, *De Brahm's Report*, 229, 238 – 39.

36. Keith Thomas, *Man and the Natural World*, 51 – 148, 273 – 80.

37. Swann, *Dictionary of English and Folk-Names*, 2 (tawny and barn owls), 12 (barnacle goose), 13 (barn owl), 18

(bittern), 42 (carrion crow), 55 (heron), 91–92 (nightjar), 96 (nightjar), 97–98 (golden eagle), 131 (snipe), 138 (corncrake), 149 (owls), 151–52 (magpie), 164 (swan), 166 (bittern), 167 (nightjar), 180 (pied wagtail), 184 (nightjar), 186 (green woodpecker), 187–88 (raven), 198–99 (robin), 201 (rook), 231–33 (swallow); Terence Hanbury White, *Book of Beasts*, 105–8 (eagle); Keith Thomas, *Man and the Natural World*, 51–148, 273–80; Alice Parmalee, *All the Birds*, 97–99; Hartert et al., *Hand-List of British Birds*.

38. Lawson, *New Voyage to Carolina*, 140–55.

39. McNamara, "Feathered Scribe." On the dicky (dickey) bird: this term has been in use since the eighteenth century for generic small birds such as sparrows, pipits, warblers, and others (*OED Online*, s.v. "dicky-bird," accessed September 1, 2006). On the dunnock and the hedge sparrow, see Cocker and Mabey, *Birds Britannica*, 333–34 (cf. Swann, *Dictionary of English and Folk-Names*, 79, 120).

40. Alexander Wilson, *American Ornithology*, 5:74–75.

41. Lewis, "Democracy of Facts."

42. Lévi-Strauss, *Le Totémism Aujourd'hui*, 128; Lévi-Strauss, *Totemism*, 89; Lévi-Strauss, *Savage Mind*, 1, 3, 9. For the root of this interest, see Durkheim and Mauss, *Primitive Classification*. Lévi-Strauss wrote: "On comprend enfin que les espèces naturelles ne sont pas choisies parce que 'bonnes à manger' mais parce que 'bonnes à penser'" (*Le Totémism Aujourd'hui*, 128). In his translation, Rodney Needham produced Lévi-Strauss's best-known "quotation" — the two phrases in single quotation marks, which became "good to eat" and "good to think" (*Totemism*, 89). I prefer "good for thinking," "good to think about," or "good to reflect on." Thanks to Michele Hayeur Smith, Davis Hammond, John Bourgoin, and an anonymous reader for their differing opinions.

43. Quinn, "First Colony: John White," 447–53; Geary, "Appendix II"; Hulton, *America 1585*. See also Christy, "Topsell's 'Fowles of Heauen'"; Swanton, "Newly Discovered Powhatan Bird Names"; Gilliam, "Powhatan's Dearest Bird"; Gilliam, "Powhatan Algonkian Bird Names."

44. Quinn, "First Colony: Thomas Hariot," 358–59.

45. Strachey, *Historie of Travell*, 174–207; Harrington, "Original Strachey Vocabulary"; Barbour, *Complete Works*, 2:78. Thanks to David Harris Sacks for discussion of "divedapper," defined as a "small diving waterfowl," and "copit crown," probably "copple-crown," defined as a "tuft of feathers on a fowl's head; a crest" (also *OED Online*, s.v. "dive-dapper," "copple-crown," accessed September 1, 2006).

46. Humes and Humes, *Chickasaw Dictionary*.

47. Munro and Willmond, *Chickasaw*.

48. Pickens, "Contributions to Catawba Ethnozoology," and Pickens, "Another Contribution to Catawba Ethnozoology." That the great horned owl and the barred owl were considered different sexes of one species is perhaps indicative of the limited extent of a single informant's knowledge. Thanks to Robbie Ethridge for the discussion of turkey and chicken in this paragraph.

49. Mooney, *Myths of the Cherokee*, 280–86 and passim; Witthoft, "Bird Lore"; Witthoft, "Some Eastern Cherokee Bird Stories"; Fradkin, *Cherokee Folk Zoology*, 150–86 and passim.

50. On the absence of an "omniscient informant," see Gardner, "Birds, Words, and a Requiem." On naming and taxonomy, see Krech, "Traditional Environmental Knowledge."

51. Speck and Witthoft, "Some Notable Life-Histories" (Pamunkey); Sillitoe, "From Head-Dresses to Head-Messages"; Feld, "Cockatoo, Hornbill, Kingfisher"; Forth, *Nage Birds*, 115–37; Krech, "Traditional Environmental Knowledge."

52. On range in naming birds and salience, see Diamond and Bishop, "Ethno-

ornithology of the Ketengban People"; Hunn, "Sahaptin Bird Classification"; Berlin, Boster, and O'Neill, "Perceptual Bases of Ethnobiological Classification"; and Bulmer, "Mystical and Mundane."

SUBSISTENCE

1. Archer, "Description of the People," 103 ("kill fowle"); Beverley, *History and Present State*, 210.

2. Swanton, *Indians*, 283–87, 292 (Solis on the Caddo), 295, 298–99; Hudson, *Southeastern Indians*, 280; Speck, *Ethnology of the Yuchi Indians*, 19. See also Robertson, "Account," 77, 83; John Smith, "Map of Virginia," 359. On fish and shellfish, see Goggin and Sturtevant, "Calusa."

3. John Smith, "Map of Virginia," 357; Strachey, *Historie of Travell*, 80; Lawson, *New Voyage to Carolina*, 216; Swanton, *Indians*, 257–58, 259–60, 265, 277, 298, 368–70; Schorger, *Wild Turkey*, 42–61 (five million), 241–69 (strutting, etc.). Inland, turkeys were especially numerous and sometimes the only bird mentioned in lists of game (e.g., Swanton, *Early History*, 184). As for dressing and cooking, Lawson (*New Voyage to Carolina*, 58) reported, "The *Indians* dress most things after the Wood-Cock fashion, never taking the Guts out"; Bartram (Harper, *Travels*, 152) noted that the Seminole called roasted turkey "the white man's dish." On eggs, see Campbell, "Choctaw Subsistence."

4. Swanton, *Indians*, 259, 298, 371, map 13 (end); Schorger, *Passenger Pigeon*.

5. Lawson, *New Voyage to Carolina*, 50–51.

6. Lawson, *New Voyage to Carolina*, 217.

7. Alexander Wilson, *American Ornithology*, 2:104.

8. Neumann, "Human-Wildlife Competition"; Neumann and Goodwin and Associates, "Human-Wildlife Competition." Neumann undermines his argument when he fails to mention the early observations of Laudonnière, Ribault, Strachey, Banister, De Brahm, Le Page, and others. After I had written the analy-

sis here, an anonymous reader of the manuscript led me to an important synthesis of recent zooarchaeological work, H. Edwin Jackson's " 'Darkening the Sun.' "

9. Nicholson, "Bone Degradation, Burial Medium"; Nicholson, "Bone Degradation in a Compost Heap."

10. Neill, Gut, and Brodkorb, "Animal Remains"; Penelope H. Weigel, "Great Auk Remains"; Robert D. Weigel, "Bird Remains"; Paul W. Parmalee, *Animal Remains*; Shufeldt, "Fossil Birds"; Hamon, "Northern Birds"; Brodkorb, "Great Auk"; Van der Schalie and Parmalee, "Animal Remains"; Cleland, "Faunal Remains"; Paul W. Parmalee, "Additional Noteworthy Records"; Guilday, *Biological and Archaeological Analysis*; Barkalow, "Vertebrate Remains"; Bruce D. Smith, *Middle Mississippi Exploitation*; Byrd, "Tchefuncte Subsistence"; Springer, "Analysis"; Larson, *Aboriginal Subsistence Technology*; Milanich and Fairbanks, *Florida Archaeology*, 100, 127, 154, 159, 172, 184, 244; Fradkin, "Bird Remains"; Reitz, "Vertebrate Fauna"; Scott, "Analysis"; Welch, "Mississippian Emergence"; House, "Powell Canal"; Hoffman, "Episodic Zooarchaeology"; Jenkins, "Use of Vertebrate Fauna"; Paul W. Parmalee, "Archaeological Avian Assemblage"; Scott and Jackson, "Early Caddo Ritual." See also Hudson, *Southeastern Indians*, 20, 47.

11. Speck, *Catawba Texts*, 76 – 78.

12. Speck, *Catawba Texts*, 78; Feduccia, *Catesby's Birds*, 54 ("to all other").

13. Adair, *History*, 169 – 73.

14. Adair, *History*, 169 – 73. On Adair: Hudson, "James Adair as Anthropologist"; Braund, "Introduction." For the listed birds, see Douglas, *Purity and Danger*; Hunn, "Abominations of Leviticus Revisited"; Bulmer, "Uncleanness."

15. Adair, *History*, 403; Swanton, *Indians*, 371 ("we Shou'd"); see also Wright, "Early Records . . . III," 79; Hudson, *Southeastern Indians*, 302, 317. Archaeologists found few bird remains in one central Florida site where they had expected many; a taboo on consumption or an artifact of soil conditions (Milanich and Fairbanks, *Florida Archaeology*, 184)?

16. Mooney and Olbrechts, *Swimmer Manuscript*, 120; Hawkins, *Sketch of the Creek Country*, 78.

17. Cushman, *History*, 214; Swanton, *Indians*, 289 (Choctaw story); Swanton, "Social and Religious Beliefs," 253 – 55. For some reason, the twentieth-century Catawba were reported to consider consumption of the mourning dove a "sin" (Speck, *Catawba Hunting*, 25 – 26).

18. Witthoft, "Bird Lore," 374; Fradkin, *Cherokee Folk Zoology*, 387 – 88.

19. Hudson, *Southeastern Indians*, 318. My argument draws on Douglas, *Purity and Danger*; Hunn, "Abominations of Leviticus Revisited"; Bulmer, "Uncleanness"; Douglas, "Pangolin Revisited."

20. Strachey, *Historie of Travell*, 79 – 80.

21. Swanton, *Early History*, 42 (Martyr), 356 (eagle — Laudonnière).

22. Lawson, *New Voyage to Carolina*, 35, 149 – 50; Bushnell, "Drawings by A. DeBatz." McAtee ("Birds in Lawson's 'New Voyage' ") and Feduccia (*Catesby's Birds*, 41) conclude that these were sandhill cranes.

23. Strachey, *Historie of Travell*, 79 – 80.

24. Lawson, *New Voyage to Carolina*, 35, 149 – 50, 153.

25. Cleland, "Faunal Remains," 51; Patricia Galloway, selected translations of Le Page du Pratz (personal communication, March 2004; cf. Tregle, *History of Louisiana*, 277); Swanton, *Indians*, 251 (the turkey was "rarely tamed"), 253, 299, 346. On fowl including ducks, see Sauer, *Agricultural Origins and Dispersals*, 32, 57 – 60, 73.

26. John Smith, "Map of Virginia," 349; Lawson, *New Voyage to Carolina*, 153; Schorger, *Wild Turkey*, 479.

27. Crawford, "Turkey"; Schorger, *Wild Turkey*, 136 – 46, 463 – 81; Wright, "Early Records of the Wild Turkey," 353; Stangel, Leberg, and Smith, "Systematics and Population Genetics"; Andrew F. Smith, *Turkey*, xvii, 6, 9 (quotation from Sahagún), 10, 14 – 38, 54 – 55, 83 – 84, 87.

28. Bushnell, "Drawings by A. DeBatz"; George, *Animals and Maps*, 50, 134, 163, 166, 193; Hulton, *Work of Jacques Le Moyne de Morgues*, 2:P103 (these turkeys were arguably based on both wild and domesticated forms); Cumming, *Southeast in Early Maps*, map 26 (Gerard Mercator and Jodocus Hondius, 1606, map of Virginia and Florida); Schorger, *Wild Turkey*, 102 – 12, 464 – 65, 468; Andrew F. Smith, *Turkey*, 10, 22; Eiche, *Presenting the Turkey*; Leopold, "Nature of Heritable Wildness," 180 – 83; Lovett E. Williams Jr., "Recurrent Color Aberrancy"; McIlhenny, *Wild Turkey*, 84 (R. W. Schufeldt quoting J. D. Caton); R. Wayne Bailey, "Notes on Albinism"; Pelham and Dickson, "Physical Characteristics," 33 – 34.

29. Swanton, *Indians*, 283 – 88, 351; Zeuner, *History of Domesticated Animals*, 443 – 55; Crawford, "Domestic Fowl." The first chickens in the New World might have come from Polynesia and arrived in southern South America in the fourteenth century (Wilford, "First Chickens in Americas").

30. Virginia DeJohn Anderson, "Animals into the Wilderness"; Wing, "Evidences for the Impact"; Barbour, *Complete Works*, 1:242 ("a cock and a hen"); Hann, *History of the Timucua Indians*, 99. The eighteenth- and nineteenth-century Caddo also seem to have accepted and raised chickens without hesitation (Swanton, *Source Material . . . Caddo*, 86, 196).

31. Lawson, *New Voyage to Carolina*, 62 ("keep many"); Gravier, "Relation ou journal du voyage," 149.

32. Simoons, *Eat Not This Flesh*, 144 – 67. There is no evidence from this time that native people engaged in cockfights.

33. Romans, *Concise Natural History*, 138; Usner, "Frontier Exchange Economy," 183.

34. Romans, *Concise Natural History*, 138 – 39 ("so scarce").

35. Romans, *Concise Natural History*, 145 ("very abundant"); Swanton, *Indians*,

286 (Bartram); Ethridge, *Creek Country*, 159, 177.

36. Hawkins, *Sketch of the Creek Country*, 18, 21 ("great many"), 23, 26, 28 – 29, 50 ("great number"), 61, 75; Swanton, *Indians*, 263 (Seminoles).

37. Tambiah, "Animals Are Good"; Bahti, "Animals in Hopi Duality"; O'Laughlin, "Mediation of Contradiction"; Simoons, *Eat Not This Flesh*, 144 – 67.

38. Adair, *History*, 171 – 72.

39. Swanton, "Early Account," 67; Swanton, *Source Material . . . Choctaw*, 235; Adair, *History*, 172 – 73 ("eaten a"), 403, 498 – 99. On unclean birds, see Bulmer, "Uncleanness."

40. Adair, *History*, 185, 265.

41. Cushman, *History*, 267 – 68; Debo, *Rise and Fall*, 40 – 41; McKee and Schlenker, *Choctaws*, 50 – 59; Carson, *Searching for the Bright Path*, 88 – 93. Stanley Brandes also cautions, in an essay on animal metaphors among the people of Tzintzuntzan in Mexico, that the relationship between people and animals is not always the key to meaning; thus, the people of Tzintzuntzan call an illegal migrant to the United States *pollo*, "chicken," because the person guiding him is *coyote*, an animal that takes chickens away in the night, and a sensitive child *gallina culeca*, "nesting hen," because of the relationship of the hen to her eggs (Brandes, "Animal Metaphors").

42. Munro and Willmond, *Chickasaw*, 15 – 16.

43. Patricia Galloway's selected translations of Le Page du Pratz (personal communication, March 2004; cf. Tregle, *History of Louisiana*, 273). Muscovy duck possessed a great variety of vernacular names. Known as Turkish duck, India duck, and musk duck, its common name might be a corruption of an ethnonym of Indians in Colombia (Clayton, "Muscovy Duck"; Donkin, *Muscovy Duck*; Sauer, *Early Spanish Main*, 59, 71, 115; Martin and Maudlin, *Dictionary of Creek/Muskogee*, 44, 112 [*fuco sule*]).

44. John James Audubon, *Ornithological Biography*, 1:35, 348.

45. Alexander Wilson, *American Ornithology*, 4:33 – 34.

46. Alexander Wilson, *American Ornithology*, 4:34.

47. Laudonnière, *Three Voyages*, 62; Hann, *History of the Timucua Indians*, 93.

48. Quinn, "First Colony: John White," 422.

49. Adair, *History*, 399 – 400.

50. Harper, *Travels of William Bartram*, 123; Waselkov and Braund, *William Bartram*, 55; Swanton, *Source Material . . . Choctaw*, 46.

51. Feduccia, *Catesby's Birds*, 94 – 95; Lawson, *New Voyage to Carolina*, 149.

52. Ewan and Ewan, *John Banister*, 382; Feduccia, *Catesby's Birds*, 94 – 95; Alexander Wilson, *American Ornithology*, 5:59; John James Audubon, *Ornithological Biography*, 1:117 – 19.

53. Mooney, *Myths of the Cherokee*, 454; Speck, *Gourds of the Southeastern Indians*, 40 – 41, 51 – 52, 73 – 75, fig. 80 opp. 86, 91. The chimney swift nested in hollow trees — Audubon described with "amazement" the sound of an estimated nine thousand inside a seventy-foot rotting sycamore — and, speculatively, some early American Indian structures (John James Audubon, *Ornithological Biography*, 2:329 – 33; Graves, "Avian Commensals in Colonial America").

54. John James Audubon, *Ornithological Biography*, 1:279.

55. Romans, *Concise Natural History*, 132 – 33 ("blow it").

56. Swanton, *Indians*, 585 – 86; Fradkin, *Cherokee Folk Zoology*, 259 – 60; Bushnell, *The Choctaw of Bayou Lacomb*, 19 – 20; Swanton, *Source Material . . . Choctaw*, 52; Speck, "Creek Indians of Taskigi Town," 110 ("about as long").

57. Speck, "Cane Blowgun," 201 ("early evening").

58. Swanton, *Indians*, 251, 329 – 31, 573 – 74; Bruce D. Smith, "Middle Mississippi Exploitation"; Speck, *Catawba Hunting*, 13 – 15 (boys also used slings

and crossbows as toys); Speck, *Ethnology of the Yuchi Indians*, 22; Quinn, "First Colony: John White," 431, 433; Rountree, *Powhatan Indians of Virginia*, 41; Witthoft, "Bird Lore;" Fradkin, *Cherokee Folk Zoology*, 255 – 59, 263 – 64; Bottoms and Painter, "Bola Weights"; Bottoms and Painter, "Bolas and Birds"; Feiler, *Jean-Bernard Bossu's Travels*, 146 – 47; Wright, "Early Records . . . II"; Speck, Hassrick, and Carpenter, *Rappahannock Taking Devices*, 5 – 7, 12.

59. Lawson, *New Voyage to Carolina*, 17 ("firing"); Swanton, *Indians*, 329 ("Fire hunting was used for small game, generally including turkeys"); Speck, *Catawba Hunting*, 13.

60. Dickinson, *New Travels*, 44; Gilmore, "Hunting Habits."

61. Swanton, *Source Material . . . Choctaw*, 65, 74; Swanton, "Social Organization," 37 (Whooping Creek); Hawkins, *Sketch of the Creek Country*, 43, 50 – 51, 62 (Woc-co-coie, Pin-e-hoote, Pad-gee-li-gau, Wattooluhhaugau hatche); Martin and Maudlin, *Dictionary of Creek/Muskogee*, on great blue heron, turkey, red-headed woodpecker. On orthography: *v* is the mid-back rounded vowel that is the sound of *u* in "but" in English; thanks to Celeste Sullivan for discussion.

62. Swanton, *Indians*, 298 – 99.

63. Beverley, *History and Present State*, 210 – 11; Lawson, *New Voyage to Carolina*, 240; Hudson, *Southeastern Indians*, 270; Swanton, *Source Material . . . Choctaw*, 45. Migrating birds might once have figured more prominently in Choctaw reckoning of the passage of months and seasons (see Cushman, *History*, 193).

64. Le Page du Pratz, *History of Louisiana*, 2:352 – 84 (accessed March 7, 2006); cf. Tregle, *History of Louisiana*, 336 – 41; Swanton, *Indians*, 260 – 61.

MATERIAL CULTURE

1. Nicholson, "Bone Degradation, Burial Medium"; Nicholson, "Bone Degradation in a Compost Heap."

2. J. Daniel Rogers et al., "Identification of Feathers."

3. According to Sturtevant, representations were at first "tupinambized" and then evolved through a succession of allegorical feathered Americas and feathered-headdress images deriving initially from the Lakota, or Sioux, and applying ultimately to all North American Indians (as in powwows and processions); see Sturtevant, "La tupinambisation."

4. The visual record in the South runs from John White and Jacques Le Moyne de Morgues (and Theodore de Bry's engravings) to Alexandre de Batz, Joshua Reynolds, William Verelst, John Trumbull, Charles Bird King, George Catlin, the engravings in Thomas McKenney and James Hall's *History of the Indian Tribes of North America*, Alfred Boisseau, and others. See Honour, *New Golden Land*; Hulton, *Work of Jacques Le Moyne de Morgues*; Hulton, *America 1585*; Sturtevant, "First Visual Images"; Bushnell, "Drawings by A. DeBatz"; Feest, "Virginia Indian in Pictures"; Fundaburk, *Southeastern Indians*.

5. This entire topic deserves greater attention. See Downs, "British Influences"; Swanton, *Indians*, 468; Samuel Cole Williams, *Lieut. Henry Timberlake's Memoirs*, 134 ("adorned"); Krech, "Feather Use."

6. Hakluyt, *Divers Voyages*, 57 ("wear garlandes"); Swanton, *Indians*, 253, 499, 504–7, 541. Strachey apparently noted that Powhatan women wore feathers in their hair, but according to Swanton, this "was not as common as is supposed by white romancers" (*Indians*, 499; cf. Le Moyne's illustrations).

7. Robertson, "Account," 186n56; Garcilaso de la Vega, the Inca, "La Florida," 149, 266. Garcilaso mentions plumes more than do other chroniclers of the de Soto expedition; problematically, his account is secondhand, literary, and perhaps influenced by conventional representations of the Inca, among whom he had prior experience, as well as by European conventions of plume use.

8. Garcilaso de la Vega, the Inca, "La Florida," 290, 322, 327–28 (cf. Swanton, *Indians*, 430).

9. Quinn, "First Colony: John White," 427–43 passim.

10. Swanton, *Early History*, 73.

11. Swanton, *Early History*, 347 ("many pieces" [Le Moyne]; "esteem" [Le Challeux]).

12. Beverley, *History and Present State*, 161–62; Archer, "Description of the People," 103 ("long fethers"); Percy, "George Percy's Discourse," 137; Percy, "Fragment Published in 1614," 147.

13. John Smith, "Map of Virginia," 355; see also Barbour, *Complete Works*, 3:115. Strachey's (*Historie of Travell*, 74) account covers the same ground as Smith's except that he mentions a "buzzard," which was probably a buteo: men wore "the whole skyn of a hawke stuffed, with the winges abroad, and Buzzardes or other fowles whole wings, and to the feathers they [would] fasten a little Rattle." Beverley (*History and Present State*, 194), drawing on Smith, also remarked on a man with "the skin of a Bird with the Wings abroad dry'd, ty'd on his Head." See also Rountree, *Powhatan Indians of Virginia*, 70 (Archer); Swanton, *Indians*, 441–42, 502.

14. Swanton, *Indians*, 476 ("claws"), 501. A tiercelet was probably an accipiter or falcon.

15. Swanton, *Source Material . . . Caddo*, 142–46.

16. Strachey, *Historie of Travell*, 74 ("with a great pride"); Percy, "George Percy's Discourse," 136–37 ("a Birds Claw"). See also Rountree, *Powhatan Indians of Virginia*, 70–71 and n. 113; Kupperman, *Indians and English*, 63.

17. Lawson, *New Voyage to Carolina*, 203; Swanton, *Early History*, 149, 348.

18. Romans, *Concise Natural History*, 72–73, 122; Adair, *History*, 71 ("fasten"); Alexander Moore, *Nairne's Muskhogean Journals*, 48; Swanton, *Indians*, 253, 499, 505–6, 510; Fradkin, *Cherokee Folk Zoology*, 264; Harper, *Travels of William Bartram*, 318.

19. Speck, *Ethnology of the Yuchi Indians*, 46–48; Swanton, *Indians*, 497–98, 508–10; Hudson, *Southeastern Indians*, 264–65.

20. Harper, *Travels of William Bartram*, 318.

21. Romans, *Concise Natural History*, 146.

22. Tregle, *History of Louisiana*, 364–65.

23. Harper, *Travels of William Bartram*, 319–20 ("almost naked"); True, *Memoir of Dº. d'Escalante Fontaneda*, 30.

24. Swanton, *Source Material . . . Choctaw*, 43–44, 199 (italics added). *Ōpa*, a "large owl" (Byington, *Dictionary of Choctaw*), was probably either the (hooting) great horned or barred owl; yet for the Chickasaw, *ōpa* was the short-eared owl. In Europe, pheasants from India and guinea fowl from Africa were both called peafowl; Europeans transported guinea fowl to the American South (Andrew F. Smith, *Turkey*, 17–18, 54).

25. Swanton, *Source Material . . . Choctaw*, 44, 102, 191.

26. Robertson, "Account," 83; Lyon, "Canete Fragment," 308; Hudson, *Knights of Spain*, 146–84. Martyr also referred to "feather mantles of various colors" (Swanton, *Early History*, 44).

27. Swanton, *Indians*, 459–61 and 439–80 passim; Swanton, "Social Organization," 332–33; Brinton, *Notes on the Floridian Peninsula*, 104–5; Fradkin, *Cherokee Folk Zoology*, 263–64. A note on buffaloes: The heart of bison range was in the prairies and plains in the West, but buffaloes ranged nearly to the east coast and were occasionally encountered in the Southeast in the eighteenth and nineteenth centuries.

28. John Smith, "Map of Virginia," 355. Strachey's nearly identical account reads: "Some women wore mantells, made both of Turkey feathers and other fowle so prettely wrought and woven with threeds that nothing could be discerned but the feathers, which were exceeding warme and very handsome" (*Historie of Travell*, 72).

29. Lawson, *New Voyage to Carolina*, 197, 200.

30. Swanton, *Source Material . . . Caddo*, 38, 140.

31. Swanton, *Indians*, 462, 473; Tregle, *History of Louisiana*, 44, 272–73, 363 (perukes or wigs); Brannon, "Dress," 88 (La Salle on turkey-feather robes).

32. Swanton, *Indians*, 454; Hudson, *Southeastern Indians*, 267–68; Fradkin, *Cherokee Folk Zoology*, 263–64.

33. Swanton, *Indians*, 455.

34. Romans, *Concise Natural History*, 138; probably derivative of Le Page du Pratz.

35. Adair, *History*, 411–12; cf. Cushman, *History*, 330.

36. Swanton, *Indians*, 455.

37. Harper, *Travels of William Bartram*, 319.

38. Markham, *Hawkins' Voyages*, 62 ("fresh rivers"); Ian W. Brown, "Calumet Ceremony in the Southeast," 313; Blakeslee, "Origin and Spread," 759; John James Audubon, *Ornithological Biography*, 5:255–56; Bent, *Life Histories of North American Marsh Birds*, 1–12; Allen, Palmer, and Reilly, "Greater Flamingo."

39. Feduccia, *Catesby's Birds*, 29–30, 48–49; John James Audubon, *Ornithological Biography*, 4:188, 5:62; Allen et al., "Scarlet Ibis"; McAtee, "Folk Names," 83.

40. Swanton, *Early History*, 233 ("hit a flying bird," from an account of the Tristan de Luna expedition that set off to colonize Florida in 1559); Hudson, *Knights of Spain*, 88–127.

41. Swanton, *Indians*, 251, 571–82; Garcilaso, "La Florida," 70–71 ("made of thick feathers"), 291; John Smith, "Map of Virginia," 357; Barbour, *Complete Works*, 3:117; Strachey, *Historie of Travell*, 108; Ewan and Ewan, *John Banister*, 382; Beverley, *History and Present State*, 229; Rountree, *Powhatan Indians of Virginia*, 32, 41–42; Adair, *History*, 413; Speck, *Ethnology of the Yuchi Indians*, 21 ("swift and sure"); Fradkin, *Cherokee Folk Zoology*, 258, 263.

42. Sears, "Food Production"; Cleland, "Faunal Remains," 60; Woodrick, "Appendix D"; Hudson, *Southeastern Indians*, 54; Speck, Hassrick, and Carpenter, *Rappahannock Taking Devices*, 13 (turkey rib or leg-bone fishhook).

43. John Smith, "Map of Virginia," 371. See also Strachey, *Historie of Travell*, 62; Woodrick, "Appendix D."

44. Speck, *Ethnology of the Yuchi Indians*, 52. See also De Vorsey, *De Brahm's Report*, 111.

45. Tregle, *History of Louisiana*, 277, 365; Swanton, *Source Material . . . Caddo*, 187.

46. Swanton, "Early Account," 64; Swanton, *Source Material . . . Choctaw*, 233; Hawkins, *Sketch of the Creek Country*, 31.

47. Swanton, *Indians*, 552; Speck, "Catawba Medicines and Curative Practices," 184. According to one report, the burning quill might have left tracings in the hot clay, but Vincas Steponaitis (personal communication, March 28, 2004), among others, is skeptical that a burning quill could leave a mark, and one anonymous reviewer remarked correctly that a quill would effectively mark an unfired pot.

48. The Cherokee: Mooney and Olbrechts, *Swimmer Manuscript*, 68–69; Mooney, "Cherokee Ball Play," 121–22; Fradkin, *Cherokee Folk Zoology*, 305. The Creek: Alexander Moore, *Nairne's Muskhogean Journals*, 61.

49. Feduccia, *Catesby's Birds*, 40–41; Swanton, "Social Organization," 449.

50. Swanton, *Indians*, 444.

51. Ewan and Ewan, *John Banister*, 373; Wheeler, *Treasure of the Calusa*, 151, 156.

52. Le Page du Pratz, *History of Louisiana*, 3:260–61 (accessed March 7, 2006).

53. Braund, *Deerskins and Duffels*, 123–24.

54. Feiler, *Jean-Bernard Bossu's Travels*, 152–53.

55. Swanton, *Source Material . . . Caddo*, 199–200; Hawkins, *Sketch of the Creek Country*, 253 ("1 hat"); Waselkov, "French Colonial Trade" (the four occasions were 1719, 1759, 1760, and 1763). In Quebec in the same period, fifty plumes turn up in a list of goods needed for Indians (de Marly, *Dress in North America*, 79).

56. Alexander Wilson, *American Ornithology*, 7:112.

57. McClellan, *History of American Costume*, 148–491 passim, 409 ("shuttlecock"); Warwick et al., *Early American Dress*, 56–226 passim; de Marly, *Dress in North America*, 35–38, 45–47, 51 ("stylish").

58. Foreman, *Indians Abroad*; Warren, *Fashion Accessories since 1500*; Ribeiro and Cumming, *Visual History of Costume*; Ribeiro, *Dress in Eighteenth-Century Europe*; Ashelford, *Dress*; Ribeiro, *Art of Dress*; Ribeiro, *Gallery of Fashion*; Krech, "Feather Use."

59. Swanton, *Early History*, 176; Foreman, *Indians Abroad*, 46 ("natural").

IMAGERY

1. Lévi-Strauss, *Totemism*, 89; Lévi-Strauss, *Savage Mind*.

2. Bullen, "Carved Owl Totem"; Milanich and Fairbanks, *Florida Archaeology*, 168; Purdy, *Indian Art of Ancient Florida*; Fundaburk and Foreman, *Sun Circles and Human Hands*, plate 142.

3. Cushing, "Preliminary Report," 384, 426–27 ("a thin board"); Kolianos and Weisman, *Florida Journals*, 60 ("crowning find"); Milanich, "Temporal Placement." On other south Florida wooden sculptures of birds or painting on boards, see Sturtevant, "Last of the South Florida Aborigines," 148–49; Goggin, "Tekesta Indians of Southern Florida"; Hann, *Missions to the Calusa*, 422.

4. Cushing, "Preliminary Report," 384, 426–27; Gore, "Cushing's 'Bird-God of War.'"

5. Proctor and Lynch, *Manual of Ornithology*, 70–74.

6. Fundaburk and Foreman, *Sun Circles and Human Hands*, plates 21, 34, 37 (Moundville). With regard to speech, there is a Mayan convention relating speech (through scrolls spilling from

avian bills) to birds or bird manifestations of rulers or gods. A recent find in Mesoamerica that explores the connection is from near La Venta, some two thousand years before Key Marco (Pohl, Pope, and Nagy, "Olmec Origins of Mesoamerican Writing"). McAtee ("North American Bird Records," 59) mentions a note from seventeenth-century Virginia about use of the pileated woodpecker tongue for a toothpick, although whether by the English or the Powhatan is not clear. On hyoidal extension, see Proctor and Lynch, *Manual of Ornithology*, 127.

7. Goggin, "Manifestations"; Larson, "Examination" (Larson incorrectly concluded that the belted kingfisher is represented on these ornaments); Branstetter, "Montague Tallant Collection"; Wheeler, *Treasure of the Calusa*, 122 – 23, 135 – 36.

8. Partially obscured by the woodpecker's back is an enigmatic paddlelike (bi-lobed?) object. On crested woodpeckers, see Jerome A. Jackson, *Ivory-Billed Woodpecker*; Bull and Jackson, *Pileated Woodpecker*; Fradkin, *Cherokee Folk Zoology*, 417 ("lazy and stupid").

9. Lawson, *New Voyage to Carolina*, 196 (Carolina Indians); Swanton, *Indians*, 453 (Catesby, possibly derivative, on Siouans and the Chickasaw), 488 (Cofitachequi), 532 (Algonquian), 536 (Caddoan); Percy, "Fragment published in 1614," 142; Strachey, *Historie of Travell*, 72 (Powhatan); Swanton, *Source Material . . . Caddo*, 143, 155.

10. Reiger, " 'Plummets' "; Reiger, "Artistry, Status and Power"; Wheeler, *Treasure of the Calusa*, 17, 132 – 33, 158.

11. Earl C. Townsend Jr., *Birdstones*; Faulkner, "Tennessee Birdstones"; Weisman, "Popeyed Bird-Head Effigy"; Richard F. Townsend, "American Landscapes," 22, 26.

12. Hudson, *Southeastern Indians*, 34 – 119; Gibson, "Broken Circles"; Gibson, *Ancient Mounds of Poverty Point*; Milanich and Fairbanks, *Florida Archaeology*, 89 – 144; Fundaburk and Foreman,

Sun Circles and Human Hands, plate 112; Hudson, *Black Drink*.

13. The idea that people or ideas from Mexico influenced the Southeastern Ceremonial Complex (formerly, Southern or Buzzard Cult) has receded greatly in recent years in favor of endemic origins. The literature on Mississippian, SECC, and bird-man artifacts is voluminous. In addition to the essays in Galloway's *Southeastern Ceremonial Complex* — in particular Strong's "Mississippian Bird-Man Theme" — I have found the following especially useful: Larson, "Unusual Figurine from the Georgia Coast"; Kelly and Larson, "Explorations at Etowah"; Larson, "Southern Cult Manifestations"; Larson, "Mississippian Headdress"; Howard, *Southeastern Ceremonial Complex*; Stephen Williams, *Waring Papers*; Larson, "Archaeological Implications"; Peebles, "Moundville and Surrounding Sites"; James A. Brown, "Spiro Art"; James A. Brown, "Southern Cult Reconsidered"; Jones, "Southern Cult Manifestations"; Knight, Brown, and Lankford, "On the Subject Matter"; Cobb, "Mississippian Chiefdoms"; Kneberg, "Engraved Shell Gorgets"; Hudson, *Southeastern Indians*, 34 – 97, 122 – 83; Brose, "Interpretation of the Hopewellian Traits"; Milanich and Fairbanks, *Florida Archaeology*; McCane-O'Connor, "Prehistoric Ceramics"; Fuller and Silvia, "Ceramic Rim Effigies"; Lee Ann Wilson, "Southern Cult Images"; Luer, "Mississippian-Period Popeyed Bird-Head Effigies"; Luer, "Safety Harbor Incised Bottle"; Fundaburk and Foreman, *Sun Circles and Human Hands*; Kehoe, *America before the European Invasions*; James A. Brown, "Cahokian Expression," 106.

14. Knight, "Farewell." Thanks to Robbie Ethridge for the source.

15. See especially Galloway, *Southeastern Ceremonial Complex*; Knight, Brown, and Lankford, "On the Subject Matter"; Bierer, *Indians and Artifacts*; Fundaburk and Foreman, *Sun Circles and Human Hands*.

16. Schorger, *Wild Turkey*, 154 – 58, 248 – 52; Andrew F. Smith, *Turkey*, 5 – 6.

17. Another being was the so-called *piasa*, a composite serpent, raptor, and predatory cat. See Howard, *Southeastern Ceremonial Complex*, 37 – 53; Strong, "Mississippian Bird-Man Theme"; Knight, Brown, and Lankford, "On the Subject Matter"; James A. Brown, "Archaeology of Ancient Religion"; Hudson, *Southeastern Indians*, 128 – 32, 144 – 47; James A. Brown, "Cahokian Expression," 106, 118 – 19, and passim.

18. Alexander Wilson, *American Ornithology*, 9:121; Stephen Williams, *Waring Papers*; Howard, *Southeastern Ceremonial Complex*, 37 – 45; Galloway, *Southeastern Ceremonial Complex*; Clayton M. White et al., *Peregrine Falcon*, 2 ("nature's most"). A raptor is a carnivorous bird of prey that hunts or scavenges. Accipiters like Cooper's or sharp-shinned hawks possess tail proportions and banding patterns suggestive of SECC imagery but lack moustachial stripes. The eastern form of the peregrine became gravely endangered because of DDT; today many peregrines in the east are introduced western forms, or their descendants, which have much broader moustachial stripes.

19. On talons, see, e.g., Larson, "Examination."

20. Larson, "Mississippian Headdress"; Larson, "Archaeological Implications"; Knight and Steponaitis, "New History of Moundville"; Richard F. Townsend, "American Landscapes," 33 – 34; Swanton, "Social and Religious Beliefs," 251; Swanton, *Source Material . . . Choctaw*, 200, 212; Bushnell, *Choctaw of Bayou Lacomb*, 18.

21. Hudson, *Southeastern Indians*, 139 – 42; Douglas, *Purity and Danger*; Douglas, *Implicit Meanings*.

DESCENT AND POWER

1. Witthoft, "Will West Long"; Witthoft, "Bird Lore," 379.

2. Lawson, *New Voyage to Carolina*, 204 ("or some such"); Adair, *History*, 84,

220, 392, 508; Cushman, *History*, 76, 375; Swanton, "Social and Religious Beliefs," 187; Swanton, "Social Organization," 107. There seem to be few, if any, associations between birds and marriage, although in French Louisiana, a man at marriage wore a "tuft of feathers fastened to his hair" (Tregle, *History of Louisiana*, 345); Swanton, *Source Material . . . Choctaw*, 105, 122; Speck, "Creek Indians," 116; De Vorsey, *De Brahm's Report*, 109 (on the title Raven); Hawkins, *Sketch of the Creek Country*, 60, 361; Stiggins, *Creek Indian History*, 64 (war names); Parsons, *Notes on the Caddo*, 58.

3. Swanton, *Indians*, 654–61; Hewitt, "Notes on the Creek Indians," 128; Hudson, *Southeastern Indians*, 192–94, 236–37; Swanton, *Source Material . . . Choctaw*, 79; Swanton, "Social Organization," 108–70, 270–73; Swanton, *Source Material . . . Caddo*, 165–66. Two Timucuan clans were named for birds: Buzzard and Quail (Swanton, *Early History*, 371; Milanich and Fairbanks, *Florida Archaeology*, 222).

4. Swanton, "Social Organization," 111–273 passim; Hudson, *Southeastern Indians*, 184–202.

5. Swanton, "Social and Religious Beliefs," 192–98, 201 ("There were some people . . ."), 211. Tcowe'cak is probably the chimney swift; cf. *chotillak*, "chimney swallow" (Humes and Humes, *Chickasaw Dictionary*).

6. Charles Hudson (personal communication, May 23, 2005) suggests that the text also implies what he has always suspected, that Indians in the South "held the conception of a world of birds that symbolically paralleled the world of people." In this regard it might have shared basic assumptions of the anthropocentric worlds of mammals, fish, and other animals deemed important elsewhere in native America.

7. Speck, *Ethnology of the Yuchi Indians*, 70–71; Swanton, "Social Organization," 168–69. Something might have been lost in the translation to English; in

a society premised on matrilineal kinship, the correct metaphor would be, "You have killed my mothers and maternal uncles."

8. Moiety comes from the French *moitié* (half). Swanton, "Social Organization," 111–273 passim, 164 ("spring crane"); Swanton, *Indians*, 251, 664; Walker, "Creek Confederacy before Removal," 382–83. On color symbolism, see Hudson, *Southeastern Indians*, 132, 331–**32**, 358–60, 374, 410, and passim.

9. Robertson, "Account," 92; Rangel, "Account," 290. See also Brannon, "Dress."

10. Garcilaso, "La Florida," 69.

11. Robertson, "Account," 112–13.

12. Biggar, *Jean Ribaut*, 79 ("trymed"); Laudonnière, *Three Voyages*, 20; Swanton, *Early History*, 79, 234 ("most beautiful"), 351, 356; Swanton, *Indians*, 528, 649; Longe, "Small Postscript," 22. Laudonnière also remarked on what he called "hermaphrodites," or transvestites who "paint[ed] their faces and fluff[ed] out their hair with feathers," which he somehow thought was "in order to make themselves as repulsive as possible" (*Three Voyages*, 13).

13. Tregle, *History of Louisiana*, 354, 357; Hudson, *Southeastern Indians*, 331.

14. Tregle, *History of Louisiana*, 365–66.

15. Swanton, *Source Material . . . Caddo*, 157.

16. Swanton, *Indians*, 501 (Harriot plate 3).

17. John Smith, "Map of Virginia," 355; Rountree, *Powhatan Indians of Virginia*, 69–70, 101–2.

18. Strachey, *Historie of Travell*, 65. See also Swanton, *Indians*, 645. Unfortunately, "A Match-coat from Virginia: Feathers-Deer-skin" in Tradescant's collection in the Ashmolean Museum has long since disappeared (Bushnell, "Virginia," 38 (cf. Ewan and Ewan, *John Banister*, 394).

19. Hudson, *Southeastern Indians*, 204; Walker, "Creek Confederacy before Removal," 388–89.

20. Gerrard and Bortolotti, *Bald Eagle*; Stalmaster, *Bald Eagle*; Palmer, "Golden Eagle," 197–99; Watson, *Golden Eagle*, 90 and passim; Kochert et al., *Golden Eagle*; Buehler, *Bald Eagle*; Bent, *Life Histories of North American Birds of Prey*, pt. 1, 309 (William Brewster).

21. Gerrard and Bortolotti, *Bald Eagle*, 2–7; Watson, *Golden Eagle*, 258–59; Feduccia, *Catesby's Birds*, 34–35.

22. A Timucuan chief presented two young eagles to a leader of Laudonnière's expedition. Did he realize that this was the king of birds for the French (Swanton, *Indians*, 346)?

23. Adair, *History*, 409; Hudson, *Knights of Spain*, 69.

24. Harper, *Travels of William Bartram*, 326.

25. Adair, *History*, 87. See also Swanton, *Indians*, 331, 715.

26. Feiler, *Jean-Bernard Bossu's Travels*, 161.

27. Cuming, "Journal of Sir Alexander Cuming," 135, 136, 143; Samuel Cole Williams, *Lieut. Henry Timberlake's Memoirs*, 63–64; Hudson, *Southeastern Indians*, 164.

28. Foreman, *Indians Abroad*, 50; Jason B. Jackson, Fogelson, and Sturtevant, "History," 32.

29. Williams, *Lieut. Henry Timberlake's Memoirs*, 103, 107; Hudson, *Southeastern Indians*, 164, 168.

30. Swanton, *Source Material . . . Caddo*, 232.

31. Foreman, *Indians Abroad*, 58.

32. Swan, "Position and State," 265; Swanton, "Social Organization," 182.

33. de Milford, *Memoir*, 156–57.

34. Swanton, "Social Organization," 243 ("a wooden eagle"); Swanton, "Religious Beliefs and Medical Practices," 503.

35. Harper, *Travels of William Bartram*, 96, 287.

36. Knight, *Moundville Expeditions*, 382–87; Harper, "*Vultur sacra* of William Bartram."

37. Hewitt, "Notes on the Creek Indians," 134.

38. Osceola was often portrayed wearing several plumes, two black and one white, for example; he was evidently painted in one portrait with two ostrich and one crane/egret feather (McCarthy, "Portraits of Osceola"; Goggin, "Osceola," 167 [quotations from Catlin]; Kersey, *Pelts, Plumes, and Hides*, 39 [ostrich plumes]). See also http://www.nativetech.org/seminole/turbans/index.php.

39. Speck, "Catawba Religious Beliefs, Mortuary Customs, and Dances," 39–40; Speck and Schaeffer, "Catawba Kinship and Social Organization."

WAR AND PEACE

1. For discussion I am grateful to Fred Fausz (personal communication, e-mail April 28, 2006, based on his in-process work, "Jamestown Massacre of 1622"). Nemattanew and Jack of the Feathers are spelled variously. Barbour, *Complete Works* 2:293 ("immortall . . . make it known"); Fausz and Kukla, "Letter of Advice," 108–9, 117; Beverley, *History and Present State*, 52–53 ("often dress"); Fausz, "George Thorpe," 113 ("all covered"); Rountree, *Powhatan Indians*, 77–78 and notes; Fausz, "Opechancanough," 30; Rountree, *Pocahontas's People*, 57, 61, 69, 71–73, 302.

2. Strachey, *Historie of Travell*, 73. Banister remarked on young men preparing for war by painting their bodies red and black and "strewing swans down upon their heads" in order to "appear terrible to the beholders" (Ewan and Ewan, *John Banister*, 381). Beverley—drawing from Banister—also commented on men who, about to dance prior to going to war, painted themselves various colors and "to make themselves appear yet more ugly and frightful, [strew] Feathers, Down, or the hair of Beasts, upon the Paint while it [was] still moist, and capable of making these light substances stick fast on" (*History and Present State*, 192). Swanton (*Indians*, 529) believes that Strachey's "Carnation byrd, which they call Ahshowcutteis"

was the redstart, but a more obvious candidate is the resident northern cardinal. Herneshew was then a common name for heron.

3. Robertson, "Account," 110. One member of the expedition complained that if he happened to kill an Indian, he found "nothing to take from him except a bow and a plume, as if they were any use to me" (Garcilaso, "La Florida," 401).

4. Garcilaso, "La Florida," 320–21, 394, 461–62, 476, 486. The first two places mentioned were Coste and Pacaha. Garcilaso's account is difficult to judge. An interesting metaphorical (if not literal) use of birds was recorded when Indians guiding de Soto spoke about a town so large "that its people, shouting, made flying birds fall" (Hernández de Biedma, "Relation," 226).

5. Robertson, "Account," 155–56.

6. Garcilaso, "La Florida," 507–8.

7. Swanton, *Early History*, 352; Swanton, *Source Material . . . Caddo*, 190, 196.

8. Lawson, *New Voyage to Carolina*, 201.

9. Romans, *Concise Natural History*, 133 (the use of bacchant—an inspired votary of Bacchus, thus a drunken reveler—is one of many examples of use of classical imagery and allegory to make sense of American Indians; like many, it is misplaced); Larson, "Historic Guale Indians"; Swanton, *Indians*, 697; Swanton, "Early Account," 66; Swanton, *Source Material . . . Choctaw*, 163; *OED Online*, s.v. "bacchant," accessed September 1, 2006.

10. Adair, *History*, 197. See also Swanton, *Indians*, 696; Swanton, "Social and Religious Beliefs," 235; Hudson, *Southeastern Indians*, 325.

11. Harper, *Travels of William Bartram*, 154.

12. Adair, *History*, 380; Swanton, "Early Account," 66; Swanton, *Source Material . . . Choctaw*, 162, 166; Swanton, "Social Organization," 413.

13. Quoting John Stuart, in Adair, *History*, 489. Braund believes these to have

been tundra swans, but see discussion on pp. 16 and 206n17.

14. Swanton, *Indians*, 696; Hudson, *Southeastern Indians*, 326; Lankford, *Native American Legends*, 113–16.

15. Mooney, *Myths of the Cherokee*, 281–83; Hudson, *Southeastern Indians*, 129, 163.

16. Speck, "Creek Indians of Taskigi Town," 118; Swanton, *Source Material . . . Caddo*, 234.

17. Beverley, *History and Present State*, 196.

18. Witthoft, "Bird Lore," 380; Kimberly G. Smith, Withgott, and Rodewald, *Red-Headed Woodpecker*; Hudson, *Southeastern Indians*, 386 (Hudson's *dalala* is the red-headed woodpecker).

19. Swanton, "Social Organization," 436; Adair, *History*, 505.

20. Swanton, *Early History*, 233, 255–56.

21. Adair, *History*, 111–12, 199–200. See also Swanton, "Social and Religious Beliefs," 238–39; Hudson, *Southeastern Indians*, 257.

22. Swanton, *Source Material . . . Caddo*, 181–82.

23. Swanton, "Social Organization," 36, 299, 441–43; Hawkins, *Sketch of the Creek Country*, 215, 400 ("the white road"), 493 ("white smoke"); Martin and Maudlin, *Dictionary of Creek/Muskogee*, 9.

24. Alexander Moore, *Nairne's Muskhogean Journals*, 40–42 (brackets in original).

25. Lawson, *New Voyage to Carolina*, 175; von Gernet and Timmins, "Pipes and Parakeets"; Hall, "Anthropocentric Perspective"; Turnbaugh, "Calumet Ceremonialism"; Blakeslee, "Origin and Spread"; Springer, "Ethnohistoric Study"; Paper, *Offering Smoke*; Ian W. Brown, "Calumet Ceremony in the Southeast"; Ian W. Brown, "Calumet Ceremony in the Southeast as Observed Archaeologically"; Hall, *Archaeology of the Soul*.

26. Adair, *History*, 412–13; Swanton, *Indians*, 546; Swanton, "Social Organization," 435; Swanton, *Source Material . . .*

Caddo, 158; Swanton, *Source Material . . . Choctaw*, 169; Swanton, "Early Account," 67.

27. See Ian W. Brown, "Calumet Ceremony in the Southeast," 313; compare Blakeslee, "Origin and Spread," 759.

28. Le Page's flight feathers fit the snow goose, the white ibis, the white pelican, or the whooping crane, but not any eagle. Tregle, *History of Louisiana*, 45, 271 ("very rare"), 273–74 ("Perching Duck"), 370–71 ("by the pipe"), 371 ("a fan made").

29. von Gernet, "*Nicotiana* Dreams"; see also von Gernet, "North American Indigenous *Nicotiana* Use."

30. Marquette, "Voyages du P. Jacques Marquette," 129, 131, 133 (http://puffin .creighton.edu/jesuit/relations/relations _59.html, accessed April 14, 2006). See Hall, *Archaeology of the Soul*, 168; von Gernet and Timmins, "Pipes and Parakeets," 38–40.

31. Mooney, *Myths of the Cherokee*, 286–87, 454; Swanton (*Indians*, 675) made a simple error in stating that Bat and Flying Squirrel won this game for the animals.

32. Swanton, *Myths and Tales*, 22–23.

33. Swanton, *Myths and Tales*, 23; Lankford, *Native American Legends*, 241.

34. Swanton, *Indians*, 674–86; Hudson, *Southeastern Indians*, 408–21.

35. Romans, *Concise Natural History*, 134; Feiler, *Jean-Bernard Bossu's Travels*, 169–70; Swanton, *Source Material . . . Choctaw*, 140, 150 (feathers later apparently obsolete).

36. Tregle, *History of Louisiana*, 341.

37. Swanton, *Indians*, 664, 677; Swanton, "Social Organization," 190, 460 ("masterful"), 462.

38. Swanton, "Social Organization," 244 ("emblematic"); Swanton, *Indians*, 617; Hann, *History of the Timucua Indians*, 109; Hann and McEwan, *Apalachee Indians*, 122–35.

39. Harper, *Travels of William Bartram*, 234 ("high waving plumes"); Hudson, *Southeastern Indians*, 409; John James

Audubon, *Ornithological Biography*, 1:117; 2:177–78.

SPIRITUALITY

1. Quinn, "First Colony: John White," 427, 429, 440, 442–43; Hulton, *America 1585*, 79, 117, 182, 189; Strachey, *Historie of Travell*, 95–96; John Smith, "True Relation," 188; John Smith, "Map of Virginia," 365–66; Swanton, *Indians*, 477 (Harriot). Even though Rountree (*Powhatan Indians*, 78, 100–102) regards "the connection between feathers and religious power, at least for the Powhatans" as "very poorly documented," the evidence points rather to an association between birds and religion for these and other Indian people in the South.

2. Beverley, *History and Present State*, 203, 212 ("a black bird"). Rumee Ahmed (personal communication May 23, 2006) suggests, "[The story about Mahomet's pigeon (or dove)] seems very common in Medieval European polemical works against Islam" but is without evidence "in either Muslim historical or hadith works as far as I know. There is also an apocryphal story about a pigeon that the prophet kept, and the two stories are possibly conflated to make 'Mahomet's pigeon.'"

3. Lawson, *New Voyage to Carolina*, 25. With regard to his intentions, Beverley wrote more evenhandedly about American Indians than did many of his contemporaries.

4. Adair, *History*, 131. See also Swanton, *Indians*, 251.

5. Nunez, "Creek Nativism," 14.

6. Le Page du Pratz, *History of Louisiana*, 3:20 (accessed March 7, 2006; cf. Neitzel, *Archeology of the Fatherland Site*, 71); Swanton, *Source Material . . . Caddo*, 146, 157, 214–16, 223.

7. Swanton, "Sun Worship in the Southeast"; Speck, "Catawba Religious Beliefs," 39; Daniel Rogers and Sabo, "Caddo," 625; Parsons, *Notes on the Caddo*, 43, 51–52. This reflection on birds and religion is informed by Evans-Pritchard, *Nuer Religion*, 123–43; Turner,

"'We Are Parrots,'"; Balzer, "Flights of the Sacred"; Armstrong, *Folklore of Birds*; Armstrong, *Life and Lore*; Rowland, *Birds with Human Souls*; Thomas, *Man and the Natural World*, among others.

8. Sears, "Food Production"; Sears, *Fort Center*; Milanich and Fairbanks, *Florida Archaeology*, 187.

9. Robertson, "Account," 57; Garcilaso, "La Florida," 301. See Milanich and Hudson, *Hernando de Soto*, 63.

10. Le Page du Pratz, *History of Louisiana*, 3:18 (accessed March 7, 2006; cf. Neitzel, *Archeology of the Fatherland Site*, 70); Tregle, *History of Louisiana*, 351–52; Swanton, *Indians*, 613.

11. On imitating the Natchez, see Swanton, *Indians*, 419; Bushnell, "Drawings by A. DeBatz," plate 1.

12. Neitzel, *Archeology of the Fatherland Site*, 69–71.

13. Adair, *History*, 213. See also Swanton, *Indians*, 613.

14. Lawson, *New Voyage to Carolina*, 28; Strachey, *Historie of Travell*, 100; Rountree, *Powhatan Indians of Virginia*, 113, 139; Swanton, *Indians*, 724, 746; Swanton, "Religious Beliefs and Medical Practices," 513 ("great eagle"); Neitzel, *Archeology of the Fatherland Site*, 78; Swanton, *Source Material . . . Caddo*, 204.

15. Swanton, *Indians*, 537, 726, 729; Swanton, *Source Material . . . Choctaw*, 189; Lawson, *New Voyage to Carolina*, 188.

16. Buckley, *Black Vulture*; Kirk and Mossman, *Turkey Vulture*; Alexander Wilson, *American Ornithology*, 9:97–98, 104–7, cf. 112

17. Feiler, *Jean-Bernard Bossu's Travels*, 202; Alexander Wilson, *American Ornithology*, 9:97–98, 104–7, cf. 112.

18. Mooney and Olbrechts, *Swimmer Manuscript*, 272; Mooney, *Myths of the Cherokee*, 284; Swanton, *Indians*, 251; McAtee, "North American Bird Records," 59 ("old Aches"); Hudson, *Southeastern Indians*, 340.

19. Milanich and Sturtevant, *Francisco Pareja's 1613 Confessionario*, 23, 44 (blue jay); Hudson, *Southeastern Indians*, 178

(woodpecker); Swanton, *Source Material . . . Choctaw,* 199 (sapsucker [*biskinik*]); Swanton, "Catawba Notes," 628 (grouse); de Baillou, "Contribution," 93 – 102 (goose); Speck, *Catawba Texts,* 34 – 36 (small birds, cardinal), 39 – 40 (crow); Longe, "A Small Postscript," 46 (screech-owl); Fradkin, *Cherokee Folk Zoology,* 400 – 402.

20. Romans, *Concise Natural History,* 132. An "owl of the large kind" was probably either the great horned owl or, less likely, the barred owl.

21. Harper, *Travels of William Bartram,* 320.

22. Swanton, *Indians,* 252; Hudson, *Southeastern Indians,* 340.

23. Swanton, *Indians,* 618.

24. Adair, *History,* 84; Romans, *Concise Natural History,* 132. Both Adair and Romans published their works in 1775.

25. Willughby, *Ornithology,* 24; Edwards, *Gleanings of Natural History,* 3:334 – 35; Linné, *Systema Naturae,* 72 – 78; Waters, *Concise History of Ornithology,* 176 – 88.

26. John James Audubon, *Ornithological Biography,* 1:49.

27. Adair, *History,* 84, 377 – 78; Romans, *Concise Natural History,* 132; Hudson, *Southeastern Indians,* 240; Wells, *100 Birds,* 261 – 62; John James Audubon, *Ornithological Biography,* 1:99; Choate, *Dictionary of American Bird Names,* 82, 156.

28. Swanton, *Source Material . . . Caddo,* 222, 225.

29. I am grateful to Arlene Fradkin (personal communication, April 8, 2006) for discussion of this section. Longe, "A Small Postscript," 44.

30. Audubon encountered only two Bewick's wrens in Louisiana in the 1820s, remarking, "Where it comes from, and whither it goes to breed, are quite unknown to me" (John James Audubon, *Ornithological Biography,* 1:96).

31. Stouff, *Sacred Beliefs,* 34 – 35 and passim.

32. On anomaly, see Douglas, *Purity and Danger;* Douglas, *Implicit Meanings;* and Douglas, "Pangolin Revisited."

33. Beverley, *History and Present State,* 214. This bird received its name (Pawcorance) because it apparently sounded the name of an altar stone where offerings were made. John Smith, "Map of Virginia," 367; Gilliam, "Powhatan's Dearest Bird."

34. Feduccia, *Catesby's Birds,* 71 – 72.

35. Hewitt, "Notes on the Creek Indians," 156 – 57; Speck, "Creek Indians of Taskigi Town," 135 (according to Speck, *stikini* is "little screech owl," but others have it as great horned owl); Speck, "Catawba Religious Beliefs," 36 – 37; Nunez, "Creek Nativism," 149 ("flying about"); Swanton, "Social and Religious Beliefs," 252, 271.

36. Bushnell, *Choctaw of Bayou Lacomb,* 33; Swanton, *Source Material . . . Choctaw,* 198 – 99 (common owl), 216 – 17; Campbell, "Choctaw Afterworld," 149. The identification of the "common owl" is uncertain; a "large owl" (Byington, *Dictionary of Choctaw*), it was perhaps the great horned or barred owl — but for the Chickasaw, "ōpa" was the short-eared owl.

37. Mooney, "Sacred Formulas of the Cherokees," 354; Mooney and Olbrechts, *Swimmer Manuscript,* 29; Witthoft, "Some Eastern Cherokee Bird Stories," 180; Witthoft, "Bird Lore," 379; Alan Kilpatrick, *Night Has a Naked Soul,* 4, 8 – 11, 31; Longe, "A Small Postscript," 46 ("cut to pieces"); Fradkin, *Cherokee Folk Zoology,* 168 – 69, 399 – 402; Hudson, *Southeastern Indians,* 126.

38. Speck, *Catawba Texts,* 24 – 26, 36 – 37; Swanton, "Catawba Notes," 628; Speck, "Catawba Religious Beliefs."

39. Swanton, *Source Material . . . Caddo,* 221, 224; Parsons, *Notes on the Caddo,* 33 – 34, 57 – 58. Also on owls, see Milanich and Sturtevant, *Francisco Pareja's 1613 Confessionario,* 24, 26; Swanton, *Early History,* 383.

40. König, Weick, and Becking, *Owls;*

Marks, Evans, and Holt, *Long-Eared Owl;* Bent, *Life Histories of North American Birds of Prey,* pt. 2, 163 (Brewster).

41. Swann, *Dictionary of English and Folk-Names,* 13, 208 ("sign of death"); Armstrong, *Folklore of Birds,* 113 ("witchcraft, death and doom"); Bent, *Life Histories of North American Birds of Prey,* pt. 2, 140 – 53 (barn owl); McAtee, "Folk Names of Florida Birds," 121 – 22 (monkey-face owl); Rowland, *Birds with Human Souls,* 115 – 20; Douglas, *Purity and Danger;* Douglas, *Implicit Meanings;* Hunn, "Abominations of Leviticus Revisited," 110 – 11; Bulmer, "Uncleanness."

42. Speck, *Ethnology of the Yuchi Indians,* 112 – 31, 127 ("all bent over").

43. Speck, *Ethnology of the Yuchi Indians,* 112 – 31, 129 ("allowed liberties").

44. Rountree, *Powhatan Indians of Virginia,* 98; Lawson, *New Voyage to Carolina,* 44.

45. Speck, "Catawba Religious Beliefs," 48 – 49, 53 – 54; Swanton, "Social and Religious Beliefs," 257; Swanton, *Source Material . . . Choctaw,* 193, 222 – 23; Hudson, *Southeastern Indians,* 403 – 5.

46. Speck, "Creek Indians of Taskigi Town," 135; Swanton, "Religious Beliefs," 549ff.; Speck, *Ceremonial Songs,* 163, 169 – 71, 178 – 82, 186 – 90.

47. Swanton, "Religious Beliefs and Medical Practices," 546 – 613, 548 ("white day . . . yard of peace"); Hewitt, "Notes on the Creek Indians," 150 – 53; Speck, "Creek Indians," 141 ("white egrets"); Howard, *Southeastern Ceremonial Complex,* 80 – 150; Swanton, *Indians,* 633 ("a high pole," a quotation from Hodgson, an English missionary in Creek country in 1820); Bushnell, "Account of Lamhatty"; Swanton, "Green Corn Dance," 180; Hudson, *Southeastern Indians,* 367 – 75 (Chickasaw priests etc.).

48. Swanton, "Religious Beliefs," 609; Swanton, "Green Corn Dance," 182; Speck, "Ceremonial Songs," 186 – 90 ("rather spectacular").

49. Weslager, "Nanticokes and the Buzzard Song."

BIRD SPIRITS AND SPIRIT-BIRDS

1. Speck, "Creek Indians of Taskigi Town," 122, 131–32. (The phrase and song "they chatter" is said to be repeated "a number of times"; four is selected here. Orthography: the second "tins" is *ti* + nasalized *i* + *s*. Martin is "djil djil," which might be an onomatope, because its Creek name bears no resemblance.) Hewitt, "Notes on the Creek Indians," 155; Swanton, "Religious Beliefs and Medical Practices," 636–70; Speck, "Ceremonial Songs," 213, 219–20, 237–40; Paredes, "Folk Culture," 100. In recent times, chickens were believed to cure chicken pox, and a quail's head placed in the mouth of an infant guaranteed that he or she would speak well.

2. Adair, *History*, 204–5 (in using "cherubimical," Adair yet again sought connection with the Old Testament — in this case the divine two- or four-winged creatures able, if need be, to transport Jehovah); Swanton, "Social and Religious Beliefs," 258–72; Speck, "Notes on Chickasaw Ethnology," 54.

3. Lawson, *New Voyage*, 226–27; Swanton, *Source Material . . . Caddo*, 220.

4. In addition to the work of James Mooney, John Witthoft, Will West Long, and Jack, Anna, and Alan Kilpatrick, that of Frans Olbrechts (on Mooney's materials) and Raymond D. Fogelson should be mentioned (and is cited in the pages that follow). Ethnographers of the Cherokee (and Cherokees themselves) have long remarked that some men and women knew far more than most about traditional culture, the "walking encyclopediae" or "curators of the myths and stories," the ones whom Cherokees themselves said "knew most" (Mooney and Olbrechts, *Swimmer Manuscript*, 88–89).

5. For *idi:gawé:sdi*, see Mooney, "Sacred Formulas of the Cherokees"; Mooney and Olbrechts, *Swimmer Manuscript*; Jack Kilpatrick and Anna Kilpatrick, *Walk in Your Soul*; Jack Kilpatrick and Anna Kilpatrick, *Run toward the Nightland*. To be effective, the incanta-tions must be delivered in Cherokee (Jack Kilpatrick and Anna Kilpatrick, *Walk in Your Soul*, 13).

6. Mooney, "Sacred Formulas of the Cherokees," 340.

7. Jack Kilpatrick and Anna Kilpatrick, *Run toward the Nightland*, 56–57; Jack Kilpatrick and Anna Kilpatrick, *Walk in Your Soul*, 28.

8. Mooney, "Sacred Formulas of the Cherokees," 342–43; Jack Kilpatrick and Anna Kilpatrick, *Walk in Your Soul*, 8.

9. Mooney, "Sacred Formulas of the Cherokees," 397; Jack Kilpatrick and Anna Kilpatrick, *Run toward the Nightland*, 110, 159, 172–73, and passim; John James Audubon, *Ornithological Biography*, 1:249.

10. Jack Kilpatrick and Anna Kilpatrick, *Walk in Your Soul*; Jack Kilpatrick and Anna Kilpatrick, *Run toward the Nightland*.

11. Jack Kilpatrick and Anna Kilpatrick, *Walk in Your Soul*, 62–67.

12. Jack Kilpatrick and Anna Kilpatrick, *Run toward the Nightland*, 54; Jack Kilpatrick and Anna Kilpatrick, *Walk in Your Soul*, 20–21.

13. Jack Kilpatrick and Anna Kilpatrick, *Run toward the Nightland*, 59 ("Now! Listen!"); Jack Kilpatrick and Anna Kilpatrick, *Walk in Your Soul*, 21–29, 51–52 (*tsugv:tsala:la* is variously the black-and-white warbler [Eastern Cherokees] and various orioles [Oklahoma Cherokees] as well as a beautiful spirit bird resembling the northern bobwhite).

14. Mooney, *Myths of the Cherokees*, 280–94; Mooney and Olbrechts, *Swimmer Manuscript*, 36, 65–66, 156, 179, 285; Fradkin, *Cherokee Folk Zoology*, 288–302, 346, 386–421.

15. Mooney, "Sacred Formulas of the Cherokees," 341, 355–56; Mooney and Olbrechts, *Swimmer Manuscript*, 43–50, 76, 178, 181, 186, 189, 191, 214, 220–21, 264, 266–67, 295–96; Hudson, *Southeastern Indians*, 129.

16. Jack Kilpatrick and Anna Kilpatrick, *Notebook of a Cherokee Shaman*, 123–24 ("Pileated Woodpecker"); John James Audubon, *Ornithological Biography*, 2:177–78.

17. Mooney, "Sacred Formulas of the Cherokees," 354; Mooney and Olbrechts, *Swimmer Manuscript*, 29; Witthoft, "Some Eastern Cherokee Bird Stories," 180; Witthoft, "Bird Lore," 379; Alan Kilpatrick, *The Night Has a Naked Soul*, 4, 8–11, 31; Hudson, *Southeastern Indians*, 126.

18. Jack Kilpatrick and Anna Kilpatrick, *Walk in Your Soul*, 59 ("Now! The whip-poor-will") and passim; Jack Kilpatrick and Anna Kilpatrick, *Run toward the Nightland*, 110, 159, 172–73, and passim; Alan Kilpatrick, *The Night Has a Naked Soul*, 9, 87–88 ("Bring me your soul").

19. Mooney, *Myths of the Cherokee*, 401–2; Mooney and Olbrechts, *Swimmer Manuscript*, 30; Jack Kilpatrick and Anna Kilpatrick, *Friends of Thunder*, 147–48; Alan Kilpatrick, *The Night Has a Naked Soul*, 9–10; Hudson, *Southeastern Indians*, 179–82.

20. Jack Kilpatrick and Anna Kilpatrick, *Friends of Thunder*, 4; Fogelson, "Change, Persistence, and Accommodation," 222.

21. Fogelson, "Change, Persistence, and Accommodation," 220–21. Hoot owl is a vernacular name for the barred owl (McAtee, "Folk Names of Florida Birds," 122).

SACRED AND SECULAR NARRATIVES

1. Urban and Jackson, "Mythology and Folklore."

2. Swanton, "Mythology," 286–87; Brightman, "Chitimacha."

3. Lankford, *Native American Legends*, 126.

4. Swanton, *Myths and Tales*, 7, 131–33, 182–83, 222; Lankford, *Native American Legends*, 149–50, 160–61.

5. Lankford, *Native American Legends*, 59, 61–63 (Tunica, Cherokee Cardinal); Swanton, *Myths and Tales*, 169 (Snipe); Jack Kilpatrick and Anna Kilpatrick, *Friends of Thunder*, 136–37 (Cherokee Shrike, Cardinal, Chickadee).

6. Mooney, *Myths of the Cherokee*, 316 – 19, 466 – 69; Jack Kilpatrick and Anna Kilpatrick, *Friends of Thunder*, 136 – 37.

7. Speck, *Ethnology of the Yuchi Indians*, 103 – 4, 138; Swanton, *Myths and Tales*, 84 – 85; Mooney, *Myths of the Cherokee*, 239 – 42, 430.

8. Swanton, *Source Material . . . Choctaw*, 200, 212; Bushnell, *Choctaw of Bayou Lacomb*, 18.

9. Swanton, *Myths and Tales*, 123 ("a bird like a wren"); for *cehcekwuce*, see Martin and Maudlin, *Dictionary of Creek/Muskogee*.

10. The widely found tale is known as "The Bungling Host." Swanton, *Myths and Tales*, 55 – 211 passim, 254 – 55 ("good for me"); Jack Kilpatrick and Anna Kilpatrick, *Friends of Thunder*, 26 – 29.

11. Swanton, *Myths and Tales*, 121, 175 – 77; Lankford, *Native American Legends*, 109 – 11. In a tale said by Swanton (*Myths and Tales*, 81 – 82) to be European, a red-headed woodpecker flies up to Lightning for help in completing a task, clearly an indigenous role for this bird.

12. Speck, "Creek Indians of Taskigi Town," 145 – 46; Swanton, "Religious Beliefs and Medical Practices," 487 – 88; Martin and Maudlin, *Dictionary of Creek/Muskogee*.

13. Cushman, *History*, 225 – 27; Swanton, *Source Material . . . Choctaw*, 202 – 10.

14. Swanton, *Source Material . . . Caddo*, 27; Swanton, *Source Material . . . Choctaw*, 202 – 11; Speck, *Catawba Texts*, 23; Cushman, *History*, 223 – 24 (Puchi Yushubah); Lankford, *Native American Legends*, 144 – 46; Alice Parmalee, *All the Birds*, 53 – 58. The passenger pigeon had red irises, a black bill, and a slate blue head (Schorger, *Passenger Pigeon*, 231 – 32). The red-billed pigeon has red irises, a red bill, and is dark bluish purple in color. A Mexican species, it is not found today north (or east) of the lower Rio Grande, but its former range possibly intersected with the Choctaw.

15. Swanton, *Myths and Tales*, 123 – 24.

16. Swanton, *Early History*, 192.

17. Swanton, *Myths and Tales*, 118 – 213 passim; Lankford, *Native American Legends*, 64 – 65.

18. Swanton, "Social Organization," 36; Lankford, *Native American Legends*, 113 – 16.

19. Swanton, *Myths and Tales*, 37, 89 – 91, 154, 192, 246 – 47; Mooney, *Myths of the Cherokee*, 284 – 87, 315 – 16, 466; Lankford, *Native American Legends*, 74 – 79, 125; see also Jack Kilpatrick and Anna Kilpatrick, *Friends of Thunder*, 70 – 76.

20. Mooney, *Myths of the Cherokee*, 254 – 55 (Hummingbird), 288 – 89 (Kingfisher), 293 (Turkey Vulture), 401 – 3 and passim; Speck, "Catawba Religious Beliefs," 32 (Flicker — Catawba); Speck, *Catawba Texts*, 5 (Robin), 5 – 6 (Flicker); Witthoft, "Bird Lore"; Witthoft, "Some Eastern Cherokee Bird Stories"; Fradkin, *Cherokee Folk Zoology*, 288 – 302, 346, 386 – 421; Jack Kilpatrick and Anna Kilpatrick, *Friends of Thunder*, 24 – 25; Lankford, *Native American Legends*, 126 – 27 (Buzzards — Caddo).

21. Mooney, *Myths of the Cherokee*, 290 – 91; Swanton, *Myths and Tales*, 42, 102, 157, 169 – 70, 201 – 2, 248 – 49, 253, 259 – 60; Lankford, *Native American Legends*, 129 – 31; Jack Kilpatrick and Anna Kilpatrick, *Friends of Thunder*, 10 – 12.

22. Swanton, *Myths and Tales*, 10 – 19, 54, 57, 134 – 35, 178 – 81, 230 – 39.

23. Swanton, *Myths and Tales*, 2 – 7, 215 – 18, 227 – 30, 237, 241 – 42; Greenlee, "Folktales of the Florida Seminole," 144 (Rabbit).

24. Swanton, *Myths and Tales*, 59, 127, 139, 142, 175, 187, 219 – 22, 234 – 39; Speck, *Catawba Texts*, 22; Jack Kilpatrick and Anna Kilpatrick, *Friends of Thunder*, 24 – 25, 32 – 35.

25. Swanton, *Myths and Tales*, 47 – 48, 109, 210, 259.

26. Swanton, *Myths and Tales*, 57 – 58.

27. Among the unidentified are the Koasati *tciktcinigasi* (wren?) and *tcukbi-labila* (chuck-will's-widow); thanks to an anonymous reader for the latter. Seemingly also invisible are gulls, but the Yuchi mistakenly took the first white people they saw for gulls, because they emerged from sea foam (Swanton, *Myths and Tales*, 200, 202; Lankford, *Native American Legends*, 136).

HUMAN IMPACT ON BIRDS

1. Steadman, "Prehistoric Extinctions of Pacific Island Birds"; Steadman, White, and Allen, "Prehistoric Birds from New Ireland"; Diamond, "Blitzkrieg against the Moas"; Holdaway and Jacomb, "Rapid Extinction of the Moas"; Athens et al., "Avifaunal Extinctions."

2. Krech, *Ecological Indian*.

3. Krech, *Ecological Indian*, 29 – 43; Grayson, "Pleistocene Avifaunas"; Steadman and Martin, "Extinction of Birds."

4. Broughton, *Prehistoric Human Impacts*.

5. Some observers, including ones awed by numbers of birds, deployed hyperbole to entice settlers to North America.

6. Hawkins, *Sketch of the Creek Country*, 61, 64.

7. John James Audubon, *Ornithological Biography*, 1:35, 127, 243, 331, 399, 434, 466; 2:11, 21, 292, 316; 3:128 – 30, 169; Corning, *Journal of John James Audubon*, 55, 81 – 82, 88, 123 – 24; Maria R. Audubon, *Audubon and His Journals*, 2:246 – 54, 353 – 54, 365 – 66.

8. Swanton, *Indians*, 739; Paul W. Parmalee and Perino, "Prehistoric Archaeological Record"; Fundaburk and Foreman, *Sun Circles and Human Hands*, 35. The spoonbill record is not unique for the region.

9. John Smith, "True Relation," 199, 205; John Smith, "Map of Virginia," 363, 371, 395, 424. See also Strachey, *Historie of Travell*, 115; Beverley, *History and Present State*, 51; Rountree, *Powhatan Indians of Virginia*, 109.

10. Ewan and Ewan, *John Banister*, 385; Hudson, *Southeastern Indians*, 76, 316;

Fundaburk and Foreman, *Sun Circles and Human Hands*, 34.

11. Swanton, *Indians*, 738.

12. John Smith, "Map of Virginia," 360 ("Hares, Partridges"); Barbour, *Complete Works*, 2:118, 298 ("the Deere . . . all is one"); Swanton, *Indians*, 630 ("meeres"), 644 (meered meant limited or bounded; see OED *Online*, s.v. "mere," accessed September 1, 2006). Strachey and Edward Waterhouse echoed Smith. Strachey remarked, "[A]t all tymes and seasons they destroy [game]. . . . Hares, Patridges, Turkeys, fatt or leane, young or old in eggs in breeding tyme, or however, they devowre, at no tyme sparing any that they can katch in their power" (*Historie of Travell*, 82–83). And just after the Jamestown massacre of 1622, Waterhouse speculated that if the English retaliated for the attack, then the supply of wild turkeys would increase, because "the Indians never put difference of destroying the Hen, but kill[ed] them whether in season or not, whether in breeding time, or sitting on their egges, or having newly hatched, it [was] all one to them" (Waterhouse, "Declaration," 557).

13. Krech, *Ecological Indian*, 151–71.

14. Romans, *Concise Natural History*, 138–39; Usner, *Indians, Settlers, and Slaves*, 173–74; Wright, "Early Records . . . III," 79–80 ("It was strange"; "The wild Turkeys"). On the decline of deer, see Krech, *Ecological Indian*, 151–71.

15. Wright, "Early Records . . . IV"; Andrew Smith, *Turkey*, 50; Mosby and Handley, *Wild Turkey in Virginia*, 3–17; John James Audubon, *Ornithological Biography*, 1:15.

16. Wood, "Changing Population"; Krech, *Ecological Indian*, 96, 265–66n43; Silver, *New Face on the Countryside*, passim.

17. John James Audubon, *Ornithological Biography*, 4:3.

18. Schroeder and Robb, *Greater Prairie-Chicken*.

19. Gerrard and Bortolotti, *Bald Eagle*, 2–7; Stalmaster, *Bald Eagle*, 149–60;

Palmer, "Golden Eagle," 218–29; Watson, *Golden Eagle*, 230–31; Buehler, *Bald Eagle*.

20. Great auk remains were found in at least one southern midden, but the range of this extinct species was predominantly far to the north.

21. Hamel, *Bachman's Warbler*.

22. Schorger, *Passenger Pigeon*; Blockstein, *Passenger Pigeon*.

23. Paul W. Parmalee ("Archaeological Avian Assemblage," 82 and passim) finds passenger pigeon remains at all levels in a site in northern Alabama dated 7000 BC to AD 1000; see also H. Edwin Jackson, "'Darkening the Sun.'"

24. See Schorger, *Passenger Pigeon*; and note 23 above.

25. Lawson, *New Voyage*, 50–51, 217; Adair, *History*, 361, 405. Schorger (*Passenger Pigeon*, 133–40) details incidents in which northern Indians involved in the squab trade destroyed passenger pigeon roosts and left many dead birds to rot on the ground.

26. Schorger, *Passenger Pigeon*.

27. Snyder and Russell, *Carolina Parakeet*.

28. Snyder, *Carolina Parakeet*, 6–31, 88 and passim; Alexander Wilson, *American Ornithology*, 4:91–92; Feduccia, *Catesby's Birds*, 64–66 (I depart from Feduccia's conclusion that Wilson's experience killing parakeets provides insight on Indian harvesting); McKinley, "Carolina Parakeet in the Upper Missouri"; McKinley, "Archaeozoology of the Carolina Parakeet"; McKinley, "Carolina Parakeet in Georgia"; McKinley, "Carolina Parakeet in the Virginias"; McKinley, "Historical Review"; McKinley, *Carolina Parakeet in Florida*; Guilday, "Biological and Archaeological Analysis," 36–37.

29. Jerome A. Jackson, *Ivory-Billed Woodpecker*.

30. Alfred M. Bailey, "Ivory-Billed Woodpecker's Beak"; Wetmore, "Evidence" (Wetmore concludes unwisely that the foot "was of no particular interest" to Indians and that it must have been from a bird that occurred naturally in

what is now Ohio); Paul W. Parmalee, "Vertebrate Remains from the Cahokia Site"; Paul W. Parmalee, "Remains"; Van der Schalie and Parmalee, "Animal Remains"; Paul W. Parmalee, "Vertebrate Remains from an Historic Archaeological Site"; Alice Parmalee, "Additional Noteworthy Records"; Guilday, "Biological and Archaeological Analysis," 35–36; Murphy and Farrand, "Prehistoric Occurrence"; O'Shea, Schrimper, and Ludwickson, "Ivory-Billed Woodpeckers"; Paul W. Parmalee, "Archaeological Avian Assemblage," 81–82; Wade, *Arts*, 99.

31. Feduccia, *Catesby's Birds*, 88.

32. Alexander Wilson, *American Ornithology*, 4:23–24.

33. John James Audubon, *Ornithological Biography*, 1:343–46 (ivory-billed); 2:77 (pileated); 3:93 (great blue heron), 206–7 (whooping crane).

34. Alexander Wilson, *American Ornithology*, 4:23.

35. Jerome A. Jackson, *In Search*.

36. On decline and extinction, see Schorger, *Passenger Pigeon*; Blockstein, *Passenger Pigeon*; Saikku, "'Home in the Big Forest'"; Saikku, "Extinction of the Carolina Parakeet"; Snyder and Russell, *Carolina Parakeet*; Cokinos, *Hope Is the Thing*; Hoose, *Race*; Jerome A. Jackson, *In Search*.

37. Doughty, *Feather Fashions and Bird Preservation*, 16; Price, *Flight Maps*, 57–58; cf. Grunwald, *Swamp*, 120.

38. Covington, *Seminoles of Florida*, 148, 153, 169; Kersey, *Pelts, Plumes, and Hides*, 18, 30, 36, 39–41, 52, 57, 61, 65, 76 ("it did not take"), 81, 117, 131–32; Dimock and Dimock, *Florida Enchantments*, 299 ("enough of the old birds"); Grunwald, *Swamp*, 120; Doughty, *Feather Fashions and Bird Preservation*, 97–115, 125–34, 148–56 and passim; Price, *Flight Maps*, 57–109.

VISIBLE AND INVISIBLE BIRDS

1. Swanton, *Indians*, 251–53; Keith Thomas, *Man and the Natural World*, 63–81; Armstrong, *Folklore of Birds*; Arm-

strong, *Life and Lore*; Rowland, *Birds with Human Souls*.

2. Lawson, *New Voyage to Carolina*, 147; Feduccia, *Catesby's Birds*, 106 (Wilson), 107.

3. Bedichek, *Adventures with a Texas Naturalist*, 200–239; Byington, *Dictionary of Choctaw*; Martin and Maudlin, *Dictionary of Creek/Muskogee*; Munro and Willmond, *Chickasaw*.

4. Fogelson "Change, Persistence, and Accommodation," 222.

AFTERWORD

1. Contreras and Bernstein, *We Dance Because We Can*, 11 (Joshua Squirrel), 17 (Jim Sawgrass).

2. On the 2005 powwow calendar: http://www.powwows.com, http://www.gatheringofnations.com/powwows, http://www.powwow-power.com/powwows.shtml (accessed September 2, 2005).

3. Lerch, "Indians of the Carolinas"; Campisi, "Resurgence and Recognition."

4. On regalia and costume: Contreras and Bernstein, *We Dance Because We Can*, 10–17, 32–35, 42–47, 58–59, 68–73, 76–81, 90–93, 102–3, 112–17. For history of the powwow in the south, see Paredes, "Emergence"; Paredes, "Back from Disappearance"; Paredes, "Kinship and Descent"; Goertzen, "Purposes of North Carolina Powwows"; Jason Baird Jackson, "East Meets West"; Cook, Johns, and Wood, "Monacan Nation Powwow."

Bibliography

Adair, James. *The History of the American Indians.* Edited by Kathryn E. Holland Braund. Tuscaloosa: University of Alabama Press, 2005.

Allen, Robert P., Ralph S. Palmer, and E. M. Reilly Jr. "Greater Flamingo." In Palmer, *Handbook of North American Birds,* 1:542–50.

Allen, Robert P., Ralph S. Palmer, E. M. Reilly Jr., and A. W. Schorger. "Scarlet Ibis." In Palmer, *Handbook of North American Birds,* 1:529–32.

American Gourd Society. http://www.americangourdsociety.org/.

American Ornithologists' Union. *Checklist of North American Birds.* 7th ed. Washington, D.C., 1998.

Anderson, David G., and Kenneth E. Sassaman. "Early and Middle Holocene Periods, 9500 to 3750 BC." In Fogelson, *Handbook of North American Indians,* 87–100.

Anderson, Virginia DeJohn. "Animals into the Wilderness: The Development of Livestock Husbandry in the Seventeenth-Century Chesapeake." *William and Mary Quarterly* 59 (2002): 377–408.

Archer, Gabriel. "Description of the People." In Barbour, *Jamestown Voyages,* 1:102–4.

———. "A relation . . . written . . . by a gent. Of ye Colony." In Barbour, *Jamestown Voyages,* 1:80–98.

Armstrong, Edward A. *The Folklore of Birds.* 2nd ed. New York: Dover, 1970.

———. *The Life and Lore of the Bird, in Nature, Art, Myth, and Literature.* New York: Crown Publishers, 1975.

Ashelford, Jane. *Dress in the Age of Elizabeth I.* New York: Holmes and Meier, 1988.

Athens, J. Stephen, H. David Tuggle, David J. Welch, and Jerome V. Ward.

"Avifaunal Extinctions, Vegetation Change, and Polynesian Impacts in Prehistoric Hawai'i." *Archaeology in Oceania* 37 (2002): 57–78.

Audubon, John James. *The Birds of America: From Original Drawings by John James Audubon.* Vol. 1. London: John James Audubon, 1827–30.

———. *The Birds of America: From Original Drawings by John James Audubon.* Vol. 2. London: John James Audubon, 1831–34.

———. *The Birds of America: From Original Drawings by John James Audubon.* Vol. 3. London: John James Audubon, 1834–35.

———. *The Birds of America: From Original Drawings by John James Audubon.* Vol. 4. London: John James Audubon, 1835–38.

———. *Ornithological Biography.* 5 vols. Edinburgh: A. Black, 1831–49.

Audubon, Maria R. *Audubon and His Journals.* 2 vols. New York: Charles Scribner's Sons, 1897. Reprint, New York: Dover, 1994.

Bahti, Mark Tomas. "Animals in Hopi Duality." In *Signifying Animals: Human Meaning in the Natural World,* edited by Roy Willis, 134–39. New York: Routledge, 1994.

Bailey, Alfred M. "Ivory-Billed Woodpecker's Beak in an Indian Grave in Colorado." *Condor* 41, no. 4 (1939): 164.

Bailey, R. Wayne. "Notes on Albinism in the Eastern Wild Turkey." *Journal of Wildlife Management* 19 (1955): 408.

Balzer, Marjorie. "Flights of the Sacred: Symbolism and Theory in Siberian Shamanism." *American Anthropologist* 98 (1996): 305–18.

Banko, Winston E., and Arlie W. Schorger. "Trumpeter Swan." In

Palmer, *Handbook of North American Birds,* 2:55–71 (1976).

Barbour, Philip, ed. *The Complete Works of Captain John Smith (1580–1631).* 3 vols. Chapel Hill: University of North Carolina Press, 1986.

———, ed. *The Jamestown Voyages under the First Charter, 1606–1609.* 2 vols. Cambridge: Cambridge University Press for the Hakluyt Society, 1969.

Barkalow, Frederick S., Jr. "Vertebrate Remains from Archeological Sites in the Tennessee Valley of Alabama." *Southern Indian Studies* 24 (1972): 3–41.

Bartram, William. *Travels through North and South Carolina, Georgia, East and West Florida, the Cherokee country, the extensive territory of the Muscogulges, or Creek confederacy, and the country of the Chactaws; containing an account of the soil and natural production of those regions; together with observations on the manners of the Indians.* Philadelphia: James and Johnson, 1791.

Bedichek, Roy. *Adventures with a Texas Naturalist.* Rev. ed. Austin: University of Texas Press, 1961.

Bent, Arthur Cleveland. *Life Histories of North American Birds of Prey: Order Falconiformes.* Bulletin of the United States National Museum 167. Washington, D.C.: U.S. Government Printing Office, 1937. Reprinted as *Life Histories of North American Birds of Prey,* pt. 1, New York: Dover, 1961.

———. *Life Histories of North American Birds of Prey: Order Falconiformes and Strigiformes.* Bulletin of the United States National Museum 170. Washington, D.C.: U.S. Government Printing Office, 1938. Reprinted as *Life*

Histories of North American Birds of Prey, pt. 2, New York: Dover, 1961.

———. *Life Histories of North American Marsh Birds: Orders Odontoglossae, Herodiones and Paludicolae.* Bulletin of the United States National Museum 135. Washington, D.C.: U.S. Government Printing Office, 1926. Reprint, New York: Dover, 1963.

Berlin, Brent, James Boster, and John P. O'Neill. "The Perceptual Bases of Ethnobiological Classification: Evidence from Aguaruna Jívaro Ornithology." *Journal of Ethnobiology* 1 (1981): 95–108.

Beverley, Robert. *The History and Present State of Virginia.* Edited by Louis B. Wright. Chapel Hill: University of North Carolina Press, 1947.

Bierer, Bert W. *Indians and Artifacts in the Southeast.* Columbia, S.C.: Bierer Publishing, 1978.

Biggar, H. M., ed. *Jean Ribaut: The Whole and True Discouerye of Terra Florida: A Facsimile Reprint of the London Edition of 1563.* Deland, Fla.: Florida State Historical Society, 1927.

Blakeslee, Donald J. "The Origin and Spread of the Calumet Ceremony." *American Antiquity* 46 (1981): 759–68.

Blockstein, David E. *Passenger Pigeon (Ectopistes migratorius).* The Birds of North America, edited by A. Poole and F. Gill, no. 611. Philadelphia: Academy of Natural Sciences; Washington, D.C.: American Ornithologists Union, 2002.

Bottoms, Edward, and Floyd Painter. "Bolas and Birds during the Early Woodland Period in Southeastern Virginia." *Chesopiean* 27, no. 2 (1989): 2–5.

———. "Bola Weights from the Dismal Swamp Region of Virginia and North Carolina." *Chesopiean* 10, no. 1 (1972): 19–30.

Brandes, Stanley. "Animal Metaphors and Social Control in Tzintzuntzan." *Ethnology* 3 (1984): 207–16.

Brannon, Peter A. "The Dress of the Early Indians of Alabama." *Arrow Points* 5, no. 5 (1922): 84–93.

Branstetter, Laura. "The Montague Tallant Collection of Historic Metal Artifacts." *Florida Anthropologist* 48, no. 4 (1995): 291–99.

Braund, Kathryn E. Holland. *Deerskins and Duffels: The Creek Indian Trade with Anglo-America, 1685–1815.* Lincoln: University of Nebraska Press, 1993.

———. Introduction. In *The History of the American Indians,* by James Adair, edited by Kathryn E. Holland Braund, 1–53. Tuscaloosa: University of Alabama Press, 2005.

Brightman, Rob. "Chitimacha." In Fogelson, *Handbook of North American Indians,* 642–52.

Brinton, Daniel G. *Notes on the Floridian Peninsula, Its Literary History, Indian Tribes and Antiquities.* Philadelphia: Joseph Sabin, 1859. Reprint, New York: Paladin Press, 1969.

Brodkorb, Pierce. "Great Auk and Common Murre from a Florida Midden." *Auk* 77 (1960): 342–43.

Brose, David S. "From the Southeastern Ceremonial Complex to the Southern Cult: 'You Can't Tell the Players without a Program.'" In Galloway, *Southeastern Ceremonial Complex,* 27–37.

———. "An Interpretation of the Hopewellian Traits in Florida." In *Hopewell Archaeology: The Chillicothe Conference,* edited by David S. Brose and N'omi Greber, 141–49. Kent, Ohio: Kent State University Press, 1979.

Broughton, Jack. *Prehistoric Human Impacts on California Birds: Evidence from the Emeryville Shellmound Avifauna.* Ornithological Monographs 56. Washington, D.C.: American Ornithologists' Union, 2002.

Brown, Ian W. "The Calumet Ceremony in the Southeast: Its Archaeological Manifestations." *American Antiquity* 54 (1989): 311–31.

———. "The Calumet Ceremony in the Southeast as Observed Archaeologically." In *Powhatan's Mantle: Indians in the Colonial Southeast,* edited by Gregory A. Waselkov, Peter H. Wood, and M. Thomas Hatley, revised and expanded edition, 371–419. Lincoln: University of Nebraska Press, 2006.

———. "Prehistory of the Gulf Coastal Plain after 500 BC" In Fogelson, *Handbook of North American Indians,* 574–85.

Brown, James A. "The Archaeology of Ancient Religion in the Eastern Woodlands." *Annual Review of Anthropology* 26 (1997): 465–85.

———. "The Cahokian Expression." In *Hero, Hawk, and Open Hand: American Indian Art of the Ancient Midwest and South,* edited by Richard F. Townsend, 105–23. Chicago: Art Institute of Chicago; New Haven, Conn.: Yale University Press, 2004.

———. "On Style Divisions of the Southeastern Ceremonial Complex: A Revisionist Perspective." In Galloway, *Southeastern Ceremonial Complex,* 183–204.

———. "The Southern Cult Reconsidered." *Mid-Continental Journal of Archaeology* 1, no. 2 (1976): 115–35.

———. "Spiro Art and Its Mortuary Contexts." In *Death and the Afterlife in Pre-Columbian America: A Conference at Dumbarton Oaks, October 27, 1973,* edited by Elizabeth P. Benson, 1–32. Washington, D.C.: Dumbarton Oaks Research Library and Collections, 1975.

Buckley, Neil J. *Black Vulture (Coragyps atratus).* The Birds of North America, edited by A. Poole and F. Gill, no. 411. Philadelphia: Academy of Natural Sciences; Washington, D.C.: American Ornithologists' Union, 1999.

Buehler, David A. *Bald Eagle (Haliaeetus leucocephalus).* The Birds of North America, edited by A. Poole and

F. Gill, no. 506. Philadelphia: Academy of Natural Sciences; Washington, D.C.: American Ornithologists' Union, 2000.

Bull, Evelyn L., and Jerome A. Jackson. *Pileated Woodpecker (Dryocopus pileatus)*. The Birds of North America, edited by A. Poole and F. Gill, no. 148. Philadelphia: Academy of Natural Sciences; Washington, D.C.: American Ornithologists' Union, 1995.

Bullen, Ripley P. "Carved Owl Totem, De Land, Florida." *Florida Anthropologist* 8, no. 3 (1955): 60–73.

Bulmer, Ralph. "Mystical and Mundane in Kalam Classification of Birds." In *Classifications in Their Social Context*, edited by Roy Ellen and David Reason, 57–80. London: Academic Press, 1979.

———. "The Uncleanness of the Birds of Leviticus and Deuteronomy." *Man* 24 (1989): 304–21.

Bushnell, David I., Jr. "The Account of Lamhatty." *American Anthropologist* 10 (1908): 568–74.

———. *The Choctaw of Bayou Lacomb, St. Tammany Parish, Louisiana*. Smithsonian Institution, Bureau of American Ethnology Bulletin 48, 19–20. Washington, D.C.: U.S. Government Printing Office, 1909.

———. "Drawings by A. DeBatz in Louisiana, 1732–1735." In *Smithsonian Miscellaneous Collections* 80, no. 5 (1927): 1–15.

———. "Virginia — From Early Records." *American Anthropologist* 9 (1907): 31–44.

Byington, Cyrus. *Dictionary of Choctaw*. Edited by John R. Swanton and Henry S. Halbert. Smithsonian Institution, Bureau of American Ethnology Bulletin 46. Washington, D.C.: U.S. Government Printing Office, 1915.

Byrd, Kathleen Mary. "Tchefuncte Subsistence: Information Obtained from the Excavation of the Morton Shell Mound, Iberia Parish, Louisiana." *Southeastern Archaeological Conference Bulletin* 19 (1976): 70–75.

Campbell, Thomas Nolan. "The Choctaw Afterworld." *Journal of American Folklore* 72 (1959): 146–54.

———. "Choctaw Subsistence: Ethnographic Notes from the Lincecum Manuscript." *Florida Anthropologist* 13, no. 1 (1959): 9–24.

Campisi, Jack. "Resurgence and Recognition." In Fogelson, *Handbook of North American Indians*, 760–68.

Carson, James Taylor. *Searching for the Bright Path: The Mississippi Choctaws from Prehistory to Removal*. Lincoln: University of Nebraska Press, 1999.

Catesby, Mark. *The Natural History of Carolina, Florida and the Bahama islands: Containing the figures of birds, beasts, fishes, serpents, insects and plants; . . . Together with their descriptions in English and French*. Etched by Mr. Catesby himself from his own paintings and drawings. London: printed at the expence of the author; and sold by W. Innys and R. Manby, by Mr. Hauksbee, and by the author, at Mr. Bacon's in Hoxton, 1731–43.

———. *The Natural History of Carolina, Florida, and the Bahama Islands: Containing the figures of birds, beasts, fishes, serpents, insects, and plants: particularly, those not hitherto described, or incorrectly figured by former authors, with their descriptions in English and French*. Revised by Mr. Edwards. Etched by Mr. Catesby himself from his own paintings and drawings. London: Printed for Benjamin White, at Horace's Head, in Fleetstreet, 1771.

Choate, Ernest A. *The Dictionary of American Bird Names*. Rev. ed. Boston: Harvard Common Press, 1985.

Christy, Bayard H. "Topsell's 'Fowles of Heauen.'" *Auk* 50 (1933): 275–83.

Clayton, G. A. "Muscovy Duck." In *Evolution of Domesticated Animals*, edited by Ian L. Mason, 340–44. London: Longman, 1984.

Cleland, Charles E. "Faunal Remains from Bluff Shelters in Northwest Arkansas." *Arkansas Archaeologist* 6, nos. 2–3 (1965): 39–63.

Cobb, Charles R. "Mississippian Chiefdoms: How Complex?" *Annual Review of Anthropology* 32 (2003): 63–84.

Cocker, Mark, and Richard Mabey. *Birds Britannica*. London: Chatto and Windus, 2005.

Cokinos, Christopher. *Hope Is the Thing with Feathers*. New York: Tarcher/Putnam, 2000.

Contreras, Don, and Diane Morris Bernstein. *We Dance Because We Can: People of the Powwow*. Marietta, Ga.: Longstreet Press, 1996.

Cook, Samuel R., John L. Johns, and Karenne Wood. "The Monacan Nation Powwow: Symbol of Indigenous Survival and Resistance in the Tobacco Row Mountains." In Ellis, Lassiter, and Dunham, *Powwow*, 201–23.

Corning, Howard, ed. *Journal of John James Audubon: Made during His Trip to New Orleans in 1820–21*. Boston: Odd Club of Odd Volumes, 1929.

Covington, James W. *The Seminoles of Florida*. Gainesville: University Press of Florida, 1993.

Crawford, Roy D. "Domestic Fowl." In *Evolution of Domesticated Animals*, edited by Ian L. Mason, 298–310. New York: Longman, 1984.

———. "Turkey." In *Evolution of Domesticated Animals*, edited by Ian L. Mason, 325–34. New York: Longman, 1984.

Cuming, Alexander. "Journal of Sir Alexander Cuming: An Account of the Cherokee Indians, and of Sir Alexander Cuming's Journey amongst Them," with an introduction and annotations by Samuel Cole Williams. In *Early Travels in the Tennessee Country, 1540–180*, edited by Samuel

Cole Williams, 115–43. Johnson City, Tenn.: Watauga Press, 1928.

Cumming, William P. *The Southeast in Early Maps.* 3rd ed. Chapel Hill: University of North Carolina Press, 1998.

Cushing, Frank H. "Preliminary Report on the Exploration of Ancient Key Dwellers' Remains on the Gulf Coast of Florida." *Proceedings of the American Philosophical Society* 35, no. 153 (1897): 329–432.

Cushman, Horatio Bardwell. *History of the Choctaw, Chickasaw and Natchez Indians.* Edited by Angie Debo. Norman: University of Oklahoma Press, 1999.

de Baillou, Clemens. "A Contribution to the Mythology and Conceptual World of the Cherokee Indians." *Ethnohistory* 8 (1961): 93–102.

Debo, Angie. *The Rise and Fall of the Choctaw Republic.* Norman: University of Oklahoma Press, 1961.

de Marly, Diana. *Dress in North America.* Vol. 1, *The New World, 1492–1800.* New York: Holmes and Meier, 1990.

de Milford, Louis LeClerc. *Memoir, or A Cursory Glance at My Different Travels and My Sojourn in the Creek Nation.* Edited by John Francis McDermott. Chicago: R. R. Donnelley and Sons, 1956.

De Vorsey, Louis, Jr., ed. *De Brahm's Report of the General Survey in the Southern District of North America.* Columbia: University of South Carolina Press, 1971.

Diamond, Jared. "Blitzkrieg against the Moas." *Science* 287, no. 5461 (March 24, 2000): 2170–71.

Diamond, Jared, and K. David Bishop. "Ethno-ornithology of the Ketengban People, Indonesian New Guinea." In *Folkbiology*, edited by Douglas L. Medin and Scott Atran, 17–45. Cambridge Mass.: MIT Press, 1999.

Dickinson, Samuel Dorris, ed. *New Travels in North America by Jean-Bernard Bossu, 1770–1771.*

Natchitoches, La.: Northwestern State University Press, 1982.

Dimock, Anthony Weston, and Julian Anthony Dimock. *Florida Enchantments.* New York: Outing Publishing, 1908.

Donkin, R. A. *The Muscovy Duck, Cairina moschata domestica.* Rotterdam: A. A. Balkema, 1989.

Doughty, Robin W. *Feather Fashions and Bird Preservation: A Study in Nature Protection.* Berkeley: University of California Press, 1975.

Douglas, Mary. *Implicit Meanings: Essays in Anthropology.* London: Routledge and Kegan Paul, 1975.

———. "The Pangolin Revisited: A New Approach to Animal Symbolism." In *Signifying Animals: Human Meaning in the Natural World*, edited by Roy Willis, 25–36. New York: Routledge, 1994.

———. *Purity and Danger.* London: Routledge and Kegan Paul, 1966.

Downs, Dorothy. "British Influences on Creek and Seminole Men's Clothing, 1733–1858." *Bulletin of the Florida Anthropological Society* 33 (1980): 46–65.

Durkheim, Emile, and Marcel Mauss. *Primitive Classification.* London: Cohen and West, 1963.

Early, Ann. "Prehistory of the Western Interior after 5000 BC" In Fogelson, *Handbook of North American Indians*, 560–73.

Edwards, George. *Gleanings of Natural History.* 3 vols. London: Royal College of Physicians, 1758–64.

Eiche, Sabine. *Presenting the Turkey: The Fabulous Story of a Flamboyant and Flavourful Bird.* Florence: Centro Di, 2004.

Ellis, Clyde, Luke Eric Lassiter, and Gary H. Dunham, eds. *Powwow.* Lincoln: University of Nebraska Press, 2005.

Emerson, Thomas. "Water, Serpents, and the Underworld: An Exploration into Cahokian Symbolism." In Galloway,

Southeastern Ceremonial Complex, 45–92.

Ethridge, Robbie. *Creek Country: The Creek Indians and Their World.* Chapel Hill: University of North Carolina Press, 2003.

Evans-Pritchard, Edward Evan. *Nuer Religion.* Oxford: Clarendon Press, 1956.

Ewan, Joseph, and Nesta Ewan. *John Banister and His Natural History of Virginia, 1678–1692.* Urbana: University of Illinois Press, 1970.

Faulkner, Charles H. "Tennessee Birdstones." *Tennessee Archaeologist* 21, no. 2 (1965): 39–54.

Fausz, J. Frederick. "George Thorpe, Nemattanew, and the Powhatan Uprising of 1622." *Virginia Cavalcade* 28, no. 3 (1979): 110–17.

———. "Opechancanough: Indian Resistance Leader." In *Struggle and Survival in Colonial America*, edited by David G. Sweet and Gary B. Nash, 21–37. Berkeley: University of California Press, 1981.

Fausz, J. Frederick, and Jon Kukla. "A Letter of Advice to the Governor of Virginia, 1624." *William and Mary Quarterly* 34 (1977): 104–29.

Feduccia, Alan, ed. *Catesby's Birds of Colonial America.* Chapel Hill: University of North Carolina Press, 1985.

Feest, Christian F. "The Virginia Indian in Pictures, 1612–1624." *Smithsonian Journal of History* 2, no. 1 (1967): 1–30.

Feiler, Seymour, ed. *Jean-Bernard Bossu's Travels in the Interior of North America, 1751–1762.* Norman: University of Oklahoma Press, 1962.

Feld, Steven. "Cockatoo, Hornbill, Kingfisher." In *Man and a Half*, edited by Andrew Pawley, 207–13. Aukland: Polynesian Society, 1991.

Fitzpatrick, John W., et al. "Ivory-Billed Woodpecker (*Campephilus principalis*) Persists in Continental North America." *Science* 308, no. 5727 (June 3, 2005): 1460–62.

http://www.sciencemag.org.revproxy
.brown.edu/cgi/content/full/1114103/
DC.

Fitzpatrick, John W., Martjan
Lammertink, M. David Luneau Jr.,
Tim W. Gallagher, and Kenneth V.
Rosenberg. "Response to Comment
on 'Ivory-Billed Woodpecker
(*Campephilus principalis*) Persists
in Continental North America.'"
Science 311, no. 5767 (March 17, 2006):
1555. http://www.sciencemag.org/
cgi/content/full/311/5767/1555b.

Fogelson, Raymond D. "Change,
Persistence, and Accommodation in
Cherokee Medico-Magical Beliefs."
In *Symposium on Cherokee and
Iroquois Culture*, edited by William N.
Fenton and John Gulick, Smithsonian
Institution, Bureau of American
Ethnology Bulletin 180, 215 – 25.
Washington, D.C.: U.S. Government
Printing Office, 1961.

———, ed. *Handbook of North
American Indians*. Vol. 14, *Southeast*.
Washington, D.C.: Smithsonian
Institution, 2004.

Foreman, Carolyn. *Indians Abroad,
1493 – 1938*. Norman: University of
Oklahoma Press, 1943.

Forth, Gregory. *Nage Birds: Classification
and Symbolism among an Eastern
Indonesian People*. New York:
Routledge, 2004.

Fradkin, Arlene. "Bird Remains from
Two South Florida Prehistoric Sites."
Florida Scientist 43, no. 2 (1980):
111 – 15.

———. *Cherokee Folk Zoology: The
Animal World of a Native American
People, 1700 – 1838*. New York:
Garland, 1990.

Fuller, Richard S., and Diane E. Silvia.
"Ceramic Rim Effigies in Southwest
Alabama." *Journal of Alabama
Archaeology* 30, no. 1 (1984): 1 – 48.

Fundaburk, Emma Lila, ed. *Southeastern
Indians: Life Portraits; A Catalogue of
Pictures, 1564 – 1860*. Luverne, Ala.:
Emma Lila Fundaburk, 1958.

Fundaburk, Emma Lila, and Mary
Douglass Foreman, eds. *Sun Circles
and Human Hands: The Southeastern
Indians, Art and Industries*.
Tuscaloosa: University of Alabama
Press, 2001.

Gallagher, Tim. *The Grail Bird: The
Rediscovery of the Ivory-Billed
Woodpecker*. Boston: Houghton-
Mifflin, 2006.

Galloway, Patricia. *Choctaw Genesis,
1500 – 1700*. Lincoln: University of
Nebraska Press, 1996.

———, ed. *The Hernando de Soto
Expedition: History, Historiography,
and "Discovery" in the Southeast*.
Lincoln: University of Nebraska
Press, 1997.

———. *The Southeastern Ceremonial
Complex: Artifacts and Analysis; The
Cottonlandia Conference*. (Exhibition
catalog by David Dye and Camille
Wharey.) Lincoln: University of
Nebraska Press, 1989.

Garcilaso de la Vega, the Inca. "La
Florida." In *The De Soto Chronicles:
The Expedition of Hernando de Soto
to North America in 1539 – 1543*, edited
by Lawrence A. Clayton, Vernon
James Knight Jr., and Edward C.
Moore, 2 vols., 2:25 – 560. Tuscaloosa:
University of Alabama Press,
1993.

Gardner, Peter M. "Birds, Words, and
a Requiem for the Omniscient
Informant." *American Ethnologist* 3
(1976): 446 – 68.

Gathering of Nations. http://www
.gatheringofnations.com/powwows
(accessed September 1, 2006).

Geary, James A. "Appendix II: The
Language of the Carolina Algonkian
Tribes." In *The Roanoke Voyages,
1584 – 1590: Documents to Illustrate
the English Voyages to North America
under the Patent Granted to Walter
Raleigh in 1584*, edited by David E.
Quinn, 2 vols., Works Issued by the
Hakluyt Society, 2nd ser., no. 104,
2:873 – 900. London: Hakluyt Society,

1955. Reprint, Nendeln, Liechtenstein:
Kraus Reprint, 1967.

George, Wilma. *Animals and Maps*.
London: Secker and Warburg, 1969.

Gerrard, Jon M., and Gary R. Bortolotti.
*The Bald Eagle: Haunts and Habits of
a Wilderness Monarch*. Washington,
D.C.: Smithsonian Institution Press,
1988.

Gibson, Jon L. *The Ancient Mounds of
Poverty Point*. Gainesville: University
Press of Florida, 2000.

———. "Broken Circles, Owl Monsters,
and Black Earth Midden." In *Ancient
Earthen Enclosures*, edited by Robert
C. Mainfort Jr. and Lynne P. Sullivan.
Gainesville: University Press of
Florida, 1998.

Gilliam, Charles Edgar. "Powhatan
Algonkian Bird Names: The
Aushouetta (Topsell) or the
Ahshowcutters (Strachey);
Richmondena cardinalis." *Journal of the
Washington Academy of Sciences* 37, no.
1 (1947): 1 – 2.

———. "Powhatan's Dearest Bird."
Garden Gossip 25, no. 5 (1950):
11, 25.

Gilmore, Harry W. "Hunting Habits of
the Early Nevada Paiutes." *American
Anthropologist* 55 (1953): 148 – 53.

Goertzen, Chris. "Purposes of North
Carolina Powwows." In Ellis, Lassiter,
and Dunham, *Powwow*, 275 – 302.

Goggin, John M. "Manifestations of a
South Florida Cult in Northwestern
Florida." *American Antiquity* 12, no. 4
(1947): 273 – 76.

———. "Osceola: Portraits, Features, and
Dress." *Florida Historical Quarterly* 33
(1955): 161 – 92.

———. "The Tekesta Indians of Southern
Florida." *Florida Historical Quarterly*
18 (1940): 274 – 84.

Goggin, John M., and William C.
Sturtevant. "The Calusa: A Stratified,
Nonagricultural Society (with Notes
on Sibling Marriage)." In *Explorations
in Cultural Anthropology: Essays in
Honor of George Peter Murdock*, edited

by Ward H. Goodenough, 179–219. New York: McGraw-Hill, 1964.

Gore, Robert H. "Cushing's 'Bird-God of War': Solving a Key Marco Mystery." *Florida Anthropologist* 48, no. 3 (1995): 194–99.

Graves, Gary R. "Avian Commensals in Colonial America: When Did *Chaetura pelagica* Become the Chimney Swift?" *Archives of Natural History* 31 (2004): 300–307.

Gravier, Jacques. "Relation ou Journal du voyage en 1700 depuis le Pays des Illinois Jusqu'a l'Embouchure du Fleuve Mississipi." In *The Jesuit Relations and Allied Documents: Travels and Explorations of the Jesuit Missionaries in New France, 1610–1791*, edited by Reuben Gold Thwaites, 65:100–179. Cleveland: Burrows Brothers, 1899.

Grayson, Donald. "Pleistocene Avifaunas and the Overkill Hypothesis." *Science* 195, no. 4279 (February 18, 1977): 691–93.

Greenlee, Robert F. "Folktales of the Florida Seminole." *Journal of American Folklore* 58, no. 228 (1945): 138–44.

Grunwald, Michael. *The Swamp*. New York: Simon and Schuster, 2006.

Guilday, John. *Biological and Archaeological Analysis of Bones from a 17th Century Indian Village (46 PU 31), Putnam County, West Virginia*. Report of Archaeological Investigations 4. Morgantown: West Virginia Geological and Economic Survey, 1971.

Hakluyt, Richard, ed. *Divers Voyages Touching the Discovery of America, and the Islands Adjacent*. London: Hakluyt Society Publications, 1850.

Hall, Robert L. "An Anthropocentric Perspective for Eastern United States Prehistory." *American Antiquity* 42 (1977): 499–518.

———. *An Archaeology of the Soul: North American Indian Belief and Ritual*. Urbana: University of Illinois Press, 1997.

———. "The Cultural Background of Mississippi Symbolism." In Galloway, *Southeastern Ceremonial Complex*, 239–78.

Hally, David J., and Robert C. Mainfort. "Prehistory of the Eastern Interior after 500 bc." In Fogelson, *Handbook of North American Indians*, 265–85.

Hamel, Paul B. *Bachman's Warbler (Vermivora bachmanii)*. The Birds of North America, edited by A. Poole and F. Gill, no. 150. Philadelphia: Academy of Natural Sciences; Washington, D.C.: American Ornithologists' Union, 1995.

Hamon, J. Hill. "Northern Birds from a Florida Indian Midden." *Auk* 76, no. 4 (1959): 533–34.

Hann, John H. "Hernando de Soto in Apalachee: Archaeology and History; Introduction to the Documentary Record." In *Hernando de Soto among the Apalachee: The Archaeology of the First Winter Encampment*, edited by Charles R. Ewen and John H. Hann, 117–46. Gainesville: University Press of Florida, 1998.

———. *A History of the Timucua Indians and Missions*. Gainesville: University Press of Florida, 1996.

———, ed. and trans. *Missions to the Calusa*. Gainesville: University Press of Florida, 1991.

Hann, John H., and Bonnie G. McEwan. *The Apalachee Indians and Mission San Luis*. Gainesville: University Press of Florida, 1998.

Hariot, Thomas. *Der ander Theyl der newlich erfunden Landtschafft Americae*. Frankfurt am Main: Johann Feyerabend, for Theodore de Bry, 1591.

Harper, Francis, ed. *The Travels of William Bartram*. Athens: University of Georgia Press, 1958.

———. "The *Vultur sacra* of William Bartram." *Auk* 53 (1936): 381–92.

Harrington, John P. "The Original Strachey Vocabulary of the Virginia Indian Language." *Anthropological Papers*, no. 46, 189–202. Smithsonian

Institution, Bureau of American Ethnology Bulletin 157. Washington, D.C.: U.S. Government Printing Office, 1955.

Hartert, Ernst, F. C. R. Jourdain, N. F. Ticehurst, and H. F. Witherby. *A Hand-List of British Birds*. London: Witherby and Company, 1912.

Hawkins, Benjamin. *A Sketch of the Creek Country, in the Years 1798 and 1799 and The Letters of Benjamin Hawkins, 1796–1806*. Collections of the Georgia Historical Society, vol. 3, part 1, Savannah: Georgia Historical Society, 1848; and Georgia Historical Society Collections, vol. 9, Savannah: Georgia Historical Society, 1916. Reprinted in one volume. Spartanburg, S.C.: Reprint Company, 1974.

Hernández de Biedma, Luys. "Relation of the Island of Florida." In *The De Soto Chronicles: The Expedition of Hernando de Soto to North America in 1539–1543*, edited by Lawrence A. Clayton, Vernon James Knight Jr., and Edward C. Moore, 2 vols., 1:221–46. Tuscaloosa: University of Alabama Press, 1993.

Hewitt, John Napoleon Brinton. "Notes on the Creek Indians," edited by J. R. Swanton. *Anthropological Papers*, no. 10, 119–59. Smithsonian Institution, Bureau of American Ethnology Bulletin 123. Washington, D.C.: U.S. Government Printing Office, 1939. Reprinted in *A Creek Source Book*, edited by William C. Sturtevant. New York: Garland, 1987.

Hill, Geoffrey E., Daniel J. Mennill, Brian W. Rolek, Tyler L. Hicks, and Kyle A. Swiston. "Evidence Suggesting That Ivory-Billed Woodpeckers (*Campephilus principalis*) Exist in Florida." *Avian Conservation and Ecology* 1, no. 3:2. http://www.ace-eco.org/vol1/iss3/art2/ (accessed October 1, 2006).

Hoffman, Rob. "Episodic Zooarchaeology: Intrasite Variability in a Faunal Assemblage from Reelfoot Lake, West Tennessee." *Tennessee Anthropologist* 15 (1990): 132–43.

Holdaway, Richard N., and Chris Jacomb. "Rapid Extinction of the Moas (*Aves: Dinornithiformes*): Model, Test, and Implications." *Science* 287, no. 5461 (March 24, 2000): 2250–54.

Honour, Hugh. *The New Golden Land: European Images of America from the Discoveries to the Present Time*. New York: Pantheon, 1975.

Hoose, Phillip. *The Race to Save the Lord God Bird*. New York: Farrar, Straus and Giroux, 2004.

House, John. "Powell Canal: Baytown Period Adaptation on Bayou Macon, Southeast Arkansas." In *The Mississippian Emergence*, edited by Bruce D. Smith, 9–26. Washington, D.C.: Smithsonian Institution Press, 1990.

Houston, C. Stuart, and Mary I. Houston. "The 19th Century Trade in Swan Skins and Quills." *Blue Jay* 55, no. 1 (1997): 24–34.

Howard, James H. *The Southeastern Ceremonial Complex and Its Interpretation*. Missouri Archaeological Society Memoir 6. Stillwater: Oklahoma State University, 1968.

Hudson, Charles, ed. *Black Drink: A Native American Tea*. Athens: University of Georgia Press, 1979.

———. "James Adair as Anthropologist." *Ethnohistory* 24 (1977): 311–28.

———. *The Juan Pardo Expeditions: Exploration of the Carolinas and Tennessee, 1566–1568*. Washington, D.C.: Smithsonian Institution Press, 1990.

———. *Knights of Spain, Warriors of the Sun: Hernando de Soto and the South's Ancient Chiefdoms*. Athens: University of Georgia Press, 1997.

———. *The Southeastern Indians*. Knoxville: University of Tennessee Press, 1978.

Hudson, Charles, and Carmen Chaves Tesser, eds. *The Forgotten Centuries: Indians and Europeans in the American South, 1521–1704*. Athens: University of Georgia Press, 1994.

Hulton, Paul. *America 1585: The Complete Drawings of John White*. Chapel Hill: University of North Carolina Press; London: British Museum Publications, 1984.

———, ed. *The Work of Jacques Le Moyne de Morgues, a Huguenot Artist in France, Florida and England*. Vols. 1 and 2. London: British Museum Publications, 1977.

Humes, Jesse, and Vinnie May (James) Humes. *A Chickasaw Dictionary*. Norman, Okla.: Chickasaw Nation, 1973.

Hunn, Eugene. "The Abominations of Leviticus Revisited: A Commentary on Anomaly in Symbolic Anthropology." In *Classifications in Their Social Context*, edited by Roy Ellen and David Reason, 103–16. London: Academic Press, 1979.

———. "Sahaptin Bird Classification." In *Man and a Half*, edited by Andrew Pawley, 137–47. Aukland: The Polynesian Society, 1991.

Jackson, H. Edwin. "'Darkening the Sun in Their Flight': A Zooarchaeological Accounting of Passenger Pigeons in the Prehistoric Southeast." In *Engaged Anthropology: Research Essays on North American Archaeology, Ethnobotany, and Museology*, edited by Michelle Hegmon and B. Sunday Eiselt, Anthropological Papers 94, Museum of Anthropology, University of Michigan, 174–99. Ann Arbor: Museum of Anthropology, University of Michigan, 2005.

Jackson, Jason Baird. "East Meets West: On Stomp Dance and Powwow Worlds in Oklahoma." In Ellis, Lassiter, and Dunham, *Powwow*, 172–97.

Jackson, Jason B., Raymond D. Fogelson, and William C. Sturtevant, "History of Ethnological and Linguistic Research." In Fogelson, *Handbook of North American Indians*, 31–47.

Jackson, Jerome A. *In Search of the Ivory-Billed Woodpecker*. Washington, D.C.: Smithsonian Books, 2004.

———. *The Ivory-Billed Woodpecker* (Campephilus principalis). The Birds of North America, edited by A. Poole and F. Gill, no. 711. Philadelphia: Academy of Natural Sciences; Washington, D.C.: American Ornithologists' Union, 2002.

———. "Ivory-Billed Woodpecker (*Campephilus principalis*): Hope, and the Interfaces of Science, Conservation, and Politics." *Auk* 123 (2006): 1–15.

Jeffries, Richard. "Regional Cultures, 700 BC to AD 1000." In Fogelson, *Handbook of North American Indians*, 115–27.

Jenkins, Cliff. "The Use of Vertebrate Fauna in the Subsistence System during the Transition from Late Woodland to Mature Mississippian: The Tibbee Creek Site (22-Lo-600), Lowndes County, Mississippi." *Mississippi Archaeology* 28, no. 2 (1993): 45–74.

Johnsgard, Paul. "The Triumphant Trumpeter." *Natural History* 87, no. 9 (1978): 72–79.

Jones, B. Calvin. "Southern Cult Manifestations at the Lake Jackson Site, Leon County, Florida: Salvage Excavation of Mound 3." *Midcontinental Journal of Archaeology* 7, no. 1 (1982): 3–44.

Kehoe, Alice Beck. *America before the European Invasions*. New York: Longman, 2002.

Kelly, Arthur Randolf, and Lewis H. Larson Jr. "Explorations at Etowah, Georgia, 1954–1956." *Archaeology* 10 (1957): 39–48.

Kersey, Harry A., Jr. *Pelts, Plumes, and Hides: White Traders among the Seminole Indians, 1870–1930*.

Gainesville: Florida Atlantic University, 1975.

Kidder, Tristram R. "Prehistory of the Lower Mississippi Valley after 800 BC." In Fogelson, *Handbook of North American Indians*, 545–59.

Kilpatrick, Alan. *The Night Has a Naked Soul: Witchcraft and Sorcery among the Western Cherokees*. Syracuse, N.Y.: Syracuse University Press, 1997.

Kilpatrick, Jack Frederick, and Anna Gritts Kilpatrick. *Friends of Thunder: Folktales of the Oklahoma Cherokees*. Norman: University of Oklahoma Press, 1995.

———. *Notebook of a Cherokee Shaman*. Washington, D.C.: Smithsonian Institution Press, 1970.

———. *Run toward the Nightland: Magic of the Oklahoma Cherokees*. Dallas: Southern Methodist University Press, 1967.

———. *Walk in Your Soul: Love Incantations of the Oklahoma Cherokees*. Dallas: Southern Methodist University Press, 1965.

Kirk, David A., and Michael J. Mossman. *Turkey Vulture (Cathartes aura)*. The Birds of North America, edited by A. Poole and F. Gill, no. 339. Philadelphia: Academy of Natural Sciences; Washington, D.C.: American Ornithologists' Union, 1998.

Kneberg, Madeline. "Engraved Shell Gorgets and Their Associations." *Tennessee Archaeologist* 15, no. 1 (1959): 1–39.

Knight, Vernon James, Jr. "Farewell to the Southeastern Ceremonial Complex." *Southeastern Archaeology* 25, no. 1 (2006): 1–5.

———, ed. *The Moundville Expeditions of Clarence Bloomfield Moore*. Tuscaloosa: University of Alabama Press, 1996.

Knight, Vernon James, Jr., James A. Brown, and George E. Lankford. "On the Subject Matter of Southeastern Ceremonial Complex Art."

Southeastern Archaeology 20 (2001): 129–41.

Knight, Vernon James, Jr., and Vincas P. Steponaitis, eds. *Archaeology of the Moundville Chiefdom*. Washington, D.C.: Smithsonian Institution, 1998.

———. "A New History of Moundville." In Knight and Steponaitis, *Archaeology of the Moundville Chiefdom*, 1–25.

Kochert, Michael N., K. Steenhof, C. L. McIntyre, and E. H. Craig. *Golden Eagle (Aquila chrysaetos)*. The Birds of North America, edited by A. Poole and F. Gill, no. 684. Philadelphia: Academy of Natural Sciences; Washington, D.C.: American Ornithologists' Union, 2002.

Kolianos, Phyllis E., and Brent R. Weisman, eds. *The Florida Journals of Frank Hamilton Cushing*. Gainesville: University Press of Florida, 2005.

König, Claus, Friedhelm Weick, and Jan-Hendrik Becking. *Owls: A Guide to the Owls of the World*. New Haven, Conn.: Yale University Press, 1999.

Krech, Shepard, III. "Dodo." In Krech, McNeill, and Merchant, *Encyclopedia of World Environmental History*, 1:330–31.

———. *The Ecological Indian: Myth and History*. New York: W. W. Norton, 1999.

———. "Feather Use in the American South: A European Connection?" Manuscript in the author's possession, n.d.

———. "On Feathered America." Paper delivered at the annual meeting of the American Anthropological Association, New Orleans, November 24, 2002.

———. "Traditional Environmental Knowledge." In Krech, McNeill, and Merchant, *Encyclopedia of World Environmental History*, 3:1213–16.

Krech, Shepard, III, John McNeill, and Carolyn Merchant. *Encyclopedia of World Environmental History*. 3 vols. New York: Routledge, 2004.

Kroeber, Alfred Louis. Review of *The American Indian*, by Clark Wissler. *American Anthropologist* 20 (1918): 203–9.

Kupperman, Karen Ordahl. *Indians and English: Facing Off in Early America*. Ithaca, N.Y.: Cornell University Press, 2000.

Lankford, George E. *Native American Legends: Southeastern Legends; Tales from the Natchez, Caddo, Biloxi, Chickasaw and Other Nations*. Little Rock: August House, 1987.

Larson, Lewis H., Jr. *Aboriginal Subsistence Technology on the Southeastern Coastal Plain during the Late Prehistoric Period*. Gainesville: University Press of Florida, 1980.

———. "Archaeological Implications of Social Stratification at the Etowah Site, Georgia." In *Approaches to the Social Dimensions of Mortuary Practices*, edited by James A. Brown, Memoirs of the Society for American Archaeology 25, 58–67. Issued as *American Antiquity* 36, no. 3, pt. 2 (1971).

———. "The Etowah Site." In Galloway, *Southeastern Ceremonial Complex*, 133–41.

———. "An Examination of the Significance of a Tortoise-Shell Pin from the Etowah Site." In *Archaeology of Eastern North America: Papers in Honor of Stephen Williams*, edited by James B. Stoltman, Mississippi Department of Archives and History Archaeological Report 25, 169–85. Jackson: Mississippi Dept. of Archives and History, 1993.

———. "Historic Guale Indians of the Georgia Coast and the Impact of the Spanish Mission Effort." In *Tacachale: Essays on the Indians of Florida and Southeastern Georgia during the Historic Period*, edited by Jerald Milanich and Samuel Proctor, 120–40. Gainesville: University Press of Florida, 1978.

———. "A Mississippian Headdress from

Etowah, Georgia." *American Antiquity* 25 (1959): 109–12.

———. "Southern Cult Manifestations on the Georgia Coast." *American Antiquity* 23 (1958): 426–30.

———. "Unusual Figurine from the Georgia Coast." *Florida Anthropologist* 8, no. 3 (1955): 75–81.

Laudonnière, René. *Three Voyages.* Translated and edited by Charles E. Bennett. Gainesville: University Press of Florida, 1975.

Lawson, John. *New Voyage to Carolina.* Edited by Hugh Talmage Lefler. Chapel Hill: University of North Carolina Press, 1967.

Leopold, A. Starker. "The Nature of Heritable Wildness in Turkeys." *Condor* 46 (1944): 133–97.

Le Page du Pratz, M. (Antoine-Simon). *Histoire de la Louisiane: Contenant la découverte de ce vaste pays; sa description géographique; un voyage dans les terres; l'histoire naturelle; les moeurs, coûtumes & religion des naturels, avec leurs origins . . .* 3 vols. Paris: Chez De Bure, l'Aîné . . . , 1758.

———. *The History of Louisiana / L'Histoire de la Louisiane* (1758). Selections translated by Gordon Sayre. Gordon Sayre, University of Oregon, http://www.uoregon.edu/~gsayre/LPDP.html (accessed March 7, 2006).

Lerch, Patricia. "Indians of the Carolinas since 1900." In Fogelson, *Handbook of North American Indians,* 328–36.

Lévi-Strauss, Claude. *The Savage Mind.* Chicago: University of Chicago Press, 1966.

———. *Totemism.* Boston: Beacon Press, 1963.

———. *Le totémisme aujourd'hui.* Paris: Presses Universitaires de France, 1962.

Lewis, Andrew J. "A Democracy of Facts, an Empire of Reason: Swallow Submersion and Natural History in the Early American Republic." *William and Mary Quarterly* 62 (2005): 663–96.

Linné, Carl von. *Systema Naturae.* Paris: Sumptibus Michaelis-Antonii David, 1744.

Lockwood, W. B. *The Oxford Dictionary of British Bird Names.* Oxford: Oxford University Press, 1993.

Longe, Alexander. "A Small Postscript on the Ways and Manners of the Indians Called Charikees, the Contents of the Whole So that You May Find Everything by the Page." Modern version edited by David H. Corkran. *Southern Indian Studies* 21 (October 1969): 3–49.

Luer, George M. "Mississippian-Period Popeyed Bird-Head Effigies in West-Central and Southwest Florida." *Florida Anthropologist* 45, no. 1 (1992): 52–62.

———. "A Safety Harbor Incised Bottle with Effigy Bird Feet and Human Hands from a Possible Headman Burial, Sarasota County, Florida." *Florida Anthropologist* 46, no. 4 (1993): 238–50.

Lyon, Eugene. "The Canete Fragment: Another Narrative of Hernando de Soto." In *The De Soto Chronicles: The Expedition of Hernando de Soto to North America in 1539–1543,* edited by Lawrence A. Clayton, Vernon James Knight Jr., and Edward C. Moore, 2 vols., 1:307–10. Tuscaloosa: University of Alabama Press, 1993.

Magnel, Francis. "Francis Magnel's Relation of the First Voyage and the Beginnings of the Jamestown Colony." In Barbour, *Jamestown Voyages,* 1:151–57.

Markham, Clements R., ed. *The Hawkins' Voyages during the Reigns of Henry VIII, Queen Elizabeth, and James I.* New York: Burt Franklin, 1970.

Marks, J. S., D. L. Evans, and D. W. Holt. *Long-Eared Owl* (Asio otus). Birds of North America, edited by A. Poole and F. Gill, no. 133. Philadelphia: Academy of Natural Sciences; Washington, D.C.: American Ornithologists' Union, 1994.

Marquette, Father Jacques. "Voyages du P. Jacques Marquette, 1673–75." In *The Jesuit Relations and Allied Documents: Travels and Explorations of the Jesuit Missionaries in New France, 1610–1791,* edited by Reuben Thwaites, 59:86–211 (documents 136–138). Cleveland: Burrows Brothers, 1900.

Martin, Jack B., and Margaret McKane Maudlin. *A Dictionary of Creek/Muskogee.* Lincoln: University of Nebraska Press, 2000.

Mason, Ian L., ed. *Evolution of Domesticated Animals.* London: Longman, 1984.

McAtee, Waldo Lee. "The Birds in Lawson's 'New Voyage to Carolina,' 1709." *Chat,* December 1955, 74–77; June 1956, 23–27.

———. "Folk Names of Florida Birds." *Florida Naturalist,* April 1955, 35–37, 64; July 1955, 83–87, 91; October 1955, 103, 121–23.

———. "North American Bird Records in the 'Philosophical Transactions,' 1665–1800." *Journal of the Society for the Bibliography of Natural History* 3 (1953–60): 56–60.

———. "The North American Birds of Virginia Chroniclers, 1588–1686." *Journal of the Society for the Bibliography of Natural History* 3 (1953–60): 92–101.

McCane-O'Connor, Mallory. "Prehistoric Ceramics: The Weeden Island Tradition." *American Indian Art Magazine* 5, no. 2 (1980): 48–53, 77.

McCarthy, Joseph Edward. "Portraits of Osceola and the Artists Who Painted Them." *Papers* (Jacksonville Historical Society) 2 (1949): 23–44.

McClellan, Elisabeth. *History of American Costume, 1607–1870.* New York: Tudor, 1937.

McIlhenny, Edward A. *The Wild Turkey and Its Hunting.* Garden City, N.Y.: Doubleday, Page, 1914.

McKee, Jesse O., and Jon A. Schlenker, *The Choctaws: Cultural Evolution of a Native American Tribe*. Jackson: University Press of Mississippi, 1980.

McKenney, Thomas, and James Hall. *History of the Indian Tribes of North America: With Biographical Sketches and Anecdotes of the Principal Chiefs*. Philadelphia: E. C. Biddle, 1837.

McKinley, Daniel. "Archaeozoology of the Carolina Parakeet." *Central States Archaeological Journal* 24, no. 1 (1977): 5 – 26.

——. *The Carolina Parakeet in Florida*. Gainesville: Florida Ornithological Society, 1985.

——. "The Carolina Parakeet in Georgia." *The Oriole* 42, no. 2 (1977): 21 – 25.

——. "The Carolina Parakeet in the Upper Missouri and Mississippi River Valleys." *Auk* 82 (1965): 215 – 26.

——. "The Carolina Parakeet in the Virginias: A Review." *Raven* 49 (1978): 1 – 10.

——. "Historical Review of the Carolina Parakeet in the Carolinas." *Brimleyana* 1 (1979): 81 – 98.

McNamara, Kevin R. "The Feathered Scribe: The Discourses of American Ornithology before 1800." *William and Mary Quarterly* 47 (1990): 210 – 34.

Melosi, Martin. "Environment." In Wilson and Ferris, *Encyclopedia of Southern Culture*, 315 – 21.

Merrell, James H. *The Indians' New World: Catawbas and Their Neighbors from European Contact through the Era of Removal*. Chapel Hill: University of North Carolina Press, 1989.

Milanich, Jerald T. "Prehistory of Florida after 500 BC." In Fogelson, *Handbook of North American Indians*, 191 – 203.

——. "Prehistory of the Lower Atlantic Coast after 500 BC." In Fogelson, *Handbook of North American Indians*, 229 – 37.

——. "The Temporal Placement of Cushing's Key Marco Site, Florida." *American Anthropologist* 80 (1978): 682.

Milanich, Jerald T., and Charles H.

Fairbanks. *Florida Archaeology*. New York: Academic Press, 1980.

Milanich, Jerald T., and Charles Hudson. *Hernando de Soto and the Indians of Florida*. Gainesville: University Press of Florida, 1993.

Milanich, Jerald T., and William C. Sturtevant, eds. *Francisco Pareja's 1613 Confessionario: A Documentary Source for Timucuan Ethnography*. Translated by Emilio F. Moran. Tallahassee: Division of Archives, History, and Records Management, Florida Department of State, 1972.

Mitchell, Carl D. *Trumpeter Swan (Cygnus buccinator)*. The Birds of North America, edited by A. Poole and F. Gill, no. 105. Philadelphia: Academy of Natural Sciences; Washington, D.C.: American Ornithologists' Union, 1994.

Mooney, James. "The Cherokee Ball Play." *American Anthropologist* 3 (1890): 105 – 32.

——. *Myths of the Cherokee*. New York: Dover, 1995.

——. "The Sacred Formulas of the Cherokees." In *Smithsonian Institution, Bureau of American Ethnology, Seventh Annual Report for 1885 – 1886*, 301 – 97. Washington, D.C.: U.S. Government Printing Office, 1891.

Mooney, James, and Frans M. Olbrechts. *The Swimmer Manuscript: Cherokee Sacred Formulas and Medicinal Prescriptions*. Smithsonian Institution, Bureau of American Ethnology Bulletin 99. Washington, D.C.: U.S. Government Printing Office, 1932.

Moore, Alexander, ed. 1988. *Nairne's Muskhogean Journals: The 1708 Expedition to the Mississippi River*. Jackson: University Press of Mississippi, 1988.

Moore, Clarence B. "Aboriginal Remains from the Black Warrior River." *Journal of the Academy of Natural Sciences* 13 (1905): 125 – 244.

——. "Moundville Revisited." *Journal*

of the Academy of Natural Sciences of Philadelphia 13 (1907): 337 – 405.

Moorehead, Warren King. *Etowah Papers I: Exploration of the Etowah Site in Georgia*. New Haven, Conn.: Yale University Press, 1932.

Mosby, Henry S., and Charles O. Handley. *The Wild Turkey in Virginia: Its Status, Life History, and Management*. Richmond, Va.: Commission of Game and Inland Fisheries, Pittman Robertson Projects — Division of Game, 1943.

Muller, Jon. "The Southern Cult." In Galloway, *Southeastern Ceremonial Complex*, 11 – 26.

Munro, Pamela, and Catherine Willmond. *Chickasaw: An Analytical Dictionary*. Norman: University of Oklahoma Press, 1994.

Murphy, James, and John Farrand. "Prehistoric Occurrence of the Ivory-Billed Woodpecker (*Campephilus principalis*), Muskingum County, Ohio." *Ohio Journal of Science* 79, no. 1 (1979): 22 – 23.

Neill, Wilfred T., H. James Gut, and Pierce Brodkorb. "Animal Remains from Four Preceramic Sites in Florida." *American Antiquity* 21 (1956): 383 – 95.

Neitzel, Robert S. *Archeology of the Fatherland Site: The Grand Village of the Natchez*. Anthropological Papers of the American Museum of Natural History 51, pt. 1. New York: American Museum of Natural History, 1965.

Neumann, Thomas W. "Human-Wildlife Competition and the Passenger Pigeon: Population Growth from System Destabilization." *Human Ecology* 13, no. 4 (1985): 389 – 410.

Neumann, Thomas W., and R. Christopher Goodwin and Associates. "Human-Wildlife Competition and Prehistoric Subsistence: The Case of the Eastern United States." *Journal of Middle Atlantic Archaeology* 5 (1989): 29 – 57.

Nicholson, Rebecca A. "Bone Degradation, Burial Medium and Species Representation: Debunking the Myths, an Experiment-Based Approach." *Journal of Archaeological Science* 23 (1996): 513–33.

———. "Bone Degradation in a Compost Heap." *Journal of Archaeological Science* 25 (1998): 393–403.

Nunez, Theron A., Jr. "Creek Nativism and the Creek War of 1813–1814." *Ethnohistory* 5, no. 3 (1958): 292–301.

Obermeyer, Rick, ed. "Turbans in 19th Century Seminole Men's Clothing." In *NativeTech: Native American Technology and Art*. http://www.nativetech.org/seminole/turbans/index.php.

O'Laughlin, Bridget. "Mediation of Contradiction: Why Mbum Women Do Not Eat Chicken." In *Women, Culture, and Society*, edited by Michelle Zimbalist Rosaldo and Louise Lamphere, 301–18. Stanford, Calif.: Stanford University Press, 1974.

O'Shea, John M., George Schrimper, and John K. Ludwickson. "Ivory-Billed Woodpeckers at the Big Village of the Omaha." *Plains Anthropologist* 27 (1982): 245–48.

Palmer, Ralph S. "Golden Eagle." In Palmer, *Handbook of North American Birds*, 5:180–231 (1988).

———, ed. *Handbook of North American Birds*. 5 vols. New Haven, Conn.: Yale University Press, 1962–1988.

Paper, Jordan. *Offering Smoke: The Sacred Pipe and Native American Religion*. Moscow: University of Idaho Press, 1988.

Paredes, J. Anthony. "Back from Disappearance: The Alabama Creek Indian Community." In *Southeastern Indians since the Removal Era*, edited by Walter L. Williams, 123–41. Athens: University of Georgia Press, 1979. Reprinted in *A Creek Source Book*, edited by William C. Sturtevant. New York: Garland, 1987.

———. "The Emergence of Contemporary Eastern Creek Indian Identity." In *Social and Cultural Identity: Problems of Persistence and Change*, edited by Thomas K. Fitzgerald, Southern Anthropological Society Proceedings 8, 63–80. Athens: University of Georgia Press, 1974. Reprinted in *A Creek Source Book*, edited by William C. Sturtevant. New York: Garland, 1987.

———. "The Folk Culture of the Eastern Creek Indians: Synthesis and Change." In *Indians of the Lower South: Past and Present*, edited by John K. Mahon, Proceeding of the Fifth Annual Gulf Coast Historical and Humanistic Conference, 93–111. Pensacola, Fla.: Gulf Coast History and Humanities Conference, 1975.

———. "Kinship and Descent in the Ethnic Reassertion of the Eastern Creek Indians." In *The Versatility of Kinship: Essays Presented to Harry W. Basehart*, edited by L. S. Cordell and S. Beckerman, 165–94. New York: Academic Press, 1979. Reprinted in *A Creek Source Book*, edited by William C. Sturtevant. New York: Garland, 1987.

Parmalee, Alice. *All the Birds of the Bible: Their Stories, Identification, and Meaning*. New Canaan, Conn.: Keats, 1959.

Parmalee, Paul W. "Additional Noteworthy Records of Birds from Archaeological Sites." *Wilson Bulletin* 79, no. 2 (1967): 155–62.

———. *Animal Remains from the Banks Site, Crittenden County, Arkansas*. Tennessee Archaeological Society Miscellaneous Paper 5. Knoxville: Tennessee Archaeological Society, 1959.

———. "An Archaeological Avian Assemblage from Northwestern Alabama." *Archaeozoologia* 5, no. 2 (1993): 77–92.

———. "Remains of Rare and Extinct Birds from Illinois Indian Sites." *Auk* 75 (1958): 169–76.

———. "Vertebrate Remains from an Historic Archaeological Site in Rock Island County, Illinois." *Transactions of the Illinois State Academy of Science* 57 (1964): 167–74.

———. "Vertebrate Remains from the Cahokia Site, Illinois." *Transactions of the Illinois State Academy of Science* 50 (1957): 235–42.

Parmalee, Paul W., and Gregory Perino. "A Prehistoric Archaeological Record of the Roseate Spoonbill in Illinois." *Central States Archaeological Journal* 18 (1971): 80–85.

Parsons, Elsie Clews. *Notes on the Caddo*. Memoirs of the American Anthropological Association 57. Menasha, Wis.: American Anthropological Association, 1941.

Peebles, Christopher S. "Moundville and Surrounding Sites: Some Structural Considerations of Mortuary Practices II." In *Approaches to the Social Dimensions of Mortuary Practices*, edited by James A. Brown, Memoir of the Society for American Archaeology, 68–91. Issued in *American Antiquity* 36, no. 3, pt. 2 (1971).

Pelham, Paul H., and James G. Dickson. "Physical Characteristics." In *The Wild Turkey: Biology and Management*, edited by James G. Dickson, 32–45. Mechanicsburg, Pa.: Stackpole Books, 1992.

Percy, George. "Fragment Published in 1614." In Barbour, *Jamestown Voyages*, 1:146–47.

———. "George Percy's Discourse." In Barbour, *Jamestown Voyages*, 1:129–46.

Perdue, Theda, and Michael D. Green. *The Columbia Guide to American Indians of the Southeast*. New York: Columbia University Press, 2001.

Phillips, Philip, and James A. Brown. *Pre-Columbian Shell Engravings from the Craig Mound at Spiro, Oklahoma*. Vol. 1. Cambridge, Mass.: Peabody Museum Press, 1978. Copyright 1978 by the President and Fellows of Harvard College.

———. *Pre-Columbian Shell Engravings from the Craig Mound at Spiro, Oklahoma.* Vol. 2. Cambridge, Mass.: Peabody Museum Press, 1984. Copyright 1984 by the President and Fellows of Harvard College.

Pickens, Andrew Lee. "Another Contribution to Catawba Ethnozoology." In "Indian and Nature Lore from Old Catawba Country, or Out-of-Doors in the Southern Piedmont: Indians, Animals, Plants." *Neighborhood Research* 18, nos. 1–5 (1957).

———. "Contributions to Catawba Ethnozoology." In "Indian and Nature Lore from Old Catawba Country, or Out-of-Doors in the Southern Piedmont: Indians, Animals, Plants." *Neighborhood Research* 18, nos. 1–5 (1957).

Pohl, Mary E. D., Kevin O. Pope, and Christopher von Nagy. "Olmec Origins of Mesoamerican Writing." *Science* 298, no. 5600 (December 6, 2002): 1984–87.

Price, Jennifer. *Flight Maps: Adventures with Nature in Modern America.* New York: Basic Books, 1999.

Proctor, Noble S., and Patrick J. Lynch. *Manual of Ornithology: Avian Structure and Function.* New Haven, Conn.: Yale University Press, 1993.

Purdy, Barbara A. *Indian Art of Ancient Florida.* Gainesville: University Press of Florida, 1996.

Quinn, David Beers, ed. "Arthur Barlowe's Discourse of the First Voyage." In *The Roanoke Voyages, 1584–1590: Documents to Illustrate the English Voyages to North America under the Patent Granted to Walter Raleigh in 1584,* 2 vols., Works Issued by the Hakluyt Society, 2nd ser., no. 104, 1:91–117. London: Hakluyt Society, 1955. Reprint, Nendeln, Liechtenstein: Kraus Reprint, 1967.

———, ed. "The First Colony: John White." In *The Roanoke Voyages, 1584–1590: Documents to Illustrate the English Voyages to North America under the Patent Granted to Walter Raleigh in 1584,* 2 vols., Works Issued by the Hakluyt Society, 2nd ser., no. 104, 1:390–464. London: Hakluyt Society, 1955. Reprint, Nendeln, Liechtenstein: Kraus Reprint, 1967.

———, ed. "The First Colony: Thomas Hariot." In *The Roanoke Voyages, 1584–1590: Documents to Illustrate the English Voyages to North America under the Patent Granted to Walter Raleigh in 1584,* 2 vols., Works Issued by the Hakluyt Society, 2nd ser., no. 104, 1:314–87. London: Hakluyt Society, 1955. Reprint, Nendeln, Liechtenstein: Kraus Reprint, 1967.

Rangel, Rodrigo. "Account of the Northern Conquest and Discovery of Hernando de Soto." In *The De Soto Chronicles: The Expedition of Hernando de Soto to North America in 1539–1543,* edited by Lawrence A. Clayton, Vernon James Knight Jr., and Edward C. Moore, 2 vols., 1:247–306. Tuscaloosa: University of Alabama Press, 1993.

Reed, John Shelton. "The South: What Is It? *Where* Is It?" In *The South for New Southerners,* edited by Paul Escott and David Goldfield, 18–41. Chapel Hill: University of North Carolina Press, 1991.

Reiger, John F. "Artistry, Status and Power: How 'Plummet'-Pendants Probably Functioned in Pre-Columbian Florida — and Beyond." *Florida Anthropologist* 52, no. 4 (1999): 227–40.

———. "'Plummets' — An Analysis of a Mysterious Florida Artifact." *Florida Anthropologist* 43, no. 4 (1990): 227–39.

Reitz, Elizabeth J. "Vertebrate Fauna from Four Coastal Mississippian Sites." *Journal of Ethnobiology* 2, no. 1 (1982): 39–61.

Ribeiro, Aileen. *The Art of Dress: Fashion in England and France 1750 to 1820.* New Haven, Conn.: Yale University Press, 1995.

———. *Dress in Eighteenth-Century Europe, 1715–1789.* New York: Holmes and Meier, 1984.

———. *Gallery of Fashion.* Princeton, N.J.: Princeton University Press, 2000.

Ribeiro, Aileen, and Valerie Cumming. *The Visual History of Costume.* London: B. S. Batsford, 1989.

Robertson, James Alexander. "The Account by a Gentleman from Elvas." In *The De Soto Chronicles: The Expedition of Hernando de Soto to North America in 1539–1543,* edited by Lawrence A. Clayton, Vernon James Knight Jr., and Edward C. Moore, 2 vols., 1:19–218. Tuscaloosa: University of Alabama Press, 1993.

Rogers, Daniel, and George Sabo III. "Caddo." In Fogelson, *Handbook of North American Indians,* 616–31.

Rogers, J. Daniel, Carla J. Dove, Marcy Heacker, and Gary Graves. "Identification of Feathers in Textiles from the Craig Mound at Spiro, Oklahoma." *Southeastern Archaeology* 21 (2002): 245–51.

Rogers, Philip M., and Donald A. Hammer. "Ancestral Breeding and Wintering Ranges of the Trumpeter Swan (*Cygnus buccinator*) in the Eastern United States." *North American Swans* 27, no. 1 (1993): 13–29.

Rolingson, Martha Ann. "Prehistory of the Central Mississippi Valley and Ozarks after 500 BC." In Fogelson, *Handbook of North American Indians,* 534–44.

Romans, Bernard. *A Concise Natural History of East and West Florida.* Edited by Kathryn E. Holland Braund. Tuscaloosa: University of Alabama Press, 1999.

Rountree, Helen C. *Pocahontas's People: The Powhatan Indians of Virginia through Four Centuries*. Norman: University of Oklahoma Press, 1990.

———. *The Powhatan Indians of Virginia: Their Traditional Culture*. Norman: University of Oklahoma Press, 1989.

Rowland, Beryl. *Birds with Human Souls: A Guide to Bird Symbolism*. Knoxville: University of Tennessee Press, 1978.

Saikku, Mikko. "The Extinction of the Carolina Parakeet." *Environmental History Review* 14, no. 3 (1990): 1–18.

———. "'Home in the Big Forest': Decline of the Ivory-Billed Woodpecker and Its Habitat in the United States." In *Encountering the Past in Nature*, edited by Timo Myllyntaus and Mikko Saijkku, 94–140. Athens: Ohio University Press, 2001.

Sassaman, Kenneth E., and David G. Anderson. "Late Holocene Period, 3750 to 650 BC." In Fogelson, *Handbook of North American Indians*, 101–14.

Sauer, Carl O. *Agricultural Origins and Dispersals*. 2nd ed. Cambridge, Mass.: MIT Press, 1969.

———. *The Early Spanish Main*. Berkeley: University of California Press, 1966.

Sayre, Gordon, trans. and ed. *Antoine-Simon Le Page du Pratz: The History of Louisiana* (selections). http://www .uoregon.edu/~gsayre/LPDP.html (accessed September 1, 2006).

Scarry, John F., ed. *Political Structure and Change in the Prehistoric Southeastern United States*. Gainesville: University Press of Florida, 1996.

Schorger, Arlie William. *The Passenger Pigeon: Its Natural History and Extinction*. Madison: University of Wisconsin Press, 1955.

———. *The Wild Turkey: Its History and Domestication*. Norman: University of Oklahoma Press, 1966.

Schroeder, M. A., and L. A. Robb. *Greater Prairie-Chicken (*Tympanuchus cupido*)*. The Birds of North America, edited by A. Poole and F. Gill,

no. 36. Philadelphia: Academy of Natural Sciences; Washington, D.C.: American Ornithologists' Union, 1993.

Scott, Susan L. "Analysis, Synthesis, and Interpretation of Faunal Remains from the Lubbub Creek Archaeological Locality." In *Studies of Material Remains from the Lubbub Creek Archaeological Locality*, vol. 2 of *Prehistoric Agricultural Communities in West Central Alabama*, edited by Christopher S. Peebles, 272–390. Ann Arbor: University of Michigan, 1983.

Scott, Susan L., and H. Edwin Jackson. "Early Caddo Ritual and Patterns of Animal Use: An Analysis of Faunal Remains from the Crenshaw Site (3M16), Southwestern Arkansas." *Arkansas Archeologist* 37 (1996): 1–38.

Sears, William H. "Food Production and Village Life in Prehistoric Southeastern United States." *Archaeology* 24 (1971): 322–29.

———. *Fort Center: An Archaeological Site in the Lake Okeechobee Basin*. Gainesville: University Press of Florida, 1982.

Shufeldt, R. W. "Fossil Birds Found at Vero, Florida, with Descriptions of New Species." In *Florida Geological Survey — Eighth Annual Report*, 35–42 and plates. Tallahassee: Florida Geological Survey, 1917.

Sibley, D., L. R. Bevier, M. A. Patten, and C. S. Elphick. "Comment on 'Ivory-Billed Woodpecker (*Campephilus principalis*) Persists in Continental North America.'" *Science* 311, no. 5767 (March 17, 2006): 1555. http:// www.sciencemag.org/cgi/content/ full/311/5767/1555a.

Sillitoe, Paul. "From Head-Dresses to Head-Messages: The Art of Self-Decoration in the Highlands of Papua New Guinea." *Man* 23 (1988): 298–318.

Silver, Timothy. *New Face on the Countryside: Indians, Colonists and Slaves in South Atlantic Forests,*

1500–1800. Cambridge: Cambridge University Press, 1990.

Simoons, Frederick J. *Eat Not This Flesh: Food Avoidances from Prehistory to the Present*. Madison: University of Wisconsin Press, 1994.

Smith, Andrew F. *The Turkey: An American Story*. Chicago: University of Illinois Press, 2006.

Smith, Bruce D. *Middle Mississippi Exploitation of Animal Populations*. Anthropological Papers, Museum of Anthropology, University of Michigan 57. Ann Arbor: University of Michigan, 1975.

———. "Middle Mississippi Exploitation of Animal Populations: A Predictive Model." *American Antiquity* 39 (1974): 274–91.

———. "The Origins of Agriculture in the Americas." *Evolutionary Anthropology* 3 (1995): 174–84.

Smith, John. "A Map of Virginia [including "The Proceedings of the English Colonie in Virginia . . ."]." In Barbour, *Jamestown Voyages*, 2:321–464.

———. "A True Relation." In Barbour, *Jamestown Voyages*, 1:165–208.

Smith, Kimberly G., James Withgott, and Paul G. Rodewald. *Red-Headed Woodpecker (*Melanerpes erythrocephalus*)*. The Birds of North America, edited by A. Poole and F. Gill, no. 518. Philadelphia: Academy of Natural Sciences; Washington, D.C.: American Ornithologists' Union, 2000.

Smith, Marvin. "Early Historic Period Vestiges of the Southern Cult." In Galloway, *Southeastern Ceremonial Complex*, 142–46.

Snyder, Noel F. R. *The Carolina Parakeet: Glimpses of a Vanished Bird*. Princeton, N.J.: Princeton University Press, 2004.

Snyder, Noel F. R., and Keith Russell. *Carolina Parakeet (*Conuropsis carolinensis*)*. The Birds of North America, edited by A. Poole and

F. Gill, no. 667. Philadelphia: Academy of Natural Sciences; Washington, D.C.: American Ornithologists' Union, 2002.

Speck, Frank G. "The Cane Blowgun in Catawba and Southeastern Ethnology." *American Anthropologist* 40 (1938): 198–204.

———. *Catawba Hunting, Trapping and Fishing.* Joint Publications of the Museum of the University of Pennsylvania and the Philadelphia Anthropological Society 2. Philadelphia: Museum of the University of Pennsylvania, 1946.

———. "Catawba Medicines and Curative Practices." In *Twenty-fifth Anniversary Studies*, edited by D. S. Davidson, 179–97. Philadelphia: Philadelphia Anthropological Society, 1937.

———. "Catawba Religious Beliefs, Mortuary Customs, and Dances." *Primitive Man* 12, no. 2 (1939): 21–57.

———. *Catawba Texts.* New York: Columbia University Press, 1934.

———. *Ceremonial Songs of the Creek and Yuchi Indians.* University of Pennsylvania, Anthropological Publications of the University Museum, vol. 1, no. 2, 157–245. Philadelphia: University Museum, 1911.

———. "The Creek Indians of Taskigi Town." *Memoirs of the American Anthropological Association* 2 (1907): 99–164. Reprinted in *A Creek Source Book*, edited by William C. Sturtevant. New York: Garland, 1987.

———. *Ethnology of the Yuchi Indians.* University of Pennsylvania, Anthropological Publications of the University Museum, vol. 1, no. 1. Philadelphia: University Museum, 1909. Reprint, Atlantic Highlands, N.J.: Humanities Press, 1979.

———. *Gourds of the Southeastern Indians: A Prolegomenon on the Lagenaria Gourd in the Culture of the Southeastern Indians.* Boston: New England Gourd Society, 1941.

———. "Notes on Chickasaw Ethnology and Folk-Lore." *Journal of American Folklore* 20, no. 76 (1907): 50–58.

Speck, Frank G., Royal Hassrick, and Edmund Carpenter. *Rappahannock Taking Devices: Traps, Hunting and Fishing.* Joint Publication no. 1 of the Museum of the University of Pennsylvania and the Philadelphia Anthropological Society. Philadelphia: University Museum, 1946.

Speck, Frank G., and C. E. Schaeffer. "Catawba Kinship and Social Organization with a Resume of Tutelo Kinship Terms." *American Anthropologist* 44 (1942): 555–75.

Speck, Frank G., and John Witthoft. "Some Notable Life-Histories in Zoological Folklore." *Journal of American Folklore* 60, no. 238 (1947): 345–49.

Springer, James Warren. "An Analysis of Prehistoric Food Remains from the Bruly St. Martin Site, Louisiana, with a Comparative Discussion of Mississippi Valley Faunal Studies." *Mid-Continental Journal of Archaeology* 5 (1980): 193–223.

———. "An Ethnohistoric Study of the Smoking Complex in Eastern North America." *Ethnohistory* 28 (1981): 217–35.

Stalmaster, Mark V. *The Bald Eagle.* New York: Universe Books, 1987.

Stangel, Peter W., Paul L. Leberg, and Julia I. Smith. "Systematics and Population Genetics." In *The Wild Turkey: Biology and Management*, edited by James G. Dickson, 18–28. Mechanicsburg, Pa.: Stackpole Books, 1992.

Steadman, David W. "Prehistoric Extinctions of Pacific Island Birds: Biodiversity Meets Zooarchaeology." *Science* 267, no. 5201 (February 24, 1995): 1123–31.

Steadman, David W., and Paul S. Martin. "Extinction of Birds in the Late Pleistocene of North America." In *Quaternary Extinctions*, edited by Paul S. Martin and Richard G. Klein, 466–77. Tucson: University of Arizona Press, 1984.

Steadman, David W., J. Peter White, and Jim Allen. "Prehistoric Birds from New Ireland, Papua New Guinea: Extinctions on a Large Melanesian Island." *Proceedings of the National Academy of Sciences* 96, no. 4 (March 2, 1999): 2563–68.

Stiggins, George. *Creek Indian History.* Birmingham, Ala.: Birmingham Public Library Press, 1989.

Stouff, Faye. *Sacred Beliefs of the Chitimacha Indians.* Edited by Maureen Pitre. Baton Rouge: Nashoba tek Press, 1995.

Strachey, William. *The Historie of Travell into Virginia Britania (1612)*, edited by Louis B. Wright and Virginia Freund. London: Hakluyt Society, 1953.

Strong, John A. "The Mississippian Bird-Man Theme in Cross-Cultural Perspective." In Galloway, *Southeastern Ceremonial Complex*, 211–37.

Sturtevant, William C. *A Creek Source Book.* New York: Garland, 1987.

———. "First Visual Images of Native America." In *First Images of America: The Impact of the New World on the Old*, edited by Fredi Chiappelli, coedited by Michael J. B. Allen and Robert L. Benson, 2 vols., 1:417–54. Berkeley: University of California Press, 1976.

———. "Last of the South Florida Aborigines." In *Tacachale: Essays on the Indians of Florida and Southeastern Georgia during the Historic Period*, edited by Jerald Milanich and Samuel Proctor, 141–62. Gainesville: University Press of Florida, 1978.

———. "La tupinambisation des Indiens d'Amerique du nord." In *Les Figures de l'Indien*, edited by Gilles Thérien,

293 – 303. Montreal: Université du Québec à Montréal, 1988.

Swan, Caleb. "Position and State of Manners and Arts in the Creek, or Muscogee Nation in 1791." In *Historical and Statistical Information respecting the History, Condition, and Prospects of the Indian Tribes of the United States*, edited by Henry Rowe Schoolcraft, 6 vols., 5:251 – 83. Philadelphia: Lippincott, Grambo, 1855.

Swann, H. Kirke. *A Dictionary of English and Folk-Names of British Birds*. London: Witherby, 1913. Reprint, Detroit: Gale Research, 1968.

Swanton, John R. "Catawba Notes." *Journal of the Washington Academy of Sciences* 8, no. 19 (1918): 623 – 29.

———. "An Early Account of the Choctaw Indians." *Memoirs of the American Anthropological Association* 5, no. 2 (April – June, 1918): 53 – 72.

———. *Early History of the Creek Indians and Their Neighbors*. Smithsonian Institution, Bureau of American Ethnology Bulletin 73. Washington, D.C.: U.S. Government Printing Office, 1922. Reprint, Gainesville: University Press of Florida, 1998.

———. "The Green Corn Dance." *Chronicles of Oklahoma* 10, no. 2 (1932): 170 – 95.

———. *The Indians of the Southeastern United States*. Smithsonian Institution, Bureau of American Ethnology Bulletin 137. Washington, D.C.: U.S. Government Printing Office, 1946. Reprint, Classics in Smithsonian Anthropology 2. Washington, D.C.: Smithsonian Institution Press, 1979.

———. "Mythology of the Indians of Louisiana and the Texas Coast." *Journal of American Folklore* 20, no. 79 (1907): 285 – 89.

———. *Myths and Tales of the Southeastern Indians*. Smithsonian Institution, Bureau of American

Ethnology Bulletin 88. Washington, D.C.: U.S. Government Printing Office, 1929. Reprint, Norman: University of Oklahoma Press, 1995.

———. "Newly Discovered Powhatan Bird Names." *Journal of the Washington Academy of Sciences* 24, no. 2 (1934): 96 – 99.

———. "Religious Beliefs and Medical Practices of the Creek Indians." *Forty-second Annual Report of the Bureau of American Ethnology [for] 1924 – 1925*, 473 – 672. Washington, D.C.: U.S. Government Printing Office, 1928.

———. "Social and Religious Beliefs and Usages of the Chickasaw Indians." *Forty-fourth Annual Report of the Bureau of American Ethnology to the Secretary of the Smithsonian Institution, 1926 – 1927*, 169 – 273. Washington, D.C.: U.S. Government Printing Office, 1928.

———. "Social Organization and Social Usages of the Indians of the Creek Confederacy." *Forty-second Annual Report of the Bureau of American Ethnology [for] 1924 – 1925*, 23 – 472. Washington, D.C.: U.S. Government Printing Office, 1928.

———. *Source Material for the Social and Ceremonial Life of the Choctaw Indians*. Smithsonian Institution, Bureau of American Ethnology Bulletin 103. Washington, D.C.: U.S. Government Printing Office, 1931.

———. *Source Material on the History and Ethnology of the Caddo Indians*. Smithsonian Institution, Bureau of American Ethnology Bulletin 132. Washington, D.C.: U.S. Government Printing Office, 1942. Reprint, Norman: University of Oklahoma Press, 1996.

———. "Sun Worship in the Southeast." *American Anthropologist* 30 (1928): 206 – 13.

Tambiah, Stanley J. "Animals Are Good to Think and Good to Prohibit." *Ethnology* 8 (1969): 423 – 59.

Thomas, David Hurst, ed. *Columbian*

Consequences. Vol. 2, *Archaeological and Historical Perspectives on the Spanish Borderlands East*. Washington, D.C.: Smithsonian Institution Press, 1990.

Thomas, Keith. *Man and the Natural World: A History of the Modern Sensibility*. New York: Pantheon Books, 1983.

Townsend, Earl C., Jr. *Birdstones of the North American Indian: A Study of These Most Interesting Stone Forms, the Area of Their Distribution, Their Cultural Provenience, Possible Uses and Antiquity*. Indianapolis: privately printed, 1959.

Townsend, Richard F. "American Landscapes, Seen and Unseen." In Townsend, *Hero, Hawk, and Open Hand*, 15 – 35.

———, ed. *Hero, Hawk, and Open Hand: American Indian Art of the Ancient Midwest and South*. Chicago: Art Institute of Chicago; New Haven, Conn.: Yale University Press, 2004.

Tregle, Joseph G., Jr., ed. *The History of Louisiana*. Translated from the French of M. Le Page du Pratz. London, 1774. Baton Rouge: Louisiana State University Press, 1975.

True, David O., ed. *Memoir of Doˉ. d'Escalante Fontaneda, Written in Spain, about the Year 1575*. Translated with notes by Buckingham Smith. Coral Gables, Fla.: Glade House, 1945.

Trumbull, John Trumbull. *Autobiography, Reminiscences, and Letters of John Trumbull from 1756 to 1841*. New Haven, Conn: B. L. Hamlen; New York: Wiley and Putnam, 1841.

Turnbaugh, William A. "Calumet Ceremonialism as a Nativistic Response." *American Antiquity* 44 (1979): 685 – 91.

Turner, Terence. " 'We Are Parrots,' 'Twins Are Birds': Play of Tropes as Operational Structure." In *Beyond Metaphor: The Theory of Tropes in Anthropology*, edited by James W.

Fernandez, 121–58. Stanford, Calif.: Stanford University Press, 1991.

Urban, Greg, and Jason Baird Jackson. "Mythology and Folklore." In Fogelson, *Handbook of North American Indians*, 707–19.

Usner, Daniel H., Jr. "The Frontier Exchange Economy of the Lower Mississippi Valley in the Eighteenth Century." *William and Mary Quarterly* 44 (April 1987): 165–92.

———. *Indians, Settlers, and Slaves in a Frontier Exchange Economy: The Lower Mississippi Valley before 1783*. Chapel Hill: University of North Carolina Press, 1992.

Van der Schalie, Henry, and Paul W. Parmalee. "Animal Remains from The Etowah Site, Mound C, Bartow County, Georgia." *Florida Anthropologist* 13, nos. 2–3 (1960): 37–54.

von Gernet, Alexander. "*Nicotiana* Dreams: The Prehistory and Early History of Tobacco in Eastern North America." In *Consuming Habits: Drugs in History and Anthropology*, edited by J. Goodman, P. E. Lovejoy, and A. Sherratt, 67–87. London: Routledge, 1995.

———. "North American Indigenous *Nicotiana* Use and Tobacco Shamanism: The Early Documentary Record, 1520–1600." In *Tobacco Use by Native North Americans: Sacred Smoke and Silent Killer*, edited by J. C. Winter, 59–80. Norman: University of Oklahoma Press, 2000.

von Gernet, Alexander, and Peter Timmins. "Pipes and Parakeets: Constructing Meaning in an Early Iroquoian Context." In *Archaeology as Long-Term History*, edited by Ian Hodder, 31–42. Cambridge: Cambridge University Press, 1987.

Wade, Edwin L., ed. *The Arts of the North American Indian: Native Traditions in Evolution*. New York: Hudson Hills Press, 1986.

Walker, Willard B. "Creek Confederacy

before Removal." In Fogelson, *Handbook of North American Indians*, 373–92.

Warren, Geoffrey. *Fashion Accessories since 1500*. London: Unwin Hyman, 1987.

Warwick, Edward, Henry C. Pitz, and Alexander Wyckoff. *Early American Dress*. New York: Benjamin Bloom, 1965.

Waselkov, Gregory A. "French Colonial Trade in the Upper Creek Country." In *Calumet and Fleur-de-Lys: Archaeology of Indian and French Contact in the Midcontinent*, edited by John A. Walthall and Thomas E. Emerson, 35–53. Washington, D.C.: Smithsonian Institution Press, 1992.

Waselkov, Gregory A., and Kathryn E. Holland Braund, eds. *William Bartram on the Southeastern Indians*. Lincoln: University of Nebraska Press, 1995.

Waterhouse, Edward. "A Declaration of the State of the Colony and . . . a Relation of the Barbarous Massacre." Thomas Jefferson Papers Series 8. Virginia Records Manuscripts. 1606–1737, 54-571, p. 557. http://memory.loc.gov/cgi-bin/ampage?collId=mtj8&fileName=mtj8pagevc03.db&recNum=572.gif (accessed April 24, 2006; nonfunctional September 1, 2006).

Waters, Michael. *A Concise History of Ornithology*. New Haven, Conn.: Yale University Press, 2003.

Watson, Jeff. *The Golden Eagle*. London: T. and A. D. Poyser, 1997.

Weber, David J. *The Spanish Frontier in North America*. New Haven, Conn.: Yale University Press, 1992.

Weidensaul, Scott. *The Ghost with Trembling Wings: Science, Wishful Thinking, and the Search for Lost Species*. New York: North Point Press, 2002.

Weigel, Penelope Hermes. "Great Auk Remains from a Florida Shell Midden." *Auk* 75, no. 2 (1958): 215–16.

Weigel, Robert D. "Bird Remains from

South Indian Field, Florida." *Florida Anthropologist* 12, no. 3 (1959): 73–74.

Weisman, Brent R. "A Popeyed Bird-Head Effigy of Stone from the Homosassa River, Citrus County, Florida." *The Florida Anthropologist* 46, no. 1 (1993): 53–55.

Welch, Paul D. "Mississippian Emergence in West-Central Alabama." In *The Mississippian Emergence*, edited by Bruce D. Smith, 197–225. Washington, D.C.: Smithsonian Institution Press, 1990.

Wells, Diana. *100 Birds and How They Got Their Names*. Chapel Hill, N.C.: Algonquin Books of Chapel Hill, 2002.

Weslager, Clinton A. "Nanticokes and the Buzzard Song." *Bulletin of the Archaeological Society of Delaware* 4, no. 2 (1945): 14–17.

Wetmore, Alexander. "Evidence for the Former Occurrence of the Ivory-Billed Woodpecker in Ohio." *Wilson Bulletin* 55 (1943): 55.

Wheeler, Ryan J. *Treasure of the Calusa: The Johnson/Willcox Collection from Mound Key, Florida*. Monographs in Florida Archaeology 1. Tallahassee, Fla.: Rose Printing, 2000.

Whan, William, and Gerry Rising. "Did Trumpeter Swans Ever Breed in Eastern North America?" http://www.acsu.buffalo.edu/~insrisg/nature/swans.html (accessed July 31, 2006).

White, Clayton M., Nancy J. Clum, Tom J. Cade, and W. Grainger Hunt. *Peregrine Falcon (Falco peregrinus)*. The Birds of North America, edited by A. Poole and F. Gill, no. 660. Philadelphia: Academy of Natural Sciences; Washington, D.C.: American Ornithologists' Union, 2002.

White, Terence Hanbury. *The Book of Beasts*. London: Jonathan Cape, 1954.

Widmer, Randolph. "The Relationship of Ceremonial Artifacts from South Florida with the Southeastern

Ceremonial Complex." In Galloway, *Southeastern Ceremonial Complex*, 166–80.

Wilford, John Noble. "First Chickens in Americas Were Brought from Polynesia." *New York Times*, June 5, 2007, D3.

Williams, Lovett E., Jr. "A Recurrent Color Aberrancy in the Wild Turkey." *Journal of Wildlife Management* 28 (1964): 148–52.

Williams, Samuel Cole. *Lieut. Henry Timberlake's Memoirs, 1756–1765.* Marietta, Ga.: Continental Book Company, 1948.

Williams, Stephen, ed. *The Waring Papers: The Collected Works of Antonio J. Waring, Jr.* Papers of the Peabody Museum of Archaeology and Ethnology 58. Cambridge, Mass.: Harvard University, 1968.

Willughby, Francis. *The Ornithology of Francis Willughby of Middleton in the County of Warwick.* London: John Martyn, 1678.

Wilson, Alexander. *American Ornithology, or, The Natural History of Birds in the United States: Illustrated with plates, engraved and colored from original drawings taken from nature.* 9 vols. Philadelphia: Bradford and Inskeep, 1808–14.

Wilson, Charles Reagan, and William Ferris, ed. *Encyclopedia of Southern Culture.* Chapel Hill: University of North Carolina Press, 1989.

Wilson, Lee Anne. "Southern Cult Images of Composite Human and Animal Figures." *American Indian Art Magazine* 11, no. 1 (1985): 46–57.

Wing, Elizabeth S. "Evidences for the Impact of Traditional Spanish Animal Uses in Parts of the New World." In *The Walking Larder: Patterns of Domestication, Pastoralism, and Predation*, edited by Juliet Clutton-Brock, 72–79. London: Unwin Hyman, 1989.

Wissler, Clark. *The American Indian: An Introduction to the Anthropology of the New World.* New York: Douglas C. McMurtrie, 1917.

Witthoft, John. "Bird Lore of the Eastern Cherokee." *Journal of the Washington Academy of Sciences* 36, no. 11 (1946): 372–84.

———. "Some Eastern Cherokee Bird Stories." *Journal of the Washington Academy of Sciences* 36, no. 6 (1946): 177–80.

———. "Will West Long, Cherokee Informant." *American Anthropologist* 50 (1948): 355–59.

Wood, Peter H. "The Changing Population of the Colonial South: An Overview by Race and Region, 1685–1790." In Wood, Waselkov, and Hatley, *Powhatan's Mantle*, 35–103.

Wood, Peter H., Gregory A. Waselkov, and M. Thomas Hatley, eds. *Powhatan's Mantle: Indians in*

the Colonial Southeast. Lincoln: University of Nebraska Press, 1989.

Woodrick, Anne. "Appendix D: Bone Artifacts." In Susan L. Scott, *Analysis, Synthesis, and Interpretation of Faunal Remains from the Lubbub Creek Archaeological Locality, in Prehistoric Agricultural Communities in West Central Alabama*, by Susan L. Scott, vol. 2, *Studies of Material Remains from the Lubbub Creek Archaeological Locality*, edited by Christopher S. Peebles, 380–90. Ann Arbor: University of Michigan/Heritage, Conservation; Atlanta: Recreation Service, Interagency Archeological Services, 1983.

Wright, Albert Hazen. "Early Records of the Wild Turkey." *Auk* 31 (1914): 334–58.

———. "Early Records of the Wild Turkey, II." *Auk* 31 (1914): 463–73.

———. "Early Records of the Wild Turkey, III." *Auk* 32 (1915): 61–81.

———. "Early Records of the Wild Turkey, IV." *Auk* 32 (1915): 207–24.

Young, Gloria, and Michael Hoffman, eds. *The Expedition of Hernando de Soto West of the Mississippi, 1541–1543.* Fayetteville: University of Arkansas Press, 1993.

Zeuner, Frederick E. *A History of Domesticated Animals.* London: Hutchinson, 1963.

Index

Page numbers in *italics* represent illustrations.

chuck-will's-widow, *194*, 205n2

chúwquaréo (red-winged blackbird), *28*

clans, lineage practices of, 102–4

clothing. *See* attire

Cofitachequi chiefdom, 64, 69, 86–87

colors: of birds, 15, 71, 73; for bird spirits/
spirit-birds, 158; black, 79, 126, 158;
black-and-white, 78; blue and yellow,
158; brown, 158; green, 79; purple, 158;
in rituals/ceremonies, 153; as status
signifiers, 120

—red: calumet decoration, 126; moieties,
104; for power or victory, 158; for war,
60–61, 103, 112, *122*, 123

—white: for American military rank,
78–79; for Great Sun, 60–61; moieties,
104; for peace, 103, 112, 122–23, 153, 158;
for serenity/happiness, 158; worn in
ball games, 128

commerce. *See* trade/commerce

commodification. *See* trade/commerce

Congaree, 40–41

Contreras, Don, 201

Coosa chiefdom, 64, 104

coots, *19*

cormorants, 37, *88*, 176

Cory, Charles Barney, Sr., *Mikasuki
Seminole men* (photo), *116*

coyotes, in myths/legends, 172, 209n42

cranes (sandhill or whooping), 37, 41, *42*,
42–43, *43*, 59, 120, 187

Creek: in Alabama (state), 9; on bird clan
name, 103; bird taboos, 40; clothing/
adornment, 66, *67*, 77, 112–13, 120,
129; eagle emblem, 112; feather usage,
75, 125; folklore/beliefs, 138–39, 146,
168–69, 171; food/diet, 45–46; language
family, 205n9; myths/legends, 128,
140–41, 146, 169, 171; personal names,
58, 101; rituals/ceremonies, 153;
symbolism, of birds in war, 121–22

—portraits: Chief Tomo Chachi Mico
and nephew, *108*; Chief William
McIntosh (White Warrior), *113*; Jim
Sawgrass, *200*

—trade: in cloth/deerskin, 77–78; in
poultry, 46

Cuming, Alexander, 81

curlews, *16*, *43*, 73

Cusabo language family, 205n9

Cushing, Frank Hamilton, *82*, 83–85

Cuyp, Albert, *Domestic Fowl*, *44*

Cypress, Wilson, *59*

de Batz, Alexandre, 126

—artworks: *Desseins de Sauvages de
Plusieurs Nations, Nlle. Orleans 1735*,
41, *43*, *124*; *Temple des Sauvages . . .
Cabane du chef*, *135*

De Brahm, William, 22, 23

de Bry, Theodor, artworks of: *Pageantry
with Which a Chosen Queen is Brought
to the King*, *106*; *Queen of the Florida
Island, with Feather Head Covering*, *70*;
That in Which They Train Their Youth,
127; *That Which Outina Considers
Military Order of March When He Goes
to War*, *100*

deer, 35, 178

Dickens, Charles, 79

"dicky birds," 25–26, 29

diet. *See* food/diet

disease/sickness, 7–8, 46, 138, 157, 161–65

Douglas, Mary, 142

doves, 20

ducks: archaeological remains of,
37; in early imagery, 96; hunting
and domestication of, 58; hybrids
(*mulards*), 49; mergansers, 26, *28*, *38*,
88, *105*; Muscovy (*Cairina moschata*),
48–49, 209n43; wood ducks, 96

—illustrations: bufflehead, *23*;
canvasback, *16*; goldeneye, *23*; mallards,
16; Muscovy, *49*; summer, *16*, *90*, *195*;
tree-nesting, *90*; tufted/ring-necked,
23; wood ducks, *16*, *195*

Dumont, Jean Benjamin François,
Louisiana Indians, *75*

eagles: anthropomorphization of,
24; archaeological remains of, 37;
in architecture, 110; in ball game
regalia, 129; Bartram's description of,
112–13; commodification of, 110–11;
curative powers of, 157; extirpation of,
181–82; feathers of, on calumets, 126;
illustrations of, *97*, *108–10*, *182*; in magic
formulas, 158, 160; prohibition against
eating of, 39; symbolism of, 107–13,
121, 192

eggs, 39–40, 43, 46

egrets (herns), 23, 37

Elvas (chronicler), 104, 120

Eno language family, 205n9

Etowah, Ga., 85, 89, 134

Europeans: and bird symbolism, 191;
conceptions of, about natural world,
24; domesticated birds brought to
New World by, 49; early records of,
about birds, 11–12, 22–26; English
people, 24, 29–30, 148; Indian views of,
47; indigenous peoples as viewed by,
63–64; myths/legends of, about birds,
25, 51, 148; sickness introduced by, 7–8;
and turkeys, 43, 179

—commodification: and destruction of
bird populations, 16–17; fashion trade
with native people, 76–81

farming, 6–8, 49–55, 183

feathers. *See also* attire

—decoration for: arrows, awls, fans, and
pouches, 73–76; calumets, 75, 120, 125;
canoes, 104, 120; darts, 55; dwellings,
65; mortuaries, 135; staff of office, *116*;
war banners, 123; weapons, 121–22

—implements/artifacts: arrow fletching,
59, 73–74, 75, *127*; fans, 66, 74–75, *75*, 79,
81, 105, *106*, 126; oil skimmer, 75; *pelote*
(feather blanket), 104; quills, 16, 75;
wands, *118*

—medicinal use: as emetic, 75; as
prophylactics, 161

—sources: ostriches, *114*; roosters, 45;
roseate spoonbills, 73; turkeys/raptors,
41, 62, 71, 75

fire, 58, 181

Five Civilized Tribes, and Trail of Tears, 8

flamingos, *67*, 71–72, *74*, *197*

Florida, 7, 9, 20, 22, 189

flycatchers, 25, *25*, 26, 33, 158, *161*, 192

Fogelson, Raymond D., 158, 164, 199

folklore/beliefs: conceptions of natural
world, 23–26, 32–33, 39–40; decline/
loss of, 4, 164–65; disease causes and
cures, 157; hereditary elite, as divine, 7;
invoking birds to woo women, 158–61,
161, *162*; persistence of bird stories,
25–26, 32–33, 39–40. *See also* myths/
legends